PAGE 50

ON THE ROAD

YOUR COMPLETE DESTINATION GUIDE
In-depth reviews, detailed listings
and insider tips

Around
Yellowstone
p133

Yellowstone
National Park
p52

Grand Teton
National Park
p173

Around
Grand Teton
p209

THIS EDITION WRITTEN AND RESEARCHED BY

Bradley Mayhew

Carolyn McCarthy

Welcome to Yellowstone & Grand Teton

Yellowstone

Yellowstone National Park is the crown jewel of the Greater Yellowstone Ecosystem and the destination of nearly every visitor to the region. The real showstoppers are the geysers and hot springs – nature's crowd pleasers – but at every turn this land of fire and brimstone breathes, belches and bubbles like a giant kettle on the boil. The park's highways traverse these geysers, through meadows and forests, past roadside herds of bison and campsites aromatic with pine needles and family campfires. In between lies the country's largest collection of elk, the continent's oldest, largest wild bison herds and a pristine wilderness roamed by wolves, grizzlies, moose and antelope.

Grand Teton & Beyond

South of Yellowstone is Grand Teton National Park, probably the most famous natural skyline in the United States and the nation's most iconic mountain range. These vertical peaks, reflected in a string of gorgeous glacial lakes, come the closest to most people's picture-postcard image of alpine splendor and will send a shiver of excitement down the spine of even the least vertically inclined.

Opportunities to venture into the back-country abound in both parks, whether it's on foot, horseback, boat, ski or snowshoe. Buckle up and climb the Tetons, canoe around sublime Shoshone Lake, mountain bike to the summit views of Mt Washburn

There's nowhere in the world quite like Greater Yellowstone. From its raging geysers to howling wolf packs, the land stands alone as one last pocket of a wild, primeval America.

(left) Morning Glory Pool (p85) in Upper Geyser Basin, Yellowstone National Park.
(below) A young grizzly bear investigating a meadow in Grand Teton National Park.

or hike for days through the remote back-country – the choice is yours.

The parks' wonders don't stop at their boundaries. The two parks and their surrounding protected areas form a larger, interconnected area six times the size of Yellowstone: the Greater Yellowstone Ecosystem. Here you'll find blue-ribbon trout streams, fabulous hiking trails and a scattering of charming Wild West towns with their gaze set firmly on the great outdoors.

The Essential Outdoor Vacation

More than three million people a year are drawn here, so if you are traveling in July and August be prepared to share the parks' charms, as well as their campgrounds and parking spots. Yet even in high summer it's not difficult to shake the crowds. Park the car and head off down a trail, if only for a mile or two, and the parks will embrace you in their rejuvenating beauty.

Whatever your interests, some memories are shared – the taste of s'mores over a campfire, the nose-wrinkling smell of sulfurous steam and the electrifying thrill you get when hearing your first wolf howl. A journey to Yellowstone is a great vacation, but also a modern pilgrimage to two of America's most admirable and enduring national landmarks.

›Yellowstone & Grand Teton National Parks Top Experiences ›

Beartooth Highway
Spectacularly scenic approach to Yellowstone (p139)

Lamar Valley
Yellowstone's best wildlife-watching (p64)

Grand Canyon of the Yellowstone
Dramatic waterfalls and canyon colors (p65)

Mammoth Terraces
Travertine terraces and grazing elk (p92)

Bozeman
Home to Montana's most entertaining museum (p158)

Big Sky
One of America's best ski resorts (p162)

Gallatin River
Fly-fishing nirvana (p162)

Norris Geyser Basin
Geysers, springs and mudpots (p75)

MONTANA
WYOMING

Custer National Forest

Gallatin National Forest

Beaverhead-Deerlodge National Forest

Lee Metcalf Wilderness

Stillwater River

Gallatin River

Paradise Valley

Gallatin Valley

Lamar Valley

Grand Canyon of the Yellowstone

Beartooth Hwy

Red Lodge

Fishtail

Absarokee

Big Timber

Livingston

Bozeman

Big Sky

Cooke City

Mammoth

Tower-Roosevelt Junction

Gardiner

Canyon Village

Norris Geyser Basin

West Yellowstone

Hebgen Lake

ELEVATION

	12,000ft
	10,000ft
	8000ft
	6000ft
	4000ft
	2000ft
	1000ft
	0

40 km
20 miles

0
0

Ⓝ

Teton Crest Trail
The region's ultimate alpine walk (p196)

Mormon Row
Superbly photogenic views of the Tetons (p182)

Dubois

Jackson

Grand Prismatic Spring
The park's most beautiful thermal feature (p85)

Old Faithful & Upper Geyser Basin
The world's densest collection of geysers (p79)

Bechler Basin
Remote waterfalls, wildlife and backcountry soaks (p104)

Grand Teton
Ascend the mighty Grand and look down on the Tetons (p174)

Henry's Lake

Buffalo Bill Reservoir

North Absaroka Wilderness

Washakie Wilderness

Shoshone National Forest

Absaroka Range

Yellowstone River

Lake Village

Yellowstone Lake

Heart Lake

Yellowstone National Park

Grant Village

Old Faithful

Madison Lake

WYOMING

IDAHO

Targhee National Forest

John D Rockefeller Jr Memorial Parkway

Colter Bay Village

Jackson Lake

Grand Teton National Park

Grand Teton (13,770ft) ▲

Teton Village

20 TOP EXPERIENCES

Wildlife-spotting in the Lamar Valley

1 Known as the 'Serengeti of North America,' the lush Lamar Valley (p64) is home to the densest collection of big animals in Yellowstone. A dozen pullouts offer superb views over grazing herds of bison and elk, but search the treelines closer with a spotting scope and you'll likely also spot a lone grizzly on the prowl or a pack of wolves on the hunt. Come at dawn or dusk for the best action and be prepared to stand transfixed as nature plays out before your eyes.

Old Faithful & Upper Geyser Basin

2 The world's most famous geyser (p78) erupts every 90 minutes or so, so you have plenty of time to view it from several angles – from the main boardwalk, from the balcony of the Old Faithful Inn and from Observation Hill. The surrounding geyser basin offers dozens of other spectacular spouters; some that erupt dramatically just once a day, others that thrash continually in a violent rage. Check the new visitor center for predicted eruption times and bring a book if you want to catch a biggie like Beehive or Grand, as it may take a while.

Paddling the Teton's Alpine Lakes

3 Whether soloing in a kayak or bundling the family into a canoe, paddling is a great way to glide into nature at your own pace. When your arms tire, shore up on empty beaches for a picnic or a swim. With a permit you can also backcountry camp. Jackson Lake is the Teton's biggest lake; families might prefer to manage the smaller scale of Leigh and String Lakes. For an adventurous multi-day alternative in Yellowstone, try gorgeous Shoshone Lake, the region's largest backcountry lake. String Lake, below

Grand Canyon of the Yellowstone

4 The sublime canyon colors and dramatic 308ft drop of the Lower Falls are the big draws of Yellowstone's very own grand canyon (p65). There are several different ways to view the canyon: get close to the drop-off at the Brink of the Lower Falls, take in the big picture at Artist Point or descend on steps to feel the spray on your face at Uncle Tom's. Best of all, take the rim's hiking trails to appreciate the views away from the car and the crowds.

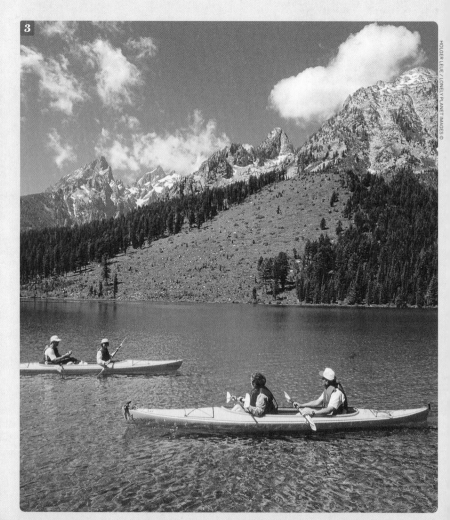

HOLGER LEUE / LONELY PLANET IMAGES ©

Climbing Grand Teton

5 Buck the trend and look down on the Tetons on a guided ascent. The birthplace of American mountaineering, the chiseled and weathered Grand continues to be among America's premier climbing destinations. The two-day affair starts with a steep 7-mile approach past wildflower fields and waterfalls. Rest up, because a 3am wake-up call heralds summit day, with views of the sprawling wilderness of three states. Climbers need some prior instruction, but it can be gained locally before the climb (p198).

Museum of the Rockies, Bozeman

6 Greater Yellowstone's most entertaining museum (p158) is the perfect combination of fun and learning. The jaw-dropping dinosaur collection is what really catches the imagination, from the collection of sea monsters and fossilized dinosaur nests to the reconstructed Montanoceratops and the world's largest T-Rex skull. There's a fine planetarium and the new Yellowstone for Kids interactive displays are a great place to start or end a park vacation. Budget at least half a day.

Grand Prismatic Spring

7 Yellowstone's most beautiful thermal feature is this swimming-pool-sized hot spring (p85), 10 miles north of Old Faithful. The shimmering turquoise blue waters are impressive enough but it's the surrounding multicolored rings of algae that push it out of this world. As the water temperature changes, so do the colors of the thermophiles, creating a rainbow of oranges, yellows and greens. From above, the springs looks like a giant eye weeping exquisite multicolored tears. For the best overviews, climb the hill behind the springs from the Fairy Falls hike.

Backpacking the Tetons

8 Don't expect any breaks, from the trailhead it's all uphill. But the payback? Rolling glades alight with wildflowers, snow-lipped ridges and clear alpine lakes – some of the most luscious, life-affirming scenery in the Tetons lies a day's hike in – and once there, who wants to hurry home? Backpackers can spend a week on the popular Teton Crest Trail, rambling over the lofty spine of the Tetons. The shorter – but still challenging – Alaska Basin has fistfuls of summer blooms and Dall sheep as your companions.

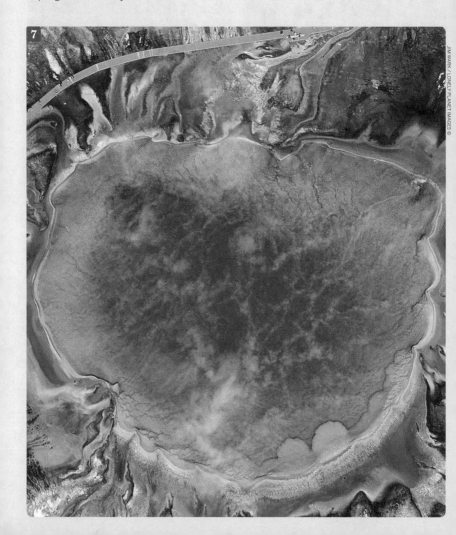

7

JIM WARK / LONELY PLANET IMAGES ©

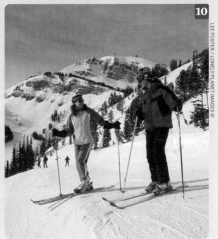

Moose Watching

9 Majestic, massive and gawky as over-grown teenagers, moose are a sight to behold. Bulls can weigh twice as much as a Harley Davidson motorcycle, with massive, cupped antlers, each weighing up to 50lb, which are shed after the fall rut. You'll find them wherever willows grow, since it's their food of choice. They can also be found around lakes and marshes. In the Tetons, they're common around Willow Flats and Cottonwood Creek, and in Yellowstone look for them in the Bechler region and the Gallatin River drainages.

Skiing Jackson Hole or Big Sky

10 Winter is the perfect time to combine a park visit with some serious mountain fun. The region's downhill action centers on Jackson Hole (p219) in Wyoming and Big Sky (p162) in Montana, two of the continent's best resorts. Jackson Hole offers great runs near Jackson town and airport, whereas Big Sky boasts over 5500 acres of runs and also offers one of country's best cross-country resorts. Don't limit yourself to skiing, there are dinner sleigh rides and dogsledding in Big Sky and backcountry yurts, and even heli-skiing options in Jackson Hole. Jackson Hole, above

CHEYENNE ROUSE / LONELY PLANET IMAGES ©

Family Hiking

11 Nature trails, hikes to beaches, lookout points, lakes and geysers... adventure just comes naturally to kids, who will be thrilled by their first sighting of a backcountry bison or belching mudpots. Junior Rangers can earn badges and nature know-how, while Yellowstone's new Young Scientist Program ups the ante by helping kids explore the park with a specialized tool kit in hand. Before heading out, know the endurance level of your kids and choose your trail wisely, see p41 for our suggestions. Grand Tetons, above

Wildflowers

12 Break out the hiking boots in June and you'll discover that the hillsides across the region have quietly exploded with a mosaic of attention-grabbing wildflowers. Golden yellow balsamroots, mauve lupines, fire-red paintbrush and pink monkey flowers are just a few of the spectacular blooms competing for your attention in meadows from the Gallatins to the Tetons. Know your blooms and you might spot more wildlife – grizzlies love beargrass, while hummingbirds are drawn to fire-red Indian paintbrush. Head to higher elevations in July for even more blooms. Grand Teton National Park, top right

Bechler Basin Waterfalls

13 Hidden in the remote southwest corner of the park, close to nowhere and accessed by a single bone-crunching dirt road, Bechler hides Yellowstone's most spectacular collection of waterfalls. Union, Dunanda, Colonnade and Cave Falls are the better-known destinations but there are dozens of other thundering falls, feathery cascades and hidden hot springs that entice hardy backpackers and day hikers to brave the fearsome mosquitoes and boggy trails. Come in August and September for the best conditions. Cave Falls (p105), right

JOHN ELK III / LONELY PLANET IMAGES ©

RICHARD CUMMINS / LONELY PLANET IMAGES ©

Mormon Row

14 A favorite of photographers, this gravel strip of old homesteads and wind-thrashed barns (p182) backed by the Teton's jagged panorama lies just east of Hwy 191. Sure, you could drive it, but the ultra-scenic and pancake-flat loop makes for one nice bike ride. In the 1890s, early settlers were drawn to this landscape of lush sagebrush for homesteading. The flats are also popular with bison and pronghorn, the latter have used this corridor for seasonal migrations to the Yukon for over 6000 years.

Mammoth Terraces

15 Northern Yellowstone's major thermal feature is a graceful collection of travertine terraces and cascading hot pools. Some terraces are bone dry, while others sparkle with hundreds of minuscule pools, coral-like formations and a fabulous palette of colors that could come from an Impressionist painting. The miniature mountain of thermal action is in constant flux. Get bonus views of several terraces by taking the little-trod Howard Eaton Trail, or ski it in winter, when you'll likely share the terraces with elk; see p92.

Norris Geyser Basin

16 Yellowstone's hottest and most active geyser basin and its tallest geyser (in fact the world's tallest at 400ft) are not at Old Faithful but further north in Norris Geyser Basin (p75). Boardwalks lead around the bone-white plain, past hissing fumaroles, jet blue pools, colorful runoffs and rare acidic geysers. The Yellowstone hot spot is so close to the surface here that the land actually pulsates. Stay at the nearby campground and you can stroll over from your campsite at sunset while looking out for elk along the Gibbon River.

Fly Fishing the Gallatin River

17 Montana is sacred ground for fly-fishing enthusiasts, and the region's blue-ribbon streams don't get much better than the Gallatin River, immortalized by Robert Redford in his film *A River Runs Through It*. The region's dozen or so fly-fishing shops are well stocked with lovingly crafted caddis flies and woolly buggers and can fill you in on current best fishing spots, including the nearby Madison, Yellowstone or Firehole Rivers. Most places offer guided trips and some offer casting clinics. Madison River, above

Yellowstone in Winter

18 Winter is perhaps Yellowstone's most magical season, but come prepared for the serious cold. Geysers turn nearby trees into frozen ice sculptures, frosty-bearded bison warm themselves by steaming hot springs and the wildlife is easier to spot in the whiteness. Take a snowcoach trip to Canyon, ski past exploding geysers or snowshoe out through the muffled silence to a frozen waterfall, then finish the day sipping hot chocolate in front of a roaring fire at the Old Faithful Snow Lodge.

Backpacking Yellowstone

19 Perhaps the best way to appreciate the park is to pack up your tent and join the elite 1% of visitors who experience the scale and silence of Yellowstone's backcountry. Only when you wander on foot through wolf and grizzly country do you truly sense the primeval wildness of Yellowstone's remoter reaches. Traverse the Gallatin range in the park's northwest, backpack out to Heart Lake or take an adventurous expedition-style trek through the remote southeastern Thorofare, as far from a road as you can get in the Lower 48. Heart Lake Trail, right

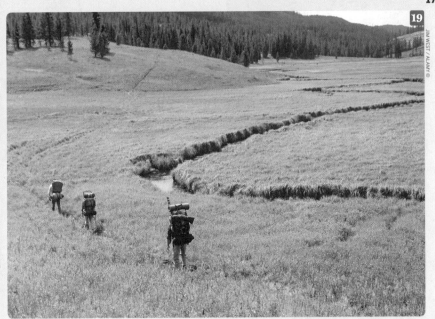

JIM WEST / ALAMY ©

19

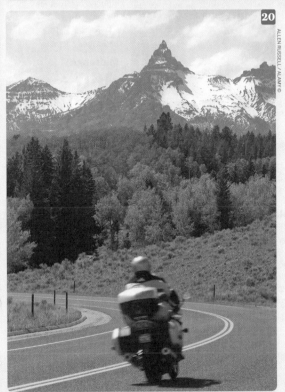

ALLEN RUSSELL / ALAMY ©

20

Beartooth Highway

20 Depending on who's talking, the Beartooth Hwy (p139) is either the best way to get to Yellowstone, the most exciting motorbike ride in the West or the most scenic highway in America. We'd say it is all three. The head-spinning tarmac snakes up the mountainside to deposit you in different world, high above the treeline, onto a rolling plateau of mountain tundra, alpine lakes and Rocky Mountain goats. The views are superb, the fishing awesome and the hiking literally breathtaking.

need to know

Entrance Fees

» $25 per vehicle ($20 motorcyclist or snowmobile), covers both parks for seven days; $12 per person on foot, bicycle or snowcoach.

Number Of Visitors

» Yellowstone: 3.6 million (2010)

» Grand Teton: 2.7 million (2010)

When to Go

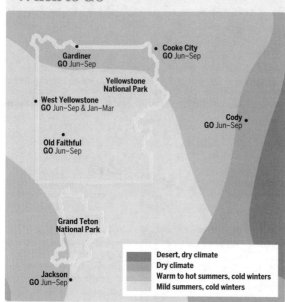

Cooke City
GO Jun–Sep

Gardiner
GO Jun–Sep

Yellowstone
National Park

West Yellowstone
GO Jun–Sep & Jan–Mar

Cody
GO Jun–Sep

Old Faithful
GO Jun–Sep

Grand Teton
National Park

Jackson
GO Jun–Sep

Desert, dry climate
Dry climate
Warm to hot summers, cold winters
Mild summers, cold winters

Your Daily Budget

Budget less than
$60

» Campgrounds $12 to $20 per carload, RVs $35 to $50

» Budget hotel outside the park $70

» Free hiking and backcountry permits

Midrange
$60–170

» Rooms in Yellowstone $100 to $200, with a few cabins in Roosevelt from $65

» Restaurant meal $20-30

» Rafting/Wild West cookout for a family of four $180-210.

Top end over
$170

» Splurge in Jackson and Jenny Lake.

» Guided fly-fishing trip costs $225 per day in a group of two

» Winter tour in Yellowstone from $300 per person per day

High Season
(Jun–Aug)

» Cool nights and hot days (very hot on the plains).

» Over half the parks' visitors arrive. Prices peak at gateway towns, park campgrounds fill by lunchtime and reservations are essential.

Shoulder
(May, mid-Sep–Oct)

» Cooler months bring fewer crowds (and more discounts) but unpredictable weather. September is generally excellent.

» Some activities and campgrounds close.

» Some roads don't open until the end of May.

Low Season
(late Dec–Mar)

» Only 5% of visitors see Yellowstone in winter.

» Campgrounds are closed and transport is limited to snowcoaches or guided snowmobiles.

Year Founded

» Yellowstone: 1872 (the world's first national park)

» Grand Teton: 1929

Money

» ATMs at all accommodations and many general stores.

» Credit/debit available everywhere.

» Tipping expected on horse rides, rafting trips and at dude ranches.

Cell Phones

» Coverage good in Grand Teton (except the canyons).

» Patchy coverage in Yellowstone outside of the main junctions.

Driving

» Most roads are sealed; speed limit 45mph, dropping to 25mph at busy junctions.

» Parking spots at popular trailheads fill up by 11am July and August.

Websites

» **Yellowstone National Park** (www .nps.gov/yell)

» **Grand Teton National Park** (www .nps.gov/grte)

» **Lonely Planet** (www .lonelyplanet.com) Destination information, hotel bookings, traveler forums and more.

» **Xanterra** (www .yellowstonenational parklodges.com) Yellowstone lodges, campgrounds and more.

» **Grand Teton Lodge Company** (www.gtlc. com) Campsites, dining and activities.

» **Montana Tourism** (www.visitmt.com, www.wintermt.com)

» **Wyoming Tourism** (www.wyomingtourism .org, www.state.wy.us)

Exchange Rates

Australia	A$1	US$1.05
Canada	C$1	US$1.02
Euro Zone	€1	US$1.41
Japan	¥100	US$1.22
New Zealand	NZ$1	US$0.82
UK	£1	US$1.62

For current exchange rates see www.xe.com.

Important Numbers

Yellowstone National Park	☏307-344-7381
Old Faithful Visitor Center	☏307-344-2751
Grand Teton National Park	☏307-739-3300
Xanterra reservations	☏307-344-7311
Grand Teton Lodge Company	☏307-543-3100

Opening Dates

» **Yellowstone National Park** The north entrance at Gardiner is open year-round, as is the northern Gardiner to Cooke City road via Mammoth and Roosevelt. Roads open in May on a staggered schedule. Most campgrounds, park services and visitor centers close October to May.

» **Grand Teton National Park** Open year-round, though most of Teton Park Rd is closed to vehicles in winter. Most campgrounds and visitor centers (except the Craig Thomas Discovery & Visitor Center) close October to May.

Coping with the Crowds

Our advice? Firstly get out of the car – you'll lose 90% of tourists simply by walking a mile from the road. Follow the park animals and get up early, rest at lunchtime and stay out late. Be at the trailhead at 8am for the best light, fewer tourists and more parking spaces. Get active during the hour just before sunset, when others are rushing back to set up their campsites and the wildlife is back out again. Then eat dinner at 9pm when restaurant tables are wide open. Roads are generally busiest between 11am and 3pm.

Finally, head out of the park. While the Gallatin National Forest may not have the same sexy ring as Yellowstone National Park, the hikes are just as superb and you'll have the trails to yourself.

if you like...

Wildlife

To spot a grizzly, wolf or bighorn sheep you need to know the terrain, the season and the workings of an animal's brain. Then again, you'll probably see bison, elk or even a bear without even undoing your seatbelt.

Lamar and Hayden Valleys
Big herds of bison, wolf packs and the occasional grizzly make these Yellowstone's prime animal hangouts. Join a ranger for wildlife-watching in Hayden (p62)

Grizzly & Wolf Discovery Center, West Yellowstone
Didn't see a grizzly or wolf in the park? Don't despair – you're guaranteed an up-close sighting in this nonprofit educational center (p167)

Guided tour A course with the Yellowstone Institute or a tour with a professional naturalist will really add to your understanding of Yellowstone's complex ecosystem (p35)

Mustang tour, Cody For something a bit different try this day trip to spot wild mustangs cavorting on the high Wyoming desert (p147)

Thermal Features

For many, Yellowstone's biggest draw is its otherworldly collection of spouters, gushers, bubblers and burpers, which together constitute over three quarters of the world's weirdest thermal features.

Old Faithful The iconic old geyser isn't the biggest or the most beautiful in Yellowstone, but it is impressive and dependable. Try to view it from various angles, including Observation Hill (p81)

Grand Prismatic Spring Simply put, the park's most beautiful thermal feature, a swimming-pool-sized spring ringed by an incredible array of rainbow colors (p85)

A backcountry geyser There's something really special about watching a geyser away from the crowds of Old Faithful. Hike out to Lone Star or another backcountry geyser for your own private show (p102)

Mammoth Hot Springs The graceful tiered terraces and colorful coral-like formations have a subtle beauty (p60)

Scenic Drives

There's hardly a mile in Yellowstone country that isn't pull-off-the-road, drop-dead gorgeous. If we had to choose our favorite drives, these are the ones that make us almost happy to pay park prices for our gas.

Beartooth Hwy An astounding drive above the tree line from Red Lodge to Cooke City, known as the most scenic road in America (p139)

Gallatin Valley Blending scenes from Robert Redford's *A River Runs Through It* with twin mountain ranges and some lovely ranchlands (p162)

Paradise Valley Rolling ranchlands and snowy peaks create the perfect approach from Livingston to Yellowstone's north entrance. It's not called Paradise for nothin' (p151)

Signal Mountain Summit Rd Dramatic panoramas over the Snake River to the Tetons, from 800ft above Jackson Hole's valley floor (p181)

Hwy 191 & Teton Park Rd More fantastic views of the Tetons from the flats of Jackson Hole Valley, with the chance of spotting pronghorn, deer or moose. (p185)

» Rafting on Snake River, Jackson (p214)

Backcountry Trips

Yellowstone's wildest corners are as far from a road as you can get in the Lower 48. A certain know-how is essential here: you need to know what you are doing if you want to sleep with the grizzlies.

Teton Crest Trail Superlative mountain scenery on this four-day trek along the high spine of the Tetons (p195)

Gallatin Range Yellowstone's northeast corner offers superb backpacking trips over mountain passes to lakes and snowcapped peaks (p113)

Beartooth Plateau With over a thousand lakes dotted around this alpine tundra, the Beartooths offer routes from overnighters to a fantastic full traverse (p141)

Shoshone Lake Yellowstone's largest backcountry lake offers golden lakeshore campsites for a great multiday trek or (even better) paddle (p118)

Heart Lake Thermal features, a peak ascent and more lakeshore campsites, just a day's walk from the road (p108)

The Good Life

Just because you're in the Wild West doesn't mean you have to rough it all the time. Take a break with the following indulgences.

Couloir Linger over a four-course dinner with wine pairings and gape at the views from Jackson Hole's only mountain-top restaurant, which also offers in-kitchen dining with special pampering from the chef (p221)

Atelier Ortega Bakers in crisp whites serve up elaborate French desserts and sumptuous chocolates for takeaway (p217)

Spring Creek Ranch Snuggle by the fireplace of a luxuriant cabin, sink into the spa or order sunset cocktails with screaming Teton views at the Granary restaurant (p215)

Rainbow Ranch Lodge Share one of the lodge's 5000 bottles of wine in the romantic outdoor Jacuzzi before retiring to the gourmet restaurant or one of the ultra-stylish pondside luxury rooms. (p165)

Winter

Only a fraction of Yellowstone's visitors see the park during its most alluring season. Many repeat visitors rank it their favorite season, despite some logistical complications (snowcoaches and skinny skis are the main ways of getting around).

Old Faithful Ski out past frozen ghost trees to frozen waterfalls and exploding geyers, before returning to the Snow Lodge for hot chocolate (p120)

Big Sky & Jackson Hole Mountain Resort The region's premier downhill runs also offer excellent Nordic trails and dinner sleigh rides (p162 & p220)

West Yellowstone The region's Nordic ski and snowmobiling capital, West is also the kick-off point for snowcoach tours into Yellowstone Park (p169)

Canyon yurt camp Take a snowcoach to your own private backcountry yurt and spend a couple of days skiing around the wildlife-rich backcountry (p121)

If you like... hot-spring soaking, we suggest Yellowstone's Boiling River (p61), Chico Hot Springs (p152), Granite Hot Springs (p222) or a backcountry soak at Bechler's Ferris Fork (p113).

Learning

The more you learn about the Yellowstone ecosystem, the more interesting it becomes. With courses from wolf watching to the inner workings of a supervolcano, you'll never look at the land in the same way again.

Yellowstone Institute & Teton Science School Both offer a fantastic range of year-round courses, from photography to backpacking 101, led by real experts (p35)

Junior rangers Kids will love earning their ranger badge through parkwide projects and activities (p42)

Fly-fishing course The photogenic streams of the Yellowstone, Gallatin and Madison are the ideal place to perfect your cast, with a private guide or in a group (p37)

Kayaking course Several rafting companies in Gardiner and Jackson offer fun kayaking courses on the Yellowstone and Snake Rivers (p155 and 184)

The Wild West

Montana and Wyoming still carry the ghosts of the American West, proud home to cowboys, ranches, rodeos and Native American powwows.

Cody, WY Investigate the cabins of Butch and Sundance at Old Trail Town, then saddle up to the bar of Buffalo Bill's Irma Hotel, before dancing up a storm to honkytonk tunes at Cassie's (p144)

Stay at a dude ranch From sunset trail rides to recuperative spa treatments, nothing creates more memories than staying at a ranch. The best are in the Wapiti and Gallatin Valleys and Jackson Hole (p258)

Roosevelt Country Ride the rumbleseat on a stagecoach ride before tucking into steak and beans at the park's favorite cowboy cookout (p128)

Jackson Rhinestone cowboys, staged shootouts and gourmet chow make Jackson the posterchild for Wyoming's New West (p210)

An Adrenaline Rush

Aside from an unexpected brush with a grizzly, there are plenty of ways to get the pulse racing in the Yellowstone region. Bring a spare pair of underpants. You'll need them.

Climbing Grand Teton A two-day guided climb takes you to the best views in the West and gives you a real sense of achievement (p198)

White-water rafting From wild rides on the Gallatin and Snake Rivers to family floats on the Yellowstone, these are family trips the kids will love (p162 & p211)

Paragliding Jackson Hole Get unrivalled Teton views on a tandem flight from Jackson Hole Mountain Resort (p220)

Big Sky Ziplines, trampoline bungees and chairlift-assisted mountain-bike runs mean summer now rivals winter at this ski resort (p162)

month by month

March

Mid-March marks the end of the park's winter season, as the snowplows start to clear Yellowstone's roads. Yellowstone's wildlife has the park pretty much to itself.

 Spring Cycling
From the second Monday in March to the third Thursday in April most of Yellowstone's roads are closed to motor traffic, but West Yellowstone to Mammoth road is open to cyclists. There are no facilities and possible snow but it's a wonderful opportunity to cycle traffic-free.

April

As Yellowstone starts to shake off winter, the park's roads start to open, starting with the West Entrance and western sections of the Grand Loop Rd (see p57 for details).

 Backcountry Reservations
On April 1 reservations are taken for Yellowstone's backcountry campsites (see p105), so if you have a specific time for a specific route, make sure your reservations are in today.

May

Rain and snowmelt create high rivers and full waterfalls, with snow at higher elevations. Wildlife-viewing is good, with baby elk and bison finding their feet, but many hiking trails are boggy.

 Elkfest Antler Auction
Head to Jackson to kit out your cabin in Rocky Mountain style. Boy scouts collect and sell shed antlers to raise money to buy winter feed for the National Elk Refuge in a weekend of activities (www.elkfest.org) a week before Memorial Day.

 Memorial Day
The last Sunday in May marks the beginning of high season. Park entrances, roads and access routes are now open, the last being the road between Tower and Canyon over Dunraven Pass (8859ft) and the Beartooth Hwy, which can delayed for a week or more by heavy snow.

June

Summer arrives at last, as average highs hit 70°F and wildflowers start to bloom at lower elevations. The last of the park accommodations open by mid-June. Mosquitoes can be bothersome until mid-August.

 Plains Indian Powwow
The region's Native American culture is celebrated in mid-June at Cody's Buffalo Bill Historical Center, as dancers, drummers and artisans gather in a colorful celebration of Shoshone and other traditions.

 Rodeo!
Rodeo is the major cultural event of the Yellowstone year. Cody's nightly summer rodeo kicks off June 1, as does Jackson's biweekly version, with more rodeos pulling into Gardiner and West Yellowstone mid-month.

Custer's Last Stand Reenactment

Hundreds of historical re-enactors head to the Battle of Little Bighorn from June 24 to 26 for the anniversary of Custer's Last Stand. Admission to the battlefield is free on the 25th.

July

Temperatures reach 80°F in lower elevations, with Cody and Billings around 10°F hotter. Afternoon thunderstorms are common but the high country is snow-free, allowing high-altitude wildflowers to bloom. One million people visit Yellowstone Park in July.

Cody Stampede

The July 4 weekend brings crowds to the park and rodeo to the park's gateways. The Cody Stampede (www.codystampederodeo.com) is the region's biggest bash but there are also rodeos in Livingston and Red Lodge.

Music Festivals

July is the month for live music. The Grand Teton Music Festival adds some classical class to Teton Village, the Yellowstone Jazz Festival funks up Cody, while Targhee Fest hits Idaho's Teton Valley mid-month.

August

As visitor numbers peak, moose and elk retreat into the backcountry. Days are long, with daylight remaining until about 9:30pm. August is a prime hiking month, when wildflowers are in full bloom at higher altitudes.

Christmas in August

Stumble into Yellowstone's Old Faithful Inn on August 25 and face the surreal sight of Christmas decorations and carol singers. The tradition dates back to the turn of the last century, when a freak August snowstorm stranded a group of visitors in the Upper Geyser Basin.

Smoking Waters Mountain Man Rendezvous

Yellowstone's biggest mountain man rendezvous is a 10-day reenactment of an 1859 gathering and includes tomahawk-throwing competitions, cowboy poetry and black-powder sharpshooting. Red Lodge has a smaller rendezvous at the end of July, as does Jackson in May.

Crow Fair

Over 1000 tepees of the Apsaalooke Nation are erected in the Crow Agency, west of Billings, on the third weekend in August, for the annual Crow Fair (www.crow-fair.com). Highlights include dramatic Native American dances, rodeo and plenty of fried tacos.

September

Fall colors, the sounds of bugling elk, lack of mosquitoes and off-season discounts make September a great month to visit, despite chilly nights. Ranger programs peter out after Labor Day, as park accommodations start to close.

Running of the Sheep

Tiny Reed Point, Montana, hosts the annual 'Running of the Sheep', an admirably dorky, far less exciting version of Pamplona's Running of the Bulls. A parade and evening street dance ramp up the action.

November

All Yellowstone park roads close on the first Monday in November, except for the Gardiner–Cooke City road. In Grand Teton US 26/89/191 remains open all winter to Flagg Ranch but parts of Teton Park Rd and the Moose–Wilson road close, as does Grassy Lake Rd.

Yellowstone Ski Festival

Thanksgiving week heralds the Yellowstone Ski Festival (www.yellowstoneskifestival.com) at West Yellowstone, a great time for ski buffs and newcomers to the sport. Highlights include ski clinics (for kids, too) and gear demos. Nordic skiing kicks off around this time.

itineraries

Mammoth
Bunsen Peak
Norris Geyser Basin
Yellowstone National Park
Madison River
Fairy Falls
Old Faithful Inn
Yellowstone Lake
Lone Star Geyser
John D Rockefeller Jr Memorial Parkway
Grand Teton National Park
Jackson Lake
String Lake/ Leigh Lake
Oxbow Bend
Lake Solitude
Jenny Lake Dr
Mormon Row

One Week
Yellowstone & Grand Teton Overview

Starting in **Mammoth**, take the morning to climb **Bunsen Peak** for the fantastic views, before paying a brief visit to Mammoth Hot Springs and driving to **Norris Geyser Basin**. Continue on to your reserved campsite at Madison for some early-evening elk- and bison-spotting or fly-fishing on the **Madison River**.

Spend the next two days in Geyser Country, hiking to either **Fairy Falls** or Sentinel Meadows for backcountry geysers and bison. Overnight at historic **Old Faithful Inn** to experience the Upper Geyser Basin in the moonlight and the next day cycle out to **Lone Star Geyser** to catch a backcountry eruption.

Drive south into Grand Teton and search for trumpeter swans and herons at **Oxbow Bend**. **Jenny Lake Dr** is worth a linger for its awesome views of the Central Tetons. Enjoy a family shoreline at forested **String and Leigh Lakes** or join the crowds for Grand Teton's most popular day hike: around Jenny Lake and up Cascade Canyon to **Lake Solitude**. Finally, cycle around **Mormon Row** for some classic shots of barns and bison before heading south to Jackson for a day off to recover from it all!

PLAN YOUR TRIP ITINERARIES

Mammoth Hot Springs

Roosevelt Lodge

Yellowstone National Park

Willow Park

Lamar Valley

Dunraven Pass ▲ Mt Washburn

Norris Geyser Basin

Porcelain Basin

Cascade Lake Picnic Area
Grand Canyon of the Yellowstone

— — Yellowstone Loop, North
—■—■— Yellowstone Loop, South

Hayden Valley

Firehole Swimming Area

Grand Prismatic Spring

Continental Divide

Lake Yellowstone Hotel

Old Faithful

Yellowstone Lake

Shoshone Lake

One Day
Yellowstone Loop, North

❯ This route through the north of the park takes in some premier wildlife-watching, views of the Grand Canyon and a sampler of geysers and hot springs. You can join this loop anywhere but you'll need to start early and stay out late to fit it all in.

Head straight to the **Lamar Valley** around dawn to look for wolves, coyotes or bison. Grab a Hiker's Breakfast at **Roosevelt Lodge** then drive up to **Dunraven Pass** to make the three- to four-hour return hike up **Mt Washburn** for the park's best views. Picnic amid the pines at shady **Cascade Lake** picnic area or grab lunch on the go at Canyon.

Gawp at the thundering falls and rusted colors of the **Grand Canyon of the Yellowstone** from Uncle Tom's Trail and Artist Point on the southern rim road, before driving across the Solfatara Plateau to the geysers and hot springs of superheated **Norris Geyser Basin**. Then swing north towards Mammoth, stopping en route to watch for afternoon moose at **Willow Park**. Stroll the boardwalks at dusk to admire surreal Palette Springs and Canary Springs at **Mammoth Hot Springs**, before collapsing in the bar for a well-deserved Old Faithful Ale.

One Day
Yellowstone Loop, South

❯ The southern loop takes in epic Yellowstone Lake, the park's greatest geysers and a dip in the Firehole River. You can also start this loop at West Yellowstone, adding on 28 miles. For a two-day trip combine the northern and southern loop options to take in most of the park's roadside highlights.

Wake up by **Yellowstone Lake** and join the birds on a lakeshore stroll. Drive west from West Thumb up over the **Continental Divide** before descending into Geyser Country. Check predicted eruption times at the visitor center to catch **Old Faithful** and another of the Upper Geyser Basin spouters. Head north to Midway Geyser Basin and admire **Grand Prismatic Spring**, blowing off steam with the kids in the thermally heated **Firehole Swimming Area** further north.

Continue north to the **Porcelain Basin** hot springs at Norris, grabbing a picnic lunch at peaceful Norris Meadows picnic area, before swinging east to savor views of the **Grand Canyon of the Yellowstone** from Uncle Tom's Trail and Artist Point. Swing south through the **Hayden Valley** for some prime sunset wildlife-watching before returning to enjoy the park's best food at **Lake Yellowstone Hotel Dining Room**.

- ┅┅┅ Teton in a Day
- ▬▬▬ Jackson Hole & the Tetons

Indian Arts Museum
Jackson Lake Lodge
Willow Flats
Log Chapel of the Sacred Heart
Grand Teton National Park
Inspiration Point
Moose Ponds
Plains & Panoramas Route
Taggart Lake Trailhead
Schwabacher's Landing
Dornan's Chuckwagon
Menor's Ferry
Hole in One Biking Loop
Jackson: Center for the Arts; Snake River Brewing Co; Snake River Grill
Stagecoach Bar
Nora's Fish Creek Inn
Snake River Canyon
Jackson Peak

One Day
Teton in a Day

❯ Incredible alpine scenery is the main attraction of the Tetons. To soak it all up, those short on time should focus on road-tripping the major highlights. Start with a hearty breakfast in Moose at **Dornan's Chuckwagon**, a pioneer-style camp serving flapjacks al fresco with great Teton views. Then glimpse the area's fascinating homesteading history at historic **Menor's Ferry**; audio tours are available for mobile phones.

Get off the road and into the wilderness with a short hike in ragged hills to glacial moraines cupping **Taggart** and **Bradley Lakes**. Bring swimsuits – you can take a dip from Taggart's eastern edge if it's warm enough. After, spread your blanket at the edge of the pines and picnic by the **Log Chapel of the Sacred Heart**.

For excellent photographs, **Schwabacher's Landing** offers the best panoramas of the Teton's toothy Cathedral group. Nearby, there's incredible Native American beadwork at the **Indian Arts Museum**. End your outing watching wildlife at **Willow Flats**; there's usually a moose munching in the dusky light. Finally, cap your day at **Jackson Lake Lodge** with a huckleberry margarita at the Blue Heron.

Four Days
Jackson Hole & the Tetons

❯ The adrenaline center of Jackson Hole is best savored with a passion for action. First, fuel up with a classic breakfast of pan-fried trout at Wilson's **Nora's Fish Creek Inn**. Then saddle your road bike to ride the **Hole in One loop** – extra points for starting from Wilson. Post-ride, opt for an OB-1 at the award-winning **Snake River Brewing Company**.

On day two, hit the most scenic hike in the park, **Inspiration Point**. Take the ferry across Jenny Lake for an easy return. Detour to **Moose Ponds** to snag a glimpse of its namesake ungulates. For sunset views, rumble your pickup along the dirt roads and main corridors of the **Plains & Panoramas route**.

On day three, paddle **Snake River Canyon** on a white-water raft trip. Later you can treat yourself to a pan-roasted elk chop and ultra-decadent desserts at **Snake River Grill** and take in some culture at the modern **Center for the Arts**.

On your final day, join the locals powering up **Jackson Peak**, with valley views of the Teton Range. Make your last night count: The best roadhouse around, **Stagecoach Bar** packs with revelers moving to live country and western, rock or reggae.

Museum of the Rockies

Chico Hot Springs

Paradise Valley

Red Lodge

Gardiner
Beaver Ponds
Mammoth

Yellowstone River Picnic Area

Beartooth Lake

Willow Park

Lamar Valley

Beartooth Hwy

Fossil Forest Trail

Norris Geyser Basin

South Rim Trail & Ribbon Lake

Hayden Valley

Yellowstone National Park

Geyser Basins

Elephant Back Mountain

Old Faithful Inn

Yellowstone Lake
West Thumb Geyser Basin

Legend:
- - - Yellowstone, Big Loop
—■—■ Yellowstone to Paradise

Four Days
Yellowstone, Big Loop

From Mammoth head to some early-morning wildlife viewing in the **Lamar Valley** before enjoying the crowd-free views of the Narrows on the **Yellowstone River Picnic Area** hike. Continue south to Canyon to take the **South Rim and Ribbon Lake** hike before overnighting in Canyon Village.

The next day try some more early-morning wildlife-watching in **Hayden Valley** before continuing south to hike **Elephant Back Mountain** for great views of Lake Yellowstone. After lunch at Lake Hotel or a lakeshore picnic on the sand bars around Gull Point, continue south, stopping at the hot springs of **West Thumb Geyser Basin** before heading west across the continental divide to overnight at **Old Faithful Inn**.

Spend day three visiting the **geyser basins**, and the next day drive to Mammoth via **Norris Geyser Basin**, arriving at lunchtime to stroll the travertine terraces at **Mammoth** and either take a guided walk through historical Fort Yellowstone or a dusk hike to spot wildlife on the **Beaver Ponds** trail.

One Week
Yellowstone to Paradise

Add this three-day scenic drive onto the previous four-day park itinerary and you'll get a fantastic week of scenic drives, park highlights and even a trip through Paradise.

From **Red Lodge**, budget half a day to drive America's most scenic 70 miles, the **Beartooth Hwy**, stopping to stretch your legs or try some fishing at **Beartooth Lake**. Overnight in Cooke City, then enter the park at the Northeast Entrance for some early wildlife-watching in **Lamar Valley** and a hunt for petrified trees on the **Fossil Forest Trail**, then join the previous itinerary at Canyon.

Heading north from Mammoth on day six, squeeze in a morning rafting trip or horseback ride from **Gardiner** before continuing north through the lovely **Paradise Valley** to reminisce over a hot soak and gourmet dinner at **Chico Hot Springs**. Continue on to Bozeman on your last day to spend a few hours at the **Museum of the Rockies** and some last-minute shopping.

Alternatively, spend all your time in the park and throw in some more backcountry hiking, preferably the Sepulcher Mountain hike, an overnight hike to Heart Lake or even the fantastic three-day trekking or canoe trip around Shoshone Lake.

Activities

Top Activities in Greater Yellowstone

Hiking Stroll back in geologic time on the Fossil Forest Trail or scramble the heights of Avalanche Peak.

Canoeing Paddle the placid waters of Shoshone or Jackson Lake.

Fishing Land the big one while wading in one of Yellowstone's famous rivers.

Wildlife watching Observe wolves on the prowl or bears at play.

Horseback riding Kick up trail dust on an equestrian tour of the backcountry.

Nature walks Trek with a ranger to score the inside scoop on wildlife.

Snowboarding Carve a path through the powder at great resorts like Big Sky and Jackson Hole.

Cross-country skiing Glide through the alabaster landscape of winter.

Alive, sweeping and often stunning – this wilderness is a playground for the outdoor enthusiast. And playing – not gazing from the car – is the best way to discover what's on offer. Just feast your eyes, and your pulse will accelerate. Ranging from the Tetons' ragged spires to Yellowstone's vast meadows, this natural refuge is home to the highest concentration of thermal features in the world – plus marauding wolves, bison herds and cutthroat trout. Wildlife is prolific and often present when visitors undertake quieter sports like fishing, hiking and canoeing. Thrill-seekers can go white-water rafting, climbing, paragliding or kayaking.

Summer

Every animal that burrows and snoozes the long winter away snaps to life at the prospect of a Yellowstone summer, and we should be no exception. It's time to lace up your boots and rekindle your friendship with the wild. It's well worth setting aside a few nights in the backcountry; camping equipment is readily available throughout the region (see p279). When your hiking boots get battered, saddle up, stargaze or try the region's water sports.

Hiking & Backpacking

Hiking means escaping the crowds to enjoy abundant alpine vistas, cascading waterfalls, wildlife and thermal features. You could say the backcountry is yours for the taking. Yellowstone National Park boasts over

THE CONTINENTAL DIVIDE TRAIL

Extending from New Mexico to Canada, this 3100-mile **thru trail** (CDT; www.cdtrail. org) bisects beautiful sections of the Teton Wilderness and Yellowstone. Hiking it is a great option for hearty thru-hikers who think big. Obtaining backcountry permits for the Yellowstone section can be tricky, as hikers must know their dates and pick up the permit in advance, but rangers are generally understanding. Due to snow, this portion of the trail usually opens around July 1. Check the website for maps, trip planning and volunteer opportunities. Useful guidebooks to the trail include *Continental Divide Trail Guidebook Vol 3*, available from the Continental Divide Trail Society (www.cdtsociety.org).

900 miles of maintained trails, and you can peruse Grand Teton National Park's sublime alpine scenery via its 200 miles of hiking trails, yet less than 1% of visitors sleep out in the backcountry. Popular campsites fill up fast, however, so plan in advance or keep your itinerary flexible.

See the hiking charts on p32 and p34 for a list of hikes and details of their distance, difficulty rating and features. You can find additional hiking options in the Around Yellowstone and Around Grand Teton chapters.

Closures & Seasonal Conditions

In Yellowstone, fire outbreaks or bear activity can close trails without warning at any time. At the higher elevations, trails may be snow-covered until late July. August and September are the driest months, and May and June are the wettest. Ticks proliferate on low-elevation trails between mid-March and mid-July, so wear insect repellent and long pants. Mosquitoes are most intense in June and July, petering out by mid-August. September is an excellent month for hiking.

In Grand Teton National Park, higher elevations often remain snow-covered until late July, and high passes such as Paintbrush Divide and Hurricane Pass remain under snow as late as mid-August. Become familiar with using an ice tool; it may be necessary in early summer.

Permits

Backcountry permits are required for overnight trips in Yellowstone and Grand Teton. These can be acquired at visitor centers and ranger stations. In Yellowstone, backcountry campers must watch a bear-safety video and review regulations with a ranger before obtaining a permit, or provide a card of proof that you've received a previous permit.

Hike Ratings

There are hikes for every ability level in Greater Yellowstone. The duration for hikes listed in this guide refers to walking time only and doesn't include breaks. Our trail descriptions follow the following guidelines:

Easy Manageable for nearly all walkers, an easy hike is under 4 miles, with fairly even, possibly paved terrain, and no significant elevation gain or loss.

Moderate Fine for fit hikers and active, capable children; moderate hikes have a modest elevation gain.

Difficult For fit and experienced hikers only. Trails might be strenuous, long and even indistinct in places. Expect significant elevation gain, and scrambling may be necessary.

Day Hikes

Almost every part of the Greater Yellowstone region offers outstanding hiking. Don't overlook the longer trails – you can fashion short day hikes by following the first couple of miles of a longer trail.

Day hikes are well-marked, well-maintained trails, often with restroom facilities. In some forested areas these trails may be marked by a series of blazed trees; in Yellowstone trees bear orange metal tags; on rocky moraines look for cairns.

For more information on day hikes in Yellowstone and Grand Teton, see p89 and p188.

Overnight Hikes

The wonders and solitude of the remote backcountry make it well worth hauling in overnight gear. Both parks offer backpacking trips for all skill levels.

If you're not used to hiking with a pack, start with one of the easier options (for suggestions see the boxed text p106). Backcountry campsites, such as those found at

Yellowstone's Ribbon Lake or Grand Teton's Leigh and Bearpaw Lakes are less than a two-hour hike from the trailhead. For hiking and kayaking combinations, try the remote southwest wilderness.

Outside Yellowstone's eastern entrance, the wild and largely inaccessible Absaroka Range (part of the Shoshone National Forest) offers fine extended backcountry hikes into Yellowstone. The Thorofare Region, southeast of Yellowstone Lake, offers Yellowstone's most remote terrain, ideal for committed, self-sufficient backpackers. These remote wildernesses – also the habitat of grizzlies – are favored by horse packers, as the distances are large, the terrain rugged and the trails seldom used. Hunters frequent these areas in late September and early October, so wear orange clothes and expect sites to fill up.

Backcountry Safety

Hikers and campers must reckon with the elements and their own frame of mind. Be prepared for Yellowstone's unpredictable weather – you may go to bed under a clear sky and wake up under 2ft of snow, even in August. Afternoon weather is particularly volatile in the Tetons, so get an early start. By knowing your limitations and the route you plan to take, you can pace yourself accordingly.

Check the forecast before setting off and keep watch on the weather. Don't rely on your cell phone for emergency contact, as coverage may be spotty.

The most cautious safety measures suggest never hiking alone. Regardless, always let someone know where you are going and how long you plan to be gone. Use sign-in boards at trailheads or ranger stations. Travelers looking for hiking companions can post notices at ranger stations, outdoor-equipment stores, campgrounds and hostels.

For tips on animal encounters and other issues, see the Health & Safety chapter (p271).

Rock Climbing & Mountaineering

American mountaineering was born in the Tetons when Paul Petzoldt built the country's first guiding school here in 1929. These huge granite faces continue to be among America's premier climbing destinations. Excellent short routes abound, as well as the classic longer summits like Grand Teton, Mt Moran and Mt Owen, along famous routes like the Upper Exum Ridge and Owen-Spalding route. The best season for climbing is mid-July through August.

A prime resource for climbers in the Tetons during summer is the American Alpine Club's Climbers' Ranch (☑307-733-7271; www.americanalpineclub.org). In addition to serving as a hostel for climbers and hikers (p205), the organization's extensive library and knowledgeable staff prove excellent resources. Look for slideshows and educational events in summer. If you plan to rely heavily on the expertise of the Climbers' Ranch, membership is recommended.

The best ice climbing in the region is found at the South Fork of the Shoshone River, 40 miles southwest of Cody. The season runs from November to April, with the coldest weather offering the best conditions.

Recommended Guide Services

Exum Mountain Guides (☑307-733-2297; www.exumguides.com) At Jenny Lake, with one-day mountaineering courses for beginners and intermediates. A course or previous experience is necessary to attempt Grand Teton on a guided climb. The most popular climbs are daylong ascents of South (12,514ft) and Middle Teton (12,804ft), and two-day climbs of Grand Teton (13,770ft).

Jackson Hole Mountain Guides (☑307-733-4979, 800-239-7642; www.jhmg.com) In Jackson, offers similar instruction to Exum and guided trips in the Tetons.

Montana Alpine Guides (www.adventure montana.com) In Bozeman. Offers climbing courses plus guided climbs and backpacking trips.

Montana Mountaineering Association (www.montanamountaineering.org) In Bozeman, offers courses in ice climbing in Hyalite Canyon, plus backcountry skiing and mountaineering.

Cycling
Road Cycling

Road biking is recommended from late April to October, when the parks' roads, topping out at 8860ft, are probably free of snow. Cyclists will find campsites reserved for hikers and cyclists at almost all campgrounds in Yellowstone National Park. Riding can be more diverse and less stressful outside the park, away from the RV parades.

HIKING IN YELLOWSTONE NATIONAL PARK

NAME	REGION	DESCRIPTION	DIFFICULTY
Avalanche Peak	Lake Country	Relentlessly steep, this ascent above the treeline offers unparalleled views of the Absarokas and Yellowstone Lake	difficult
Beaver Ponds Trail	Mammoth Country	Rolling hike from Mammoth Junction through sagebrush and wildflowers to five secluded ponds	easy-moderate
Bechler Meadows & Falls	Bechler Region	A solitary walk through lush forest, with big falls and wildlife-watching opportunities	easy-moderate
Bechler River Trail	Bechler Region	A wild backcountry adventure filled with rivers, cascades, hot springs and prolific wildlife	moderate
Bunsen Peak & Osprey Falls	Mammoth Country	Short uphill climb to mountain-top views, with an optional canyon descent to up-close views of a little-visited waterfall	moderate (difficult with extension)
Cascade Lake & Observation Peak	Canyon Country	Wet hike through meadows and grazing bison, then up the side of a mountain for expansive views	moderate
Elephant Back Mountain	Lake Country	This easy ascent follows a well-trodden path to fine lake views	moderate
Fairy Falls & Twin Buttes	Geyser Country	Flat stroll through lodgepole forest to a 197ft waterfall and a little-visited geyser	easy
Fossil Forest Trail	Roosevelt Country	Steep unmaintained trail to several 50-million-year-old petrified trees and fine views	moderate-difficult
Heart Lake & Mt Sheridan	Lake Country	Solitude at this backcountry lake near thermal features; challenge-seekers can climb Mt Sheridan (3145ft)	easy-moderate
Lone Star Geyser	Geyser Country	Bike or stroll along an old service road to a fine backcountry geyser that erupts every three hours	easy
Lost Lake	Roosevelt Country	A peaceful hike to a secluded lake and a petrified tree – perfect for anyone staying at Roosevelt Lodge	easy
Mt Washburn	Canyon Country	The park's most popular trail, offering epic views of Yellowstone caldera, and a mountain-bike route option	moderate
Mt Washburn & Sevenmile Hole	Canyon Country	Shuttle hike from mountain peak to canyon floor through the heart of grizzly country	moderate-difficult
Mystic Falls & Biscuit Basin	Geyser Country	Loop hike from a colorful geyser basin to a pretty waterfall, with a more challenging return option	easy
North Shoshone Lake & Shoshone Geyser Basin	Geyser Country	Part of the Continental Divide Trail to a remote geyser basin and stunningly silent backcountry lake	moderate
Pelican Valley	Lake Country	Birdwatchers favor this rolling stroll through meadows and sagebrush in the heart of bear country	moderate
Sentinel Meadows & Queen's Laundry Geyser	Geyser Country	Loop hike past bison and hot springs to an historic backcountry geyser, with some off-trail sections	easy
Sepulcher Mountain	Mammoth Country	A varied and scenic loop with superb views and a secret peek at Mammoth's hidden thermal features	difficult
South Rim Trail & Ribbon Lake	Canyon Country	Fine family hike or a first overnighter to moose habitat and views of Yellowstone Canyon	easy
Yellowstone River Picnic Area Trail	Roosevelt Country	Crowdless views of the lower Yellowstone Canyon; a must for amateur geologists	easy

 Wildlife Watching View Great for Families Fishing Waterfall Thermal Features Bicycles

DURATION	DISTANCE	ELEVATION CHANGE	FEATURES	FACILITIES	PAGE
3½-5hr	4 miles	2100ft			p99
2½hr	5 miles	350ft			p89
3½hr	8 miles	negligible			p104
4 days	28 miles	1100ft			p112
6-7hr	10.2 miles	2100ft (extra 800ft descent & ascent with extension)			p90
4-5hr	10.4 miles	1400ft			p97
2-2½hr	3.5 miles	800ft			p98
3-4hr	6 miles	negligible			p102
2½-3½hr	3.5 miles	800ft			p94
1-2 days	16 miles	345/3145ft			p108
1½-2½hr	4.8 miles	negligible			p102
2hr	3.3 miles	600ft			p93
4hr	6.4 miles	1400ft			p96
2 days	15.6 miles	2800ft			p106
1½-2hr	3 miles	700ft			p100
2 days	20 miles	600ft			p109
6-8hr	16 miles	negligible			p98
2½hr	3.2 miles	negligible			p101
7 hr	11.5 miles	3400ft			p91
3-4hr	6.4 miles	negligible			p95
1½-2hr	4 miles	350ft			p93

Restrooms Drinking Water Ranger Station Backcountry Campsite Picnic Sites Grocery Store Nearby

HIKING IN GRAND TETON NATIONAL PARK

NAME	REGION	DESCRIPTION	DIFFICULTY
Avalanche Canyon & Lake Taminah	Central Tetons	This challenging hike runs the gamut of good stuff: lake swims and killer views	difficult
Death Canyon	Moose-Wilson Rd	An ethereal river valley flanked by granite climbing walls	moderate
Garnet Canyon	Central Tetons	This climbers' route hauls the heartiest hikers into a world of rock and ice	difficult
Hermitage Point	Colter Bay Region	A wild and windswept point facing the multi-fanged Mt Moran	easy-moderate
Lake Solitude	Central Tetons	Alpine scenery and altitude gain: this ultra-popular grind scales to a mountain lake via a gradual climb	moderate-difficult
Leigh & Bearpaw Lakes	Central Tetons	A fun, flat, family outing skirting a forest-clad, crystal-clear swimming hole	easy-moderate
Paintbrush Divide	Central Tetons	This pretty grind lifts you into the alpine scenery above tree-level	moderate
Phelps Lake	Moose-Wilson Rd	A lovely and flat forested amble around a beautiful lake	easy-moderate
Surprise & Amphitheater Lakes	Central Tetons	One of the park's oldest trails, this classic leg-burner with valley views is a crowd pleaser	difficult
Taggart & Bradley Lakes	Central Tetons	Glacial lakes set in wildflower meadows and thick pine forest	easy-moderate
Two Ocean Lake & Grand View Point	Colter Bay Region	A fresh alternative with lush forest, wildflowers and good birdwatching	easy-moderate

🦌 Wildlife Watching   👁 View   👪 Great for Families   〰 Waterfall   🚻 Restrooms   🚰 Drinking Water

Most park roads are rough and narrow and do not have shoulders; expect careless drivers with one eye on the bison and another on the map.

In spring, Yellowstone National Park opens its roads exclusively to cyclists (see p114); it's a great time to pedal the park. Still, snowbanks cover many roadsides through June, making cycling more challenging.

For recommended rides in Yellowstone and Grand Teton National Park, see p114 and p197. The *Bicycling in Yellowstone National Park* brochure has a map with suggested routes, and some information is available on the park website. Bicycle repairs and parts are not available inside the park; it's typically 20 to 30 miles between services.

In Grand Teton National Park, a multi-use pathway totaling 41 miles has begun implementation along Teton Park Rd. The section between Moose and Jenny Lake (7.6 miles) has been completed and work is underway to link this section with Jackson.

Cycling Tours

The annual fall Cycle Tour (www.cycleyellowstone.com; per person $55), organized by the Chamber of Commerce in West Yellowstone, offers a van-supported ride to destinations within the park that change yearly. Teton Mountain Bike Tours (☎307-733-0712; www.tetonmtbike.com) offers family-friendly guided mountain-bike tours of Grand Teton and Yellowstone. Half-day tours cost around $60 and include transportation, bike hire and helmet. Wilderness Ventures (☎307-733-2122; www.wildernessventures.com) leads multi-sport trips for teens.

Mountain Biking

Ski resorts offer lift-serviced trails. West Yellowstone has an excellent network of trails both inside and outside Yellowstone National Park, including the Rendezvous Ski Trails (p169). There is also good single track in the Absaroka and Gallatin Ranges, accessible from Paradise Valley (p153). Regional mountain-biking hubs are Bozeman and Jackson.

DURATION	DISTANCE	ELEVATION CHANGE	FEATURES	FACILITIES	PAGE
6-7hr	11 miles	2300ft			p192
5hr	8-10 miles	1360ft			p193
9hr	12 miles	4800ft			p191
4hr	9.2 miles	negligible			p188
6-7hr	14.4 miles	2240ft			p190
3½hr	7.4 miles	negligible			p189
2-3 days	17.8 miles	3775ft			p195
3½hr	7 miles	negligible			p193
5-6hr	9.6 miles	3000ft			p191
3hr	5.9 miles	560ft			p192
3½hr	6.4 miles	400ft			p189

Ranger Station   Backcountry Campsite   Boat Shuttle   Picnic Sites

PLAN YOUR TRIP ACTIVITIES

Regulations

In the national parks, cyclists may ride on all public roads and a few designated service roads but aren't allowed on any trails or in backcountry areas. Bikes are restricted from entering designated wilderness areas, but may otherwise ride on national forest trails. Trail etiquette requires that cyclists yield to other users.

Wildlife Tours

These worthwhile outings can provide much insight into the inner workings of the parks and their inhabitants. Start with naturalist-guided trips and courses from the Yellowstone Institute (p79) or **Teton Science School** (☎888-945-3567, 307-733-2623; www.wildlifeexpeditions.org; Jackson).

Outstanding smaller outfits include the following:

Austin-Lehman Tours (www.austinlehman.com) High-quality tours, based in Billings.

Grub Steak Expeditions (www.grubsteaktours.com) Cody-based company run by a former park ranger.

The Wild Side (☎406-223-2152; www.wolftracker.com; 412 Water St, Gardiner) Biologist-led guided wolf watching and supported spring and fall treks.

Yellowstone Safari Company (☎866-586-1155; www.yellowstonesafari.com) Biologist-led trips, based in Bozeman.

Yellowstone Wildlife Safari Co (☎800-SAFARIS; www.safariyellowstone.com) In Livingston.

Horseback Riding & Pack Trips

If you're eager to break in your Wranglers on a saddle, consider the wide range of options available, starting from two-hour rides to multiday cattle drives, and rustic operations where guests sweep the stables to ritzy guest ranches with hot tubs and umbrella drinks.

Horseback riding satisfies a primal romantic notion: you can mosey along through beautiful countryside, crossing rivers and ascending steep slopes that would have cost dearly on foot. Overnights have an added element of adventure; essentially you are backpacking but without carrying a load. Depending on your experience and comfort level, you may be allowed to help care for your animal.

In Yellowstone Park there are corrals at Mammoth, Roosevelt and Canyon Junction. Grand Teton has rides from Jackson Lake Lodge and Colter Bay (p199). Ranches in the Wapiti (p149) and Gallatin (p164) Valleys operate horseback rides for nonguests.

Check out the **Dude Ranchers' Association** (www.duderanch.org) for helpful information and links. The following state organizations provide information for licensed outfitters:

Idaho Outfitters & Guides Association (✆208-342-1919, 800-494-3246; www.ioga.org; 711 N 5th St, Boise, ID)

Montana Outfitters & Guides Association (✆406-449-3578; www.moga-montana.org; 2 North Last Chance Gulch,Helena, MT)

Wyoming Outfitters & Guides Association (✆307-527-7453; www.wyoga.org; 1716 8th St, Cody)

Rafting

Cold water, adrenaline and stunning scenery make rafting a prime summer draw. It's a great group activity; teens in particular will be ever grateful for trading in the minivan for a splashier ride. Commercial outfitters in Grand Teton and outside the parks offer options ranging from inexpensive half-day trips to overnight and multiday expeditions.

Paddlers can choose from large rafts for 12 or more people, or smaller rafts for six; pick the latter if you prefer paddling, otherwise your full-time job is 'holding on.' Full-day trips run from $50 to $90 depending on location, and overnight trips can cost $100 to $200 per person.

White-water trips are not without risk. It's not unusual for participants to fall out of the raft in rough water, although serious injuries are rare and the vast majority of trips are without incident. All trip participants are required to wear US Coast Guard–approved life jackets, and even nonswimmers are welcome. All guides are trained in lifesaving techniques.

River classifications vary over the course of the year, depending on the water level. Higher water levels, usually associated with spring runoff, make a river trip more challenging.

Best Rafting Destinations

» America's longest free-flowing river, Yellowstone River flows through the Paradise Valley from Gardiner (p155).

» Exciting Gallatin River trips (p163) start near Big Sky.

» The Snake River has white-water trips south of Jackson (p214).

» Wildlife-watching float trips down the Snake through Grand Teton National Park (boxed text, p184).

» The Shoshone River west of Cody flows through the scenic Absaroka Range (p146).

Canoeing & Kayaking

Exploring the wilderness on water shows the breadth of beauty and solitude beyond the roads. Yellowstone offers exciting opportunities for paddlers: families can take a load off little legs and cool off, while romantics can paddle up to hidden camps on remote beaches.

One stunning destination is the pine-rimmed Shoshone Lake (p109), the largest backcountry lake in the lower 48. It's popular with boaters who arrive via the Lewis River Channel and also visit the remote Shoshone Geyser Basin. The vast Yellowstone Lake offers access to the remotest reaches of the park, where you can hike into the rarely visited southeast corner. Inquire at Bridge Bay Marina on Yellowstone Lake about boat charters or potential shuttles to the southeast corner.

Grand Teton's Jackson Lake offers scenic backcountry paddling (p199), with several islands to explore and hiking in the little-visited northwest corner. Novice and family paddlers favor String and Leigh Lakes (p200), and Lewis Lake in Yellowstone. Wildlife watching is superlative on Two Ocean Lake.

At Colter Bay in Grand Teton you can rent canoes, but they can't go far, as trips are limited to the bay. For a longer trip, it's best to rent from an outdoor shop such as **Dornan's** (✆307-733-2522; www.dornans.com) at Moose.

Kayakers can paddle the Snake River (boxed text p184), with sections appropriate for a range of abilities and top-notch wildlife watching. Kayak rentals and instruction are available in Jackson and Colter Bay in the Tetons, and also in Gardiner, Montana.

Fishing

Boasting some of the country's best rivers, Greater Yellowstone takes fly-fishing very seriously, particularly in Montana, where Robert Redford's *A River Runs Through It* was filmed.

Yellowstone offers more than 400 fishable waters with cutthroat, rainbow, brown, brook and lake (Mackinaw) trout; Arctic grayling; and mountain whitefish. Fishing season runs from Memorial Day weekend to the first Sunday in November, except on Yellowstone Lake, which opens June 15. Bait angling is generally banned. Catch and release is standard in many areas and has played a major part in boosting fish stocks. Pick up a copy of the relevant state or park fishing regulations before you head out.

The park's best fishing streams are the Gibbon, Madison and Yellowstone Rivers, though you can't really go wrong anywhere – see p118 for more information. Slough Creek has gained a reputation as angling heaven. The Madison, Gibbon and Firehole Rivers in Yellowstone are fly-fishing only.

In Grand Teton National Park, Leigh and Jenny Lakes are stocked with lake, brown, brook and Snake River cutthroat trout. One of the best fishing spots is on the Snake River just below the Jackson Lake dam (with parking on both sides of the river). Ice fishing is growing in popularity, although spring and fall offer the best fishing.

Outside the parks, the Madison is the region's most acclaimed river, though it's also the most mobbed, especially during early July's salmon fly hatch. Fishing shops offer equipment and guides, and float trips proliferate around the region's prime fishing areas. Hit them up for tips on where to fish and what flies to pack. Fly 'afishionados' should check out the free casting clinics at Jacklins Fly Shop in West Yellowstone (p168) every summer Sunday evening.

Fishing Licenses

A Yellowstone National Park fishing permit is required to fish in the park. Anglers 16 years and older must purchase a $15 three-day permit, a $20 seven-day permit or a $35 season permit. To fish in Grand Teton National Park, only a Wyoming fishing

> ## MEET THE RANGERS
>
> In addition to patrolling, rangers give over 4000 programs yearly (mostly June to Labor Day). Park newspapers *Yellowstone Today* and *Grand Teton* list all events and schedules.
>
> » **Guided Ranger Walks** Excellent free hikes and interpretation with an experienced ranger. Reserve in advance.
>
> » **Ranger Programs** Stargaze, learn to track or explore the workings of hot-water wilderness with an insider at these free, short outings (about one hour). Campers shouldn't miss the nightly wheelchair-accessible Campfire Talks in the campgrounds. One-hour programs cover cool topics like entertaining creature-features or local Native American history.

license is required (with a $10.50 conservation stamp for all but one-day licenses).

Wyoming

Outside of the two parks, Wyoming generally offers fishing all year round. Fishing licenses are purchased according to whether you want them for daily (nonresident/resident $14/6) or yearly (nonresident/resident $92/24) use. For details contact the Wyoming Game & Fish Department (☑307-777-4600; http://gf.state.wy.us).

Montana

Fishers must have a conservation license (nonresident/resident $10/8), good for life, and a fishing license. A seasonal license (nonresident/resident $44/18) is good for one year; a two-day stamp costs $15. Contact the Bozeman division of Montana Fish, Wildlife & Parks (☑406-994-4042; http://fwp.mt.gov/fishing; 1400 South 19th, Bozeman, MT) for both.

Idaho

Local vendors and the Idaho Department of Fish & Game (☑208-334-3700; http://fishandgame.idaho.gov) issue fishing licenses. Daily licenses cost $13 for the first day and $6 for additional consecutive days; or purchase a full-season license (nonresident/resident $98/26).

Winter

While the grouse roost in snowdrifts and bison huddle in frosted masses, the skiing, snowshoeing and wildlife-watching options are excellent. Though an increasingly popular season, winter still only attracts a fraction of summer's numbers. Winter sports are practiced from the end of November to April, though February and March generally offer the best snow conditions. In Yellowstone and Grand Teton National Parks, winter activities include cross-country skiing, backcountry skiing, skate skiing (with short skis on groomed hardpack trails), snowshoeing and snowmobiling. One useful resource is the **Montana Winter Guide** (www.wintermt.com).

Downhill Skiing & Snowboarding

Impressive snowfalls and wild and lovely terrain make the northern Rockies a premier downhill destination. Most resorts offer a range of winter activities as well as top-notch ski and snowboard instruction. Cheaper packages are offered in the more precarious early season between November/early December or late-season from March to April, when the skiing is usually quite good.

Resorts

Jackson Hole (www.jacksonhole.com) Offers world-class terrain and heart-thumping views.

Big Sky (www.bigskyresort.com) Boasting vast terrain, Montana's premier resort.

RESPONSIBLE BACKCOUNTRY USE

Backcountry environments are fragile and cannot support careless activity, especially in the wake of heavy visitation. We recommend following the Leave No Trace principles (www.lnt.org/programs/principles.php).

Hiking

» To prevent further erosion, always stay on the trail and don't create shortcuts. Staying on muddy trails will prevent damage to the surrounding terrain.

Campsites

» Use old campsites instead of clearing new ones.

» Camp at least 200ft from the nearest lake, river or stream.

Campfires

» If there is already a fire ring, use it. Burn only dead and downed wood.

» Build fires at least 9ft away from flammable material (including grass and wood).

» Watch fires at all times and extinguish them completely.

Water & Toilets

» Always use toilets established at trailheads, campgrounds or along trails.

» Where no toilet exists, bury human waste in a 6in-deep 'cat hole' at least 300ft from the nearest lake or watercourse.

» Pack out toilet paper in a sealed plastic bag.

» Avoid soaps and detergents – sand or a kitchen scouring pad clean pots remarkably well. In high-altitude lakes even biodegradable soap may not degrade.

» Tip dishwater far from streams and separate food residue with a small basin or strainer. Put these residuals in the trash – leaving it or dirty dishes might attract bears.

Access

» Please do not camp (or collect firewood) on private land without permission, and leave stock gates as you find them.

Grand Targhee (www.grandtarghee.com) Family-friendly and famed for deep champagne powder.

Moonlight Basin (www.moonlightbasin.com) The local's fave, Lonesome Peak gets 400in of light, dry powder each season.

Snow King (www.snowking.com) A mini-resort with tubing and night skiing in downtown Jackson.

Red Lodge Mountain (www.redlodge mountain.com) Thoroughly local, but with expanding terrain and a snowboard park; a good time.

Cross-country & Backcountry Skiing

Nothing approximates heaven more than gliding through snow-covered wilderness under a sharp, blue sky. Nordic (or cross-country) skiing offers a great workout in stunning settings, and saves bucks on lift tickets. The national park and forest services maintain summer hiking trails as cross-country trails during winter, offering terrific solitude and wildlife-watching opportunities.

Backcountry skiing takes skiers to more difficult terrain than regular Nordic gear can handle. The equipment – either telemark (single-camber skis with edges and free-heel bindings) or rondonee (an alpine hybrid system allowing for free-heeled ascents), fitted with climbing skins for ascents – allows skiers to travel cross-country and down steep slopes, though telemark is much better suited to cross-country terrain. Newcomers to the sport should take a lesson (available at most ski resorts) and get in some resort runs before tackling the backcountry. In addition, backcountry skiers must be well versed in avalanche safety.

In late November, the West Yellowstone Ski Festival brings Nordic skiers from around the world and offers demos and clinics.

Dedicated Trails

Land controlled by the NPS, US Forest Service, Bureau of Land Management and private owners supports hundreds of miles of cross-country trails. In Yellowstone, shuttles offer ski drops in Mammoth and Old Faithful. Stay off the groomed roads meant for motorized travel. Otherwise, skiers will find ungroomed backcountry trails with orange markers.

Grand Teton National Park grooms 14 scenic miles of track between Taggart-Bradley Lakes parking area and Signal Mountain. Trails are usually marked with orange flags.

For trails, see p201. Backcountry skiers must take more precautions. Avalanches are a major hazard in the canyons and upper areas of the Tetons.

The Best of the Backcountry

» The Rendezvous Trail System (p169) in West Yellowstone (also the winter training ground for the US Nordic team).

» A snowcoach takes you to the Old Faithful Snow Lodge (p127) for skiing around the kaleidoscope-hued geyser basins, around the Grand Canyon of the Yellowstone and up Mt Washburn.

» Near West Yellowstone, the Fawn and Bighorn Pass Trails connect to form a loop of around 10 miles through elk wintering areas.

» Lone Mountain Ranch (p162) at Big Sky has 46.5 miles of privately groomed trails.

» Red Lodge Nordic Center (p137) has 9 miles of trails.

Snowshoeing

In Yellowstone and elsewhere you can generally snowshoe anywhere – the problem is getting to the trailhead. Try not to mark groomed cross-country trails with your snowshoes, though; stay a few paces from any groomed areas. You can access trails from the Mammoth–Cooke City road all winter, and ski shuttles run to snowbound parts of the park from Mammoth and Old Faithful. Most resorts and hotels rent snowshoes. For more information, see p201.

Rangers lead snowshoe hikes from West Yellowstone's Riverside trail (BYO snowshoes) and Grand Teton's Discovery Center (snowshoes provided). Lone Mountain Ranch (p162) at Big Sky has exclusive snowshoe trails.

Snowmobiling

The park service enforces a daily cap of snowmobiles in Yellowstone National Park, and they must be accompanied by a commercial guide. In Grand Teton, snowmobiling is allowed only on the frozen surface of Jackson Lake. A good alternative is offered by the surrounding national forests, which still offer hundreds of miles of trails.

Snowmobile policies are under constant revision; check with the park for updates. Yellowstone's snowmobile travel season runs from late December to early March.

Book trips a week or two in advance as spaces are limited. All roads except for the North Entrance through the Northeast Entrance (open only to wheeled vehicles) are groomed for oversnow vehicles. The road from the West Entrance to Madison to Old Faithful is shared with cross-country skiers; ride with caution.

All snowmobiles in both parks must meet best available technology (BAT) standards. Speed limits are generally 45mph. Snowmobiles are not allowed in any wilderness areas. If you are new to snowmobiling, bear in mind that it's much more comfortable to ride solo than to double up. When renting, check the cost of clothing rental and insurance, and whether the first tank of gas is free. Backrests and heated handgrips are desirable extras.

Outside the Parks

West Yellowstone is the 'snowmobile capital of the world.' Here you can legally drive snowmobiles in town and attend March's World Snowmobile Expo (www.snowmobile expo.com). Check with the West Yellowstone Chamber of Commerce Information Center (☑406-646-7701; www.westyellowstonechamber. com; Canyon St) for a free *Winter Guide to Yellowstone Country* map with hundreds of miles of snowmobiling routes.

There are over 1000 miles of snowmobile trails between West Yellowstone and Idaho's Targhee National Forest. One is the popular 34-mile Two Top Mountain Loop, the country's first National Recreational Snowmobile Trail. Flagg Ranch Resort (p201) is the southern snowmobiling gateway to Yellowstone (for commercial tours only).

Cooke City (p143) is another regional hub for snowmobiling activity.

Snowcoach Tours

Converted vans on snow tracks, snowcoaches provide transportation in and around the park in winter, also providing a useful service for skiers. Snowcoach tours depart daily from West Yellowstone (p167), Flagg Ranch Resort (p202) and Mammoth; most stop at Old Faithful and all stop for wildlife-watching opportunities. Xanterra (www.travelyellow stone.com; tours from $55) operates park-based tours. Other operators are listed on p170.

Dogsledding

If you have always wanted to travel by paw power, several companies offer day and half-day trips in national forest areas. In Big Sky, Spirit of the North (☑406-682-7994; www.huskypower.com) offers 8-mile half-day adventures with you in the driver's seat. In Chico, check out Absaroka Dogsled Treks (☑406-333-4933; www.extrememontana. com). In Jackson, Continental Divide Dogsled Adventures (☑800-531-MUSH; www.dog sledadventures.com) runs day trips or overnight trips in yurts (Central Asian–style circular tents).

Travel with Children

Hikes For Little Legs

Most kids will enjoy the following adventures, all within 2 miles of a road:

Wraith Falls
A 79ft cascade on the Mammoth to Tower–Roosevelt road.

Ribbon Lake
Great moose-spotting in Yellowstone.

Trout Lake
Cutthroat spawn in early summer in the park's northeast corner.

String & Leigh Lakes
Perfect for canoeing in Grand Teton.

Pelican Creek Trail
A fantastic nature trail on the north shore of Yellowstone Lake just east of Fishing Bridge.

Natural Bridge Trail
Ride an old stagecoach road to a 50ft bridge.

Mystic Falls
Geysers and hot springs to explore in Upper Geyser Basin.

Artist Paint Pots
Bubbling mud pots near Norris Junction.

Storm Point Trail
Bison, moose and marmot north of Lake Yellowstone.

If Yellowstone's wonderland of spurting geysers, gurgling mud pots and wild animals turns adults into kids, then imagine its impact on young ones antsy to explore. In addition, Grand Teton's mountain attractions can be easily scaled down for little legs – and offer ample rewards in the form of picnics and lake swims. It is telling that a number of returning visitors first fell in love with the parks as children. Just exploring the surroundings and snuggling into tents can offer a complete departure from any humdrum everyday routine.

This chapter should give you an idea of the range of possibilities and help you to plan for all stages of your trip – from dreaming it to doing it.

Yellowstone & Grand Teton for Kids

The national parks are as kid-friendly as a destination gets, but the wilderness must be treated with respect. The National Park Service (NPS) looks after its young visitors well, with fun outings, education programs and kid-focused presentations. Children under 12 stay free in park accommodations and most restaurants offer kid menus. Activities ranging from horseback riding to whitewater rafting offer a thrill for all the family.

On the Trail

It's best for kids to set the pace. Pick a route that offers an easy out. A cool destination, like a lake or falls, offers extra incentive. Choosing a shorter route gives kids a chance to slow down and explore. A scavenger hunt list, made from features described in hike descriptions, can help keep their attention. Outfitting kids with a mini backpack, a small hiking stick or camera helps them feel part of the expedition.

National Parks Programs

Kids can earn a very cool badge through the Junior Ranger Program (www.nps.gov/yell/forkids/beajuniorranger.htm; booklet $3; ☉Jun-Labor Day), an iconic and worthwhile program. Tasks include completing an activity book with questions and games, attending a ranger talk and doing a hike. The program can be completed in two days and is aimed at five- to 12-year-olds (although adults can enjoy it too). Grand Teton's Grand Adventure Program (www.nps.gov/grte/forkids/index.htm; donation $1) also trains Junior Rangers; inquire about it at any visitor center.

Junior Rangers and their families can participate in Yellowstone Wildlife Olympics, a field day with physical challenges that pit your abilities against those of iconic wildlife (in theory, no pronghorn are injured in the making of this game). This three-hour activity is held at different visitor centers twice a week; see the park newspaper for details.

Yellowstone also launched the Young Scientist Program (www.nps.gov/yell/forteachers/youngscientist.htm), which lets kids investigate the mysteries of the park with a special toolkit in hand, completing tasks for a coveted patch or keychain. It's for ages five and up.

At the in-depth program Expedition: Yellowstone! (lodging/instruction per day $35/$60; ☉school year) kids learn about preservation, the park's natural and cultural history and current issues affecting the Greater Yellowstone Ecosystem. Includes hikes, field investigations, discussions, creative dramatics and journal writing. This four- to five-day curriculum-based residential program is for students in grades four to eight. Badger your teachers to arrange a visit; parents can come along as chaperones. It's based at Lamar Buffalo Ranch or Mammoth.

Families should take advantage of Yellowstone's ranger-led activities: half-hour programs presented at the visitor centers. Several campgrounds run family-oriented campfire programs with lectures or live music in the early evenings. See the park newspapers for details. Grand Teton's campfire program is based in Colter Bay.

Private Programs

Inside the parks, concessionaires and nonprofits run a range of family-friendly activities. For more in-depth experiences, the Yellowstone Association (☎307-344-2289; www.yellowstoneassociation.org) offers a range of excellent year-round family programs. The most popular is Yellowstone for Families, where a qualified naturalist takes families (with children aged from eight to 12 years old) animal tracking, exploring and wildlife-watching in the park. Other fun stuff includes painting at Artists' Point or taking wildlife photos.

Two-hour stagecoach rides from Roosevelt Lodge travel the sagebrush flats. Trips go several times per day and run from early June to August. Reserve with Xanterra (☎307-344-7311; adult/child $12/6).

Children's Highlights
Adventure

» Camping under the stars and toasting marshmallows

» Fishing for cutthroat trout in a pristine mountain lake or river

» Spying wildlife with binoculars or a spotting scope

» Rafting the Snake River

» Horseback riding the open range (kids eight years old and up)

» Paddling a canoe in Grand Teton National Park

» Tubing, boarding or skiing at Rocky Mountain ski resorts

» Winter outings snowshoeing or cross-country skiing in the park

» Splashing about in the warm water springs of Boiling and Firehole Rivers

» Biking the community pathway through Grand Teton National Park

» Playing in the Chico Hot Springs Pool

Entertainment

» Rodeos in Cody and Jackson for calf-roping and stage gunfights

» Bungee tramps, climbing walls and disc golf at ski resorts in summer

» Huge dinosaur skeletons at Bozeman's Museum of the Rockies and Yellowstone for Kids exhibit

» Stagecoach rides in summer and sleigh rides in winter

» Interactive exhibits of the Draper Museum of Natural History at Cody

KEEPING IT SAFE

» Use a checklist for hiking supplies, including water, sunscreen and first aid

» Kids should carry a flashlight and whistle, and know what to do if they get lost

» Keep children within sight on the trail

» Be careful roadside when everyone's eyes are on the bison, not the traffic

» Scenic overlooks with sheer drops require extra attention

» Caution kids about thermal areas before visiting them

» Discuss situations you might encounter before leaving home

» A pre-trip practice outing helps kids know what to bring and expect

» Let kids know the proper way to handle an animal encounter

» Introduce them to Leave No Trace ethics

» Make-your-own-art studio at the National Museum of Wildlife Art in Jackson

» Trying zookeeper duties at the Grizzly & Wolf Discovery Center in West Yellowstone

» Shetland ponies at the Beartooth Nature Center in Red Lodge

» Drive-in movie theater in Driggs, Idaho

Dining

» Chuckwagon dinners with oversized grills and steaming cast-iron cauldrons

» Picnics on rocky outcrops with a view to the world

» Burgers from the Red Box Car, a defunct train car in Red Lodge

» A short stack at the Running Bear Pancake House in West Yellowstone

» Hot fudge sundaes at the Pioneer Grill, a classic diner in Jackson Lake Lodge

» The Montana Candy Emporium in Red Lodge

Rainy Day Refuges

» Indoor climbing walls in Jackson, Bozeman and Cody

» The kids' workshops at Cody's Buffalo Bill Historical Center

» The IMAX theater in West Yellowstone

» The Grizzly & Wolf Discovery Center in West Yellowstone

» Jackson's movie theaters

» Public libraries in the gateway communities

Coolest Camps

In addition to the camps listed here, most ski resorts offer daycare or camp outings.

» **Field Learning** (www.tetonscience.org) Make inquiries through GPS scavenger hunts or ecology expeditions. The Teton Science School offers outstanding programs for small fries, high schoolers and families.

» **Mini Mountaineers** (www.jhmg.com/school/kids/index.php) The Kids Rock program offers kids six to 10 years old a chance to get vertical (with parents in tow) in a safe and fun outing run by mountain pros. Teens can choose programs that expand on climbing technique and teamwork. Most kids' fave? Tramping through snowfields in summer.

» **Rock Star Treatment** (www.jhrocknroll camp.com) Rock & Roll camp means jamming in day or overnight programs under the tutelage of a professional musician. Budding Claptons and the like must have a year's instrument instruction under their belts. Camp culminates in a live performance, of course.

Planning
When to Go

Yellowstone and Grand Teton really come alive in summer, with wildlife teeming in the valleys and activities in full swing. Yet, with warm and waterproof clothing it's possible to enjoy the parks year-round and still get a lot out of the experience. The tranquility of off-season can even heighten a wilderness experience. Winter can be an especially fun time, as kids try out skis, see fumaroles puff from white landscapes and snowshoe in the tracks of a hare.

What to Pack or Rent

Kids should have comfortable outdoor clothing, a bathing suit, hats for the sun, a shell jacket and warm clothing for chilly days and nights. If you are picky about your bug spray, it's best to bring it from home. Before

PLAY, LEARN & PLAN ONLINE

Kids can get in the mood for the trip with these online games and interactive activities. The official national parks websites listed below also provide extensive information on activities, events and closures for planning

» Test sleuthing skills and try park puzzles at www.nps.gov/webrangers

» For teens, travel on award-winning electronic field trips at www.windows intowonderland.org

» Scavenge for clues about Yellowstone's explosive past or play with jackelopes at the official Yellowstone site www.nps.gov/yell/forkids/index.htm

» Find the mystery animal or take the first steps toward the Junior Ranger badge at the official Grand Teton site www.nps.gov/grte/forkids/index.htm

your trip, make sure everyone has adequate hiking shoes – this could be anything from sneakers to waterproof boots, depending on the range of terrain you'll cover, just make sure it's broken-in. Sandals or Crocs can also be useful for camp. A cheap digital camera or pair of binoculars can provide lots of entertainment since there's so much wildlife to watch.

Most car-rental agencies can add a child's car seat for a nominal fee, but it is best to inquire while making your reservation. Strollers may be harder to come by, so it is best to take yours with you. However, with the crowds and unpaved trails, strollers are not that convenient. Baby backpacks are especially handy for getting beyond the boardwalk and onto the trails with tots or babies over six months old.

It's possible to rent children's bikes with helmets, ski gear and snowshoes; see the Clothing & Equipment chapter (p278) for details.

Before You Go

Keep the kids in mind as you plan your itinerary or include them in the trip planning from the get-go. If they have a stake in the plan, they will be more interested when they arrive, or so the theory goes. Kids tend to thrive with structured activities that can give them a purpose in the park. Lonely Planet's *Travel with Children,* by Cathy Lanigan, provides good information, advice and anecdotes.

Visitor centers have lots of child-oriented exhibits and can divert kids' attention through children's books, coloring books and jigsaw puzzles while you furtively check out the maps.

Book Yellowstone Association programs and area camps months in advance.

If you don't want to be tied town to a schedule while traveling, plenty of activities can be booked just a few days in advance. However, to participate in ranger programs that admit limited numbers, it's always a good idea to show up early.

Catering to Teens

The Tetons and Yellowstone offer tons of things for teens to do. If your teens do not have much outdoor experience, it may be wise to enroll them in a course. Bike rentals are available in all gateway towns and Old Faithful. Climbing gyms usually have short beginner courses appropriate for teens and ski resorts often have mountain biking or alpine slide options. Readers suggest white-water rafting and swimming – there are plenty of alpine lakes that become divine retreats when the temperatures soar. Teens of every skill level can have a blast exploring ski and snowboard runs at area resorts. All hikes included in this guide are appropriate for fit teens.

At Yellowstone National Park, the Youth Conservation Corps (www.nps.gov/yell/park mgmt/yccjobs.htm) offers teens month-long summer jobs in the park, with training in conservation and trail rehabilitation. Weekend activities include hiking, rafting, fishing and assisting scientists or field rangers. The program offers two month-long sessions in a residential setting for young people between the ages of 15 and 18 years of age. Only 30 spots are available, chosen from a random draw. Enrollment is six months prior to summer.

Travel with Pets

Best Spots for Dogs

Wilderness areas and state parks have looser restrictions, see relevant chapters for information.

Trails near Red Lodge, MT

Mountain passes, glacier lakes and basins all on national forest land within a few miles of town.

Jackson Peak

A bare summit with stunning views of the Teton Range, this day hike passes fragrant forests of Douglas fir, and Goodwin Lake in Bridger-Teton National Forest.

Jedediah Smith Wilderness

A remote area strewn with gorgeous alpine lakes and streams north of Grand Teton National Park, access via Grassy Lake Rd.

Jackson, WY

A fido-crazed town with a pet resort and hip dog park.

While vacation-time loyalty to a furry friend is admirable, national parks are a challenging place for pets. Strict restrictions limit pets to paved parking lots and picnic areas. With good reason, too, as these are some of the country's wildest places, where large, charismatic wildlife could be easily threatened by domestic animals (or vice-versa). Still, travel with pets should be as hassle-free and fun as possible. One option is to take advantage of national forest trails where dogs are allowed on a leash. There are many near Yellowstone and the Tetons and your dog will thank you for the introduction to a world of new sights and smells.

Rules & Regulations

In the national parks pets must be leashed at all times. They are not allowed on any boardwalks or backcountry trails, or more than 100ft from roads or paved paths. Needless to say, you will have to clean up after your beloved.

Also, you are not allowed to tie your pet (aka bear bait) to objects or leave him/her unattended. If temperatures are cool, a pet may stay inside a ventilated vehicle, but that's rarely the case in summer.

Service animals such as seeing eye dogs are welcome.

Health & Safety

All pets should have their vaccinations before travel. Like people, animals need conditioning for the outdoors. Break your pet in slowly with easier treks where allowed.

Adequate food, shelter and water should always be handy (but never left where it can attract wild animals). Bring a stash of plastic bags to clean up waste and have a water dish. Never let your pet get near thermal features – they won't know it's hot until it's too late.

Trails & Parks

A glance at an atlas reveals city parks or rivers and lakes that can offer pets a refreshing dip. Once there, check signs for restrictions and local leash laws.

Shoshone National Forest, Bridger-Teton National Forest, Gallatin National Forest and Caribou-Targhee National Forest all allow dogs on leashes. In Jedediah Smith Wilderness, dogs must be under voice control at all times. Always have one eye out for wildlife before your retriever exercises its instincts.

Run by a local pet-advocacy group, **Sophie's Place** (250 Scott Ln; www.pawsofjh .org; ☉daylight hours) is Jackson's only dog park; its website proves a useful resource.

Accommodations

Finding accommodations is another challenge. Pets are allowed in Yellowstone's cabins, but not in the hotels. Most campgrounds allow dogs but do not permit them to go loose.

Our lodging reviews indicate when pets are allowed, usually for a fee ($10 to $35). Reserve these accommodations well in advance, given their shortage.

Kennels

Kennels can be found in most gateway towns. If you don't see one, ask for the local veterinary clinic where staff can indicate the best local kennels or private dog-sitting services.

Look for kennels that are ABKA (American Boarding Kennel Association) certified. When choosing a kennel, ask for a walk through. Consider the following factors: the size of the sleeping space, the presence of outdoor yards or play spaces, the number of daily walks or play sessions, the size and attentiveness of the staff and the kennel's certifications. Some even have webcams, so brooding pet parents won't miss a whimper. Facilities that always keep dogs separate might keep your teacup poodle out of a tussle or prevent it from catching an illness from another dog. Some prefer some canine company to pass the time (in this case, ensure it is well supervised). Kennels may also provide lodgings for cats, birds and fish.

Visitor centers can usually provide information on local veterinary clinics.

Chinook Boarding Kennels (☎307-587-3379; www.woofyproducts.com; 134 E Cooper Ln, Cody, WY) Full-service, climate-controlled boarding and large courtyards for exercise. Has a certified groomer, private training and pet-sitting. Reservations required.

Doggie Daycare & Motel (☎406-763-5585; www.doggiedaycareandmotel.com; 421 Garnet Mt Way, Bozeman, MT) ABKA-certified dog and cat boarding, and full grooming facility, 11 miles south of Bozeman.

Happy Trails Pet Resort (☎307-733-1606; www.springcreekanimalhospital.com; 1035 W Broadway, Jackson, WY) AKBA-accredited veterinary clinic with modern kennels and cat condos for daycare or boarding. Deluxe suites have webcams and TVs.

Kennels at the Smith Family Ranch (☎406-848-7477; www.paradisevalleyvacation. com; 1828 Old Yellowstone Trail South, btwn Gardiner & Emigrant, Paradise Valley, MT) Working ranch; accommodates horses and dogs.

Querencia Kennels (☎406-333-4500; www.querencia.com; 55 Querencia Dr, Emigrant, Paradise Valley, MT) Lodge and canine boarding with ample room to romp.

Trail Creek Pet Center (☎208-354-2571; 180 S 150 East, Driggs, ID; ☉8am-6pm) AKBA-certified boarding facility with grooming and an outdoor exercise center for pets. Offers pet pick-up and drop-off.

Horse Trails & Equestrian Facilities

Yellowstone allows private stock only after July 1, due to snowy and wet conditions. While horses are not allowed in front country campgrounds, some backcountry sites accommodate horses. A favorite of riding groups, Bechler Corner has a number of sites, contact the **backcountry ranger office** (☎307-344-2160).

Bringing a horse or pack animal with you requires extensive advance planning. Download backcountry stock rules and grazing information from official national parks websites, which also list guided, multiday stock trips using horses or llamas. Contact **Yellowstone National Park** (www.nps.gov/

yell/planyourvisit/stockbusn.htm) or **Grand Teton National Park** (www.nps.gov/grte/plan yourvisit/horserides.htm).

In Grand Teton National Park late snows sometimes delay the opening of backcountry stock campsites: consult with the **parks permit office** (☏307-739-3309). Stock users often camp in national forests and travel in on day trips. Outside the park, stock camping areas in the John D Rockefeller Jr Memorial Parkway (between Flagg Ranch and Grassy Lake) do not require a permit. For stock camping in the Bridger-Teton National Forest, consult the **supervisor's office** (☏307-733-5500).

Inside Grand Teton National Park, Death Canyon Trailhead Rd boasts the only vehicle-accessible stock campsite. Backcountry stock camping is allowed in the north fork of Granite Canyon, Death Canyon, the south fork of Cascade Canyon, Paintbrush Canyon and Berry Creek. Obtain your backcountry permit at visitor centers.

regions at a glance

In many ways Yellowstone and Grand Teton couldn't be more different. Yellowstone is the big granddaddy, huge, sprawling and subtle, full of weird thermal basins, big, furry critters and wild, remote corners in which to lose yourself. Grand Teton to the south is smaller, showier and more obviously spectacular, studded with alpine lakes and vertical peaks that offer prime climbing and trekking action, just a stone's throw from civilization at Jackson Hole.

Whatever your interest, don't overlook the areas around the parks. From the ranchlands of the Paradise Valley to Jackson Hole, the scenery is just as grand and you'll find a fraction of the crowds.

Yellowstone National Park

Thermals ✓✓✓
Wildlife ✓✓✓
Activites ✓✓

Thermal Features

Fuelled by a giant magma hotspot, Yellowstone's show-stealing geysers, belching mud pots and beautiful hot springs draw the big crowds. Yep, you've decided to pitch your tent atop a giant supervolcano.

Wildlife

Geysers bring people to Yellowstone but the wildness keeps them coming back: the haunting early morning howl of a wolf or the sight of a grizzly lumbering across the valley floor.

Activities

To really explore the park you will need to unbuckle your seat belt and get a sweat on. Hiking is the perfect way to see the park but also try paddling, fly-fishing and horseback riding.

p52

Around Yellowstone

Scenery ✓✓
Museums ✓✓
Activities ✓✓✓

Scenery

The Yellowstone ecosystem doesn't end at the park gates. Surrounding the park is a network of forested mountain ranges, alpine lakes and sublime valleys that offer some superbly scenic approaches to the parks.

Museums

Not all of Yellowstone's marvels are natural. Don't miss the mind-boggling dinosaur fossils at Bozeman's Museum of the Rockies or the fine collection of historical, ethnological and ecological museums at Cody's Buffalo Bill Historical Center.

Activites

Hiking, white-water rafting, skiing, horse trekking, ziplining, snowmobiling, fly-fishing: it's hard to think of an activity you *can't* do outside Yellowstone.

p133

Grand Teton National Park

Backpacking ✓✓✓
Wildlife ✓✓
Climbing ✓✓✓

Around Grand Teton

Skiing ✓✓✓
Food ✓✓
Summer Fun ✓✓✓

Backpacking

The Tetons are simply a stunning place to strap on a backpack. From snowy cirques to cold streams and grassy glades gone Technicolor with wildflowers, this is the finest way we know to lose yourself.

Wildlife

Anyone who has seen September's elk rut, heard the high yip of coyotes or had a moose crash through their camp knows that wilderness lives large here.

Climbing

If it's adrenaline you're after, crowning these craggy spires is a euphoric undertaking. It takes time too, since most Teton approaches are an all-day affair. But you will be ascending in the footholds of America's pioneer mountaineers.

p173

Skiing

Jackson Hole is a powder-hound's paradise of silken rides and rugged terrain. With over 4000ft of continuous vertical, the smile will freeze on your face.

Food

When you play this hard, feeding that gnashing maw becomes a priority. In comes the Tetons' sumptuous, sustainable food, from local grass-fed Angus to mint couscous and organic ales. To go straight to the source, visit the farmers markets or join an Idaho farm dinner.

Summer Fun

Dirt is the word – if it ain't on you, you're not doing it right. From fat tire epics to galloping on a Wyoming ranch or just lolling in mountain wild flowers, summer is prime time.

p209

Look out for these icons:

 Our author's recommendation

 A green or sustainable option

 No payment required

See the Index for a full list of destinations covered in this book.

On the Road

Yellowstone National Park

Includes »

Best Hikes

» Mt Washburn (p96)
» Bunsen Peak (p90)
» Yellowstone River Picnic Area Trail (p93)
» Beaver Ponds Trail (p89)
» Sepulcher Mountain (p91)

Best Places to Stay & Eat

» Old Faithful Inn (p127)
» Lake Yellowstone Hotel (p126)
» Backcountry Campsite (p105)
» Mammoth Hot Springs Dining Room (p128)
» Lake Yellowstone Hotel Dining Room (p130)

Why Go?

Yellowstone National Park is the crown jewel of the Greater Yellowstone Ecosystem. From the steaming geysers and sublime lakes of the south to the golden canyons and wild-life-rich valleys of the north, the park has several distinct regions, and it's worth investing time to visit at least a couple to get a sense of the park's complex diversity.

Yellowstone's spectacular roadside sights are reward enough, but the park's real joys lie off the tarmac, at the end of a backcountry hiking or fishing trail, so try to fit in at least a couple of our hikes. From golden lakeshore sunsets or dawn mists rising over a steaming geyser basin, Yellowstone's beauty is both spectacular and subtle.

Our advice is not to try to pack everything into one visit. The crowds and traffic seem twice as bad if you're in a rush, and you'll appreciate the extra time if you have a surprise encounter with a moose or bison.

When to Go
Mammoth, WY

July & August	September & October	January–March
Warm weather and snow-free trails, but packed lodging and campgrounds.	Bugling elk, fall colors, fewer crowds and discounted rates.	Skis, snowshoes, no crowds, lots of shivering wildlife: a different side to Yellowstone.

Entrances

The following are open to vehicles 24 hours a day during open months.

The North Entrance Station is at Gardiner, Montana, and the Northeast Entrance is near Cooke City; both are open year-round.

The East Entrance is on US 14/16/20, from Cody, and the South Entrance is on US 89/191/287 north of Grand Teton National Park; both are open early May to early November.

The West Entrance is on US 20/191/287 near West Yellowstone, Montana, and is open mid-to-late April to early November.

See p57 for full details on opening dates.

DON'T MISS

One of the best free services offered by the park service is its series of **ranger-led activities**. From boardwalk strolls explaining the interior plumbing of a geyser to guided wildlife watching at dawn and short, guided hikes, the commentary given by the park's affable rangers will really add to your understanding of the park. Check times in the park newspaper *Yellowstone Today* and time your itinerary around a couple of these presentations. At the very least catch the nightly campfire talks given at most park campgrounds, some of which are aimed specifically at young families.

If you're nervous about hiking by yourself and would prefer to hike in a group, rangers also lead **guided walks** to several places in the park. Destinations vary year to year but currently include short hikes to Mystic Falls, Beaver Ponds, Lake Overlook, Storm Point, the southern rim of Yellowstone canyon and around the Upper Geyser Basin. See the Day Hikes section of this chapter (p89) for details on these hikes. Walks are limited to a couple of hours, are free and include some of the most interesting strolls in the park.

When You Arrive

» A seven-day pass to both Yellowstone and Grand Teton national parks costs $25/20 per vehicle/motorcyclist or $12 for cyclists or hikers on foot. Credit cards are accepted. An annual pass to both parks costs $50. See the boxed text, p260, for other passes.

» Visitors receive a free map and the *Yellowstone Today* newspaper, which has a schedule of ranger-led activities, park facilities, road closures and opening hours.

» Notice boards at entrances indicate which campgrounds are full or closed.

GATEWAY TOWNS

» North Entrance: Gardiner (p154)

» West Entrance: West Yellowstone (p167)

» Northeast Entrance: Cooke City (p143)

Fast Facts

» Area: 3472 sq miles

» Highest elevation: 11,358ft (Eagle Peak)

» Lowest elevation: 5282ft (Reese Creek)

Reservations

If you are camping you can get away without reservations, but for in-park accommodation and Western cookouts you should reserve up to six months in advance through **Xanterra** (307-344-7311, 866-439-7375; www. yellowstonenationalparklodges. com). Reservations open in May for the next year.

Resources

» Official park site: www .nps.gov/yell

» Lodging, restaurant and activities from the park concessionaire: www .yellowstonenationalpark lodges.com

» Useful private site: www .yellowstone.net

» Full park information on everything from geysers to hiking trails: www.yellow stonenationalpark.com

» State tourism website: www.wyomingtourism.org

Yellowstone National Park Highlights

1 Feel the tension build as you wait for **Old Faithful** (p79) to erupt

2 Contemplate the gigantic scale of the **Grand Canyon of the Yellowstone** (p65) and its thundering Lower Falls

3 Marvel at the ethereal floating rainbow colors of **Grand Prismatic Spring** (p85), Yellowstone's beautiful thermal feature

4 Wander the colorful travertine mounds of the Lower Terrace and see elk walk around the historic buildings in **Mammoth** (p59)

5 Feel your hair stand up as you spot your first wild wolf or grizzly in the **Lamar Valley** (p62)

6 Sniff the sulfur and feel the ground bubble on a boardwalk tour of **Norris Geyser Basin** (p75), home to the world's tallest geyser, Steamboat

7 Savor the views of **Yellowstone Lake** (p70) at sunset from Lake Butte Overlook, from the beach at Sedge Bay or over a Teton Ale from Lake House restaurant

8 Backpack or canoe the beautiful waters and remote thermal features of **Shoshone Lake** (p109), the largest backcountry lake in the Lower 48

To Bozeman (60mi)

Big Horn Peak

To Livingston (49mi)

Gardiner

North Entrance Station

Electric Peak (10,992ft)

Mammoth

Bunsen Peak (8564ft)

Little Quadrant Mountain (9885ft)

Road closed early November to mid/late April

Lee Metcalf Wilderness

To Ennis, MT (60mi)

Dome Mountain (9894ft)

Grizzly Lake

Mt Holmes (10,336ft)

Gallatin Rd

Hebgen Lake

Norris Campground

Norris

West Yellowstone

Riverside

Madison

West Entrance Station

Mt Haynes (8235ft)

Madison Campground

Macks Inn

Grand Prismatic Spring

Old Faithful

IDAHO

Shoshone Geyser Basin

Shoshone Lake

Douglas Knob (8544ft)

GEYSER COUNTRY

Three River Junction

Targhee National Forest

Pitchstone Plateau

BECHLER REGION

Cave Falls Campground

Grassy Lake Rd

To Ashton (4.1mi)

Jedediah Smith Wilderness

John D Rockefeller Jr Memorial Parkway

Jackson Lake

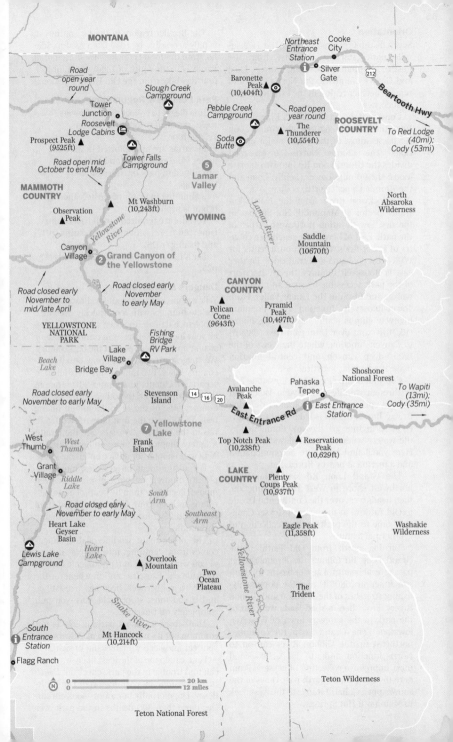

Orientation

Seven distinct regions comprise the 3472-sq-mile park (starting clockwise from the north): Mammoth, Roosevelt, Canyon, Lake and Geyser Countries, the Norris area, and remote Bechler region in the extreme southwest corner.

Conceived by Lt Daniel C Kingman in 1886, the 142-mile, figure-eight Grand Loop Rd passes most of the park's major attractions. The 12-mile Norris–Canyon road divides the Grand Loop Rd into two shorter loops: the 96-mile Lower (South) Loop and the 70-mile Upper (North) Loop.

A clockwise drive from the North Entrance begins at Mammoth Hot Springs in the dry, low-elevation northwest corner of the park. East of here is the sagebrush country of Tower-Roosevelt Junction, a center for Wild West cookouts and trail rides. Further east is Roosevelt Country, the wildest part of the park accessible by road and home to wolves and bison in the Lamar Valley. From Tower-Roosevelt Junction the mountain highway climbs south past Mt Washburn (10,243ft) and over Dunraven Pass (8859ft) to Canyon Junction, where the views of the 1200ft-deep canyon and central location make it a popular logistical base.

Continue south along the Yellowstone River through wildlife-rich Hayden Valley and the hot springs of Mud Volcano to Fishing Bridge Junction. This is Lake Country, beloved by springtime grizzlies and dominated by the watery wilderness of Yellowstone Lake. Here you'll find lakeshore accommodation and a marina at nearby Bridge Bay.

The Grand Loop Rd skirts the lake's northwest shore to West Thumb Junction, then heads west over the Continental Divide to Old Faithful in the heart of Geyser Country, home to the park's richest collection of geothermal features.

Turning north from Old Faithful, the Grand Loop Rd follows the Firehole River past several beautiful geyser basins to Madison Junction (6806ft) and the popular fly-fishing stretches of the Madison and Gibbon Rivers. From here a road leads west out of the park to the gateway town of West Yellowstone. The Grand Loop Rd continues northeast up the Gibbon River canyon to Norris Junction, home to the park's second most impressive collection of geysers. From here the road heads north past views of the snowcapped Gallatin Range to the west back to Mammoth Hot Springs.

The Bechler region, in the far southwest, is only accessible by road from Ashton, Idaho, from the John D Rockefeller Jr Memorial Parkway to the south of Yellowstone, or by a four-day hike from the Old Faithful region.

Park Policies & Regulations

» It is illegal to collect plants, flowers, rocks, petrified wood or antlers in Yellowstone.
» Firearms are now allowed in the park under valid state or federal laws but are prohibited in park or concessionaire buildings.
» Swimming in water of entirely thermal origin is prohibited.
» Permits are required for all backcountry trips (p105) and activities like boating (p117) and fishing (p118).
» For a list of campground regulations see p257.

Dangers & Annoyances

Yellowstone is grizzly country. Bears that associate humans with food quickly become a problem, a danger and then a target, so keep all your food packed away in campgrounds or strung up on a bear pole in the backcountry. We suggest carrying bear spray on all backcountry hikes. Two male hikers were killed in separate incidents in summer 2011 – one in the Canyon region, the other on the Geyser Country side of the Mary Mountain hiking trail. These were the first bear-related fatalities in the park for 25 years. See the Health & Safety chapter for more on bears and the Activities chapter for advice on hiking safely.

For all the focus on grizzlies, more people are injured by park bison (and even moose) each year than by bears. The golden rule is to keep your distance – 100yd from bears and 25yd from anything taller than a chipmunk.

The other main wildlife-related danger comes from slamming into the car in front of you while staring at a photogenic herd of roadside elk. Exercise caution whenever the desire to rubberneck becomes irresistible, and if you must stop, make sure you pull completely off the road.

Theft from trailhead parking lots is not common but it's not unheard of. Always lock your car and keep valuables out of sight.

For a catalogue of the least likely ways you can find trouble in the park, check out *Death in Yellowstone* by park historian Lee Whitlesey. The morbidly humorous book chronicles more than 300 deaths in the park over

YELLOWSTONE PARK: OPENING & CLOSING DATES

Yellowstone's opening schedule is complicated. Pin down specific opening and closing dates from websites www.nps/gov/yell and www.yellowstonenationalparklodges.com.

» **Year-round** The North Entrance at Gardiner and the north road from Gardiner to Cooke City via Mammoth and Tower-Roosevelt Junction. Mammoth Campground is also open year-round.

» **Mid- to late April** The first of the other roads to open are the West Entrance Rd and the western side of the Grand Loop Rd: Mammoth to Norris, Norris to Madison and Madison to Old Faithful. Norris to Canyon opens a week later. Old Faithful Snow Lodge opens.

» **Early May** The South and East Entrances open, followed by the road between West Thumb and Old Faithful over Craig Pass (8262ft). Old Faithful Inn opens.

» **Mid-May** Fishing Bridge RV Park, Mammoth Hotel, Old Faithful Lodge and Lake Yellowstone Hotel open.

» **End May** The road between Tower and Canyon Junctions over Dunraven Pass (8859ft) is the last park road to open, usually by Memorial Day. The Beartooth Hwy between Red Lodge and Cooke City normally opens by Memorial Day but can be delayed a week or more by heavy snowfall.

» **Early June** Canyon Village, Lake Lodge and Roosevelt Lodge open. Lewis Lake and Grant Village campgrounds are the last to open.

» **September** Park accommodation starts to close, with Canyon Village and Roosevelt Lodge first to go.

» **Mid-October** The Beartooth Hwy closes for the year, as does accommodation at Old Faithful. Slough Creek and Lewis Lake campgrounds are the last to close at the end of the month.

» **November** All park roads close on the first Monday in November, except for the Gardiner–Cooke City road.

» **Mid-December** Entrances open to snowmobiles and snowcoaches from the third Wednesday in December through to the second Monday in March, when spring plowing starts. Roads are then closed to vehicles but are open to cyclists in April. Old Faithful Snow Lodge and Mammoth Hot Springs Hotel and Dining Room open for the winter until early March.

---

the last century, ranging from the horrifying (boiled alive in a hot spring, disemboweled by a grizzly) to the ridiculous (accidentally backing a car over the edge of the Yellowstone Canyon, death from wild parsnips).

SIGHTS

Mammoth Country

Mammoth Country is renowned for its graceful geothermal terraces and the towering Gallatin Range to the northwest. As the lowest and driest region of the park, it's also the warmest and a good base for winter and early- or late-season activities.

The region's Northern Range is an important wintering area for wildlife, including the park's largest herds of elk, pronghorn, mule deer and bighorn sheep. Around half the park's population of elk winter here, attracted by the lower temperatures and lack of snow on many south-facing slopes (due to the sun and prevailing wind). The poorly aerated and drained soil supports scant vegetation, creating 'dry desert' conditions.

For visitors (and most elk) the focal point of the Mammoth region is Mammoth Junction (6239ft), 5 miles south of the park's Northwest Entrance, on a plateau above Mammoth Campground. The junction contains the region's main services, including a visitor center, backcountry office, post office, gas station, medical center and even a church and courthouse. The Mammoth Hot Springs Hotel has espresso and public showers, while the Yellowstone General Store offers groceries, souvenirs, cold beer, coffee and ice cream.

Just south of the junction is Mammoth Hot Springs, the area's main thermal

Mammoth Country

| 0 | 5 km |
| 0 | 3 miles |

Electric Creek
Reese Creek
Stephens Creek
89
Gardiner
North Entrance Station
Yellowstone River Trail
Rescue Creek Trail
Yellowstone River
Knowles Falls
Crevice Lake
Electric Peak Spur Trail
Sepulcher Mountain Trail
Beaver Ponds
Old Gardiner Rd
North Entrance Rd
Blacktail Creek Trail
Cache Lake
Sepulcher Mountain (9646ft)
Beaver Ponds Trailhead
7
8 6
Mt Everts (7841ft)
Gardner River
Glenn Creek
Upper Terrace Loop
2
Mammoth Junction
Mammoth Hot Springs
Blacktail Ponds
Rescue Creek
Fawn Pass Trail
Fawn Creek
Rustic Falls
Osprey Falls Trailhead
Sheepeater Canyon
Undine Falls
Wraith Falls
4
3
Bunsen Peak (8564ft)
Osprey Falls
Swan Lake
Gardner's Hole
Lava Creek
Blacktail Deer Creek
Bighorn Pass Trail
Panther Creek
Sheepeater Cliffs Picnic Area
Sheepeater Cliffs
5
Warming Hut
Yellowstone National Park
Lupine Creek
Antler Peak (10,023ft)
Road closed early November to early May
Grand Loop Rd
Willow Park & Moose Bogs
Indian Creek
Appolinaris Spring Picnic Area
Dome Mountain (9894ft)
Obsidian Lake
Apollinaris Spring
Arrowe Canyon Creek
Mt Holmes (10,336ft)
Grizzly Lake Trail
Beaver Lake
Obsidian Cliff
1C4
MAMMOTH COUNTRY
1C5
Mount Holmes-Winter Creek Trail
Grizzly Lake
Beaver Lake Picnic Area
Solfatara Trailhead
Lake of the Woods
Arrowe Canyon
Solfatara Creek
Winter Creek
Straten Creek
Roaring Mountain
Solfatara Creek Trail
Obsidian Creek
Grand Loop Rd
Twin Lakes
Wolf Lake
Nymph Lake
Norris Meadows Picnic Area
Howard Eaton Trail
Norris
Norris Geyser Basin
Ice Lake
Solfatara Plateau
Gibbon Geyser Basin
Norris-Canyon Rd
Gibbon River
Virginia Cascade
Gibbon Meadows

Mammoth Country

attraction. From here roads go south to Norris (21 miles) and east to Tower-Roosevelt Junction (18 miles).

MAMMOTH

Fort Yellowstone   HISTORIC SITE
Mammoth Hot Springs was known as Fort Yellowstone from 1886 to 1918, when the US Army managed the park from this collection of historic buildings. Elk regularly graze the manicured lawns of the campus-like historic and administrative centre, bringing traffic to a standstill, and the high-pitched cries of bugling elk echo around the region in fall.

If you're particularly interested in park history, pick up the *Fort Yellowstone Historic District Tour Guide* brochure (50¢) for a self-guided tour of the fort's original buildings. The tour takes in the former jail, barracks, granary and stables, most of which have been converted to employee residences. The guardhouse at the end of the row once controlled all public access into the park. If you are here on a Sunday morning, pop into the lovely English-style church (1913), where the stained-glass windows depict Old Faithful and Yellowstone Falls. (You can even get married here if you like; see boxed text p265). Other notables include the green-tiled Chinese-style roof of the chief engineer's office (nicknamed the 'pagoda') and the bear statues that guard the entrance to the post office. Rangers lead hour-long history walks daily at 6pm, departing from the visitor center.

Mammoth Visitor Center Museum MUSEUM
(☑307-344-2263; ⊙8am-7pm) In the Albright Visitor Center, this was formerly the army's bachelor quarters, but now features reproductions of 19th-century watercolors by Thomas Moran (1837–1926) and black-and-white photographs by William Henry Jackson, both of whom accompanied the 1871 Hayden expedition. Jackson's old camera is on display, as are the glass plates he developed in the field using hot water from Yellowstone's hot springs. There are also displays on the park's early visitors, lots of stuffed animals and two 20-minute videos on the parks, starting on the hour and half-hour. Don't miss the fine photographs of former superintendent Norris in his trademark buckskins and mountain man Jim Bridger (upstairs) bearing an uncanny resemblance to country singer Willie Nelson. Rangers give talks in front of the center at 3pm and some days also at 4pm.

The visitor center complex is named for Horace Albright, park superintendent between 1919 and 1929 and director of the National Park Service from 1929 to 1933.

TRUMAN EVERTS

Everts Ridge, northwest of Mammoth, is named after Truman Everts, a member of the 1870 Washburn-Langford-Doane expedition and a notable early tourist disaster story.

Separated from his group on the southern shores of Yellowstone Lake in September 1870, the 54-year-old tax inspector soon lost his bearings and promptly broke his glasses. His horse then bolted, taking all Everts' equipment with it save for a penknife and a pair of opera glasses (not quite as useless as they sound – they helped him make fire!). He kept warm at night by cuddling up to hot springs near Heart Lake, until he ended up badly burning himself. At one point he spent the night in a tree, as a pacing mountain lion stalked him from below.

After 37 days lost in the wilderness, Everts was finally discovered, shoeless, frost-bitten, emaciated, delirious and raving like a madman...but alive.

Mammoth Hot Springs Hotel   HISTORIC HOTEL

The Mammoth Hot Springs Hotel is worth a visit even if you are not staying. Piano music echoes around the lobby from 5pm followed by video or slide presentations in the side Map Room, where you can also check out the huge wall map of the United States assembled from 15 types of wood from around the world. (Residents of Maryland will be displeased to note that theirs is the only state capital not marked.) Also worth noting is the charming antique water fountain to the left of the Activities Desk.

Mammoth Hot Springs   HOT SPRINGS

The imposing Lower and Upper Terraces of Mammoth Hot Springs are the product of dissolved subterranean limestone (itself originally deposited by ancient seas), which is continuously deposited as the spring waters cool on contact with air. As guidebooks love to say, the mountain is in effect turning itself inside out, depositing over a ton of travertine (limestone deposits) here every year. The colored runoff from the naturally white terraces is due to the bacteria and algae that flourish in the warm waters. See p242 for more details on the construction of the terraces.

An hour's worth of boardwalks wend their way around the Lower Terraces and connect to the Upper Terraces Loop. The rutting Rocky Mountain elk that sometimes lounge on Opal Terrace in fall are a favorite photo opportunity.

Surreal Palette Springs (accessed from the bottom parking lot) and sulfur-yellow Canary Springs (accessed from the top loop) are the most beautiful sites, but thermal activity is constantly in flux, so check the current state of play at the visitor center. The famously ornate travertine formations that characterize the terraces of Minerva Spring have been dry since 2002 but are still beautiful. At the bottom of the terraces, by the parking area, is the phallic, dormant 36ft-high hot-spring cone called Liberty Cap, apparently named after hats worn during the French Revolution. The former spring must have had particularly high water pressure to create such a tall cone over its estimated 2500-year life span. Across the road, Opal Spring is slowly converging on a century-old residence designed by Robert Reamer (the architect of the Old Faithful Inn and Roosevelt Arch). Park strategists have to decide which to preserve – the architecture or the spring.

A 1.5-mile paved one-way road loops counterclockwise around the Upper Terraces; no vehicles longer than 25ft are permitted. The overlook affords impressive views of the Lower Terraces and Fort Yellowstone and offers access to Canary Springs and New Blue Spring. Highlights further around the loop include the spongelike Orange Spring Mound and the perfectly named White Elephant Back Terrace. The loop joins the main road near the large Angel Terrace.

Ninety-minute ranger walks leave from the Liberty Cap daily at 9:30am and there are short talks nearby at 1pm, 1:30pm and 2pm.

MAMMOTH TO TOWER-ROOSEVELT

The 18-mile road to Tower-Roosevelt Junction heads east from Mammoth over the Gardner River Bridge, where the Gardner River meets the Yellowstone River. By the roadside, just over 2 miles from Mammoth, is pretty three-tiered Undine Falls, aptly named for an alluring water nymph. For your own private views of the falls from the north side of the river, hike less than half a mile along Lava Creek trail from the nearby Lava Creek Picnic Area.

The easy 1-mile round-trip walk to Wraith Falls is a good family hike through pretty meadows and fire-burn patches. The trail begins at the pullout east of Lava Creek Picnic Area, 5 miles from Mammoth, and follows Lupine Creek for 15 minutes to the base of a 79ft cascade.

Just past Blacktail Ponds (good for spotting muskrats and waterfowl) is the Blacktail Trailhead, where trails lead down Rescue Creek or into the Black Canyon of the Yellowstone near Crevice Lake.

Two miles past here, the 0.5-mile Forces of the Northern Range Self-Guiding Trail is an accessible boardwalk that teaches kids about the environmental forces of this part of the park. Kids will get a kick from placing their hand on a wolf print.

The 6-mile one-way Blacktail Plateau Dr detours off the main highway to offer glimpses of gorgeous summer wildflowers (June and July) and golden fall colors (September). The road follows part of the Bannock Trail, a hunting route taken by Bannock Indians in the mid-19th century. The trail originated in Idaho, crossed the Yellowstone Valley at the Bannock Ford (see p93) and continued through the Lamar Valley to Soda Butte Creek before leaving what is now the park at its northeast corner and continuing to Bighorn Valley. Along the second half of this drive, near Crescent Hill, is the spot where Truman Everts was finally discovered after wandering lost in the park for 37 days (see the boxed text, p59). RVs and trailers are not allowed down the rough, unpaved road but bikes are an option if you have someone to pick you up at the other end.

Instead of taking Blacktail Plateau Dr, continue east on the main Grand Loop Rd. You'll pass Phantom Lake (one of three interconnected lakes that are normally dry by July) and an unsigned scenic overview of Hellroaring Mountain, Garnet Hill, and the Yellowstone River and Hellroaring Creek Valleys. A couple of miles further is the Hellroaring Trailhead, a short drive down a dirt road and popular with horse packers. Half a mile past here, Floating Island Lake is dense with vegetation, making it a good place to spot birds.

Just before you reach Tower-Roosevelt Junction is the 0.25-mile turnoff (no RVs or trailers) to the heavily visited Petrified Tree, surrounded by a fence like a priceless work of art. The tree is worth a quick look if you've never seen one before, but the parking lot can be cramped and busy. A nicer way to visit the tree is on an early-morning or evening hike from Roosevelt Lodge on the Lost Lake loop (p93).

MAMMOTH TO NORRIS

The 20-mile road from Mammoth to Norris passes the Upper Terraces and enters a jumbled landscape of hoodoos, formed when the 65,000-year-old travertine deposits of nearby Terrace Mountain slipped down the hillside, breaking into boulder-like fragments. (You can get an up-close look at the hoodoos on the Terrace Mountain hike or by walking the Howard Eaton trail from Glen Creek Trailhead down to Mammoth). The road climbs to the cantilevered road of the Golden Gate, named after the light-colored welded rock formed from cooled ash flows. The sprouting knob of rock on the outside of the road was actually pulled down and then replaced when the road was widened! Shortly afterwards a pullout offers views of tiny Rustic Falls, a natural funnel that was probably used by Sheepeater Indians to trap bighorn sheep.

The peak rising to the left is Bunsen Peak (8564ft), a plug of solidified magma that formed inside a long since eroded volcanic cone. Hiking and biking trails head up and around Bunsen Peak from the busy Bunsen Peak/Glen Creek Trailhead (p90 and p115). Further along on the right, delightful Swan Lake in the middle of Gardner's Hole offers good birdwatching (look for trumpeter swans in winter and early spring) and views of the Gallatins. A board helps identify the various peaks.

Two miles further south, turn off for the Sheepeater Cliffs, an amazing collection of half-million-year-old hexagonal basalt columns, stacked like building blocks. You'll find a scenic picnic area and walks along the river to more formations (no buses, trailers or RVs allowed on this road). The Sheepeaters, also known as the Tukudika, were a subtribe of the Shoshone and the park's earliest year-round inhabitants.

The road passes a nice fishing spot and wintertime warming hut near Indian Creek Campground, then continues to a series of four pullouts at Willow Park and Moose Bogs, 2 miles further south and a good place to look for some of the park's 200 or so moose. Soon after comes a pleasant picnic spot at Appolinaris Spring, once a popular stagecoach stop for parched travelers headed to Norris.

BOILING RIVER: THE PARK'S WORST-KEPT SECRET

One of the few places where you can take a legal soak in Yellowstone is Boiling River, halfway between Gardiner and Mammoth. From the parking area by the Montana–Wyoming border a trail leads 0.5 miles along the river to a point where an underground hot spring surfaces from below a limestone overhang. There are several pools along the riverside (see the boxed text p275 for the potential dangers of soaking in hot springs).

Bring a towel and flip-flops. The only changing area is the vault toilet at the parking lot. Swimming is allowed only during daylight hours, and food, pets, alcohol and nudity are prohibited. The pools are closed during high river levels (most commonly in spring).

The turnouts north of here are good places to spot pronghorn in the summer and bighorn sheep and elk in the winter. Also to the north is a sign that marks the 45th parallel, halfway between the equator and the North Pole.

Obsidian Cliff, to the left of the road, exposes the interior of a 180,000-year-old lava flow. Rapid cooling prevented the formation of crystals and fused the lava into this form of volcanic glass. Obsidian, used for spearheads and arrowheads, was widely traded by Native Americans and was one of the major reasons early peoples visited the Yellowstone region. The park service was forced to remove the cliffside trails of this National Historic Landmark due to pilfering of the obsidian – leave it alone!

Just 1 mile further, the **Beaver Lake** picnic area offers a fine spot for a picnic and some wildlife-watching. Just past here, isolated fumaroles, hot springs and other thermal features start to appear by the side of the road, heralding the approach of the thermally active Norris region.

Roaring Mountain is a huge bleached hillside pockmarked with hissing fumaroles. During its heyday around the turn of the last century, visitors could hear the roar of the fumaroles from over 4 miles away. The activity is much reduced today.

From here the road passes pretty **North** and **South Twin Lakes** and descends to beautiful **Nymph Lake**. The lake's bubbling pools, bleached white shoreline and steaming geysers lend the area a powerfully primeval air; something out of the landscapes of Tolkien or the age of the dinosaurs. Just south of here is the unsigned but superbly named **Devil's Frying Pan** springs. The smell of sulfur stays with you as the road quickly descends into the Norris Geyser Basin.

The Mammoth–Norris road is scheduled for reconstruction in 2012.

and one of the park's great wildlife-viewing areas.

The 29-mile Northeast Entrance Rd passes from Cooke City through the Lamar Valley to Tower-Roosevelt Junction (6270ft) and then continues west for 18 miles to Mammoth Hot Springs. This is the only road in the park that remains open year-round. From Tower-Roosevelt junction the Grand Loop Rd heads south to Canyon Junction, over the high Dunraven Pass.

Roosevelt Lodge (p123) has lodging, food, showers, a small grocery store and a nearby ranger station and Conoco gas station, as well as nearby hiking trails and a horse corral (see p116).

NORTHEAST ENTRANCE TO TOWER-ROOSEVELT

It's 29 miles from the Northeast Entrance to Tower-Roosevelt. A couple of miles inside the Northeast Entrance the road enters Wyoming and follows Soda Butte Creek, offering fine views of the craggy ridgeline of towering Barronette Peak (10,404ft) to the west. It was Jack Baronet who rescued Truman Everts (see boxed text p59) for a promised $600 reward; not only did he not get the reward, but the park misspelled the peak they named after him! Near Pebble Creek Campground at tiny Icebox Canyon, the lovely valley warms up and opens wide. Southeast is a ridgeline known as the Thunderer (10,554ft), after the frequent storms that gather here.

Two miles past Pebble Creek is the trailhead for the short 0.5-mile walk through fir forest and summer wildflowers to scenic **Trout Lake**, named after the abundant

Roosevelt Country

President Theodore Roosevelt visited this rugged mountainous area in the park's northeast corner during a two-week jaunt through the park in 1903, lending his name to the rustic Roosevelt Lodge by Tower-Roosevelt Junction that opened three years later. Fossil forests, the wildlife-rich Lamar River Valley, its tributary trout streams and the dramatic and craggy peaks of the Absaroka Range are the highlights in this remote, scenic and undeveloped region. The rustic cabins, stagecoach rides and Western cookouts of the Roosevelt Lodge add a cowboy flavor to the region's frontier feel. The region is also the birthplace of the park's current bison and wolf populations

Roosevelt Country

◎ **Sights**
  1 Buffalo Ranch (Yellowstone
    Institute)..............................D3

⊕ **Activities, Courses & Tours**
  2 Fossil Forest Trailhead.....................C2

⊜ **Sleeping**
  3 Pebble Creek Campground...............E2
  4 Roosevelt Lodge.................................B2
  5 Slough Creek Campground...............C2
  6 Tower Fall Campground....................B3

⊗ **Eating**
  Roosevelt Lodge Dining Room ... (see 4)
  7 Yellowstone General Store................B3

Roosevelt Country

10 km / 6 miles

Silver Gate

Northeast Entrance Station

Shoshone National Forest

Warm Creek Trailhead

Bannock Ski Trail

Warm Creek Picnic Area

Cache Creek Trail

Cache Creek

South Cache Creek

Baronette Peak (10,404ft)

Baronette Ski Trail

Amphitheatre Creek

The Thunderer (10,554ft)

Pebble Creek Trail

Pebble Creek

Soda Butte Picnic Area

Round Prairie

Leebox Canyon

Soda Butte Canyon

Bliss Pass Trail

Elk Tongue Creek

Trout Lake

Soda Butte

Lamar River Trail

Hornaday Creek

Yellowstone National Park

Druid Peak (9583ft)

Wildlife Viewing

Lamar Valley Trailhead

Rose Creek

Lamar River

Wildlife Viewing Area

Lamar Valley

Specimen Ridge Trail

Chalcedony Creek

Amethyst Mountain (9614ft)

Buffalo Fork Trail

Slough Creek Trail

Slough Creek

Wildlife Viewing Area

Lamar Canyon

Amethyst Creek

Buffalo Plateau

Buffalo Creek

Lamar Bridge

Petrified Tree

Agate Creek

Specimen Trailhead

Yellowstone River

Bannock Ford

Buffalo Ford

Picnic Area & Yellowstone River Trail

Grand Loop Rd

Yellowstone River

Antelope Creek

Chittenden Rd

Bear Management Area

Buffalo Plateau Trail

Little Buffalo Creek

Suspension Bridge

Garnet Hill Trail

Devils Den

Tower Fall

Tower Creek Trail

Wildlife Viewing Area

Hellroaring Mountain (8363ft)

Stock Bridge

Ford

Garnet Hill (7060ft)

Calcite Springs Overlook

Tower Creek

Wildlife Viewing Area

Carnelian Creek

Yellowstone River Trail

Hellroaring Trailhead

Viewpoint

Floating Island Lake

Tower Junction

Tower Ranger Station

Grand Loop Rd

Lost Lake

Lost Creek

Yellowstone River

Ford

Oxbow Creek

Blacktail Plateau Dr

THE TALLEST TALES IN THE WEST

Jim Bridger is famed as a mountain man and trapper who explored the Yellowstone region in the 1830s, but he was also the West's consummate teller of tall tales. Level-headed lowlanders may have dismissed his outrageous stories with a patronizing slap on the back, but as with most enduring stories, much of the fiction was actually based in fact.

Bridger's most famous tales told of Yellowstone's petrified trees (fact, though he couldn't resist upping the ante to 'peetrified birds singing peetrified songs'); a 'mountain of glass' that acted as a giant telescope (fiction, but based on the volcanic glass of Obsidian Cliff); a river that flowed so fast that friction made it hot on the bottom (actually thermal runoff on the Firehole River); and a spot on Yellowstone Lake where you could throw out a line and reel in a cooked fish (fact, a technique proved by early tourists at Fishing Cone, with the help of an underwater geyser).

He also told of a place where fish could cross the Rocky Mountains (actually Two Ocean Plateau, just south of the park), where a stream atop the Continental Divide branches into two, one stream leading to the Atlantic, the other to the Pacific. (Lake Isa does the same thing between Old Faithful and Yellowstone Lake but has no fish.)

cutthroats who spawn here in early summer. The 10-minute uphill hike to the pretty lake is steep enough to leave you puffing, but this is still one of the park's best short family hikes. It's popular also with anglers, who are allowed to keep their catch of rainbow (but not cutthroat) trout.

Further along the road watch (and sniff) for the whitish-yellow travertine cone of Soda Butte, the only thermal feature in this part of the park.

The road now joins the mixed sage and grasslands of the Lamar Valley, one of the park's premier wildlife viewing areas. The roadside turnouts between Pebble and Slough (pronounced 'slew') Creek campgrounds, particularly the stretch between Lamar River Trailhead and the Lamar Canyon, are prime places to spot wolves from the Agate, Lamar Canyon and Silver packs. Elk and large herds of bison also make the broad Lamar Valley their winter range, occupying separate ecological niches alongside coyotes, pronghorns and bears.

Also here is the former Buffalo Ranch, which almost singlehandedly raised Yellowstone's buffalo herds between 1907 and 1960. The buildings are now home to the excellent Yellowstone Institute (see p79).

About 6 miles before Tower–Roosevelt Junction a dirt road turns off north to Slough Creek Campground, offering fishing and hiking access. Further along the main road are several glacially formed 'kettle' ponds, which are periodically closed to protect nesting trumpeter swans. Just before Tower the road passes the popular Yellowstone River Picnic Area and hiking trail (see p93) and bridges the Yellowstone River.

For details of the road between Tower-Roosevelt and Mammoth, see p60.

TOWER JUNCTION

Calcite Springs Overlook　　　OVERLOOK

This worthwhile overlook 1.5 miles south of Tower–Roosevelt Junction offers vertiginous views of a section of the Grand Canyon of the Yellowstone known as the Narrows. A short trail leads to views north of the gorge's sulfuric yellows and smoking sides. All around are vertical basalt columns, part of a 25ft-deep lava flow that covered the area 1.3 million years ago. Below the basalt are glacial deposits; above the basalt are layers of volcanic ash. More hexagonal basalt columns hang above the roadside a little further along the main road, though parking here is limited.

You'll find dramatic (and crowd-free!) views of Calcite Springs and the Narrows from the Yellowstone River Picnic Area Trail (p93).

Tower Fall　　　WATERFALL

Two-and-a-half miles south of Tower-Roosevelt Junction, Tower Creek plunges over 132ft Tower Fall before joining the Yellowstone River. The fall gets its name from the volcanic breccia towers around it, which are like a demonic fortress and earn it the nickname The Devil's Den. Local storytellers claim that prominent Minaret Peak gets its name from one Minnie Rhett, the girlfriend of an early park visitor, but that sounds to us like one of Jim Bridger's tall tales. Iconic landscape painter Thomas Moran created one of his most famous paintings here.

A short trail leads to a viewpoint over the falls. The trail continues down 200 vertical feet to the Yellowstone River but the section to the base of the falls was recently washed away in floods so it's not really worth the effort. Stop in for well-deserved ice cream at the Yellowstone General Store on the way back. Note that the busy parking lot often fills up by the middle of the day.

Tower Fall Campground is just across the road from the parking area. The potholed and narrow section of road between Tower Fall and Tower-Roosevelt Junction is one of the worst in the park.

TOWER–ROOSEVELT TO CANYON
It's 19 miles from Tower–Roosevelt to Canyon. The Grand Loop Rd starts to climb from Tower Fall on its way to **Dunraven Pass** (8859ft), the highest part of the Grand Loop Rd and named after the British earl who traveled here in 1874 (it was Dunraven's travelogue *The Great Divide* that popularized the park in Europe). East of the road is **Antelope Creek**, prime grizzly habitat and thus closed to visitors. Several turnouts offer popular wildlife-watching opportunities here.

Named after Hiram Chittenden, one of park's early road engineers and historians, Chittenden Rd branches off to the left just before the pass. The road is a popular hiking and mountain-biking trail to the summit of **Mt Washburn** (10,243ft). A second, hiking-only trail leads to the peak from Dunraven Pass, 5 miles further south. See p96 for details of the hike to Mt Washburn and p115 for details of the mountain-bike route.

Just below Dunraven Pass is the **Washburn Hot Springs Overlook**, where an interpretive sign describes the hot springs and the surrounding Yellowstone caldera, which you now enter as you continue south. This is also a good wildlife-watching area, especially for grizzlies who wander here from the surrounding Washburn and Antelope Bear Management Areas.

Canyon Country

The Canyon area is the secondmost heavily visited part of the park after Old Faithful, due largely to the scenic grandeur of the Grand Canyon of the Yellowstone, but also due to the junction's central location and its concentration of visitor services. The impressive canyon is the star of the show and a series of scenic overlooks and a network of trails along the canyon's rims and interiors highlight its multihued beauty from a dozen angles.

CANYON VILLAGE
Canyon Village lies just east of Canyon Junction along North Rim Dr. It's the logistical base for the central part of the park and has accommodation, three restaurants, a visitor center, backcountry office, general store, outdoor gear store and ATM. The campground area has **showers** (⊙7am-1:30pm & 3pm-9:30pm), **laundry** (⊙7am-9pm) and an ice machine.

Canyon Visitor Center VISITOR CENTER
(☎307-242-2550; ⊙8am-8pm late May–mid-Oct) This modern visitor center is well worth a visit for its innovative and interactive displays on Yellowstone's geology. The highlight is a room-sized relief model of the park, on which you can visualize the terrain of your upcoming hike. Upstairs there's a sobering map of recent earthquakes in the park (an average of 2500 each year!), scratchy black-and-white videos of Old Faithful through the years, a huge satellite map of the park and a computer animation booth that details the annual bison migrations through the parks. One surprise is the artist's impression of what the park may have looked like 20,000 years ago – covered in a 4000ft-thick layer of ice. Twenty-minute movies play on the hour and half-hour and there are ranger talks for children (3pm) and adults (6pm).

GRAND CANYON OF THE YELLOWSTONE
After its placid meanderings north from Yellowstone Lake through the Hayden Valley, the Yellowstone River musters up its energy and suddenly plummets over **Upper Falls** (109ft) and then the much larger **Lower Falls** (308ft), before raging through the 1000ft-deep Grand Canyon of the Yellowstone. More than 4000ft wide at the top, the canyon snakes for 20 miles as far as the Narrows near Tower-Roosevelt Junction.

Much of the canyon's beauty comes from its subtle range of colors, from an egg white to a flamboyant salmon pink, a byproduct of iron oxidization in the rock (and not, as many assume, of sulfur deposits). As park

Canyon Country & Norris

publications note, the canyon is in effect rusting. Whiffs of steam still rise from vents in the canyon wall, hinting at the thermal activity that played a major role in the creation of the Yellowstone canyon (by weakening the rhyolite rock). The canyon is relatively recent in geological terms, carved out not by glacial erosion but by water supplied by ice dams that melted and flooded the region during the recent ice age. See the Geology chapter (p239) for more on the formation of the canyon.

The Lower Falls are twice the height of Niagara and are most impressive in spring, when the water volume can be up to 12 times that of fall. The eye-catching green notch indicates a patch of deeper and less turbulent water. At the base of the falls the reds and creams of the canyon walls turn to a mossy green, fed by the thundering spray of the river. Bring binoculars to spot ospreys that nest in the canyon from late April till early September. The falls are perhaps most spectacular in winter, when the spray freezes into a giant cone in front of the falls.

Rangers lead hikes daily at 9am from the parking lot above Uncle Tom's Trailhead and give short talks four times a day (10am for kids) at Artist Point.

NORTH RIM

Three popular scenic overlooks line the one-way 2.5-mile North Rim Dr: Lookout, Grandview and Inspiration points.

Most visitors drive between the viewpoints, but you can also hike the **North Rim Trail**, which connects all three. The trail parallels the road from Upper Falls Overlook to Inspiration Point (2.5 miles), or do it in reverse and continue 0.75 miles further to Chittenden Bridge on South Rim Dr, where it links up with the South Rim Trail. The only disadvantage to this route is that it's one way, so you'll have to either retrace your steps or arrange a designated automobile driver (thanks, Designated Automobile Driver...) to pick you up.

The first of the viewpoints leads down a steep 0.75-mile trail, descending 600ft to the **Brink of the Lower Falls** for exciting close-up views of the tumbling white water as it rushes over the lip of the falls. Heading back up isn't half as much fun as going down.

Half a mile further, popular **Lookout Point** offers the best views of the Lower Falls, while an adjacent 0.5-mile trail drops 500ft to **Red Rock** for even closer views. The average age of the crowd plummets with the elevation (it's hard on the knees). The trails here can be very slippery so watch your step. It was around here that iconic early painter Thomas Moran made the sketches for his famous painting of the canyon, allegedly weeping over the lack of colors in his palette.

The one-way road continues to **Grandview Point**, which offers views north of colorful smoking canyon walls.

A side road branches off the one-way drive to reach busy **Inspiration Point**,

---

YELLOW STONE

The name Yellowstone was not inspired by the technicolor walls of the Grand Canyon as many people think, but rather the yellowish-tan bluffs near the confluence of the Yellowstone and Missouri Rivers in western North Dakota (though some sources also suggest the bluffs near Billings). In 1798 British fur trader David Thompson anglicized the phrase 'R des roches Jaunes,' which means 'Yellow Rock (or Stone) River,' and which was used on a French map to describe the area near the Mandan villages of the upper Missouri. The French had for their part simply translated the Minetaree Indian name for the river, *Mi tsi a da zi* (Rock Yellow River).

In the region of the upper Yellowstone, near what is now the park, the Crow Indians knew the river as the Elk, but Elk National Park just doesn't have the same ring to it...

Canyon Village

which offers an overview of the length of the canyon and a small section of the lower falls. There are a few steps to descend. There used to be more, before the old lookout point fell (literally) victim to the canyon's relentless erosion.

Just before Inspiration Point is a huge granite boulder scooped up from the Beartooth Mountains 15 miles away by a glacier and deposited here 80,000 years ago. The **Glacier Boulder Trail** starts here for the 11-mile return hike to Sevenmile Hole (see p106). An easy, one-hour (2-mile) round-trip hike takes you along this trail, through forest and past intermittent canyon vistas to views of **Silver Cord Cascade**, the park's highest falls (or rather series of falls). This is a particularly fine late-afternoon hike, but keep a tight rein on the kids, as there are no barriers between them and the sheer canyon dropoffs.

UPPER FALLS VIEWPOINT

The less dramatic **Upper Falls Viewpoint** is also accessible by road: the turnoff is south of Canyon Junction and Cascade Creek on the main Grand Loop Rd to Fishing Bridge. A short walk to the right (south) leads to the Brink of the Upper Falls, though the best

Canyon Village

⊙ Sights

✪ Activities, Courses & Tours

⊜ Sleeping

✪ Eating

⌂ Shopping

views of the falls are actually from the Uncle Tom's parking area across the gorge. A five-minute walk north along the North Rim Trail (a former stagecoach road) leads to an overview of the much smaller but graceful **Crystal Falls**, the 'Hidden' or 'Third' waterfall of the Canyon region.

SOUTH RIM

South Rim Dr passes the Chittenden Bridge and Wapiti Trailhead en route to the canyon's most spectacular overlook, at Artist Point. The 3.25-mile **South Rim Trail** follows the canyon rim from Chittenden Bridge to Point Sublime via Artist Point: for details of taking in the views on foot instead of by car, see p95.

Uncle Tom's Trail is one of the region's largest parking areas and offers the best views of the Upper and Lower Falls. Uncle Tom's Trail itself is a steep route that descends 500ft to the base of the Lower Falls. The trail was constructed in 1898 by early park entrepreneur Uncle Tom Richardson, who would lead tourists across the river and down a series of trails and rope ladders for views of the falls and a picnic lunch. Sadly the rope ladders are now a thing of the past (Tom's permit was rescinded in 1903), but the 328 metal steps still descend three-quarters of the way into the canyon.

The park service once turned down an application to build an elevator here that would whisk tourists down to the canyon floor, though you may wish they had changed their mind as you make the tough return climb. Rangers lead a 1-mile stroll from here at 3pm, as well as a longer 3-mile walk at 9am.

Artist Point is probably the most famous of the canyon's viewpoints. It was not, as many people assume, named for the spot where Thomas Moran sketched his famous landscape of the falls (a copy of which is on display in the Canyon Visitor Education Center). It was actually named by the park photographer FJ Haynes for its superlative scenic views. Rangers give short talks here six times a day, with the 10am talk aimed at kids.

From Artist Point a trail leads 1 mile to **Point Sublime** for more fabulous views of the canyon walls. The 4-mile (two-hour) round-trip hike to Ribbon Lake branches off from here.

CANYON TO LAKE

South of Canyon Junction, the Grand Loop Rd winds 16 miles down to Lake Yellowstone via the excellent wildlife-watching opportunities of the Hayden Valley and the interesting Mud Volcano. This section of road makes for a good two-hour bike ride, though as always you'll have to watch out for the traffic.

HAYDEN VALLEY

The Yellowstone River is broad and shallow as it meanders gently through the vast grasslands of Hayden Valley, named after the expedition leader whose 1871 survey led to the establishment of the park the following year. This former lakebed was formed in the last ice age when a glacial outburst flooded the valley, turning the region into an arm of Yellowstone Lake. The fine silt-and-clay soil of the former lakebed prevents water from percolating into the ground, making the area marshy and impenetrable to most trees. This supports the rich shrubs and grasses favored by bison.

The Hayden is the largest valley in the park and one of its premier **wildlife-viewing** areas. With patience you're likely to see coyotes, springtime grizzlies, elk and lots of bison, plus one of the largest fall ruts. Birdwatching is equally good, including white pelicans and trumpeter swans, sandhill cranes (also at Alum Creek), ospreys, bald eagles and Canada geese. There are popular viewing areas 1 mile north of Sulfur

Cauldron and 1.5 miles north of Trout Creek, where rangers lead wildlife watching trips four times a week at 7am. Set up your spotting scope early, as the pullouts fill with cars an hour or two before dusk.

MUD VOLCANO

One of the park's most geologically volatile regions, this thermal area 10 miles south of Canyon Junction and 6 miles north of Fishing Bridge Junction contains an assortment of mud pots and other gurgling sulfurous pits. The nearby Sour Creek resurgent dome is the fuel that superheats the mud volcanoes, while the high acidity breaks down rock into mud pots rather than creating the pressurized geyser plumbing more characteristic of alkaline thermal features. During a series of earthquakes in 1979 the mud pots developed enough heat and gases to literally cook lodgepole pines and grasses on neighboring hillsides. One mud pot recently emerged from underneath the parking lot.

Mud Volcano itself has not erupted since the 1871 Langford-Washington-Doane expedition first encountered it. A crater is all that remains of the original cone. **Dragon's Mouth Spring** gets its name from the deep thumping and crashing that emanates from a hidden lair that looks like it guards the gateway to the underworld. In 1999 the pool cooled and its color changed from green to white and now gray.

The easiest way to see the other sights is to follow the 2.3-mile loop boardwalk (there are some steps) clockwise, past Mud Geyser and up Cooking Hillside. Halfway up, **Churning Cauldron** is a favorite; waves of water have created tiny beaches here. The dark colors of this and other pots are due to the presence of iron sulfides.

Black Dragon's Cauldron appeared in 1948 in a crack in the earth and has since moved south 200ft along the crack to produce an elliptical pool. The rolling motion of the water is actually due to rising gases rather than boiling water. Nearby **Sour Lake** looks like a nice place for a swim but its waters are as acidic as battery acid. Further downhill, **Grizzly Fumarole** changes throughout the year from a fumarole to a mud pot and even a muddy spring, according to the amount of moisture in the ground.

Sulfur Cauldron, just a few hundred yards north, by a pullout in the road, is one of the most acidic springs in the park, at pH 1.3. Other thermal areas, visible across the Yellowstone River, can only be reached by hiking the Howard Eaton Trail from Fishing Bridge.

Rangers lead two-hour walks around the site at 4pm, but sadly no longer go to the **Gumper**, a huge seething mud pot behind Sour Lake and off-limits to visitors.

Lake Country

Yellowstone Lake (7733ft) is Lake Country's shimmering centerpiece, one of the world's largest alpine lakes, with the largest inland population of cutthroat trout in the US. Yellowstone River emerges from the north end of the lake and flows through Hayden Valley to the Grand Canyon of the Yellowstone. The lake's south and eastern borders flank the steep Absaroka Range marking the border of the park's remote and pristine Thorofare region.

A 22-mile section of the Grand Loop Rd hugs Yellowstone Lake's shoreline between Fishing Bridge Junction to the north and West Thumb Junction to the west. Visitor centers and convenience stores are available at Fishing Bridge and Grant Village. Grant and Lake Village offer the most visitor services, including dining.

Bridge Bay Marina rents outboard motorboats and rowboats and has a fishing/grocery store, dump station, ranger station and picnic area. The busy Fishing Bridge area offers showers and laundry, as well as a gas station, groceries and camping supplies at the Yellowstone General Store.

YELLOWSTONE LAKE

The largest high-altitude lake in North America, the deep cobalt Yellowstone Lake (136 sq miles) has been a human draw for millennia; artifacts found along the lakeshore date back 12,000 years. Traditionally this was only a summering spot for native groups. The lake remains frozen almost half the year, from January to early June, though its average depth is 140ft (maximum 390ft), and parts of the lake floor boil with underwater hot springs.

In addition to excellent fishing and boating, the lake also offers prime birding and wildlife-watching. Early-summer visitors shouldn't miss an amazing display of spawning cutthroat trout at Fishing Bridge and Le-Hardy's Rapids, 3 miles north of the bridge. As crucial food sources for grizzlies and waterfowl, some spawning areas around the lakeshore are closed during spring and early summer.

Thermal activity rings the lake, and in cold weather steaming thermals blur into the water. For details on the fascinating geology of the lake see p242.

Rangers lead tours of Yellowstone Lake's shoreline daily from Fishing Bridge. For details of boating options from Bridge Bay and West Thumb see p117.

LEHARDY'S RAPIDS

These rapids are named after topographer Paul LeHardy, whose raft overturned here, spilling guns, provisions and bedding but sparing his life. Rock uplift created this steplike cascade, which formally marks the end of Yellowstone Lake. Cutthroat trout are plentiful in late springtime, where they can be seen resting in the pools before hurling themselves up the rapids to spawning grounds near Fishing Bridge. Just north of here are three picnic areas, of which the Nez Percé Ford picnic site is the nicest, with riverside tables.

FISHING BRIDGE

There has been a bridge at Fishing Bridge since 1902, but it closed to fishing in 1973 to protect spawning cutthroat trout to the benefit of resident grizzlies. Because of heavy grizzly activity, there is continuing pressure to close the area to protect this crucial habitat.

The **Fishing Bridge Visitor Center** (307-242-2450; 8am-7pm late May-late Sep) was originally built in 1931 as an information station for the first automobile tourists. The center contains displays on local birdlife (look for the great skulls on the candelabra), alongside a stuffed grizzly and a great 3D geothermal map of the park. Ranger talks are held here at 2pm and at Fishing Bridge at 5pm. Most people miss the steps behind the center that lead to a nice section of lakeshore.

LAKE VILLAGE & BRIDGE BAY

The buttercup-yellow **Lake Yellowstone Hotel**, dating from 1891, is the park's oldest building and certainly its most elegant. Robert Reamer (who also designed the Old Faithful Inn) rebuilt the hotel in 1903, adding Ionic columns and false balconies. Swank and expansive, this southern-style mansion is the perfect setting for classical concerts and pre-dinner drinks in the waterfront sunroom. There are also lovely sunset strolls in front of the hotel, including one trail that goes all the way to Fishing Bridge. Hotel tours start at 5:30pm on summer weekdays.

You'll find several spots to picnic and/or fish between Lake Village and West Thumb. Near Bridge Bay, 2-mile **Gull Point Dr** is a scenic picnic spot and popular fishing area that also offers a short bike ride for families staying at Bridge Bay. Opposite the turnoff is the road for the 3-mile biking trip to **Natural Bridge** (p115). An alternative hiking trail leads to the bridge from Bridge Bay marina.

Other nice lakeshore spots include **Sand Point** picnic area, from where trails lead 400yd down to a lagoon and black volcanic glass beach, and **Pumice Point**, a beach of dark-black sand. There are more sand bars and lagoons to explore, 2 miles, 4.5 miles and 6.5 miles further towards West Thumb.

If you fancy getting on the water, try the one-hour **sightseeing cruises** (adult/child $5/9) from Bridge Bay marina that travel to Stevenson Island and the wreck of the steamship SS *Waters* (1905). They operate at least five times daily from mid-June to mid-September and rangers accompany the first three trips of the day.

WEST THUMB GEYSER BASIN

Named for its location in the hand-shaped Yellowstone Lake, West Thumb is a small volcanic caldera spawned some 150,000 years ago inside the much larger Yellowstone caldera. Yellowstone Lake filled the crater, creating West Thumb Bay, a circular inlet on the lake's west end. The geyser basin still pours more than 3000 gallons of hot water into the lake daily.

Although West Thumb is not one of Yellowstone's prime thermal sites, its 0.5-mile shoreline boardwalk loop (with a shorter inner loop) passes through more than a dozen geothermal features. Identify its underwater features by looking for slick spots or a slight bulge in the water. Smaller thermal areas surrounding West Thumb include the roadside Pumice Point and Potts Hot Spring Basin.

At famous **Fishing Cone**, anglers once used the infamous 'hook 'n' cook' method to prepare their catch, casting fish into the boiling water. Fishing is now prohibited. Fluctuating lake levels in spring and early summer sometimes submerge the cone and Lakeshore Geyser.

Abyss Pool is one of the park's deepest springs. Nearby **Black Pool** is one of the prettiest, though it's now completely clear

Lake Country

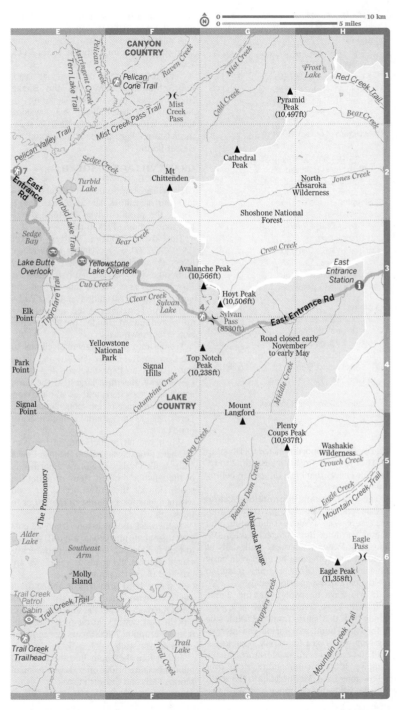

Lake Country

◉ Sights
1 Fishing Bridge Visitor Center	D2
Fishing Cone	(see 3)
2 Grant Village Visitor Center	B5
Lake Yellowstone Hotel	(see 13)
3 West Thumb Information Center	A4

◉ Activities, Courses & Tours
4 Avalanche Peak Trailhead	G3
5 Elephant Back Trailhead	C2
6 Heart Lake Trailhead	A6
7 Pelican Valley Trailhead	E2

◉ Sleeping
8 Bridge Bay Campground	C2
9 Fishing Bridge RV Park	D2
10 Grant Village	B5
11 Grant Village Campground	A5
12 Lake Lodge	C2
13 Lake Yellowstone Hotel	C2
14 Lewis Lake Campground	A7

◉ Eating
15 Fishing Bridge Yellowstone General Store	D2
16 Grant Village Dining Room	B5
17 Lake House	B5
Lake Lodge Cafeteria	(see 12)
18 Lake Yellowstone General Store	D2
Lake Yellowstone Hotel Dining Room	(see 13)

after years of supporting black thermophiles. **Thumb Paint Pots** are struggling to regain the energy that once catapulted boiling mud 25ft into the air.

The **West Thumb Information Station** (☺9am-5pm late May-late Sep), dating from 1925, serves as a summer bookstore and winter warming hut. Rangers lead a 1½-hour 'Hot Water Wilderness' walk daily at 10:30am and 4pm from here between early June and August. Other programs rotate, so see the park newspaper for details.

If you have a spare hour, the 2-mile round-trip **Lake Overlook Trail** is a good family hike that starts from the south side of the West Thumb parking lot. The interesting loop winds past forest, elk, open grassland and even some thermal features, finally climbing 400ft to commanding views over Yellowstone Lake, Mt Sheridan to the south and the wild Absorka range and Washakie

wilderness to the east. Rangers lead hikes along the route daily at 10am.

A shorter 1-mile return hike also runs from the parking lot to the shores of **Duck Lake**.

For a different angle on the geyser basin, **OARS** (www.oars.com/Wyoming) and **Snake River Kayak** (www.snakeriverkayak.com) in Jackson offer half-/full-day sea kayaking tours on Yellowstone Lake for $99/175, starting at Grant Village and paddling out to Potts Geyser Basin.

GRANT VILLAGE TO SOUTH ENTRANCE
Grant Village is a sterile scar of blockhouses and tourist facilities named after Ulysses S Grant, the president who established Yellowstone National Park in 1872.

The **Grant Villlage Visitor Center** (☎307-242-2650; ☺8am-7pm late May-late Sep) offers an exhibit on fire and an hourly 20-minute video entitled *Ten Years After the Fire,* as well as a wildlife talk at 2pm and junior ranger presentation at 11am. Early-evening presentations at the amphitheater are geared toward families; the 9:30pm version is for grown-ups.

From Grant Village the road climbs to the **Continental Divide** (7988ft) and drops into a burn area, past several trailheads. **Lewis Lake**, the third largest in the park, comes into view here, and several lakeview pullouts offer nice picnic spots. Boaters use Lewis Lake as the gateway to remote Shoshone Lake.

When you hit traffic south of the lake, you have probably arrived at the 30ft **Lewis Falls**. Walk a little way along the north side of the falls for the best views or along the south side for the closest access. In good weather, look for a glimpse of the Tetons to the south.

To the west, the Pitchstone Trailhead cuts over the remote pitchstone (ash tuft) plateau to Grassy Lake Rd, one of the park's least-visited corners. Its roadside meadows are excellent places to spot moose.

A major burn area signals the start of **Lewis Canyon**. There are lots of pullouts along the roadside, but the southernmost offers the best views. Volcanic rock that dates from an eruption 70,000 years ago comprises the canyon walls.

Just before the South Entrance, a small pullout beside a bridge offers access to small **Moose Falls** and Crawfish Creek.

The entrance station is adjacent to the Snake River Picnic Area. From here it's 18 miles to Colter Bay and 43 miles to Moose Visitor Center, both in Grand Teton National Park.

FISHING BRIDGE TO EAST ENTRANCE

There are a couple of great family hiking trails west of Fishing Bridge. At **Pelican Creek Bridge**, 1 mile east of Fishing Bridge Visitor Center, an easy 1.3-mile loop nature trail winds through lodgepole forest to a pleasant beach and lake views. Keep an eye out for moose and springtime grizzlies in the wetlands. The lakeside ponds south of the highway offer great birdwatching.

Formed by a giant steam (not lava) explosion, Storm Point, 1.5 miles further east, juts into the north end of the lake. The 2.3-mile (90 minutes) **Storm Point Trail** begins near Indian Pond, strolling through diverse wildlife habitats including meadows, shoreline and old forest. Wildlife is particularly active around dusk and dawn: try spotting bison, moose, marmots and waterfowl. Rangers lead a guided hike here at 10am. The trail closes in late spring and early summer due to bear activity and can be buggy early in summer. Just east of Storm Point, a dirt road branches north to the **Pelican Valley** Trailhead (see p98); the lush meandering meadows here rank among the park's prime grizzly habitats.

Like West Thumb, crater-shaped **Mary Bay** is the result of a thermal explosion. Both Mary Bay and neighboring Sedge Bay are peppered with underwater thermal areas, of which roiling **Steamboat Point** is the most obvious. **Sedge Bay** beach is a launching point for canoe or kayak trips south along the lake's east shoreline and is a fine place for a picnic. Birdwatchers flock to the bay's southeast corner.

As the East Entrance Rd turns away from the lake, a mile-long paved road (no buses or trailers) branches north to the **Lake Butte Overlook**, which offers grand sunset views of Yellowstone Lake and the remote Thorofare corner of the park. Further east is the less impressive Yellowstone Lake Overlook.

The main road gradually climbs up the west slope of the remote Absaroka Range past lovely **Sylvan Lake** (with a picnic area and catch-and-release fishing), Eleanor Lake and the Avalanche Peak Trailhead (p99). The road peaks at the avalanche area of **Sylvan Pass** (8530ft), dominated by 10,238ft

Top Notch Peak to the south. Look for the Howitzer gun mounted on the south side of the pass, employed to set off controlled avalanches during the dangerous winter months.

East of the pass the landscape becomes more rugged and impressive. The high barren walls of Mt Langford (10,774ft) and Plenty Coups Peak (10,937ft) rise to the south. Middle Creek, with several good fishing spots, parallels the south side of the road.

The East Entrance marks the boundary between Yellowstone National Park and Shoshone National Forest. From here the Buffalo Bill Scenic Byway leads to Cody via the Wapiti Valley (p149).

Norris

The Norris area was a former US Army outpost. The historic log Norris Soldier Station (1908), one of only three left from the era of army control of the park, now houses the **Museum of the National Park Ranger** (☑307-344-7353; ☺9am-5pm Jun-Sep), often staffed by chatty retired NPS employees. The museum's exhibits detail the evolution of the ranger profession from its military origins, including a fun mock-up of an old ranger cabin. Norris is named after Philetus W Norris, the park's second superintendent (1877–82), who is notable for constructing some of the park's first roads and for the shameless frequency with which he named park features after himself.

The Gibbon River flows through meadows in front of the building, making it a pleasant place to look for wildlife. Norris Campground is right next door.

Norris sits at the junction of roads from Madison (14 miles), Canyon (12 miles) and Mammoth (20 miles). North of the junction is Norris Campground; west is Norris Geyser Basin, with busy bathrooms, an information station and a bookstore. A pleasant 1-mile trail (no bikes) connects the basin and the campground.

NORRIS GEYSER BASIN

North and west of Norris Junction, the Norris Geyser Basin is North America's most volatile and oldest continuously active geothermal area (in existence for some 115,000 years). It's also the site of Yellowstone's hottest recorded temperatures, where three intersecting faults underlain by magma rise to within 2 miles of the surface. Barely

BEST PLACES IN YELLOWSTONE TO SPOT WILDLIFE

The following places all offer an excellent chance to get a glimpse of some seriously charismatic megafauna. Maximize your chances by arriving at dawn or dusk and renting a spotting scope from Silver Gate or Gardiner.

» **Roosevelt Country** The Lamar Valley (p62) is known as the 'American Serengeti' for its dense population of wolves, bison, grizzlies, pronghorn, elk and trumpeter swans; try also Antelope Creek (p65) for grizzlies and wolves.

» **Mammoth Country** Elk trimming the lawns at Mammoth Junction, bighorn sheep on Everett Ridge between Mammoth and the North Entrance; wildfowl at Blacktail Ponds (p60); moose at Willow Park (p61); bears and wolves in the backcountry Gallatin range.

» **Lake Country** Birdlife at Sedge Bay (p75); bison, moose, marmots and waterfowl at Storm Point (p75); springtime grizzlies and moose at Pelican Creek (p75); moose around Lewis Lake; grizzlies around Fishing Bridge in spring.

» **Norris** Elk Park (p77) for, well, elk, as well as bison.

» **Canyon Country** The Hayden Valley (p69) for bison, coyotes and bears; ospreys in the canyon; south of Mud Volcano (p70) for bison.

» **Mt Washburn** (p96) For bighorn sheep, black bears and grizzlies.

» **Geyser Country** The Firehole River and Madison Valley for bison.

1000ft below the surface, scientific instruments have recorded temperatures as high as 459°F. Norris is also home to the majority of the world's acidic geysers, fed by the basin's abundant supplies of sulfur. In Norris the earth sighs, boils and rages like nowhere else on earth.

Norris' geothermal features change seasonally, most commonly in August or September: clear pools transform into spouting geysers or mud pots and vice versa. Thermal activity is also affected by earthquake swarms and other mysterious disturbances, which generally last only a few days before things revert to 'normal.'

Norris Geyser Basin features two distinct areas: Porcelain Basin and Back Basin. Concentrate on Porcelain Basin if you are low on time. Overlooking Porcelain Basin is the tiny **Norris Museum** (☎307-344-2812; ☻9am-6pm late May-Sep), which opened as the park's first in 1930. There are ranger-led walking tours of the basin at 9:30am daily and short talks at Steamboat Geyser at 2pm, 2:30pm and 3pm.

The area's only bathrooms are in the parking lot, next to the cold-drinks machines. The parking area and toilets can get crowded, so try to schedule a visit early or late in the day.

PORCELAIN BASIN

One mile of boardwalks loop through open Porcelain Basin, the park's hottest exposed basin. (The name comes from the area's milky deposits of sinter, also known as geyserite.) The bleached basin boils and bubbles like some giant laboratory experiment and the ash-white ground actually pulsates in places. Check out the overviews from **Porcelain Terrace Overlook**, near the Norris Museum; views that, in the words of Rudyard Kipling, made it look 'as though the tide of desolation had gone out.'

As you descend from the museum, veer left before the continually blowing fumarole of **Black Growler Steam Vent**, which has shifted location several times in recent years. As with most fumaroles, this vent is higher than the basin floor and is thus without a reliable supply of water. Below here is the large but currently inactive Ledge Geyser.

Going clockwise, the boardwalk heads left past **Crackling Lake**, which bubbles like a deep-fat fryer, and the **Whale's Mouth**, a gaping blue hot spring. The swirling waters of **Whirligig Geyser** became dramatically acidic in 2000, helping support the green cyanidium algae and yellow cyanobacteria that create many of the stunning colors in its drainage channels. The color of these bacterial mats indicates the relative temperatures of the water, from very hot blues and whites (up to 199°F) to cooler yellows and greens (144°F) and even cooler beiges and dark browns (130°F to 80°F). Nearby **Constant Geyser** erupts every 20 minutes or so, but blink and you'll miss the brief eruptions.

A side path leads past Hurricane Vent to **Congress Pool**, which appeared in 1891, the year scientists convened in Yellowstone for a geologic congress. The footpath to Norris Campground leads off beside Nuphar Lake.

BACK BASIN

Two miles of boardwalks and gentle trails snake through forested Back Basin. As you exit the museum from Porcelain Basin, take the right-hand path into Back Basin. **Emerald Spring** combines reflected blue light with yellow sulfur deposits to create a striking blue-green color.

Steamboat Geyser, the world's tallest active geyser, infrequently skyrockets up to an awesome 400ft (over twice as high as Old Faithful). The geyser was dormant for half a century until 1961 and quiet again for most of the 1990s, but erupted twice in 2002 and most recently in 2005. At the time of research the geyser was splashing with frequent but minor bursts only. For a shorter loop take the right branch just past the geyser, otherwise continue clockwise around the basin.

Nearby yellow-and-green **Cistern Spring** is linked to Steamboat through underground channels, and empties for a day or two following Steamboat's eruptions. The spring is slowly drowning its surroundings in geyserite deposits.

Dramatic **Echinus Geyser** (e-*ki*-nus), the park's largest acidic geyser, erupted every couple of hours until fairly recently, with spouts reaching up to 60ft and sometimes continuing for more than an hour, but these days it's pretty quiet. You can get closer to the action here than at almost any of the park's other geysers, and if you sit in the grandstand, you may well get wet during an eruption (kids love it). The water air-cools to safe temperatures and isn't that acidic (pH 3.5, like vinegar or lemon juice) but will harm glasses and camera lenses. Furious bubbling signals an imminent eruption. Echinus is famed for its spiny geyserite deposits (echinoderms include sea urchins), characteristic of acidic solutions.

After deposits sealed its tiny 2in-wide vent, **Porkchop Geyser** exploded in 1989, blowing huge lumps of geyserite 200ft into the air. Recent rises in the ground temperature forced the park service to reroute the boardwalk around the back of Porkchop Geyser for safety purposes.

Nearby **Pearl Geyser** is one of the park's prettiest. Punsters love the British pronunciation of **Veteran Geyser** – 'Veteran Geezer.' **Minute Geyser** is a victim of early visitor vandalism and sadly no longer erupts every 60 seconds, despite its constant bubbling.

NORRIS TO MADISON JUNCTION

The 14-mile Norris to Madison Junction road quickly enters aptly named **Elk Park**, a fine place to spot elk and bison and you'll likely have to navigate a car jam here.

Just under 5 miles south of Norris Junction an easy 1-mile trail leads through burned forest to the fun mud pots and springs of **Artist Paint Pots**. The best mudpots are in the far right-hand corner.

The road crosses the Gibbon River three times, past the trailhead that leads to little-visited **Monument Geyser Basin** (see p100) and then pretty blue-green **Beryl Spring** (where the rolling action of the water comes from escaping gases rather than boiling water).

As the road and river descends off the Solfatara Plateau, you pass **Gibbon Falls**, one of the park's prettiest. For the best views of the falls you'll have to park and walk downhill along the road. Like so many of Yellowstone's waterfalls and cascades, the falls flow over hard rhyolite that marks the edge of the Yellowstone caldera.

Five miles further west a parking area on the right gives access to **Terrace Spring**, a large pool with a rolling geyser in the corner. Two lovely hot springs above form the namesake terrace. You could safely miss both Terrace and Beryl Springs if you are tight on time.

From here the road drops down to Madison Junction, with its campground and junior ranger station. The station is a good place to stop if you have kids; there are plenty of kid-friendly activities, bear skins to stroke and talks every half-hour. Spotting scopes offer a close-up look at the elk that frequent the Madison Valley. For details of the road heading west to West Yellowstone, see p87.

NORRIS TO CANYON

The 12-mile Norris–Canyon road connects the two parts of the Grand Loop Rd across the burnt forest and cooled lava flows of the Solfatara Plateau. Just past the junction the pleasant **Norris Meadows Picnic Area** offers some fine birdwatching over the plain of the meandering Gibbon River.

About 2 miles into the drive a one-way side road branches off past **Virginia Cascade**, which like Gibbon Falls lies on the caldera boundary. One story goes that the superintendent wanted to name the falls after his wife, Virginia, but the NPS was against naming park features after living people, so they compromised by naming the fall after the state of (ahem...) Virginia. The narrow 2.5-mile road follows the old stagecoach road along the Norris Cutoff and is closed to buses, trailers and RVs.

Back on the main road a small boardwalk trail marks the spot where a freak tornado ripped through the plateau in 1984. This was also the spot of the fiercest of 1988's wildfires.

Ice Lake Trail leads 0.5 miles to the peaceful namesake lake, with a handicapped-accessible backcountry site (4D3) on its southern shore. In his book *Lost in My Own Backyard,* writer Tim Cahill wrote of the lake: 'Is this a great country or what? Where else would the wilderness – or one lovely part of it – be made accessible in such a way that the disabled can spend entire sleepless nights worried about being eaten by a bear, just like any able-bodied hiker?' Excellent. Sites 4D1 and 4D2 are just a mile or so from the road and make a great first backcountry site for young families. Camping here feels like owning your own private lake. Trails continue northeast along the border of a major burn area to Wolf Lake (3 miles) and Grebe Lake (another 1.5 miles). For details on longer hike options to Cascade Lake, see p97.

Further down the Norris–Canyon road, you'll pass the Cygnet Lakes and then the Grebe Lake and Cascade Creek Trailheads, which offer an alternative route through burned forest to Grebe and Cascade Lakes.

Geyser Country

Yellowstone's Geyser Country holds the park's most spectacular geothermal features, (over half the world's total) concentrated in the world's densest concentration of geysers (over 200 spouters in 1.5 sq miles). It is Geyser Country that makes the Yellowstone plateau utterly and globally unique.

The majority of the geysers line the Firehole River, the aquatic backbone of the basin, whose tributaries feed 21 of the park's 110 waterfalls. Both the Firehole and Madison Rivers offer superb fly-fishing, and the meadows along them support large wildlife populations.

The most famous geysers always attract a crowd, but sometimes it's the smaller features that are the most interesting. The smaller geysers make up for their lack of size with great names, such as North Goggles, Little Squirt, Gizmo, Spanker, Spasmodic, Slurper and Bulger (aliases the seven dwarfs might adopt to form a criminal gang).

In the introduction to *A Lady's Life in the Rocky Mountains* (1960), historian Daniel Boorstin attributed Yellowstone Park's enormous appeal 'to the fact that its natural phenomena, which erupt on schedule, come closest to the artificiality of "regular" tourist performances.' So grab some popcorn and check show times at the visitor center.

For details of the drive from Madison Junction to Old Faithful, see p88.

UPPER GEYSER BASIN

This heavily visited basin holds 180 of the park's 200 to 250 geysers, the most famous of which is geriatric **Old Faithful**. Boardwalks, footpaths and a cycling path along the Firehole River link the five distinct geyser groups, the furthest of which is only 1.5 miles from Old Faithful.

Entering the Old Faithful parking area comes as a bit of a shock after you've spent some time in the park. As well as the visitor center, the complex boasts two gas stations, three hotels and several general stores, including the original 1897 knotty pine Hamilton Store, the oldest structure still in use in the park. The Yellowstone General Store next to the Snow Lodge has the park's best selection of groceries and sells fishing flies, spotting scopes and fishing permits.

The combined ranger station, backcountry office and medical clinic are set back from the main parking area, across the west parking lot from the visitor center. The Old Faithful Snow Lodge gift shop offers bike rentals in the summer and snowshoe and ski rentals in winter.

Rangers give a geology talk in front of Old Faithful eight times a day and offer an evening presentation in the theater at 7pm. There's a short talk for kids at 10am. Daily 90-minute geology walks depart at 5:30pm from Castle Geyser and at 8:30am from the visitor center, with a shorter walk around Old Faithful at 2:30pm.

Public **showers** (⊘6:30am-11pm) are available in the reception area at Old Faithful Inn. There are no campgrounds in the Old Faithful area.

Old Faithful Visitor Center VISITOR CENTER
(📞307-545-2750; ⊙8am-8pm mid-Apr–early Nov & mid-Dec–mid-Mar) The new, improved and environmentally friendly center offers a bookstore and information booth and shows films 30 minutes before and 15 minutes after an eruption of Old Faithful. Kids will enjoy the Young Scientist displays, which include a working laboratory geyser and experiments involving elk jaw bones. The center closes at 5pm or 6pm outside of summer.

Old Faithful Inn HISTORIC LODGE
Designed by Seattle architect Robert C Reamer and built in 1904, this is the only building in the park that looks like it actually belongs here. The log rafters of its seven-story lobby rise nearly 80ft, and the chimney of the central fireplace (actually eight fireplaces combined) contains more than 500 tons of rhyolite rock. It's definitely a worthwhile visit, even for nonguests.

The Crow's Nest, a top-floor balcony where musicians once played for dancers in the lobby below, is wonderful (but unused since 1959). Look also for the huge popcorn popper and fire tools at the back of the fireplace. The 2nd-floor observation deck offers the chance to enjoy fine views of Old Faithful geyser over a drink, and the lobby hosts occasional talks by regional authors. Free 45-minute Historic Inn tours depart from the fireplace at 9:30am, 11am, 2pm and 3:30pm.

OLD FAITHFUL
Erupting every 90 minutes or so to impatient (preliminary hand-clapping is not uncommon) visitors' delight, Old Faithful spouts some 8000 gallons of water up to 180ft in the air, though the last time we checked, the

---

WATCHING WOLVES *CAROLYN MCCARTHY*

You sit. You watch. You wait. Unlike Old Faithful, wolves don't operate on schedule. The best thing is to track reported sightings. Then you race to the nearest lookout. And watch. And wait.

We rolled out of bed at 4am, without a peep from the bluebirds, who were wisely still snoozing. What followed bordered on asinine: driving around mountain-pass pullouts in the dusky light, setting up spotting scopes in blustery winds, only to dismantle them minutes later. False alarm. We nestled into a steep overlook on Chittenden Rd, where others had already set up their post in the chill of daybreak: couples snuggled with spotting scopes while roaming children still wore pajamas. We asked the group if they had seen anything. They shrugged. 'Just grizzlies.'

Watching wolves is all about expectation. Call it the excitement of waiting for something so wild that only a few ever witness it. A Native American story says the white man rose from the hair of a dead wolf. Mongols revered them and shamanic Turks believed them to be their ancestors, while Europeans crafted suspenseful fairytales and stories of lycanthropy based on their tufted shadows and fierce incisors.

Wolves were hunted to the brink of extinction in the United States. In 1995, under much controversy, they were reintroduced into Yellowstone. At last count there were around 100 wolves, including 38 pups, down from a peak of 175 in 2003.

On Chittenden Rd, someone spotted an elk cow wandering dazed on the edge of the forest deep below us. The elk circled around, as if she was looking for something. It turned out to be her calf.

The calf was limp in the grip of the wolf, but the stunned mother elk stood her ground. What followed was dazzling. She kept charging, but the wolf kept returning to the carcass. It was not unlike a dance. But this wasn't Wild Animal Kingdom. This was happening at my feet. Sure, a mile away, but real and live in the frosted morning air.

The elk cow was brave, resilient. The wolf was patient. An alpha female wearing a radio collar, she was not young. Her fur was flecked with grey. She finally, decisively, snatched the carcass, likely taking it to feed the litter.

In moments, the onlookers packed up their spotting scopes. As the sky brightened, the regular traffic started flowing, with people clueless to the dramas of the wild that had played out while they slept.

To join a wolf course, contact the **Yellowstone Institute** (www.yellowstone association.com).

Geyser Country

0 _____ 5 km
0 _____ 3 miles

To West Entrance Station (10mi); West Yellowstone (10mi)

Purple Mountain (8433ft) ▲

Secret Valley Creek

Terrace Spring

Gibbon Falls

Grand Loop Rd

Harlequin Lake

West Entrance Rd

Madison River

Madison
Junior Ranger Station

Gibbon Canyon

4

Harlequin Lake Trailhead ▲

Firehole Falls
Swimming Area

National Park Mountain (7500ft) ▲

Firehole Canyon Dr

Firehole River

Yellowstone National Park

Firehole River Picnic Area

Mary Mountain Trail

Nez Percé Picnic Area

Nez Percé Creek

Porcupine Hills ▲

Culex Basin

Sentinel Meadows

Fountain Flat Dr

Mary Mountain West Trailhead

Queen's Laundry

Ojo Caliente Hot Spring

2

Porcupine Hills

Pocket Basin

Lower Geyser Basin

Fountain Paint Pot

Firehole Lake Dr

Twin Buttes ▲

Goose Lake

Great Fountain Geyser

Firehole Lake

Sentinel Creek

Fountain Freight Rd

Whisky Flats Picnic Area

Fairy Falls

Grand Prismatic Spring

Midway Geyser Basin

1

Midway Geyser Basin

Mallard Creek

White Creek

Fairy Creek Trail

Little Firehole Meadows

Mystic Falls Trail

See Upper Geyser Basin Map (p82)

Mystic Falls

Biscuit Basin

Upper Geyser Basin

Observation Hill

Mallard Lake

DeLacy Lakes

Summit Lake Trail

Black Sand Basin

Old Faithful Geyser

Mallard Lake Trail

Teal Lake

Craig Pass (8262ft)

3

Grand Loop Rd

Howard Eaton Trail

Kepler Cascades

Spring Creek Trail

Spring Creek Picnic Area

Lone Star Geyser

CONTINENTAL DIVIDE

Shoshone Lake

Geyser Country

old salt was in need of a dose of Viagra. Water temperature is normally 204°F and the steam is about 350°F. It's worth viewing the eruption from several different locations – the geyserside seats, the upper-floor balcony of the Old Faithful Inn and, our favorite, from a distance on Observation Hill.

Though it's neither the tallest nor the most predictable geyser in the park, Old Faithful is the most frequently erupting big geyser in Yellowstone. For over 75 years the geyser faithfully erupted every hour or so, one reason for the name the Washburn expedition gave it in 1870. The average time between shows these days is 90 minutes and getting longer, though this has historically varied between 45 and 110 minutes. The average eruption lasts around four minutes. The longer the eruption, the longer the recovery time. Rangers correctly predict eruptions to within 10 minutes about 90% of the time. And no, Old Faithful has never erupted on the hour.

After years of studying the geyser, we have our own method of calculating exactly when an eruption of Old Faithful is imminent. Just count the number of bored people seated around the geyser, the number of tourists is inversely proportional to the amount of time left until the next eruption.

If you get bored waiting for the old salt, pause a minute to consider the power of recycling – you are sitting on a boardwalk made from around three million recycled plastic water jugs.

OBSERVATION HILL

For a pre- or post-eruption overview of the entire basin, follow a branch trail from the Firehole River up a couple of hundred vertical feet to Observation Point for an alternative view of the Old Faithful eruption. From here you can descend to Solitary Geyser to rejoin the boardwalk for a 1.1-mile loop.

Solitary Geyser started off as a hot spring until it was diverted into a swimming pool in 1915 (the pool was dismantled in 1950). The lowering of the water level turned the spring into a geyser, triggering eruptions that continue to this day, even though water levels have returned to normal. Small sudden bursts occur every four to eight minutes.

GEYSER HILL

This collection of geysers closest to Old Faithful is most easily visited clockwise on the inner boardwalk loop. Not far from Old Faithful is the unmarked **Chinese Spring**, named after an Asian (actually Japanese) laundry that once operated here. Dirty clothes were put into the spring along with soap, and the owners waited for the clothes to fly out, apparently clean, in an induced eruption. Don't try a repeat performance, unless you want a citation.

Nearby, riverside **Blue Star Spring** was the site of a macabre incident in winter 1996–97, when a young bison fell into the boiling waters and died, causing the pool to smell like beef soup for days.

Consistent seepage from **Giantess Geyser** and **Vault Geyser** have created geyserite terraces that look like scaled relief maps. Giantess springs to life between two and six times a year, though when active the geyser erupts twice hourly for up to 40 hours. The surrounding area shakes from underground steam explosions just before it erupts. Vault Geyser was inactive for a decade until bursting back into life in 1998.

Doublet Pool is known for its deep blue color, thin scalloped geyserite border and the occasional thumping that emanates from collapsing steam and gas bubbles deep underground. **Aurum Geyser** ('aurum' means gold in Latin) is thought to be connected somehow to water deposits in the meadow behind it. It erupts to 20ft every 2½ to five hours.

The **Lion Geyser** group is a gathering of four interconnected geysers (two lions and two cubs), whose eruptions are preceded by a roar, hence the name. **Heart Spring** is said to resemble the shape of a human heart.

Beehive Geyser erupts twice a day, up to 190ft through its 4ft-high cone-shaped nozzle, and is the second- or third-tallest regularly active geyser in the park. Beehive has an 'indicator' – a smaller vent that when active signals the main eruption.

Erupting every 20 minutes, **Plume** is one of the easiest geysers to catch. It's also one of basin's youngest geysers, created by a steam explosion in 1922. Interestingly, its eruptions seem to have different phases at night and

Upper Geyser Basin

day. Nearby **Anemone Geyser** erupts every 15 minutes or so.

Rangers lead 90-minute walks of Geyser Hill daily at 8:30am.

MAIN LOOP

Along the tarmac trail in front of the Old Faithful Inn is **Castle Geyser**, whose huge cone, resembling a bleached sandcastle, attests to its status as the oldest geyser in the region, somewhere between 5000 and 15,000 years old (and built atop an even older spring). Castle goes off every 13 hours or so and can be predicted to within two hours; predicted times are posted by the geyser. The water eruption is followed by a noisy 30-minute steam phase, as the heat and steam energy long outlast the water supply. Nearby 42ft-deep **Crested Pool** is almost constantly boiling. This is one of the best places to get overviews of the basin.

The predictable **Daisy Geyser** lets loose at an angle up to 75ft every three hours or so and can be predicted to within 45 minutes, except when nearby Splendid Geyser erupts. Splendid is one of the largest in the region but erupts irregularly – apparently sometimes triggered by a change in atmospheric pressure, which slightly reduces the pool's boiling point. Don't confuse Daisy with the larger constantly splashing cone of **Comet**

Upper Geyser Basin

GEYSER-GAZING STRATEGIES

The first thing to do when you arrive at Old Faithful is to check the predicted geyser eruption times at the visitor center and then plan your itinerary around these. Predictions are made for the region's six main geysers – Old Faithful, Grand, Castle, Riverside, Daisy and the Lower Geyser Basin's Great Fountain – and these are also posted at Old Faithful Lodge, Old Faithful Inn and the Madison Junior Ranger Station. You can call ahead for timings on ☎307-344-2751.

Remember, though, that geysers rarely erupt on schedule, so take some snacks and sunblock for the wait. Riverside runs to within 30 minutes of predictions, but Grand is only reliable within two or three hours. Still, there's always something erupting in Upper Geyser Basin, and if you're really lucky you'll catch a biggie like Beehive or Daisy.

Budget at least half a day here to see the area around Old Faithful, and a whole day to see all the geyser basins, though you could easily spend a day or two more if you catch the geyser-gazing bug. If time is tight, concentrate on Upper and Midway Geyser Basins and skip Biscuit and Black Sand Basins.

The best loop around the Upper Geyser Basin follows the paved road one way and the boardwalk the other for a total of 3 miles. To this you can add a small hike up to Observation Point for views over the basin. There is a smaller loop around Geyser Hill, but you'll miss many of the best geysers if you limit yourself to this.

One interesting way to see the geysers is to cycle out 1.4 miles along the road to Morning Glory (where there's a bike rack), then continue on bike to Biscuit Basin via Daisy Geyser (1.3 miles). From here you can hike to Mystic Falls or cycle along the Grand Loop Rd to Black Sand Basin and get picked up there. Bikes can be rented at Bear Den Bike in the Old Faithful Snow Lodge; for details see p116.

Geyser. All three geysers are linked by underground chambers.

Grotto Geyser erupts every eight hours for anywhere between one and 10 hours. The cone takes its weird shape from trees that have been encased in the geyserite. Increased activity in Grotto generally means less activity in Giant Geyser. The picturesque **Riverside Geyser** puts on an amazing show when a 75ft column of water arcs into the Firehole River, often capped by a rainbow. Twenty-minute outpourings occur about every six hours; water spilling over the cone signals an imminent eruption.

Across the Firehole River, nearby riverside **Fan** and **Mortar Geysers** erupt infrequently but in unison, with Fan bursting water out of 17 individual jets.

Next comes beautiful Morning Glory pool, from where hardcore geyser gazers can follow a walking trail to several minor features such as **Artemisia Geyser**, named for its similarity to the color of sagebrush (*Artemisia*), and **Atomizer Geyser**, named for the large amounts of steam that follow its minor eruptions.

Heading back toward Old Faithful, take the boardwalk that branches off the cycle path to **Giant Geyser**, which produces stupendous 250ft eruptions but may be dormant for decades (it last erupted in 2010). Eruptions can last an hour, reach heights of 180ft to 250ft and expel an astonishing one million gallons of hot water with each eruption. The cessation of otherwise continuous **Bijou Geyser** nearby signals an imminent eruption of Giant Geyser.

The strikingly colorful **Chromatic Pool** and **Beauty Pool** are linked, so when one drops the other rises.

Next is **Grand Geyser**, ranking as the world's tallest predictable geyser (150ft to 180ft). It spews in bursts every eight hours or so and lasts about 12 minutes. It will often pause after nine minutes and then restart after a minute or so; the subsequent bursts are typically the most spectacular. Grand is a fountain geyser, not a cone like Old Faithful. Nearby **Turban Geyser** acts as a trigger for Grand and, along with **Vent Geyser**, continues to rage for one to two hours after Grand subsides.

Sawmill Geyser is in eruption about 30% of the time, but its extents are highly variable. Water spins violently in its crater like a circular saw. Nearby **Spasmodic** is also in eruption a third of the time and erupts from more than 20 vents.

Rangers lead 90-minute walks of the Upper Geyser Basin daily at 5:30pm.

BLACK SAND BASIN

This geyser basin, 1 mile northwest of Old Faithful, has a few interesting features. The eponymous black sand is derived from weathered volcanic glass (obsidian). You can access Black Sand Basin by car or, better, by foot from Daisy Geyser. Rangers lead hour-long walks here daily at 1pm.

Cliff Geyser is named for the geyserite wall that separates the geyser from Iron Spring Creek and is a frequent splasher. Nearby Ragged Spring frequently joins in the action with 12ft bursts. Emerald Pool looks like an exquisite flower with a lovely orange lip and gets its pretty color from yellow bacteria that blend with blue reflected from the sky. Rainbow Pool is connected to nearby Sunset Lake and is one of the more colorful in the park. The ground under the boardwalks here is literally boiling.

Unsigned Handkerchief Pool, just to the south of Rainbow Pool, was once one of Yellowstone's most famous features. Visitors would place a handkerchief in the pool and watch it get sucked down and then spat out 'clean' through a side vent. The pool stopped functioning in the 1920s, after one dimwit jammed logs into the opening, but it has since restored itself. Today it's illegal to throw anything into any of Yellowstone's thermal features.

BISCUIT BASIN

Two miles further north, Biscuit Basin was named for biscuitlike deposits that surrounded stunning Sapphire Pool, but these were destroyed during violent eruptions that followed the nearby 1959 Hebgen earthquake. If you're low on time, this is one basin you could safely miss.

The main features here are deep Jewel Geyser, which erupts every 10 minutes or so, with lovely yellow run-offs, and Shell Geyser, which is shaped like a clamshell and linked underground. Mustard Spring is named for its iron oxide–induced dark-yellow color.

A 0.5-mile hiking and biking trail leads from across the highway to Upper Geyser Basin's Daisy Geyser and a hiking-only path crosses the road to lead to Artemisia and Atomizer geysers in the Upper Geyser Basin.

The Mystic Falls Trail starts here – see p100 for details. There are free daily ranger-led hikes to the falls at 9am.

MIDWAY GEYSER BASIN

Five miles north of Old Faithful and 2 miles south of the Firehole Lake Dr entrance is Midway Geyser Basin. The key sight here is the algae-tinged indigo waters of the Grand Prismatic Spring. At 370ft wide and 121ft deep, it's the park's largest and deepest hot spring. It's also probably the most beautiful single thermal feature in the park. Boardwalks lead around the multicolored mist of the gorgeous pool and its spectacularly colored rainbow rings of algae.

For the most dramatic photos of Grand Prismatic Spring, drive south to Fairy Falls Trailhead, walk for 1 mile, and then take a faint path up the side of the fire-burned ridge (itself a lava deposit from the west rim of the caldera). From above, the spring looks like a giant blue eye, weeping exquisite multicolored tears.

The spring drains into Excelsior Pool, a huge former geyser that blew itself out of existence in the 1880s with massive 300ft explosions of water. The last eruptions here were in 1985, when the pool erupted almost continuously for 46 hours, before lulling itself back into a deep sleep. The pool continually discharges an amazing 4000 gallons of boiling water a minute into the Firehole River; according to T Scott Bryan's *The Geysers of Yellowstone,* that's enough to fill 300,000 automobile gas tanks every day. More water is expelled here in a single day than Old Faithful releases in two

---

DON'T MISS

MORNING GLORY POOL

A steamy favorite that's well worth the walk, beautiful Morning Glory Pool is named after the flower. Unfortunately, the pool is slowly changing temperature and, therefore, color, due to the tons of trash thrown into the pool by past visitors (the main access road to Old Faithful passed beside the pool until 1971). The refuse diminishes circulation and accelerates heat loss. As the pool cools, orange bacteria spreads from its sides, replacing the gorgeous blue tones. In 1950 park staff induced an eruption to empty and clean the spring, pulling out $86.27 in pennies, 76 handkerchiefs, several towels, socks, shirts and even women's underwear!

months. You can admire the colorful yellow and orange runoff as you approach the basin over the bridge.

The features are linked by a 0.5-mile accessible boardwalk; budget about 30 minutes here.

LOWER GEYSER BASIN

Separate roads access the three main sections of this sprawling thermal basin: the main Grand Loop Rd passes Fountain Paint Pot; the one-way Firehole Lake Dr loops off the main road to Great Fountain and other geysers; and Fountain Flat Dr offers access to hiking trails and minor thermal features. The latter two roads both offer the potential for a short bike ride.

FIREHOLE LAKE DRIVE

Firehole Lake Dr is a one-way, 3-mile road starting 2 miles north of Midway Geyser Basin and about 1 mile south of the Fountain Paint Pot parking lot. It passes several pretty pools and large geysers, including lovely Firehole Spring and then huge **Great Fountain Geyser**, which soars up to 200ft in a series of wide staccato bursts every 11 hours or so. Eruption times are predicted by the visitor center at Old Faithful to within a couple of hours, and you'll often find people waiting with a picnic lunch and a good book. The crater begins to overflow 90 minutes before an eruption and violent boiling signals an imminent eruption. Eruptions can last one hour.

The nearby 30ft cone of **White Dome Geyser** usually erupts every half-hour or so. The geyser is the symbol of the Yellowstone Association (see boxed text p264). Nearby **Pink Cone Geyser** gets its color from manganese dioxide deposits. A road was built right across the side of this cone in the 1930s.

Firehole Lake is a large hot spring ringed by several small geysers, including the raging waters of Artemisia Geyser and the sensuous black-and-tan smoothness of Young Hopeful.

Runoff from Firehole Lake flows into **Hot Lake** (also known as Black Warrior Lake) across the road, which offers more geysers and even a small cascade of boiling water. **Steady Geyser** is in continual eruption through one of two vents.

FOUNTAIN PAINT POT

Roughly midway between Madison Junction and Old Faithful, Fountain Paint Pot Nature Trail takes in four types of thermal features

along a 0.5-mile boardwalk loop. The Fountain Hotel, one of the park's earliest lodges, was located here until 1917.

Just past pretty Silex Spring, **Fountain Paint Pot** is a huge bowl of plopping goop that ranks as one of the biggest in the park. The action is sloppiest in spring, with some mud pots drying up by August. The area around the thermal features is slowly being drowned in deposits, while, beyond, a grassy basin supports the park's largest bison herd.

The **mud pots** are the top-billed comedians of the show. **Red Spouter** is particularly interesting, since it acts like a muddy hot spring in early summer, only to become a mud pot and then a fumarole later in the year. It only appeared after the huge Hebgen Lake earthquake of 1959. Morning and Fountain Geysers are impressive but infrequent gushers; the latter drains into Spasm Geyser.

Clepsydra Geyser has erupted almost constantly since the Hebgen Lake earthquake in 1959. The geyser was named Clepsydra (Greek for 'water clock') at the time when it used to go off every three minutes on the button. **Jelly Geyser** does indeed look like an upside-down bowl of Jell-O.

In 1981 **Celestine Pool** was the site of one of the park's most famous accidents, when a young Californian man dived headfirst into the hot spring to save his dog who had controversially decided to cool off in the enticing pool. Sadly both died as a result of their burns.

For a map of Fountain Paint Pot and Firehole Lake Dr pick up the park-service trail guide (50¢). Rangers lead tours here three times a week at 9am.

FOUNTAIN FLAT DRIVE

This former freight road turns off the Grand Loop Rd at the pleasant **Nez Percé Picnic Area** (with toilets) and continues south for 1.5 miles to a hiking and cycling trailhead. From here the road is accessible to cyclists and hikers all the way to Fairy Falls Trailhead, 4 miles away. The trail is wheelchair accessible for 2.2 miles to the Goose Lake (OD5) campsite, one of two wheelchair-accessible backcountry campsites in the park.

Just beyond a parking lot is the **Ojo Caliente Hot Spring**, which empties into the river (Ojo Caliente means 'Hot Spring' in Spanish). Just south of the bridge is the trail to Sentinel Meadows (see p101) and on either side of the bridge are trails to Pocket Basin.

Pocket Basin is one of the least-known and little-visited thermal basins in the valley. The basin is actually a miniature caldera, originally created by a hydrothermal explosion that must have been roughly on the scale of an atomic bomb. The northern trail leads past the belching mud pot of Grotto Spring and inviting Baby Bathtub Spring to the River Group, a collection of four or five geysers and hot springs that includes Cavern Spring, Bath Spring, Azure Spring, Diadem Spring and Cone Spring. Over the ridge is one of the park's largest collections of mud pots. Across the river is Mound Spring, which erupts every half-hour or so. The basin isn't on the scale of the more famous thermal features further south, but this is one place you can explore away from the boardwalks and parking lots. Remember, however, to take the normal precautions when approaching any thermal feature.

FIREHOLE CANYON DRIVE
The one-way Firehole Canyon Dr leaves the Grand Loop Rd just south of Madison Junction. The road passes 40ft-high **Firehole Falls** at the foot of towering dark rhyolite cliffs, but the main attraction here is the lukewarm **Firehole Swimming Area** (no fee), one of the few locations in the park that's open for swimming. The kids will love it. There are two toilets here but limited parking.

MADISON TO WEST YELLOWSTONE
Madison Junction sits at the confluence of the Firehole, Madison and Gibbon Rivers. Towering above the small junior ranger station is **National Park Mountain** (7500ft), which commemorates the spot where in 1870 the idea of preserving Yellowstone was allegedly first mentioned.

The Madison Valley is of interest mainly to anglers and wildlife-watchers, though all will appreciate the sublime afternoon light and active herds of deer, elk and bison. Due to the long snow-free season many elk live in the valley year-round, while bison migrate through the valley en route between their winter habitat near the park's western boundary and summer grazing in the Hayden Valley. The 14-mile road to West Yellowstone is also one of the park's busiest tourist corridors.

Two miles east of Madison, the family-friendly **Harlequin Lake Trailhead** leads 0.5 miles north to a pond. The trailhead is also a fine place to spot wildlife in the lovely valley to the south. Elk often lie in the meadows here, with only their heads poking up above the long grass. From here the road threads between volcanic bluffs, with towering Mt Haynes (8235ft) on the left and Mt Jackson on the right, past several excellent fly-fishing spots, before the valley opens up to views of the distant Gallatin Range.

Halfway along the road the Seven Mile Bridge marks the Madison River Picnic Area, popular with fly-fishers, and the Gneiss Creek Trailhead. The area south of the road here is closed to protect a trumpeter swan habitat. In 1988 this section of the park was engulfed in the North Fork fire, the largest of that summer's giant blazes.

Four miles further, **Riverside Dr** is a 1-mile, two-way road that's useful for fishing access and perhaps some family biking. Three miles later the Two Ribbons Trail is a 0.75-mile wheelchair-accessible trail that offers a fairly dull loop or point-to-point stroll through some fire burns.

Shortly after you enter Montana, about 2 miles before West Yellowstone, the dirt Barnes Rd to the north accesses several more fishing spots. And then suddenly, just like that, you are out of the wilderness and in the middle of bustling West Yellowstone (see p167).

OLD FAITHFUL TO WEST THUMB
Three miles into the 17-mile drive between Old Faithful and West Thumb is **Kepler Cascades**, where a wooden platform offers fine views of the 125ft falls. Just past the cascades turnout is the parking area for the worthwhile hike or bike ride to Lone Star Geyser (p102 and p116). The road climbs past Scaup Lake, the Spring Creek Picnic Area (site of the park's biggest stagecoach robbery in 1908) and the Continental Divide Trailhead before reaching **Isa Lake** at Craig Pass (8262ft).

Craig Pass is an unassuming spot of deep significance. Lily-choked Isa Lake sits astride both the road and the **Continental Divide** and in spring drains (or rather seeps) into both the Atlantic and Pacific drainages. The west side of the lake drains year-round into the Firehole River, which flows into the Missouri and Mississippi before finally reaching the Atlantic *to the east;* the east side (in spring only) flows into Shoshone Lake and then the Lewis, Snake and Columbia rivers and thus the Pacific Ocean *to* *the west.* The lake was named after Isabelle Jelke, the first park tourist to visit the lake, and it freezes solid in winter under around 15ft of snow.

From the pass, the road descends to the **DeLacy Creek** Picnic Area and Trailhead (see the hike description p104) and shortly afterward offers a tantalizing sliver of a view towards remote Shoshone Lake. From here the road ascends back across the Continental Divide (8391ft), before finally descending to excellent views of Yellowstone Lake and the turnoff to West Thumb. See p98 for routes onward from here.

Bechler Region

Visitors must go out of their way to find the Bechler region. Located in the remote southwest area of the park, it cannot be reached via the main entrance points or loops. Known for its numerous waterfalls and the park's highest rainfall, the remote Bechler (*Beck*-ler) region, also known as Beckler Corner or Cascade Corner, is largely the preserve of hardy backpackers, outfitters and horseback riders who brave flooded streams, monster mosquitoes and boggy marshland to access beautiful backcountry with the park's largest waterfalls and outstanding thermal soaking springs. The 8000-hectare meadow is home to diverse wildlife, including sandhill cranes, moose and coyotes. Early-season visits are impractical here – trails are often flooded into July and mosquitoes are often brutal along the river until the beginning of August.

Visitors en route to a hike in the region or traveling Grassy Lake Rd might want to detour by car or foot to the Cave Falls cascades and swimming hole (p104).

Bechler is accessed via Bechler Ranger Station or Cave Falls Trailhead, both off the mostly unpaved Cave Falls Rd via US 20, 26 miles from Ashton, Idaho, itself a two-hour drive from West Yellowstone, Montana, via ID Hwy 47 and Marysville Rd. Alternative approaches include coming from Driggs, Idaho, to the south (joining US 20) or the brutal, unpaved Grassy Lake Rd/Reclamation Rd, from the turnoff just north of Flagg Ranch, part of John D Rockefeller Memorial Parkway, 2 miles south of Yellowstone's South Entrance; allow at least two hours from Flagg Ranch.

DRIVING

There's hardly a single mile of highway on Yellowstone's 142-mile Grand Loop Rd that can't be described as scenic. The views are always fantastic, whether it's the panoramic views from Dunraven Pass, lakeshore views across Yellowstone Lake or open valley views across meandering rivers and lodgepole forests. All the main route descriptions of the park in this chapter make for excellent drives.

Geyser Trail

Duration half-day

Distance 25 miles

Start Madison

Finish Old Faithful

Nearest Town West Yellowstone

Speed Limit 45mph, sometimes dropping to 35mph; 25mph approaching Old Faithful area

Summary The drive south from Madison Campground links together several geyser basins and wildlife-watching spots with opportunities to hike, bike and even swim. Take your time on this route through the heart of Geyser Country.

GETTING AWAY FROM IT ALL

Shhh...don't tell anyone about these five seldom-visited Yellowstone sights:

» **Bechler Region** (p88, p104) The bone-crushing drive deters most visitors from this lush wilderness area, home to half the park's waterfalls.

» **Fossil Forest Hike** (p94) An unmarked turnoff and path leads up to fine views and several petrified tree stumps.

» **Imperial Geyser** (p102) Lose the crowds just 10 minutes past popular Fairy Falls.

» **Pocket Basin** (p86) Leave the boardwalks behind in this collection of off-trail hot springs and mud pots.

» **Upper Geyser Basin** (p78) Geyser eruptions seem even more magical during a full-moon stroll.

The northern approach to Old Faithful offers lots of possible stops so don't expect to cruise this route in one hit. The drive parallels the Firehole River and there are dozens of potential fly-fishing spots along this route.

Drive south from Madison Junction, past the junior ranger station, and after 2 miles take Firehole Canyon Dr to the right. This 2-mile side road takes you past rhyolite cliffs and rapids, the **Firehole Falls** and the popular **Firehole swimming area**.

Back on the main road it's another 3 miles south to Fountain Flat Dr, which branches right to give access to the pleasant Nez Percé Picnic Area, the Sentinel Meadows hike (p101), Pocket Basin backcountry geyser area (p86) and the bikeable Fountain Freight Rd.

Back on the main road, 1 mile south, the road crosses **Chief Joseph Creek**, where an interesting pullout details the flight of the Nez Percé Indians, who crossed this creek in August 1877 fleeing the US Army. For details of the two-week flight of the Nez Percé (pronounced 'Nez Purse') through Yellowstone, see boxed text, p232.

From here on you'll get your first views of the amazing thermal features ahead. A **pullout** 1 mile ahead offers a fine view of the smoking geysers and pools of Midway Geyser Basin to the right and Firehole Lake Basin on the left, as well as the meandering Firehole Valley and the occasional bison – a classic Yellowstone vista.

Just 1 mile further, take a right into Fountain Paint Pot. Another 1.5 miles south take the left on Firehole Lake Dr (p86) and make the leisurely 3-mile drive past **Great Fountain Geyser** and **Firehole Lake** to see what's on the boil.

Next up is **Midway Geyser Basin** (p85), which is worth a stop. As you continue south, you'll see the colorful runoffs from **Excelsior Pool** flowing into the Firehole River.

Two miles further is busy Fairy Falls Trailhead, a popular starting point for hikes to Fairy Falls (p102), views over Grand Prismatic Spring and bike rides along the gravel Fountain Freight Rd. You'll also likely see bison and fly-fishers in this vicinity.

It's a further 2 miles to the minor thermal sites of **Biscuit Basin** and **Black Sand Basin**, from where cyclists can get out and ride to **Old Faithful**, 1.5 miles away.

DAY HIKES

Even if you drive every road in Yellowstone you'll still see only 2% of the park. Easily the best way to get a close-up taste of Yellowstone's unique combination of rolling landscape, wildlife and thermal activity is on foot, along the more than 900 miles of maintained trails. Hiking is also the best way to escape the summer crowds. Only 10% of visitors step off the road or boardwalks, only half of those venture further than a mile and a paltry 1% overnight in the backcountry. It's one thing to photograph a bison from your car, it's quite another to hike gingerly past a snorting herd out on their turf. So pick up a map, pack some granola bars and work at least a couple of the following great hikes into your Yellowstone itinerary.

The following hikes are grouped according to region and then listed in approximate rising order of difficulty. Note that the park uses a three-character code (eg 2K7) to identify both trailheads and specific backcountry campsites, and we have included these wherever useful.

See the Hiking charts on p32 for an overview of hikes. For a rundown of our personal definitions of what is an easy, moderate and difficult hike, see p30.

Mammoth Country

Hikes in the relatively low-elevation area around the park's North Entrance highlight scenic canyons, panoramic peaks and numerous lakes, streams and waterfalls, all under the backdrop of the Gallatin Range. This is one of the park's hottest regions in summer and is one of the first regions to be snow-free in spring. Consider hiking early or late in the season or outside of midday.

Beaver Ponds Trail

Duration 2½ hours

Distance 5 miles

Difficulty Easy-moderate

Elevation Change 350ft

Start/Finish Sepulcher Mountain/Beaver Ponds Trailhead (1K1; Map p58)

Nearest Town/Junction Mammoth

Summary An enjoyable loop hike, perfect if you're overnighting at Mammoth, that climbs to five ponds and offers a good chance of spotting moose and waterfowl.

This 5-mile loop, with gentle climbs and lots of early-morning and evening wildlife, begins between Liberty Cap and a private house next to the bus parking lot at Mammoth. The trail ascends through the fir and spruce forests along **Clematis Creek** and in 2.5 miles reaches a series of five ponds amid meadows, where beavers and moose emerge in the mornings and evenings. Black bears are also a distinct possibility. Rangers offer free walks along the trail at 8am on Friday and Saturdays. Most families will be able to tackle this walk, as long as you bring mosquito repellent.

Before you get started, it's worth pausing at trailside **Hymen Terrace**, named after the Greek god of marriage and one of the prettiest of Mammoth's many hot-spring terraces. The trail is clearly signposted and follows the Sepulcher Mountain trail for the first 0.7 miles, taking a right at the first junction over a wooden bridge. Follow the trail as it starts to switchback up the hill and about 20 minutes into the hike you reach the signed junction, marking the end of the main elevation gain. Turn right for the **Beaver Ponds Loop** (left for the Sepulcher Mountain Trail).

As the path flattens, it passes through patches of moody Douglas fir forest and open meadows of wildflowers before a side trail reveals fine views over Mammoth and the sediment strata of Everts Ridge. Ten minutes later the trail crosses a 4WD service track leading up to a hilltop radio transmitter, before passing a patch of quaking aspens and descending through forest to the first of several beaver-dammed ponds (1¼ hours from the trailhead). The fifth and final pond offers fine views of Sepulcher Mountain in the background and is a good place to spot moose, elk and pronghorn. Cross the outlet at the far end of the lake and ascend to a small ridge.

From here, the trail continues across an open **sagebrush plateau**, offering views down on Gardiner town and both the modern and former stagecoach roads to the park, until you reach a ridge with fine views over the orderly buildings and manicured green lawns and white thermal terraces of Mammoth. Continue right along the ridge for more views or descend to the employee parking lot and the 4WD road to Gardiner that leads off behind the Mammoth Hot Springs Hotel. Grab a well-deserved ice cream at the general store before returning to your vehicle. You've earned it.

🏃 Bunsen Peak & Osprey Falls

Duration 2½ hours (6–7 hours with side trip)

Distance 4.2-mile round-trip (10.2 miles with side trip)

Difficulty Moderate (difficult with side trip)

Elevation Change 1300ft (2100ft with side trip)

Start/Finish Bunsen Peak Trailhead (1K4; Map p58)

Nearest Town/Junction Mammoth

Summary A short but steep hike up the side of an ancient lava plug for superb views, with the option of descending to an impressive canyon waterfall.

Bunsen Peak (8564ft) is a popular half-day hike, and you can extend it to a more demanding day hike by continuing down the mountain's gentler eastern slope to the Bunsen Peak Rd and then *waaay* down (800ft) to the base of seldom-visited Osprey Falls. It's also possible to bike 'n' hike out to Osprey Falls (see p115). The initial Bunsen Peak Trail climbs east out of Gardner's Hole to the exposed summit of Bunsen Peak, offering outstanding panoramas of Mammoth, the Gallatin Range, Swan Lake Flat and the Blacktail Deer Plateau. Even if you just make it halfway up the hill you'll be rewarded with superb views.

Bunsen Peak's trails (especially along the south slope) are free of snow much earlier than those on most other peaks in the park and thus can be negotiated as early as May with some mild glissading. Be prepared for frequent afternoon thunderstorms, which bring fierce winds and lightning year-round.

Bunsen Peak was named by the 1872 Hayden Survey for German scientist Robert Wilhelm Eberhard von Bunsen (after whom the Bunsen burner was also named), whose pioneering theories about the inner workings of Icelandic geysers influenced early Yellowstone hydrothermal research. The mountain is actually an ancient lava plug, the surrounding volcanic walls of which have partially eroded away. So, yes, you are effectively climbing up the inside of a former volcano!

From the Mammoth Visitor Center, head 4.5 miles south on Grand Loop Rd, cross the **Golden Gate Bridge**, and turn left into the unpaved parking area on the east side of the road, just beyond the Rustic Falls turnout.

The parking lot is small and fills up quickly, so get here early.

From 7250ft, the well-trodden single-track dirt trail begins just beyond a barricade on the left (north) side of unpaved **Bunsen Peak Rd**. The trail climbs immediately through sagebrush interspersed with wildflowers, then enters a young Douglas fir and lodgepole pine mosaic. You'll get early views of the Golden Gate below and to the left, and the ash-colored jumble of the hoodoos to the north. About half an hour from the trailhead a series of meadows offer views southwest to Swan Lake Flat, Antler Peak (10,023ft), Mt Holmes (10,336ft), Terraced Mountain and Electric Peak (10,992ft). Five minutes later, at one of the many switchbacks, you'll gain a great view of the eroded sandstone cliffs and spire of Cathedral Rock, with views down to the red roofs and bleached travertine mounds of Mammoth. The layered sandstone-and-shale mountain of Mt Everts (7841ft), to the north, offers proof that the area was underwater 70 to 140 million years ago. Beyond the Cathedral Rock outcrop, the switchbacks get steeper on the north side of the mountain and the exposed dome-shaped peak comes into view. Keep your eyes peeled for bighorn sheep.

The trail passes under electricity wires before radio communications equipment marks the first of three small summits, 2.1 miles from the trailhead (there are plans to remove the towers). Continue east along the loose talus ridge to the exposed easternmost summit for the best southern panoramas. Electric Peak (10,992ft), one of the largest in the Gallatin Range, looms largest to the northwest, marking the park's northern boundary, with the Absaroka Range to the northeast.

Either retrace your steps down the west slope or wind around the peak to descend the east slope to the Osprey Falls Trail.

SIDE TRIP: OSPREY FALLS & SHEEPEATER CANYON
3-4 HOURS, 6 MILES, 800FT ASCENT

From the south side of the third summit, the trail descends east through the burnt forest and volcanic talus of Bunsen Peak's eastern flank. It's 1.9 miles (one hour) downhill to the Bunsen Peak Rd. After about 45 minutes, just after you catch sight of the Bunsen Peak Rd, look for the orange marker that points you left along a subtrail to the **Osprey Falls Trailhead**.

From the marked trailhead, the 1.4-mile Osprey Falls trail wanders along the cliffs for 10 minutes before dropping like a stone into the **Sheepeater Canyon**, losing 800ft in a bit less than a mile via a series of narrow, rocky switchbacks. Finally the trail levels out by the Gardner River to reach the base of the impressive, little-visited 150ft **Osprey Falls**, set below an impressive basalt cliff and spire. You're more likely to see marmots or water ouzels in the canyon than the namesake bighorn sheep or osprey, which now prefer to nest along the Yellowstone River. The falls are a refreshing spot to linger over a packed lunch and contemplate the relentless chaos and synergy of the park's natural forces.

Retrace your steps back out of the canyon and haul yourself back up 45 minutes to Bunsen Peak Rd, from where it's a fairly dull 3.2-mile (1¼ hour) trudge along the abandoned dirt road back to the Bunsen Peak Trailhead. After 20 minutes look for a pair of antlers by the side of the trail shortly before views of the upper Gardner River. In the early morning and evening, hikers often spot wildlife (elk, bison, waterfowl and otters) in the meadows and ponds of **Gardner's Hole**, near the parking area. Look for muskrats in the roadside pond.

🏃 Sepulcher Mountain

Duration 7 hours

Distance 11.5 miles

Difficulty Difficult

Elevation Change 3400ft

Start/Finish Beaver Ponds/Sepulcher Mountain Trailhead (1K1; Map p58)

Nearest Town/Junction Mammoth

Summary A long but varied and incredibly scenic loop hike that offers superb views over half the park and gives a secret peek at hidden thermal features of the Mammoth terraces.

The first half of this three-quarter day hike is a cardio workout, gaining almost 3500ft, before descending through meadows and forest in a long but leisurely stroll back. It's a relentless climb but it's well graded, offering plenty of interest en route. The hike starts at the same trailhead as the Beaver Ponds hike so you can park anywhere in the Mammoth area. Trails Illustrated's 1:63,360 map No 303 *Mammoth Hot Springs* covers the route.

After 20 minutes the Sepulcher Mountain trail branches left away from the Beaver Ponds trail, then 25 minutes later continues straight at a junction with the Clagett Butte/Snow Pass Trail. Continue up through burnt meadows, past an easily missed pond on your right, before ascending steeply up onto a ridge where you'll get your first views of Sepulcher Mountain and the impressive Gallatin Range to the west. The trail winds below the ridgeline through patches of forest and sagebrush to a viewpoint overlooking Gardiner and the lower Paradise Valley, north of the park boundary. As you continue the ascent, look for a cairn marking the path along the ridgeline to the tomblike rocky outcrops that give Sepulcher Peak its name. At a second cairn junction take the right branch for one minute to awesome views of the Paradise Valley and a well-deserved lunch spot. The main trail and actual **summit** (9646ft) are to the left of the cairn junction, past fine views of **Electric Peak** (10,992ft) and Cache Lake below.

The trail then descends to open meadows and an equally awesome panorama over Gardner's Hole, stretching from Bunsen Peak to Fawn Pass, with views stretching across half the park as far as the Tetons. Descend the hillside on wide ribbonlike switchbacks before re-entering a patch of forest and the junction with the Cache Lake/Glen Creek/Sportsman Lake trail; take a left here.

After 15 minutes along Glen Creek you enter an open valley and branch left (east) to cross tiny Snow Pass (follow the electricity poles). Descend past a trail junction, ignoring the left branch signed for the Sepulcher Mountain Trail. As you descend here look for white chunks of travertine beside the forested trail, proof that you are skirting the Mammoth-like destroyed former hot springs of **Pinyon Terrace**.

At the trail junction by the signboard, take the left branch on the Howard Eaton trail. The final 1.3 miles take you around the back of the upper **Mammoth terraces**; take care if you decide to explore the side trails that lead to extinct cones, sinkholes and caves (emitting deadly carbon dioxide). Past Orange Mound Spring are views of some beautiful hidden white terraces (not visible from Mammoth's Upper Terraces) and Narrow Gauge Terrace, before descending past views over Mammoth to where you started, six or seven long but highly enjoyable hours ago.

Other Mammoth Country Hikes

One enjoyable loop hike is the three-hour **Terrace Mountain Loop**. Starting at Snow Pass trailhead, just south of Mammoth's Upper Terraces, the trail meanders through the interesting Hoodos, climbing high above the road to views of Rustic Falls, Mt Holmes and Swan Lake Flat, before swinging right through the open sagebrush of Glen Creek and then taking a right turn, following the electricity lines over Snow Pass and downhill past Pinyon Terrace (see the last section of the Sepulcher Mountain hike). An alternative is to start at Glen Creek trailhead.

If you can arrange a vehicle shuttle, one excellent, easy and little-seen route (all downhill!) is to follow the **Howard Eaton Trail** from Glen Creek Trailhead down past views of Rustic Falls and the Hoodos, past the junction to Snow Pass and down along the back side of Mammoth terraces to Beaver Ponds Trailhead (3.8 miles). For a description of the last section see the Sepulcher Mountain hike.

Cache Lake is a satisfying 11.2-mile, three-quarter-day hike that is long enough to give you a workout but not hard enough to wipe you out. From Bunsen Peak/Glenn Creek Trailhead (1K3), 4.5 miles south of Mammoth, the trail crosses open sagebrush country, passing turnoffs to Fawn Pass and the Sepulcher Mountain trails, along the Sportsman Lake trail. Keep an eye out for moose grazing in the lush meandering valley of Glen Creek. Turn right at the final junction with the Sportsman Lake trail and climb to the lovely lake, ringed by golden meadows and thick forest, with impressive 10,992ft Electric Peak looming to the right. It's about 2½ hours to the lake from the trailhead. Budget some time to savor the lake before retracing your steps.

An appealing shorter hike is the 8-mile return **Blacktail Deer Creek Trail**, 7 miles east of Mammoth. It descends 1100ft from the trailhead north into the Black Canyon of the Yellowstone to join the river near Crevice Lake. The return is all uphill.

Roosevelt Country

Hikes in this region are among the first in the park to be clear of snow and are accessible by road year-round. Attractions include big rolling valley views, petrified forests, meadows of wildflowers and some of the richest wildlife in the park.

🏃 Yellowstone River Picnic Area Trail

Duration 1½–2 hours

Distance 4-mile round-trip or loop

Difficulty Easy

Elevation Change 350ft

Start/Finish Yellowstone River Picnic Area (2K7; Map p63)

Nearest Town/Junction Tower-Roosevelt

Summary A lovely stroll that offers crowdless vistas over the Narrows, with much historical and geological interest.

Popular with picnickers, this scenic stroll offers fantastic views into the eroded towers and basalt formations of the Narrows and Calcite Springs, and possible glimpses of osprey and bighorn sheep: bring your binoculars. It's a good family hike but you'll need to watch for the little ones because there are lots of sheer drop-offs and no guardrails. To get to the trailhead, take the Northeast Entrance Rd across the bridge from Tower-Roosevelt to the picnic area parking lot, 1.5 miles east of the junction. Park in the lot just west of the picnic area.

Several unofficial dirt trails climb the slopes behind the picnic area but the official (signed) trail leads off from the picnic site left of the vault toilets to ascend a couple of hundred feet and deposit you puffing on the rim of the **Yellowstone canyon**. En route the trail passes several large erratic boulders, deposited in the valley over 10,000 years ago from the Beartooth Mountains by slow-moving glaciers. You'll notice along this hike how many of the Douglas firs have prospered in the moist, protective shade of these huge boulders. The hike traces the canyon's north rim for a couple of miles, providing unobscured views down past the crooked canyon walls to the **Yellowstone River** and north and east beyond rolling ridges to the peaks of the Absaroka Range.

The trail stays in open country on the ridgeline 800ft above the canyon floor for the whole route. About 20 minutes from the trailhead you may smell sulfur, a sign that you are about to pass 180-degree views of the Calcite Springs thermal area across the canyon. Ten minutes further come fine views of the breccia spires of the Narrows. Look out for bighorn sheep below the basalt columns at **Overhanging Cliff**.

The trail ends abruptly at a bald **hilltop lookout** that offers views down on the site of the Bannock Indian ford, used by the Bannock to cross the Yellowstone River during their annual hunting trips across the park. You can also see the Tower Falls region (but not the falls themselves) to the right and the fire tower atop Mt Washburn in the distance.

From here you can retrace your steps to investigate the views of the canyon for a second time, or alternatively take the trail left (northeast) for a few minutes to the three-way junction with the **Specimen Ridge Trail**. Take a left at this junction to return downhill back to the road and the picnic area. (If you have some excess energy, you could ascend partway up Specimen Ridge along the Specimen Ridge Trail for fabulous views over the Lamar Valley.)

Just before reaching the road, branch left at the trail register and cut cross-county back to the trailhead, paralleling the road to join the large erratic boulder mentioned at the start of the hike. Otherwise you'll have to hike along the road, an unpleasant end to a lovely hike.

🏃 Lost Lake

Duration 2 hours

Distance 3.3-mile loop

Difficulty Easy

Elevation Change 600ft

Start/Finish Roosevelt Lodge (Map p63)

Nearest Town/Junction Tower-Roosevelt

Summary A peaceful early-morning hike to a secluded lake and a petrified tree – perfect for families and anyone staying or dining at Roosevelt Lodge.

The Lost Lake loop trail begins directly behind Roosevelt Lodge (take the right fork), climbing about 300ft past Lost Lake to a petrified tree, from which the trail climbs onto a plateau and then descends to the Tower Ranger Station. Before you even start the hike, warm up with a quick 10-minute detour left at the trailhead to the small but pretty **Lost Creek Falls**.

From the trailhead the trail switchbacks surprisingly steeply for the first 10 minutes onto the ridge. Look out for mule deer here in the early morning. Take a right at the junction (left leads to Tower Fall Campground 2.9 miles away) and you'll come to the meadows surrounding **Lost Lake**, about 30 minutes from the trailhead. The trail traverses the length of the lake, past lily pads and dragonflies, to a good potential picnic spot at the end of the lake. If you're lucky, you might spot moose here.

From here the trail descends through meadows thick with spring wildflowers to reach the parking lot of the **Petrified Tree** (p60). Take a couple of minutes to appreciate the 50-million-year-old stone redwood (there used to be three such trees here but early tourists chipped away the other two!). If you started the hike early, you'll have the place to yourself; later in the day the parking lot will be jammed with reversing SUVs.

The trail back to Roosevelt Lodge follows the orange markers up the hill from the edge of the parking lot and ascends to an open sagebrush plateau, offering fine views ahead to Junction Butte, Specimen Ridge and the Absaroka Range to the east. The trail then descends to the **Tower Ranger Station**. You'll likely see mule deer grazing in the meadows here; at the very least you'll see a John Deere parked by the ranger station. Follow the orange trail markers and in two minutes you'll be back at the cabins of Roosevelt Lodge, where breakfast will be waiting.

🥾 Fossil Forest Trail

Duration 2½–3½ hours

Distance 3.5 miles

Difficulty Moderate–difficult

Elevation Change 800ft

Start/Finish Unmarked trailhead (Map p63)

Nearest Town/Junction Tower-Roosevelt Junction

Summary A must for amateur geologists, this unmaintained trail climbs to several petrified trees and offers fine views. Listen for howling wolves in the early morning.

This hike leads to a couple of isolated patches of petrified forest scattered along Specimen Ridge, thought to hold the word's largest collection of petrified trees. The forests were buried suddenly in ash around 50 million years ago or turned to stone by a vengeful Crow medicine man, depending on your beliefs. See p239 for more on how trees became petrified. Paleodendrochronologists (scientists who date fossilized trees, somewhat of a niche profession!) have identified dozens of different species of trees here, including tropical avocado and breadfruit, with dozens of ancient petrified forests

stacked atop even older petrified forests. Some of the trees were buried where they grew, but others were probably deposited by a mudflow caused by volcanic eruptions about 50 million years ago.

Please don't pocket any of the petrified wood here or elsewhere in the park. If you are desperate for a petrified wood souvenir, then get a permit from the **Gallatin National Forest Gardiner District Office** (✆406-848-7375; 805 Scott St, Gardiner; ☺Mon-Fri) and head to Tom Miner Basin (see boxed text, p152) in the Paradise Valley.

This trailhead isn't easy to find, so be sure not to confuse it with the Specimen Ridge Trail a couple of miles further west. The parking area is marked 'Trailhead' and is just a few hundred yards west of the Lamar Canyon bridge, 5 miles east of Tower-Roosevelt Junction and about 1 mile southwest of the turnoff to Slough Creek Campground. Look for the wheelchair-accessible parking spot.

The trail is not formally maintained by the park service, so it isn't as easy to follow as most other trails in the park, though visitor centers do have a handout on the hike if you ask nicely. There is no water along the trail. Keep an eye out for the weather; the exposed ridge is definitely not the place to be during a lightning storm. Winds can pick up in the afternoon.

From the **unmarked trailhead** the fairly clear path starts off following a dirt double track (a former service road to the nearby Crystal Valley) and then veers right after 100yd to head up the hillside for 45 minutes, through meadows of July wildflowers and past buffalo wallows to a small patch of forest. Branch right along the steeper path and after 10 minutes' uphill climb you'll reach your first petrified tree stump by a bend in the trail, about 40 minutes from the trailhead. Five minutes later comes the second stump, with a third piece lying by the side of the trail. From here it's more uphill, past a volcanic outcrop enclosing another fossilized tree and onto the ridgeline, where a side path offers a steeper alternate route down to the main loop road.

The main trail continues up the ridge and after a couple of minutes branches right on a subtrail, skirting and then traversing a small patch of forest to the stump of a **petrified giant redwood**. This fabulous tree would once have topped out at 200ft in height! Below the huge stump are two thinner but taller upright trees and views back up towards the redwood's petrified roots. Dozens more fossilized trees lie scattered along the steep forested slopes but they are dangerous to reach on the crumbling cliff face. The views over the Lamar and Yellowstone valleys are simply superb.

The subtrail continues up the hillside to join the main trail just before a small cairn; continue for 20 minutes uphill along the ridge to the summit of **Specimen Ridge**, marked by a cairn. There are wonderful views from here of bison herds in the valley below, birds of prey riding the thermals, and the Grand Canyon of the Yellowstone River in the distance. Return the way you came – the views west are stunning.

Other Roosevelt Country Hikes

From the stagecoach road just north of Tower-Roosevelt Junction, the 7.5-mile **Garnet Hill Trail** is an easy three-hour loop north of the Grand Loop Rd. The trail heads northwest along Elk Creek and then loops around Garnet Hill to return to Roosevelt Lodge. For an extension, take a left at the Garnet Hill junction, a right to cross the suspension bridge over the Yellowstone River, then drop down to Hellroaring Creek (add 2.5 miles). You can also reach the trail from Hellroaring Trailhead, 3.5 miles west of Tower-Roosevelt Junction.

For a good day hike with fine fishing, try the first part of the **Slough Creek Trail**. Head uphill past the patrol cabin to where the trail rejoins the river at the first meadow (a 4-mile round-trip), or continue to the second meadow or nearby McBride Lake (cross Slough Creek) for a 6-mile round-trip hike. Be sure to take the right branch at the junction with the trail that continues up to the Buffalo Plateau. There's also nice hiking along the fishing trails that head up Slough Creek from the campground.

Pebble Creek Trail to Warm Creek Trailhead (3K4) is a scenic 12-mile hike that requires a vehicle shuttle. The trail heads up Pebble Creek for 10 miles through burns and lovely wildflowers, crosses a pass, then drops down to the Warm Creek Trailhead and a nearby picnic area on the Northeast Entrance Rd. The hike includes several river crossings that can prove tricky in early summer.

Specimen Ridge Trail is a popular but long 19-mile hike up and along the ridge, past Amethyst Mountain, then down into the Lamar Valley. Check with rangers be-

forehand that the Lamar River ford is traversable. You'll need to arrange a shuttle.

Canyon Country

Though the surrounding backcountry draws far less attention than the Grand Canyon of the Yellowstone, it is every bit as interesting. Abundant wildlife, good camping, mesmerizing cascades and great vistas await. You can also consider the Seven Mile Hole trail as an 11-mile day hike (see p106).

South Rim Trail & Ribbon Lake

Duration 4 hours

Distance 6 miles

Difficulty Easy

Elevation Change Negligible

Start/Finish Uncle Tom's parking lot (Map p68)

Nearest Town/Junction Canyon Village

Summary An incredibly varied hike that combines awesome views of the Grand Canyon of the Yellowstone with a couple of lakes and even a backcountry thermal area.

Southeast of the Yellowstone Canyon's South Rim, a network of trails meanders through meadows and forests and past several small lakes. This loop links several of these and makes a nice antidote to seeing canyon views framed by the windshield of your car.

Park at Uncle Tom's parking area on the Canyon's South Rim Dr and, after checking out the views of the Upper Falls and the Lower Falls from Uncle Tom's Trail (p69), take the **South Rim Trail** east from Uncle Tom's Trail, along the rim of the canyon to **Artist Point** for some of the finest canyon views available.

From Artist Point take the trail east toward Point Sublime, taking in the superb views halfway along the trail, where you branch right past **Lily Pad Lake** for 0.3 miles to another junction. Branch left here and descend to **Ribbon Lake**, actually two conjoined ponds, with a good chance of spotting moose. For a close-up view of **Silver Cord Cascade**, continue on the path to the canyon rim, then head left along the canyon wall to the small falls. A faint path connects to the main trail at a small footbridge. This is the furthest point of the hike, 3.4 miles from the start.

Two secluded backcountry sites by the lake make for an easy overnighter less than 2 miles from the trailhead (4R1 is right on the lake; 4R2 is on the main trail and less private). Mosquitoes can be a problem here before mid-August, so pack some spray.

From Ribbon Lake head back to the junction with Lily Pad Lake and instead of returning the way you came, continue straight, past several minor fumaroles and hot springs to the acidic, spring-fed waters of **Clear Lake**, 1.5 miles from Ribbon Lake. Continue along the Clear Lake Trail and at the next unsigned junction take the right branch for the final 0.7 miles back to Uncle Tom's parking area.

Alternatively, the left branch continues across open grassland for just over a mile to the **Wapiti Lake Trailhead**, where you can link up with the South Rim Trail by Chittenden Bridge and return through forest to Uncle Tom's, passing fine views of the Upper Falls en route. This longer loop adds 1 mile to the hike but is a worthwhile option if you have the time.

🏃 Mt Washburn

Duration 4 hours

Distance 6.4 miles return

Difficulty Moderate

Elevation Change 1400ft

Start/Finish Dunraven Pass Trailhead (4K9; Map p66 & p107)

Nearest Junction Canyon

Summary Yellowstone's most popular day hike offers unsurpassed 360-degree mountaintop views, with the chance of spotting bighorn sheep and black bears.

This popular return hike climbs gradually to the fire lookout tower on the summit of 10,243ft **Mt Washburn** for some of the park's best views. Over 10,000 hikers do this trail annually – go early to avoid the crowds. Older teenagers should be able to do the hike.

Mt Washburn is all that remains of a volcano that erupted some 640,000 years ago, forming the vast Yellowstone caldera. Interpretive displays in the lookout tower point out the caldera extents, making this a memorable place to get a sense of the awesome scale of the Yellowstone supervolcano. The peak is named after Montana surveyor-general Henry Washburn, who rode up the peak to see the view during the Washburn, Langford and Doane expedition of 1870.

The suggested route starts from Dunraven Pass (8859ft) on the Grand Loop Rd, 4.8 miles north of Canyon and 14.2 miles south of Tower. Alternatively, begin from the larger Chittenden parking area (5 miles north of the pass) for a marginally shorter but more exposed hike (and bike trail) to the summit. Use the south side of Trails Illustrated's 1:63,360 map No 304 *Tower/Canyon*. Two USGS 1:24,000 quads also cover the route: *Canyon Village* and *Mount Washburn*.

The Washburn Bear Management Area, immediately east of the trail on the mountain's east slope, is closed annually from August 1 to November 10 and open May 10 to July 31 only by special permit from the Tower Ranger Station, so avoid wandering off-trail. Keep in mind that grizzlies flock to Mount Washburn's east slopes in large numbers during August and September in search of ripening whitebark pine nuts.

Snow often obstructs the Dunraven Pass approach through the end of June and can block the trail into July. Wildflower displays in July and August are legendary. Frequent afternoon thunderstorms bring fierce winds and lightning, so pack a windbreaker even if the weather looks clear and be ready to make a quick descent if a storm rolls in.

The wide trail follows a rough, disused road (dating from 1905) and so makes for a comfortable, steady ascent, following a series of long ribbonlike loops through a forest of subalpine firs. After 20 minutes the views start to open up. The fire tower appears dauntingly distant, but the climb really isn't as painful as it looks! Continue northeast up broad switchbacks, then follow a narrow ridge past a few stunted whitebark pines (look out for bears) to the gravel Chittenden Rd at the Mt Washburn Trail junction. At the junction the road left leads up to the three-story **fire-lookout tower**, about two hours from the trailhead. The side trail right at the junction leads down the Washburn Spur Trail to Canyon Junction (see p97).

The viewing platform and ground-level public observation room has restrooms, a calling-card-only pay phone, a public 20x Zeiss telescope, displays on the Yellowstone caldera and graphics to help you identify the peaks and valleys surrounding you. The fire tower was built in the 1930s and is still staffed from June to October. The majestic panoramas (when the weather is clear) stretch across the Yellowstone caldera south to Yellowstone Lake, Canyon and the Hayden Valley and north to the Beartooth and Absaroka Ranges. Below you are the smoking Washburn Hot Springs. Keep your eyes peeled for marmots and bighorn sheep basking near the summit. If the crowds get too much, you can always head five minutes down the Washburn Spur Trail for some peace and quiet. From the summit return the way you came.

ALTERNATIVE ROUTE: MT WASHBURN SPUR TRAIL TO CANYON
3 HOURS, 8.1 MILES, 2340FT DESCENT

If you can arrange a shuttle, consider hiking the 5.4-mile Mt Washburn Spur Trail to the junction with the Sevenmile Hole Trail and then on to the Glacial Boulder Trailhead in Canyon, a total 11.3-mile hike through the heart of grizzly country and past the Washburn Hot Springs. For an excellent overnight option, head down into the Sevenmile Hole – see p106 for details of both of these options. These hikes can be done in reverse, but this adds 850ft of ascent.

🏃 Cascade Lake & Observation Peak

Duration 4–5 hours

Distance 10.4 miles

Difficulty Moderate

Elevation Change 1400ft

Start/Finish Cascade Lake Trailhead (4K5; Map p66)

Nearest Town/Junction Canyon

Summary There's plenty of flexibility here for all levels, mixing an easy hike to Cascade Lake with fine views atop Observation Peak.

There's something for everyone on this trail, which starts just a couple of minutes' drive north of Canyon Village. The full hike climbs 1400ft to Observation Peak (9397ft), but the easier turnaround at Cascade Lake gives a level hike of only 4.4 miles return (2½ hours). You can also add on a 4-mile return side trip to Grebe Lake, should you want. If you can arrange a car shuttle, it's also possible to hike in from Cascade Lake Trailhead and hike out south to the slightly further Cascade Creek Trailhead, on the Canyon-Norris road.

Start the hike at the Cascade Lake Trailhead, 1.5 miles north of Canyon Junction, or the nearby picnic area of the same name. July is a great time for wildflowers along this route, but the trail can be wet early in the season (in which case the southern Cascade Creek trail offers a drier alternative).

The path quickly joins the trail from the picnic area and continues past the trailhead board to enter an open valley frequented by bison. The double-wide track crosses several creeks before swinging into forest to follow a meandering creek. One mile into the hike you'll hit the Cascade Creek Trail that leads here from the Canyon–Norris road. Take the right branch to Cascade Lake.

Ten minutes from the junction, the path leads into a wide valley, past backcountry site 4E4 on the left to the trail junction at the west end of the lake, less than an hour from the trailhead. The right branch leads to backcountry site 4E3 and Observation Peak; straight ahead takes you to the eastern part of the lake and on to Grebe Lake 2 miles away. The first time we did this hike we stood transfixed here for over two hours as a pack of six wolves attempted to take down a bull elk by the edge of the forest.

The lake itself opens to meadows on the west and backs on to the Solfatara Plateau and its ghost forest of burnt snags. The lake is worth exploring for its wildfowl and occasional moose. Bison often graze the meadows to the east. The lake's waters drain down Cascade Creek, eventually to plunge into the Yellowstone River in the form of Crystal Falls (see p68).

The hike up to Observation Peak, part of the Washburn Range, takes about 1¼ hours and gains 1400ft in 3 miles. After 30 minutes the trail crests a saddle and curves to the left, opening up views of the peak ahead. It loops further to a ridge line, giving you time to catch your breath before the final 20-minute climb to 4P1, one of the park's most unusual backcountry campsites, in a forested hollow just below the main peak. The site makes a fine place to enjoy dusk and dawn views, but there's no water here, so you'll have to haul up everything you need.

The views from the peak are superb; Cascade and Grebe Lakes sit below you, smoking Norris Geyser Basin is to the west and the Hayden Valley yawns to the south. Temporarily hidden below to the left are views of the Yellowstone Canyon. To the north is the Washburn Bear Management Area, classic grizzly country, so keep your eyes peeled. The ranger hut at the summit is normally boarded up. The descent back to Cascade Lake takes about one hour, from where you return to the trailhead the way you came.

YELLOWSTONE NATIONAL PARK DAY HIKES

Lake Country

Lake Country is best known for its boating opportunities, but its great hikes are also worth getting to know. Bear activity in the river inlets to Yellowstone Lake delays the hiking season here (the Pelican Valley, Natural Bridge and Heart Lake trails are closed until July), making it a limited early-season option. Check with a visitor center if you are coming in early summer and always hike with others.

🏃 Elephant Back Mountain

Duration 2–2½ hours

Distance 3.5-mile loop

Difficulty Moderate

Elevation Change 800ft

Start/Finish Elephant Back Trailhead (Map p72)

Nearest Town/Junction Lake Village

Summary This easy ascent follows a well-trodden path and rewards you with fine lake views near the top.

This popular ascent is a great short-but-sweet picnic option, suitable for families with teenagers. The trailhead is 1 mile south of Fishing Bridge Junction and 0.5 miles north of the Lake Village turnoff on the Grand Loop Rd. From Lake Hotel it is 0.25 miles one way through the woods past Section J of the hotel's cabins. Use the north side of Trails Illustrated's 1:83,333 map No 305 *Yellowstone Lake*.

The start of this lollipop loop trail parallels the Grand Loop Rd for a hundred yards, then abruptly ducks into the forest. A few minutes from the road it passes the old water pipes of Lake Village, then crosses beneath a power line and begins a steady climb. The forest floor here is thick with wildflowers, wild berries and fungi. Watch for deer and moose. After passing through 1 mile of lodgepole pines, the trail reaches a junction.

Both trails lead to the **panoramic overlook** (8600ft) of Yellowstone Lake and Stevenson Island, Pelican Valley and the Absaroka Range. The trail to the left (0.8 miles) is steeper than the trail to the right (0.9 miles). Hike clockwise up the steep one and down the easier one for an easy-on-the-knees loop. You can picnic with a view at the wooden bench at the top. Looking out, Pelican Valley's meadows lie to the left,

Stevenson Island sits in the lake ahead, and the Absaroka Range outlines the horizon in the distance.

🏃 Pelican Valley

Duration 6–8 hours

Distance 16-mile loop

Difficulty Moderate

Elevation Change Negligible

Start/Finish Pelican Valley Trailhead (5K3; Map p72)

Nearest Town/Junction Fishing Bridge

Summary Birdwatchers favor this rolling stroll through meadows and sagebrush in the heart of bear country.

Rangers recommend a minimum party of four hikers for this popular lollipop loop, among the most concentrated grizzly country in the lower 48 states. Backcountry camping is not allowed anywhere in the valley. Bring plenty to drink and a hat, since there's no shade along the trail. Hiking in the morning or late afternoon on overcast, rainy or even snowy days offers the best chance to catch a glimpse of wildlife.

Pelican Valley (including the nearby Turbid Lake trail) is closed for bear activity from April 1 to July 3 and is open for day use only (9am to 7pm) from July 4 to November 10. The July 4 opening is typically the busiest day in the valley, when animals are likely to be most skittish. Off-trail travel is prohibited on the first 2.5 miles of the trail.

The trailhead sits at a gravel parking lot on the east end of an old service road. It is off the north side of the East Entrance Rd, 3.5 miles east of Fishing Bridge and 23.5 miles west of the East Entrance. The lot is across the road from the trailhead for Storm Point and Indian Pond. Use the north side of Trails Illustrated's 1:63,360 map No 305 *Lake Yellowstone*.

The **Pelican Valley Trail** follows the abandoned Turbid Lake service road due east for a few minutes, then veers north along the forest edge to an overlook, which provides the first sight of the Pelican Creek drainage, a couple of miles away. Look for pelicans at the mouth of the creek. The trail descends through open meadow to the valley floor, passing through boggy sections. Near the poorly marked Turbid Lake Trail junction, scan the forest edge (and trail) for signs of coyotes, bison, elk and grizzlies.

REGENERATION – AFTER THE FIRE

Catastrophic wildfires swept across 1.4 million acres of the Greater Yellowstone Ecosystem in the summer of 1988 and torched one-third of Yellowstone National Park. More than 25,000 firefighters battled 51 fires during the driest summer in 112 years. The fires jumped roads, rivers and even the Grand Canyon of the Yellowstone.

Twenty-five years later, the aftermath of the fires is still very much in evidence. Yet far from marking a disaster, many observers now describe the fires as a natural event heralding a new cycle of growth.

Many plants and trees depend on high temperatures to trigger the release of their seeds (lodgepole pines require temperatures of 113 degrees to melt the resin holding theirs in place), and surveys estimated that there were as many as one million seeds per acre on the ground during the fall of 1988. It was also found that only 390 large mammals (less than 1% of the park's total) perished in the fires, the vast majority being elk (and six bears). The year after the fires, the populations of all grazing and browsing mammals flourished thanks to succulent new vegetative growth. Birds thrived on the increased numbers of insects living on dead wood. Ten years later grasses, wildflowers and shrubs were clear winners, aided by increased sunlight and soil nutrients.

For hikers, Yellowstone's scenery has been affected to a certain degree, but not all in a bad way and certainly not to the apocalyptic degree described by the media at the time. Wildflowers are blooming, many views are now unimpeded and it's now easier to see the wildlife thanks to the burns and richer grazing. Smokey the Bear would be proud.

A mile further on the trail passes the rickety remains of the **Pelican Creek Bridge**, near which you may spot cutthroat trout. Make the easy ford and climb a terrace for 1.5 miles to the bridge over **Astringent Creek**, just before another junction. The marshy area around a group of thermal springs just south of the trail offers good wildlife-watching. Continue east along the forest edge, scanning the clover patches for bear scat.

Follow the old service road northeast for 1.5 miles to another easy ford of Pelican Creek and the Upper Pelican Creek Trail junction. Stay in the meadows to the right for 0.33 miles to the Pelican Cone Trail junction, where a small stream provides the valley's best drinking water. The ill-defined trail cuts south away from the valley edge, crossing meadows to ford **Raven Creek**. Search carefully for a shallow spot. There are plenty of waist-deep swimming holes here.

Beyond Raven Creek, the poorly defined trail heads southeast through sagebrush-interspersed meadows. The trail passes through a dormant thermal area with sulfurous odors. After a patch of unburned forest, follow rolling sagebrush hills to the **Pelican Springs Patrol Cabin** and the Mist Creek Pass Trail junction. From here, it's a well-defined, undulating 5 miles back to the Pelican Bridge junction along the forested south edge of the valley.

🏃 Avalanche Peak

Duration 3½–5 hours

Distance 4-mile loop

Difficulty Difficult

Elevation Change 2100ft

Start/Finish Avalanche Peak Trailhead (5N2; Map p72)

Nearest Town/Junction Fishing Bridge

Summary Relentlessly steep, this challenging peak ascent offers unparalleled views of the Absaroka Range and Yellowstone Lake.

This thigh-burner starts off steeply, gets steeper and then continues uphill (steeply) for the entire duration. You can't say we didn't warn you... Check for closures; in early fall the trail is frequented by grizzlies foraging whitebark pine nuts.

During the late-spring snowmelt, subalpine wildflowers peak and midsummer means a profusion of high-alpine butterflies. From midsummer on get an early start since afternoon lightning storms are common. Regardless of the season, pack your hiking poles and a shell jacket for protection against gusty winds and afternoon thundershowers. You will find snowfields above the tree line through at least mid-July, even on the trail's south-facing slopes. Before then you'll need to bring snowshoes.

The trailhead sits off the East Entrance Rd, 0.5 miles west of Sylvan Pass, 19 miles east of Fishing Bridge Junction and 8 miles west of the park's East Entrance. Park in the small paved lot on the south side of the road by Eleanor Lake's west side picnic area. Use the north side of Trails Illustrated's 1:63,360 map No 305 *Yellowstone Lake*.

From the signed trailhead (8466ft) across the road, the trail climbs steeply through lush forests of spruce and fir along a small unnamed stream. Thirty minutes from the road the trail crosses the stream and traverses west across an old avalanche chute, then east again into mature whitebark pine forest. Signs mark revegetation areas where an abandoned trail used to climb straight up the chutes.

A little over a mile from the road the trail levels out and emerges at the base of a huge amphitheater-like bowl. Here, the third signed revegetation area marks a junction: a steeper, more exposed route heads off to the left (west) and a more gradual unmaintained route veers off to the right around the back side of the bowl. The main trail to the left climbs along open talus slopes to arrive at the mountain's south ridge.

Above the glacial cirques and well above the tree line, panoramic views extend north to the Beartooths and south to the Tetons. Thousands of acres just west of the peak were burned in the summer of 2003 after a lightning strike. The true summit (10,566ft) sits to the northeast along the narrow ridge beyond a series of talus wind shelters. After a summit picnic, either retrace your steps or follow a steep, unstable talus trail down the east arm of the peak to the saddle shared with jagged Hoyt Peak (10,506ft), at the Shoshone National Forest boundary. The latter is only for the sure-footed.

Descend through a series of sparsely forested rolling hills to rejoin the main trail at the foot of the bowl.

Other Lake Country Hikes

South of Grant Village the 5-mile round-trip Riddle Lake Trail traverses the Continental Divide and drops down to the lake and its marshy meadows, a favorite of moose. The trailhead is off the South Entrance Rd 3 miles south of Grant Village. Bear activity closes the trail from April 30 to July 15.

Shoshone/Dogshead Trailhead offers two ways of getting to lovely Shoshone Lake, the biggest backcountry lake in the lower 48. Popular with anglers, the 6.5-mile Shoshone Lake (Lewis River Channel) Trail follows the north shore of Lewis Lake, along the Lewis River Channel, to Shoshone Lake. Return the same way or via the shorter (4.7 miles) forested Dogshead Trail.

Norris

Check out backcountry thermal features and fine views on this short but uphill hike.

🥾 Monument Geyser Basin

Duration 2 hours

Distance 2 miles

Difficulty Moderate

Elevation Change 800ft

Start/Finish Monument Geyser Trailhead (Map p66)

Nearest Town/Junction Norris

Summary A steep but rewarding climb to a little-visited thermal feature, with fine views over Gibbon Meadows.

The semidormant chimneylike cones of Monument Geyser Basin are among the park's tallest. There's limited thermal action here these days (no geysers or spouters), but you'll likely have them all to yourself.

The short but steep hike follows the Gibbon River for 0.5 miles, then heads steeply uphill for another 0.5 miles, offering fine views of Gibbon Meadows and Mt Holmes en route. The most prominent feature in the bleached basin is Monument Geyser (also known as Thermos Bottle Geyser), which still lets off steam, unlike the other cones, which have sealed themselves up over the centuries. Budget around 45 minutes up, half an hour down and 30 minutes to explore the minor springs and fumaroles.

Geyser Country

Even the short hikes described here will get you away from the crowds at Old Faithful to some spectacular backcountry waterfalls and geysers.

🥾 Mystic Falls & Biscuit Basin

Duration 1½-2 hours

Distance 3.5-mile loop

Difficulty Easy

Elevation Change 700ft

Start/Finish Biscuit Basin (OK4; Map p80)

Nearest Town/Junction Old Faithful

Summary A short family-friendly stroll from an interesting thermal basin to a 70ft waterfall, with the option for a longer loop hike.

The shorter, out-and-back option to the base of the falls is relatively flat and thus popular with families. Due to a lack of shade, the longer loop hike to the overlook is best done in the morning or late afternoon. The trail is closed from the end of the winter season until the last Saturday of May due to the presence of bears.

The Biscuit Basin turnoff is 2 miles north of the Old Faithful overpass and 14 miles south of Madison Junction, on the west side of Grand Loop Rd. Use the north side of Trails Illustrated's 1:63,360 map No 302 *Old Faithful*.

From the parking area, head west across the Firehole River bridge. Follow the Biscuit Basin boardwalk loop 0.3 miles around to the left past several notable geysers and hot springs. Just west of Avoca Spring, the wide, sandy Mystic Falls Trail (blazed but unsigned) ducks into burned lodgepole forest dotted with wildflowers.

The undulating trail parallels, but does not cross, the Little Firehole River. Soon you'll reach the signed Summit Lake/Little Firehole Meadows junction. From here it's 0.7 miles to the left on the most direct route to the falls, saving the longer overlook loop – visible on a cliff to the right – for the return trip. Heading upstream into the canyon, the path can be muddy where seeps cross the trail. After 10 to 15 minutes the trail arrives at the bottom of the 70ft Mystic Falls, 1.2 miles from Biscuit Basin, where orange hotspring bacterial seeps are in abundance. A series of switchbacks lead to the top of the falls.

Retrace your steps to complete the family-friendly version. If you're fit or traveling without children, you can choose instead to complete the loop (which adds 1 mile and a sweaty 500ft elevation gain) by continuing 0.5 miles through more burned lodgepoles to the Fairy Creek/Little Firehole Meadows Trail junction. Turn right and descend to the Biscuit Basin Overlook for an expansive bird's-eye view of the Upper Geyser Basin and the 1988 wildfire aftermath. Follow the switchbacks downhill to rejoin the Mystic Falls Trail, then retrace your steps to Biscuit Basin.

🏃 Sentinel Meadows & Queen's Laundry Geyser

Duration 2 hours

Distance 3.2 miles return

Difficulty Easy

Elevation Change negligible

Start/Finish Freight Rd Trailhead (OK6), Fountain Flat Dr (Map p103)

Nearest Town/Junction Madison Junction

Summary Some off-trail exploring to a little-visited geyser basin, with a good chance of spotting bison.

This trail is a good choice if you fancy a bit of simple off-route trailfinding. It's flat and easy but requires some basic navigational skills. Park at the end of Fountain Flat Dr, just off the main Grand Loop Rd, 6 miles south of Madison Junction and 13 miles north of Old Faithful. From the parking lot it's 0.3 miles along the dirt road to the Ojo Caliente Spring and the bridge over the Firehole River, which is where the Sentinel Meadows Trail branches west off the gravel road. You can bike this first section and chain your bike to the bridge for your return.

Turning onto the Sentinel Meadows Trail, the trail swings away from the Firehole River, passing underneath telephone lines. The soil quickly turns to white, hinting at the thermal features lying ahead. Fifteen minutes into the hike you pass backcountry campsite OG1. The trail climbs a small hill to offer views of the valley, its three smoking thermal features and a probable scattering of bison. Mound Spring is the closest and most expansive of the springs; Steep Cone is the tallest, and Flat Cone is the furthest, across the creek. The trail ascends a second small hill, before skirting around a patch of new-growth forest, 1.7 miles from the trailhead.

This is where things get tricky. As the main trail bends to the left to hook around the forested hill, look to the right to see the steam of Queen's Laundry Geyser – this is your destination. Look out for a faint trail that parallels the main path as it swings to the south (a post in the ground makes a rough marker). This faint trail heads northwest, skirting the forest, and after 100 yards curves right over a rough log bridge. The trail peters out here and the ground gets boggy, so trace a large arc counterclockwise to the right of the bog, staying on dry ground to get to the far northern side of the geyser, by a **ruined wooden cabin**. The historic cabin is a former bathhouse, built in 1881 by park superintendent Norris as the first national park building designed solely for public use. The geyser gets its name from the bathing costumes that used to hang up to dry on strings beside the bathhouse. The deep blue geyser (really more of a pool) drains past the bathhouse into a wide cascade. Don't get too close to the geyser – act as if the normal boardwalks and warning signs were in place.

Back at the junction you can return the way you came. Alternatively, continue on the main trail as it curves east, past a pond, across a bridge, over a small rise and then along the edge of Imperial Meadows, beside an open plain favored by bison. After 20 minutes you'll see the orange arrow pointing across the boggy plain. Ignore this and continue straight (east) along the forest edge until you see a cliff-like butte straight ahead. As the trail peters out, continue straight (east) across the plain towards the right side of the hill. Take a minute to investigate **Boulder Spring**, a perpetual spouter that looks as if it's coming straight out of the hill. Several creekside pools offer potential soaking sites here.

Cross the makeshift bridge to the right and head straight under the telephone poles to rejoin the Fountain Freight Rd. The trailhead is a five-minute walk to the left and the parking lot is 10 minutes further. If you fancy some more exploration, check out the off-trail geysers of **Pocket Basin** (p86), accessed from two unmarked trails on either side of the Firehole Bridge.

🥾 Lone Star Geyser

Duration 1½–2½ hours

Distance 4.8-mile round-trip

Difficulty Easy

Elevation Change Negligible

Start/Finish Lone Star Trailhead (OK1; Map p80 & p110)

Nearest Town/Junction Old Faithful

Summary An easy level stroll along a former service road to one of the park's largest backcountry geysers. This is also a good biking trail.

This paved and pine-lined hike is popular with both day hikers and cyclists, yet is quite a contrast to the chaotic scene around Old Faithful. Isolated Lone Star erupts every three hours for between two and 30 minutes and reaches 30ft to 45ft in height, and it's definitely worth timing your visit with an eruption. Check with Old Faithful Visitor Center for predicted eruption times and bring a book or a packed lunch for the wait. If the parking lot at Lone Star Trailhead is full, park at the neighboring Kepler Cascades turnout.

From Lone Star Trailhead, above **Kepler Cascades** (where the Firehole River speeds through a spectacular gorge), take the old paved road (closed to cars) past a tiny weir that diverts water to Old Faithful village.

The road crosses the Firehole River bridge and follows the upper Firehole River, heading upstream past the Spring Creek Trail junction (1.6 miles) to end at the steep-sided, 9ft-tall **Lone Star Geyser**, after an easy 2.4 miles. Check the NPS logbook (in the wooden information box in front of the geyser) to gauge exactly when the next eruption might occur; if you catch an eruption, fill in the log for future visitors. If you have time to kill, consider following a section of the trail to **Shoshone Lake** (see p109) to check out the minor thermal areas along the Firehole River.

To completely avoid the crowds, consider taking the quieter but hillier **Howard Eaton Trail** (OK2) from 1 mile south of the Old Faithful overpass, as an alternative (if slightly longer) 5.8-mile return route. The trail joins the Shoshone Lake trail 0.3 miles beyond Lone Star geyser. You could take one route in and the other out if you can arrange a vehicle shuttle.

For nearby backcountry campsites and the overnight trip to Shoshone Lake, see p109.

🥾 Fairy Falls & Twin Buttes

Duration 3-4 hours

Distance 6 miles

Difficulty Easy

Elevation Change Negligible

Start/Finish Fairy Falls Trailhead (OK5; Map p80)

Nearest Town/Junction Old Faithful

Summary A short jaunt to one of the most accessible backcountry cascades,

Fairy Falls & Sentinel Meadows

with views over the park's most beautiful thermal feature and one of the largest backcountry geysers.

Tucked away in the northwest corner of the Midway Geyser Basin, 197ft Fairy Falls is a popular hike, largely because it's only a short jaunt from Old Faithful. Beyond Fairy Falls the lollipop loop trail continues to a hidden thermal area at the base of the Twin Buttes, two conspicuous bald hills severely charred in the 1988 fires. The geysers are undeveloped, and you're likely to have them to yourself – in stark contrast to the throngs around Grand Prismatic Spring.

The Fairy Falls (Steel Bridge) Trailhead is just west of the Grand Loop Rd, 1 mile south of the Midway Geyser Basin turnoff and 4.5 miles north of the Old Faithful overpass. The parking lot often fills up after 11am. Use the north side of Trails Illustrated's 1:63,360 map No 302 *Old Faithful*. The trail is closed until Memorial Day weekend due to the presence of bears.

Cross the **Firehole River** on the silver trestle bridge, then head northwest along Fountain Flat Dr, which is now a wide gravel cycling and hiking path. After 1 mile you'll notice multicolored steam rising from **Grand Prismatic Spring** on the right. You can't reach the boardwalk from this trail, but you can scramble up the unofficial trails to your left for an astonishing bird's-eye view of Yellowstone's most beautiful thermal feature. The park service plans to build a formal trail here as soon as funds allow. Continue 0.3 miles to a trail junction and turn left onto the narrower **Fairy Creek Trail** (if you are cycling, lock your bike here). The trail winds 1.6 miles past backcountry campsite OD1 through lodgepole forest burned in the 1988 fires.

At 197ft, **Fairy Falls** is the park's seventh-highest waterfall, but the whispy volume of water is hardly on a par with the falls on the Yellowstone River. Still, patterned streaks of white water blanket the dark lower rocks, and clumps of raspberries and fireweed flourish around a pretty pool, which makes for a fine swimming hole on a hot and sticky summer day.

After crossing a footbridge, the trail continues 0.7 miles northwest toward the prominent **Twin Buttes** and several conspicuous plumes of rising steam. Cross several marshy patches with the aid of log bridges and then take the right branch for the closest plume emanating from **Spray Geyser**, erupting frequently to a height of 6ft to 8ft. Continue west, following the outlet from **Imperial Geyser**, which is lined with orange algae. Imperial plays almost perpetually, projecting blasts of water up to 20ft into its large rainbow pool. If you care to climb onto the buttes, head across the open slopes behind Imperial Geyser for fine views. After discovering the collection of lily-choked ponds hidden in a hollow between the two summits, you can continue to either summit without much difficulty. Views to the east encompass the Lower and Midway Geyser Basins, while to the west the trail-free Madison Plateau stretches off toward the park boundary. Retrace your steps to the Fairy Falls Trailhead.

🏃 DeLacy Creek Trail

Duration 2½–3½ hours

Distance 6 miles

Difficulty Easy

Elevation Change 200ft

Start/Finish DeLacy Creek Trailhead (7K2; Map p110)

Nearest Town/Junction Old Faithful, West Thumb

Summary An easy hike through meadows and forest to the gravel shores of the park's largest backcountry lake.

The DeLacy Creek Trail offers the quickest access to Shoshone Lake, one of the park's largest and loveliest lakes (in fact, Shoshone Lake was originally called DeLacy Lake). The trailhead is on the Grand Loop Rd, east of Craig Pass near the DeLacy Creek Picnic Area, halfway between Old Faithful and West Thumb Junction. The parking area is on the north side of the road, the trail on the south.

June and July bring lovely wildflowers along the route but also plenty of boggy ground and biting insects, so bring bug repellent before August. The meadows are good habitat for moose, elk, mule deer, coyote and sandhill cranes. DeLacy Creek is the last section of the North Shoshone Lake Trail, described on p109.

The trail leads through forest for 20 minutes to a classic oxbow bend in the creek, before continuing through forest into open meadows. Ten minutes later you climb to a small hill for your first views of the lake and the valley. About 30 minutes later, just after passing the meandering lily-choked creek, you'll get to the gravelly shore of the huge **Shoshone Lake**. Enjoy a picnic on the beach and then return the way you came.

Bechler Region

Bechler boasts the highest concentration of waterfalls in Yellowstone and some of the best backcountry hot-spring soaks anywhere. Its forests also escaped the worst of the 1988 fires. The area's remoteness means it's best suited to experienced hikers taking long backcountry trips but some rewarding shorter hikes are possible. In early summer trails may be knee-deep in water, so inquire about conditions at another ranger station before driving all the way out here.

🏃 Bechler Meadows & Falls

Duration 3½ hours

Distance 8-mile loop

Difficulty Easy–moderate

Elevation Change negligible

Start/Finish Bechler Ranger Station (9K1; Map p113)

Nearest Town/Junction Driggs, Idaho

Summary A solitary walk through lush forest, with big falls and wildlife-watching opportunities.

Bechler Meadows' extensive wetlands are a wildlife magnet. Grizzlies and black bears as well as rare waterfowl such as gray owls and great blue herons are often spotted. Add substantial cascades to an already spectacular mix by starting from the Cave Falls Trailhead or by taking the Bechler Falls side trip.

This route avoids all fords, so there's no need to inquire about river levels before departing. Use the south side of Trails Illustrated's 1:63,360 map No 302 *Old Faithful*.

From Bechler Ranger Station, follow the Bechler Meadows Trail 3 miles northeast past the Boundary Creek Trail junction through lodgepole pine forest to the Bechler River/Rocky Ford cutoff junction.

If it's not too buggy, hike an extra 0.5 miles north to Bechler Meadows. You will cross a wooden suspension bridge over Boundary Creek past campsite 9B1. It's an ideal spot to look for sandhill cranes and moose, or angle around the waters for rainbow trout (permit required). See the Bechler River Trail (p112) for a suggested one- to three-day extension.

Retrace your steps to the cutoff southeast 0.7 miles past campsite 9C1 to the wide Rocky Ford at the Bechler River Trail junction. Instead of fording the river, trace the river's west bank south for 2 miles to the next junction, where a cutoff leads west 2 miles through forest back to the ranger station.

SIDE TRIP: BECHLER FALLS & CAVE FALLS
30-45 MINUTES, 3 MILES, ELEVATION CHANGE NEGLIGIBLE

Finish your hike with a 3-mile sidetrip to Bechler Falls and Cave Falls. An out-and-back hike, it will reward you with a refreshing dip in the swimming hole just past Cave Falls. This worthwhile detour heads 0.5 miles downstream from the Bechler River/Ranger Station cutoff to Bechler Falls, one of Bechler's widest and most voluminous waterfalls. Continue east on the riverbank trail 0.5 miles to the broad-spanning Cave Falls (20ft).

Other Bechler Region Hikes

At the west end of Grassy Reservoir, by the dam, trailhead 9K5 is the start of the 15.5-mile round-trip hike to Union Falls, one of the most spectacular in the national park. After a mile the trail branches right, fords Cascade Creek and then branches left (right leads to the Pitchstone Plateau Trail). After another 4 miles the trail fords Proposition Creek and then a mile later branches right onto the Union Falls Trail for another 2 miles. Feathery Union Falls are the second highest in Yellowstone National Park.

If that seems too ambitious, a shorter 3.6-mile return hike leads from the same trailhead to a series of cascades known as Terraced Falls.

At the east end of Grassy Reservoir a pullout marks the trailhead for the 6-mile round-trip hike northeast to Beula Lake. The trail crosses the South Boundary Trail en route.

All hikes are accessed from Grassy Lake Rd, south of the park.

OVERNIGHT HIKES

There's no better way to experience the raw wildness of Yellowstone than on an overnight backpacking trip. Some experience of backcountry camping is important before heading out into the wild, particularly how to hang food and be bear aware. That said, there's a huge range of challenges available, from strolls to backcountry campsites an hour from the road to multiday expedition-style traverses of the Thorofare or Gallatin range, some of the remotest terrain south of Alaska. Choose the right trip at the right time of year and arrive prepared, and there's no better way to experience the park.

If you don't fancy organizing a multi-day trek yourself, consider a company like Wildland Trekking Company (www.wildland trekking.com), which offers backpacking trips for around $250 per day, including meals, a guide and transportation from Bozeman.

Backcountry Permits

A free backcountry-use permit, available at visitor centers and ranger stations, is required for all overnight backcountry trips (day hikes don't require permits). The backcountry-use permit is site and date specific and states the campsite where you must overnight. The park's essential *Backcountry Trip Planner* lists all campsites.

About half the backcountry sites can be reserved by mail; a $20 reservation fee applies regardless of the number of nights. Booking starts on April 1, when all existing reservations are dealt with at random, and continues up to 48 hours before your start date. Reservations can be made in person at a ranger center or through the mail to Backcountry Office, PO Box 168, Yellowstone National Park, WY 82190. Applications must be on a Trip Planner Worksheet, available with the Backcountry Trip Planner on the NPS website (www.nps.gov/yell/planyourvisit/backcountrytripplanner.htm) or by contacting the central backcountry office (☎307-344-2160; YELL_Backcountry_Office@nps.gov) in

EASY BACKCOUNTRY OVERNIGHTS

Taking your kids or spouse on their first backpacking trip? The following backcountry sites are all within 2 miles of the trailhead, perfect for easy access and emergency exit.

» **Blacktail Creek** Site 1A1, 1.8 miles from Blacktail Trailhead, campfires allowed.

» **Lava Creek** 1A3, 1.4 miles from the Lava Creek Picnic Area Trailhead past Undine Falls.

» **Indian Creek** 1B1, from Indian Creek Campground/Bighorn Pass trailhead.

» **Ice Lake** 4D1 and 4D2 are on the lakeshore; 4D3 is an accessible site near the road.

» **Cascade Lake** 4E4 (see p97).

» **Norris Campground** 4F1 is 2.5 miles up Solfatara Creek.

» **Ribbon Lake** 4R1 and 4R2, from Artist Point trailhead in Canyon (see p95).

» **Lonestar Geyser** OA1 is within earshot of the geyser, and you can bike most of the way there (see p102).

» **Fairy Falls** OD1, 2.5 miles from the trailhead and part of the hike can be done on a bike (see p102).

» **Sentinel Meadows** OG1, accessed from Fountain Freight Rd (see p101).

Mammoth. Outside of summer call ☎307-344-7381.

Send the nonrefundable cash, check or money order with booking. You will receive a confirmation notice, which must be taken to a backcountry office to exchange for a permit not more than 48 hours before your trip but before 10am on the day of your trip departure.

Around 20% of backcountry-use permits are issued no more than 48 hours (effectively three nights) in advance on a first-come, first-served, walk-in basis (no $20 fee). This means that you can leave your planning to the last minute, as long as you are flexible with your itinerary. (You may, for example, have to walk further one day than you had planned if your desired site is already booked.)

The most popular areas are the Hellroaring region of the Black Canyon of the Yellowstone in spring, Slough Creek in early summer, Shoshone Lake in August, Bechler region in August/September, and Heart Lake throughout summer. It makes sense to include a back-up itinerary if applying for a popular region or trail in peak season.

There are **backcountry offices** (⊙8am-4:30pm) at Canyon Ranger Station, Mammoth Visitor Center, Grant Village, Bridge Bay Ranger Station, Bechler Ranger Station, Tower Ranger Station, Old Faithful Ranger Station, West Yellowstone Visitor Center and South Entrance Ranger Station.

Get to the office at least half an hour before closing because you have to watch an 18-minute video on backcountry safety before you can get your permit (frequent backcountry visitors can get a 'frequent flyer' card so they don't have to watch the video each time). Part of your permit goes on the dashboard of your car; the main permit stays with you on your pack.

Canyon Country

🚶 Mt Washburn & Sevenmile Hole

Duration 2 days

Distance 15.6 miles

Difficulty Moderate-difficult

Elevation Change 2800ft

Start Dunraven Pass Trailhead (4K9; Map p107)

Finish Glacial Boulder Trailhead (4K6; Map p107)

Nearest Town/Junction Canyon Village

Summary Fabulous views, a backcountry thermal feature and a descent into the Yellowstone Canyon that feels like it's '5 miles in and 7 miles out.'

This excellent overnight shuttle hike takes you to the top of one of the park's highest peaks and then down, down, down to Sevenmile Hole, a minor hydrothermal area at

Mt Washburn & Sevenmile Hole

your wits about you – this is prime grizzly habitat.

The trail descends southwest through boggy grassland grazed by elk and deer to **Washburn Hot Springs**, a small field of boiling mud pots and hissing fumaroles. Proceed past more small thermal areas to the Sevenmile Hole Trail junction, 2.9 miles from campsite 4E1.

The steep trail switchbacks down 1400ft through Douglas firs, passing a 10ft-high geyser cone before arriving at a more active thermal area. Anglers who frequently make the hike claim it feels like '5 miles in and 7 miles out.' Continue down past the easily missed turnoff to campsite 4C1, then cross a small thermal stream for the final walk to campsite 4C2 beside the **Yellowstone River**. Large springs emerge from the reddish chalky cliffs on the river's east bank. To reach campsite 4C3, ford narrow **Sulphur Creek**, then follow the riverbank past a tiny hot pool. Stock animals and wood fires are not allowed at any of the campsites. Unattended food must be out of reach of bears – if you are day-tripping down here hang (don't dump) your pack at the junction.

DAY 2: SEVENMILE HOLE TO GLACIAL BOULDER TRAILHEAD
4 HOURS, 5 MILES, 1400FT ASCENT

Back at the junction after the hard ascent, heading southwest, the trail is broader and leads along the north rim of the 1200ft-deep **Grand Canyon of the Yellowstone** for the final 2.7 miles, passing through lodgepole forest carpeted with fragrant, low-lying grouseberry shrubs. The views are increasingly spectacular as you pass the unsigned overlook of long, thin **Silver Cord Cascade**, which drops nearly 1000ft to the canyon floor. The amazing technicolor columns of the canyon's eroding sides stretch another 1 mile to the Glacial Boulder Trailhead. **Canyon Village** is 1.5 miles west along paved Inspiration Point road.

ALTERNATIVE ROUTE: GLACIER BOULDER TO SEVENMILE HOLE
6-7 HOURS, 11 MILES, 1400FT ASCENT/DESCENT

An alternative route for hiking to Sevenmile Hole starts at the Glacial Boulder Trailhead just before **Inspiration Point**. This out-and-back hike is an 11-mile round-trip and drops 1400ft in 1.5 miles; as always, the hard part is the return trip. It's a decent day hike or relaxed overnighter.

the bottom of the Grand Canyon of the Yellowstone. It's not a particularly long hike, but it does involve a lot of elevation change (most of it downhill). When the insect hatch is on, the backcountry sites at Sevenmile Hole are very popular, so book your spot well in advance.

DAY 1: MT WASHBURN & SEVENMILE HOLE
6-7 HOURS, 10.8 MILES, 1400FT ASCENT, 3500FT DESCENT

For details of the first section of this hike up to Mt Washburn, see p96.

From the four-way junction just below Washburn Peak, the **Mt Washburn Spur Trail** drops southeast along an undulating ridge past alpine wildflower meadows. After dipping through a saddle to another little gap at the tree line, bear right and descend 2.6 miles from the summit through small clearings to **Washburn Meadow** and campsite 4E1 (campfires allowed). Keep

Lake Country

🏃 Heart Lake & Mt Sheridan

Duration 1-2 days

Distance 16-mile round-trip

Difficulty Easy-moderate

Elevation Change 345ft (3145ft with side trip)

Start/Finish Heart Lake Trailhead (8N1; Map p108)

Nearest Town/Junction Grant Village

Summary A backcountry geyser and thermals, the opportunity to peak-bag or fish the lake bestow myriad options onto this straightforward hike.

While the shores of Heart Lake suffered damage from the 1988 fires, it remains a beautiful, rewarding and popular destination. An extensive thermal field extends from the northwest shore of this 2160-acre lake, showcasing boiling hot pots and a large geyser. Heart Lake provides rich habitat for waterfowl, and there are plentiful stocks of cutthroat and elusive but record-setting lake (Mackinaw) trout.

The highest summit in the Red Mountains, Mt Sheridan (10,308ft) rises high above Heart Lake's west shore, providing terrific panoramas. While the extremely fit can knock off Heart Lake and climb Mt Sheridan in a very long day hike, it's worth spending a night (or two) along the lakeshore to relax, watch the bald eagles and osprey, and explore.

Heart Lake trail is closed from April 1 to June 30 due to bear activity: reconfirm the opening date with a backcountry office. Elk carcasses from winter hardship tend to pile up here, leading to an early-season grizzly fiesta.

All west-shore campsites have a two-night limit from July 1 to September 1. Heavy snow persists along the trail up to Mt Sheridan until mid-July or later.

Use the south side of Trails Illustrated's 1:63,360 map No 305 *Yellowstone Lake*. Two 1:24,000 USGS maps also cover the route: *Heart Lake* and *Mount Sheridan*. The trailhead is 5.3 miles south of Grant Village and 16.7 miles north of the South Entrance, off South Entrance Rd. There's a toilet at the trailhead.

DAY 1: HEART LAKE TRAILHEAD TO HEART LAKE
3-5 HOURS, 8 MILES, 345FT ASCENT

Follow the sandy, mostly single-track trail southeast through strewn trunks and new-growth **lodgepole forest**. After a few miles,

Heart Lake & Mt Sheridan

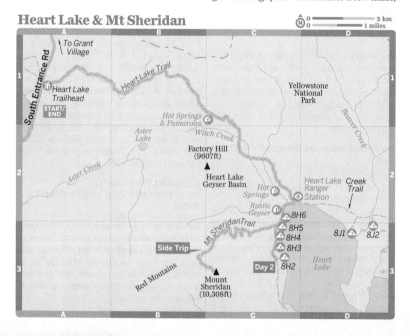

the trail rises slightly over a minor watershed to the first group of smoking fumaroles at the north foot of bald-topped **Factory Hill** (9607ft), 1½ to two hours from the trailhead. Heart Lake, 2 miles downhill, comes into view.

Wind your way down into the intensely active **Heart Lake Geyser Basin**. Numerous spurting springs and boiling pools sit a short way off to the right. The trail crosses warm Witch Creek several times to reach the Heart Lake patrol cabin, just off the lake's north shore (7450ft).

Witch Creek is a prime spot for bathing, near thermal spots. You can inquire about this and current fishing conditions at the log-cabin **ranger station** (which is staffed in summer).

Trail Creek Trail departs left (east) around the lake's northeast shore; it's a popular jumping-off point for stock users bound for the Thorofare region.

Heart Lake Trail continues right, first following the gray sand beach to cross the Witch Creek inlet on a log bridge, and then tracing the lake's west shore to reach campsite 8H6. This is the first of five sites alongside firs and spruces fringing the shoreline.

Follow the steam along an often-overgrown trail at tree line behind 8H6 to another fascinating thermal area. Here, you will spot the azure **Columbia Pool**. **Rustic Geyser** spouts up to 50ft at irregular intervals, while other springs bubble up into large calcified bathtubs.

The main trail continues past campsite 8H5 to the junction with the Mt Sheridan Trail, then proceeds about another mile south past campsites 8H4 and 8H3 to 8H2 – only 8H2 and 8H3 allow campfires. The secluded campsite 8J1, which boasts views of Mt Sheridan, is the most coveted.

There are good views across the 180ft-deep lake east to Overlook Mountain (9321ft) and southeast to flat-topped Mt Hancock (10,214ft). In the evenings, pairs of grebes often dive and court each other with mellow, lilting voices.

There are six additional campsites around Heart Lake: 8J1 (two-night limit) and 8J2 (two-night limit, stock parties only) on its northeast side, 8J4 and 8J6 on the southeast shore, 8J3 nearby along Surprise Creek, and 8H1 at the lake's southwest corner. All sites except 8H1 allow campfires.

SIDE TRIP: MT SHERIDAN
4-6 HOURS, 6 MILES, 2800FT ASCENT

The **Mt Sheridan Trail** crosses over open meadows briefly before its spiraling ascent along a steep spur largely covered in whitebark pines. Bring plenty of water; there is none available on the trail.

You will come to a saddle flanked by wind-battered firs. Continue left (southeast) up the narrowing tundra ridge over old snowdrifts to reach the 10,308ft talus-covered summit. The fire lookout (staffed in summer but otherwise locked) scans 360 degrees from Pitchstone Plateau to the west, Shoshone Lake to the northwest, Yellowstone Lake to the northeast and the jagged Tetons to the south. Snowdrifts often persist through mid-July.

DAY 2: HEART LAKE TO HEART LAKE TRAILHEAD
3-5 HOURS, 8 MILES, 345FT DESCENT

Retrace your steps from Day 1 back to the start.

Geyser Country

🏃 North Shoshone Lake & Shoshone Geyser Basin

Duration 2 days

Distance 19 miles

Difficulty Moderate

Elevation Change 600ft

Start Lone Star Trailhead (OK1; Map p110)

Finish DeLacy Creek Trailhead (7K2; Map p110)

Nearest Town/Junction Old Faithful

Summary Follow the Continental Divide Trail on this easy overnighter that combines a backcountry geyser basin with an unforgettable night by silent Shoshone Lake.

Shoshone Lake is one of the park's real hidden gems. Not only is it the largest backcountry lake in Yellowstone, at over 8000 acres, but it is also the largest lake in the lower 48 states not reachable by road. There are many possible routes around the lake, including loops from three directions (Lone Star, DeLacy Creek and Lewis Lake). Much of the first half of this route follows the Continental Divide Trail, which continues along the southern shore of the lake to the Dogshead Trailhead.

Shoshone Lake

The route described here traces the northern shore of the lake and requires a short shuttle or hitch along the Grand Loop Rd. Note that Kepler Cascades turnout is a slightly more secure overnight parking spot than the Lone Star Trailhead, since it sees much more traffic.

Between Lone Star and Shoshone Lake, the trail crosses gentle Grants Pass, which normally isn't clear of snow until late June. The lake is normally frozen until early June and some backcountry campsites are flooded into July, making mid-July the earliest reliable start date for this trip. Mosquitoes can be an irritant until August.

Use the north side of Trails Illustrated's 1:63,360 map No 302 *Old Faithful*. Two USGS quads also cover the route: *Old Faithful* and *Shoshone Geyser Basin*.

Shoshone Lake is a popular backcountry destination (about one-third of the entire park's backcountry use is concentrated along the shores of the lake), so it's worth reserving sites in advance. Campsite 8R5 in particular gets booked early because of its proximity to the Shoshone Geyser basin. Sites open to hikers along the northern shore include 8T1, 8R5, 8R3, 8R2, 8S3 and 8S2. The latter two sites make a good short overnight trip from DeLacy Creek but are too far north to be convenient for your first night on this trip. 8R2 and 8S2 are mixed hiker- and boat-accessible campsites. All of the lakeshore sites are 'no wood fire' areas.

DAY 1: LONE STAR TRAILHEAD TO 8R2/8R3

6 HOURS, 11.6 MILES, 400FT ASCENT

For the first 2.4 miles to Lone Star Geyser, see p102. Proceed past the geyser and turn left after 0.3 miles at the junction with the **Howard Eaton Trail** to head southwest. The trail passes the least-desirable campsite OA1 (campfires OK) to cross the Firehole River on a footbridge. From here you follow the

Creek, 2 miles short of the impressive Shoshone Geyser Basin.

The trail descends through the prime moose and bear habitat of **Shoshone Creek meadows**, occasionally crossing the creek on log bridges. One mile from the Bechler Junction a stock trail branches right over the creek to avoid the marshy geyser basin.

At the North Shoshone Trail junction (8.5 miles from the trailhead, 8.4 miles to DeLacy Creek) it's worth detouring for an hour to explore the geyser basin. Cross the marshy area on wooden logs and take the left branch to dump your pack in one of the bear-proof lockers. Just past here is a small beach, which offers a fine place for a snack overlooking the lake.

Return to the junction and continue straight into the geyser basin for around 0.5 miles. The surrounding meadows are fine places to spot moose and other animals at dusk.

Shoshone Geyser Basin is home to over 80 thermal features and was visited in 1839 by trapper Osborne Russell. The main ones include **Little Great Geyser**, the **Minute Man group**, **Little Bulger** and the **Orion group** further south; its **Union Geyser** used to erupt to heights of 100ft. T Scott Bryan's encyclopedic *The Geysers of Yellowstone* details 40 of the basin's geysers, none of which are marked on site.

Back at the North Shoshone Trail junction, head northeast along the trail through forest to the backcountry site along the northern shore that you've reserved. Site 8R5 appears after five minutes, while 8R3 and 8R2 are a further hour away. Just before reaching 8R3 you pass an unmarked trail that leads to a ranger patrol cabin.

DAY 2: 8R2/8R3 TO DELACY TRAILHEAD
4 HOURS, 7.6 MILES, 200FT ASCENT

From sites 8R3 and 8R2 it's another hour's walk through undulating forest to the northern shoreline. The trail parallels the lovely lake shore for half an hour before dipping back into forest to pass site 8S3. Five minutes further on a lovely little spit offers a superb place to stop and soak up the silence.

Ten minutes later the trail hits site 8S2 and the northern point of the lake as the beach curves to the right in front of large meadows. Follow the beach, looking for the occasional orange metal markers.

Fifteen minutes later the trail cuts inland to join a trail junction at the northeastern

Shoshone Lake Trail 5.8 miles south to the Shoshone Geyser Basin. The trail soon passes a small thermal field of scalding hot pools and hissing steam vents (so no, that growling isn't a grizzly bear!). Past OA1 you'll pass the most attractive off-trail campsite, OA2 (campfires OK), in 0.4 miles, and finally the best option for through-hikers, campsite OA3, in another 0.8 miles.

Climb south over the broad rolling ridge to cross the unsigned **Grants Pass** (8010ft), which marks the almost imperceptible Continental Divide. The sandy trail heads down through superb stands of tall, old-growth Engelmann spruce and whitebark pine to reach the **Bechler River (Three Rivers) Trail** junction, which is about one hour from OA3 and 1½ hours from the trailhead.

Inviting campsite 8G1 (no campfires) is a short way down the Shoshone Lake Trail, on a rise above the meadows framing Shoshone point of the lake. From here it's 3 miles along the lily ponds and meadows of De-Lacy Creek to the end of the hike, about 75 minutes away. The right-hand branch leads 4.2 miles to Dogshead Channel and Lewis Lake.

ALTERNATIVE ROUTES: DELACY CREEK LOOP & DOGSHEAD LOOP
3 & 4 DAYS, 27 & 32 MILES, ELEVATION CHANGE NEGLIGIBLE

There are plenty of other route options, including the 27-mile, three-day lollipop loop of the lake from DeLacy Creek Trailhead or the 32-mile loop of the lake from Dogshead Trailhead near Lewis Lake. You could even do a long day 18-mile return day hike from Lone Star Geyser into the Shoshone Geyser Basin. Thirteen exclusively boat-in sites along both the north and south shores offer those with floating transportation the option of spending weeks here.

Bechler Region

🏃 Bechler River Trail

Duration 4 days

Distance 28-mile round-trip

Difficulty Moderate

Elevation Change 1100ft

Start/Finish Bechler Ranger Station (9k1)

Nearest Town/Junction Driggs, Idaho

Summary Traverses wild backcountry filled with rivers, cascades and wildlife, but most come for the soaking opportunities.

Near the head of Bechler Canyon, the Ferris Fork side stream is home to several hidden waterfalls and an outstanding hot-springs soak. Anglers will be attracted by the rainbow trout. Sandals and hiking poles are extremely useful for river crossings. Bring rain gear – Bechler gets three times as much rain as the park's northern range.

Popular with horse-pack trips, backpackers and anglers, Bechler sees fierce competition for backcountry campsites in the prime months of August and September. Campsites may only be reserved for dates after July 15. In-person permits may be granted, weather permitting. Ask rangers about river ford and trail conditions – high water and swarms of bugs typically persist along this route through mid to late July. All of the

campsites mentioned here (except 9B9) limit stays to one night.

Use the south side of Trails Illustrated's 1:63,360 map No 302 *Old Faithful*. Three USGS 1:24:000 quads also cover the route: *Trischman Knob, Cave Falls* and *Bechler Falls*.

DAY 1: BECHLER RANGER STATION TO CAMPSITE 9B4
3-4 HOURS, 6.5 MILES, ELEVATION CHANGE NEGLIGIBLE

See the Bechler Meadows & Falls Trail description (p104) for directions from Bechler Ranger Station to Rocky Ford. The extremely wide crossing of the Bechler River is tricky even in low water (around mid-July) and may be completely impassable after heavy rains.

The less interesting, slightly shorter alternative is Bechler Meadows Trail, which requires a shorter, knee- to thigh-high ford near campsite 9B2 (no campfires) and treading some boggy terrain.

Beyond the ford, the Bechler River Trail heads east past the Mountain Ash Creek Trail junction. It then cuts north through forested patches and open grassy plains beside the meandering river to campsite 9B3, at the edge of a broad clearing 7 miles from the trailhead. For the first night's stay, the semiprivate, hiker-only campsite 9B4 (no campfires), located 0.5 miles further at the mouth of Bechler River Canyon, is recommended.

DAY 2: CAMPSITE 9B4 TO THREE RIVER JUNCTION
3½-4½ HOURS, 7.5 MILES, 600FT ASCENT

The trail continues to parallel the river, climbing through fir and spruce forests, birch trees and boulder fields bordering meadows thick with raspberries, thimbleberries and huckleberries. After 1.8 miles, a marked side trail descends yards to a scenic overlook of Colonnade Falls, where the Bechler River plunges 85ft in two stages. The trail steepens, passing damp campsite 9B5 to reach the spectacular Iris Falls, a 40ft curtain of water spraying thick rainbow-filled mist.

The trail ascends through more old fir and spruce forest past gliding cataracts with picturesque islets and riverside campsite 9B6 to another major ford (a 50ft-wide, waist-deep wade). Upstream, the trail sees many muddy moments as it crosses several cold minor side streams before trailside campsite 9B7. A mile upstream, just before campsite

Bechler River

DAY 3: CAMPSITE 9D1 TO FERRIS FORK HOT SPRINGS
3-4 HOURS, 4 MILES, 500FT ASCENT

Having made it all this way, you will be giddy if you have booked an extra day in the Three River Junction. When booking your trip, if you reserve another campsite in the 9B group, you can spend a day exploring.

Beyond 9D1, the trail switches back uphill 0.5 miles past 45ft **Ragged Falls** to an unsigned (but well-trodden) turnoff on the east side of the trail for **Ferris Fork Hot Springs**.

The springs' submerged thermal source emanates from the middle of a 45ft-diameter, waist-deep pool, where it mixes with chilly water from the stream's main channel, creating a royal, five-star soak.

After checking out the surrounding thermal features, you might choose to hike another 0.5 to 1.5 miles upstream along the Ferris Fork to explore a quintuplet of seldom-seen waterfalls: 33ft **Tendoy Falls**, 20ft **Gwinna Falls**, 35ft **Sluiceway Falls** and 28ft **Wahhi Falls**.

Retrace your steps down into Bechler Canyon to your chosen 9B series campsite. If you are unable to reserve a campsite for the final night, it's a lengthy but manageable 13.5-mile descent back to the ranger station.

DAY 4: BECHLER RIVER CANYON TO BECHLER RANGER STATION
4-5 HOURS, 8-12 MILES, 800FT DESCENT

Retrace your steps down the canyon to the Bechler Ranger Station via Bechler Meadows Trail, the most direct route, or the more scenic Bechler River Trail.

Other Overnight Hikes
MAMMOTH COUNTRY

One of northern Yellowstone's most popular backpacking trips is the 18.5-mile **Black Canyon of the Yellowstone** from the Hellroaring Trailhead past the fine fishing waters of the Yellowstone River. There are 18 backcountry sites along the trail (site 1Y7 is a good halfway spot). Check the status of the trail into Gardiner with park rangers, since permission to transit through private property was withdrawn in 2011, necessitating a difficult final bushwhack up dangerously exposed slopes into forest service lands.

The 19-mile trail to **Mount Holmes** (10,336ft) begins south of Indian Creek at Willow Flats Picnic Area and heads west to the summit. It can be a super-long day hike with an elevation gain of 3000ft but it's much nicer to make camp at 1C4 or 1C5 and tackle the peak the next morning. Radial

9B8 (and a pit toilet), is the last, less serious ford, below a patch of burned forest.

Another mile on, the trail passes several algae-rich thermal areas fringing **Three Rivers Meadow**, then passes inviting campsite 9B9 (no campfires and a two-night limit), with a hiker-only site tucked away on the east side of the canyon near the base of a thundering waterfall that descends from towering **Batchelder Column**. The 9B9 stock-only campsite and an NPS patrol cabin lie across a bridge on the opposite riverbank.

It's worth the steep extra mile slog up out of the lovely river flats to the canyon's wild upper valley, where hidden campsite 9D1 (no campfires, sometimes not open until August) awaits beyond a footbridge over the **Bechler's Ferris Fork**. It doesn't get any lovelier than this: camp perched on a peninsula near **Three River Junction**, overlooking the Gregg, Ferris and Phillips Forks' tumbling confluence.

hikes to Trilobite Lake look tempting but the trail is unmaintained, with lots of downed trees in the way.

Three longer east–west backpacking routes begin west of Mammoth and lead to US 191 in Montana: the 19.5-mile **Bighorn Pass Trail** begins from Indian Creek Campground, and the 21-mile **Fawn Pass Trail** and 23-mile **Sportsman Lake Trail** to its north both begin at Glen Creek Trailhead south of Mammoth. Link two of them together for a rewarding loop.

One exciting traverse is the weeklong, 40-mile **Gallatin Skyline** route that crosses the Gallatin range from west to east, from Dailey Creek in the far northwest to Mammoth, sticking to the high ridges via Shelf Lake, High Lake, Sportsman Lake and Electric Peak.

ROOSEVELT COUNTRY

The **Bliss Pass** trek, which begins 0.5 miles before Slough Creek Campground, is a pleasant overnight hike along a popular fishing stream. Head east up Elk Tongue Creek, cross Bliss Pass (8 miles from the trailhead) and descend Pebble Creek to the namesake campground for a total hike of 21 miles. Bliss Pass may be snowbound until mid-July, and fording Pebble Creek can be tricky early in the season. This is a popular horse trail. The first part of the hike follows a historic wagon trail still used by the Silver Tip Ranch; though it lies just outside the north boundary, the trail is only accessible from the park and enjoys a historic right of access. Backcountry sites along Slough Creek are limited to a maximum stay of three nights between mid-June and mid-September.

An extensive trail network branches off the upper Lamar Valley from the Lamar River Trailhead (3K1), 4.7 miles southwest of Pebble Creek Campground. The main trail is the **Lamar River Trail**, which offers good early-morning wildlife-watching. Other trails lead off this one, heading west after 1.4 miles to join the Specimen Ridge Trail, east to Cache Creek after 3.1 miles, or east to Miller Creek after 9.3 miles. The **Miller Creek Trail** eventually climbs up either Bootjack Gap or the sculptured peaks of the Hoodoo Basin for an ambitious multiday expedition into the grizzly-filled Sunlight Basin of Shoshone National Forest. The main trail continues south along the Lamar River, leading toward Wapiti Valley via the Frost Lake Trail, or to Yellowstone Lake via the prime grizzly habitat of Mist Creek.

CYCLING

Cycling on Yellowstone's roads requires taking precautions. The roads are narrow and the RVs wide: in essence, you can't underestimate the threat of a rear-view mirror. For this reason, it is best to cycle on the main loops between dawn and 9am, before the traffic starts to snarl. Entering the park in the evening or leaving in the morning has you traveling against the flow of traffic.

Another alternative is to bike early or late season before the crowds of late June and after their departure in early September. Of course, your ability to bike in the early season will depend on the weather that year. On a heavy winter snow year, spring travel can be a challenge: check the park road conditions for plowing information.

Note that from mid-March to the third Thursday in April park roads between West Yellowstone and Mammoth in Yellowstone National Park are open only to nonmotorized travel, creating a vehicle-free playground for cyclists and rollerbladers.

Yellowstone has very few trails on which mountain biking is allowed; among them are the service road to Lone Star Geyser (see p102), Natural Bridge and the Bunsen Peak Rd double-track (see p115). In general bicycles are more useful for getting around campgrounds and biking on short family-friendly paved roads, rather than adventurous downhill trips.

Mammoth Country

The **Old Gardiner Rd** between Mammoth and Gardiner offers a traffic-free ride along the late-19th-century stagecoach route into the park. After an initial uphill the dirt road then descends 1000ft in 5 miles. It's not a stunning ride but does offer a rare opportunity to cycle in peace inside the park. You'll have to arrange a car shuttle or face a long uphill back. From May to October the road is open to motorized traffic (no RVs or trailers) one-way to Gardiner; bikes can travel in either direction. From Gardiner you can continue along dirt roads up to Corwin Springs, Yankee Jim Canyon and further into the Paradise Valley – see p153.

Unpaved Blacktail Plateau Dr (Map p63) offers a fairly easy ride, though there can be a fair amount of vehicle traffic.

🚴 Bunsen Peak Road & Osprey Falls

Duration 1 hour cycling plus a 90-minute strenuous hike to Osprey Falls

Distance 6.8 miles return

Difficulty Easy

Elevation Change Negligible (800ft descent on foot to Osprey Falls)

Start/Finish Bunsen Peak Trailhead (1K4; Map p58)

Nearest Town/Junction Mammoth

Summary An easy ride on a former service road, best combined with the strenuous hike down to Osprey Falls.

Now closed to motor vehicles, 6-mile **Bunsen Peak Rd** is a dirt road popular among family bikers. Probably the best option is to combine the bike ride with a hike to Osprey Falls (see p90). To do this, lock your bike at a rack by the **Osprey Falls Trailhead**, 3.4 miles into the ride. From here it's best to return the way you came. It's a largely flat section of gravel road, with a few minor ups and downs, and offers a good family trip (though the descent and return to Osprey Falls is much harder).

From the **Osprey Falls junction** it's possible to continue downhill to a service road and vehicle maintenance depot just above Mammoth, from where you can descend along the main road and then a walking trail beside the corral to Mammoth Junction, but you'd have to arrange a car shuttle for this. Biking back up the main road to the Bunsen Peak Trailhead isn't recommended due to the gradient, traffic and lack of a bicycle lane.

Canyon Country

As well as the easy bike rides around Canyon's north and south rim roads, the Canyon region offers the park's main uphill mountain bike challenge.

🚴 Mt Washburn

Duration 3 hours

Distance 5.6 miles return

Difficulty Difficult

Elevation Change 1400ft

Start/Finish Mt Washburn North trailhead (2K6; Map p107)

Nearest Town/Junction Canyon Village

Summary This is the park's toughest mountain-bike trip, offering fabulous views from the peak and a thrilling descent.

Mt Washburn is accessed by two former service roads; the southern route from Dunraven Pass is open only to hikers but the northerly Chittenden Rd is open to hikers, cyclists and the occasional park vehicle delivering supplies to the fire tower atop **Mt Washburn**. This isn't an easy jaunt you can attempt on a $50 bike from Wal-Mart (as we did), but rather a serious high-elevation climb for well-conditioned cyclists who have the luxury of plenty of low gears to choose from. The large trailhead is just over 1 mile off the main **Grand Loop Rd** and has a vault toilet.

Access the old service road by the side of the metal gate that blocks the road to cars. The service road was originally open to early motor vehicles, though the early Model T Fords that attempted the route back then had to reverse all the way up the mountain because the engines didn't yet come with fuel pumps! The only traffic you'll see today is tourists and the occasional grizzly bear. The wonderful 1400ft descent is back along the same road. Watch out for hikers and other cyclists on the tarmac-and-gravel downhill run, as there are several blind corners. This is also prime grizzly summer habitat, so keep your eyes open for bears.

See p96 for details of the view and facilities atop the peak.

Lake Country

Pack a picnic, grab the kids and take off on an easy jaunt to Natural Bridge.

🚴 Natural Bridge

Duration 45 minutes

Distance 3-mile round-trip

Difficulty Easy

Elevation Change 110ft

Start/Finish Bridge Bay Marina

Nearest Town/Junction Bridge Bay

Summary A family-friendly ride to an interesting natural feature.

An excellent family biking trail follows an old stagecoach road that once linked West Thumb to Lake Village. The paved road starts opposite the northbound turnoff to

Gull Point Dr, just south of the Bridge Bay turnoff, but parking is found at the Bridge Bay Marina. It is 1.5 miles to **Natural Bridge**, joining the hiking trail en route. The flat route leads to rhyolite cliffs forming a natural bridge 51ft above **Bridge Creek**. You can hike the steep trail to the top but not across the fragile bridge. The trail is closed from late spring to early summer due to bear activity.

Geyser Country

In the Upper Geyser Basin bikes are allowed on the road (not the boardwalk) between Old Faithful and Morning Glory Pool (1.4 miles), and between Daisy Geyser and Biscuit Basin (1.3 miles).

You can hire bikes at Bear Den Bike in the Old Faithful Snow Lodge gift shop for $25/35 for a half/full day, with kids' bikes at $15/22.50. Bike trains (a kid's bike that hooks on the back of an adult bike) and trailers are also available. Rentals come with a helmet and a lock.

In addition to the Fountain Freight Rd route described here, the former service road to **Lone Star Geyser** makes for a fine (and flat) 5-mile, round-trip bike ride, though you'll have to dismount for the last few yards to the actual geyser. There's a bike stand at the end of the trail, where you can lock your bike. See p102 for a description of the route and geyser. Take a packed lunch for the geyser wait. Park in the Lone Star Geyser lot next to Kepler Cascades.

Fountain Freight Road

Duration 1 hour cycling (up to 4 hours with excursions)

Distance 7.4 miles return

Difficulty Easy

Elevation Change Negligible

Start/Finish Fairy Falls/Steel Bridge Trailhead (0K5; Map p103)

Nearest Town/Junction Old Faithful

Summary An easy flat bike ride on a gravel road that allows lots of stops and detours on foot – perfect for families.

The 4-mile Old Fountain Freight Rd between Fountain Flat Dr and Fairy Falls Trailhead offers an opportunity to combine some pedaling with a hike to Fairy Falls and an exploration of the Pocket Basin backcountry thermal area.

Park your car at the busy **Fairy Falls Trailhead** (which can fill up in summer) and cycle over the steel bridge (sometimes called Soldier Bridge). After 0.5 miles you'll see the blue blur of **Grand Prismatic Spring** to the right. Park the bike here and make the short but steep hike up the volcanic hillside on the left (look for the trails) for fantastic aerial views over the spring.

From here it's another 0.5 miles to the turnoff to **Fairy Falls**. You can't bike this side trail, but you can park your bike at the rack and make the 3.2-mile return detour to the waterfalls on foot (see p102).

From the turnoff to Fairy Falls, pedal north along the gravel road for 1.2 miles to **Goose Lake**, the northern shore of which makes for a good picnic spot, either now or on the way back. Continue north, past the Imperial/Sentinel Meadows Trailhead to the bridge over the Firehole River. Park your bike at the bridge and check out the **Ojo Caliente** hot spring on the north bank. It's also well worth making the short hike along the unmarked trail east on the north side of the river to the hot springs and geysers of little-visited **Pocket Basin**, just 10 minutes from the bridge. The two-hour **Sentinel Meadows and Queen's Laundry Geyser** hike also departs from here (see p101).

From the bridge turn back and cycle the 3.7 miles back to your car. If one member of your group is happy driving down to Old Faithful, the rest of you could continue south from the parking lot for 2.6 miles along the busy Grand Loop Rd to **Biscuit Basin**, where you'll find a 1.3-mile bikeable trail to **Daisy Geyser** and on to **Old Faithful**, another mile away. This makes for a 5-mile extension. In this case it's best to start this ride at its northern end, at the parking lot of Fountain Flat Dr.

OTHER ACTIVITIES

Horseback Riding

Daily **stagecoach rides** (adult/under 11yr $9.35/7.50) depart from Roosevelt Lodge three to five times daily and last around 45 minutes. For a treat, ask for the tallyho seat.

Old West **cookouts** are a fun family trip, either on horseback (one-hour trips adult/under 12 $68/57, two-hour trips $84/72) or by horse-drawn wagon ($57/46 per person); reservations are required months in advance. Trips depart daily in the late afternoon and travel to the former site of Uncle John Yancey's Pleasant Valley Hotel (1884–87), one of the park's earliest accommodations, for a gut-busting, all-you-can-eat chow-down of steak and beans accompanied by campfire music. The excursion lasts for about three hours.

Corrals next to Roosevelt Lodge offer trail rides (1/2hr $38/58), four times a day, through sagebrush country. Two-hour rides run just once a day, so reserve ahead. Children must be over eight years old. Rides can be cancelled after rain.

Horse-packing parties must obtain a backcountry-use permit for overnight trips. A horse-use permit is also required for day trips. Both are available at most ranger stations. The *Horse Packing in Yellowstone* pamphlet lists regulations. Pack animals include horses, burros, mules, ponies and llamas.

Some backcountry trails are closed to stock, and those that are open may be temporarily closed in spring and early summer due to wet conditions. Overnight pack trips are not allowed until July 1. Stock can only be kept at designated campsites. Hay is not permitted at the trailhead or in the backcountry.

Xanterra   CONCESSIONAIRE
([☎307-344-7311]; www.yellowstonenationalparklodges.com) The park concessionaire operates all the activities listed above. Reservations are recommended and can be made by phone or at activities booths at most hotels. All the activities operate from early June to early September. Xanterra also offers one-/two-hour trail rides for $38/58 at corrals just south of Canyon (eight times a day, late June to late August) and one-hour rides from corrals just north of Mammoth (four times a day, late May to early September), in the shadow of Bunsen Peak. Once again, the two-hour ride departs just once a day, so reserve ahead.

**Yellowstone Wilderness
Outfitters**   OUTFITTERS
(www.yellowstone.ws) One of several professional outfitters licensed to run day rides ($165) and multiday pack trips in the park. See the Around Yellowstone chapter for more operators.

Boating

See p105 for details on backcountry permits, which are required for all overnight boating trips in the park.

Boating is permitted May 1 to November 1, although some areas may close during the season. Motorized vessels are allowed only on Lewis Lake and parts of Yellowstone Lake. Sylvan, Eleanor and Twin Lakes, plus Beach Springs Lagoon, are closed to all boating, as are all park streams and the Yellowstone River, except on the Lewis River between Lewis and Shoshone Lakes, where hand-propelled vessels are allowed. Launching is permitted only at Bridge Bay, Grant Village (open mid-June) and Lewis Lake. Hand-carried vessels may launch at Sedge Bay. Study the *Boating Regulations* pamphlet before embarking.

A boating permit is required for all vessels, including float tubes. Permits for motorized vessels cost $10 per week or $20 per year and are available from Bridge Bay Ranger Station, Grant Village Backcountry office and the South Entrance. Permits for nonmotorized vessels cost $5 per week or $10 per year and are available from the same offices, as well as the West Entrance, Northeast Entrance, West Yellowstone Chamber of Commerce, Bechler Ranger Station and backcountry offices at Old Faithful, Canyon and Mammoth. Permits from Grant Teton National Park are honored but you need to get a free Yellowstone validation sticker.

The speed limit on Yellowstone Lake is 45mph. The limit on the south arms is 5mph, while the southernmost inlets are closed to motorboats. Landing is not allowed on the thermally affected shore between Little Thumb Creek and the south end of the West Thumb thermal area.

Certain shorelines are off-limits due to wildlife protection. Frank Island and the south end of Stevenson Island are closed from May 15 to August 15 to protect nesting ospreys and bald eagles. A 0.5-mile closure around Molly Island protects around 2000 breeding pelican who summer here between April and September. The south and east shorelines are off-limits May 15 to July 14 to prevent bear disturbance.

Unlike Grand Teton, waterskiing and jet skis are prohibited in Yellowstone. Personal flotation devices (PFDs) are required for all craft.

Boating regulations pamphlets are available at all visitor centers. General boating information is at www.nps.gov/yell/plan your visit/boating.htm.

YELLOWSTONE LAKE

The vast Yellowstone Lake just begs for extended kayak, boat and sailboat exploration, but it is important to plan your outing carefully. Drowning is the leading cause of death in Yellowstone. Water temperatures are very cold, averaging only 45°F in the summer. Moreover, sudden winds can quickly churn up 3ft to 5ft waves, capsizing small vessels, so it's preferable to paddle in the early morning or late afternoon and avoid open-water crossings. Prevailing winds come from the southwest, so if you're headed south, you'll need to set off around dawn.

One pleasant easy trip from Grant Village is the 5-mile return paddle to West Thumb Geyser Basin and Potts Geyser Basin. There's nowhere in the park to rent a kayak so you'll have to bring your own or rent from Cody, Gardiner or Jackson.

From Grant Village, the closest campsites are at Breeze Bay (8 to 10 miles away), some of which are for first- and last-night use only. The canoe and kayak put-in at Sedge Bay (Trailhead 5K4) is the closest point from which to access the lake's southeast arm (21 miles), from which you can hike to the park's remote reaches. The nearest backcountry sites start 4 miles away.

The lake also has several anchor-only sites, including two at Frank Island

Grant Village Backcountry Ranger Office   RANGER OFFICE
(☏307-242-2609; ⊙8am-5pm) An excellent resource. It distributes the Backcountry Trip Planner (www.nps.gov/yell/planyourvisit/backcountrytripplanner.htm) describing Yellowstone Lake campsites in detail, with GPS coordinates, photos and mileage from the nearest boat put-ins. Some sites have restrictions on docking, hiking etc. You may also need fishing, boating and backcountry permits (all lake campsites require a backcountry permit). Grant Village also has a marina nearby.

Bridge Bay Marina   MARINA
(☏307-242-3880; ⊙8am-8pm mid-Jun-early Sep) Offers dock slip rentals ($17 to $23 per night) and hourly rowboat ($10/45 per hour/day) and outboard ($47 per hour) rentals. If you want to spend a few days paddling around the remote southern arms of the lake, the marina operates a boat shuttle ($76 per hour, two-hour minimum) for up to six people and their kayaks to docks at Eagle Bay (7L6), Wolf Bay (7L5), Plover Point (7M4), Promontory Tip (5L8) or Columbine Creek (5E6) on the east shore of the mouth of the southeast arm. Arrange it in advance and they'll pick you up again after a few idyllic days of remote paddling.

SHOSHONE LAKE

The largest backcountry lake in the lower 48, Shoshone Lake spells paradise for hikers and kayakers. The serene lake is closed to motorized vessels and is lined with a dozen secluded boater-only campsites. On its far western edge, Shoshone Geyser Basin's pools, thermals and mud pots comprise the largest backcountry thermal area in the park. One-third of all of Yellowstone's backcountry use takes place along its shores, accessible only to hikers and hand-propelled boats.

Boaters access the lake up the channel from Lewis Lake. From mid-July to August the channel requires portage of up to 1 mile in cold water (bring appropriate footwear), though in spring you can often paddle through.

Of 20 lakeshore campsites, 13 sites are reserved for boaters, five for hikers and three are shared. All have pit toilets. Rangers claim the nicest campsites are 8Q4, 8R4 and 8R1. Wood fires are not allowed along the lakeshore.

Most boaters make their first camp on the south shore (campsites nearest to the channel are reserved for first- and last-night use only). If you need to cross the lake, do so early in the morning and at the Narrows in the center of the lake. The lake is icebound until mid-June, when flooding is possible at shoreline campsites. Backcountry boating campsites at Shoshone Lake cannot be reserved before July 1 or 15, depending on the site.

Fishing

Yellowstone is justly famous for its fly-fishing, and the park's gateway towns have dozens of excellent fly-fishing shops that can offer expert local advice on current flows, flies and hatches, or arrange fully guided trips. Where else can you cast your line in sight of a grazing bison or the steam of an exploding geyser? See p37 for general information on fishing in the region. The park concessionaire **Xanterra** (☏307-344-7311) offers full- or half-day fly-fishing guide services, as well as rod and reel rental.

BE A HERO: GO FISHING

Lake (or Mackinaw) trout were introduced to Yellowstone Lake illegally (although the park itself had stocked Lewis and Shoshone Lakes with them earlier). Since they have no natural predators, their Pac-Man-like presence has wreaked havoc on native cutthroat trout. In a year, one lake trout can eat 41 cutthroats, sushi dinners normally destined for feeding grizzlies and bald eagles. If the trend continues, the native trout population may fall to 10% of historic highs, tipping the overall ecological balance.

With a fishing rod and free time you could help redress the situation. Regulations encourage anglers to catch lake trout. The **Volunteer Fly Fishing Program** (www.nps.gov/yell/naturescience/vol_fishing.htm) puts anglers on the park's 2650 miles of streams and 150 lakes to help collect biological data through catch-and-release techniques.

Cutthroat trout, grayling and mountain whitefish, among 11 species that are native to the park, are catch-and-release only. Some areas (such as the Gibbon River below Gibbon Falls) are open to fly-fishing only. Lead weights are prohibited; only nontoxic alternatives are sanctioned.

Fishing season usually runs from June 15 to the first Sunday in November, except for streams that flow into Yellowstone Lake and some tributaries of the Yellowstone River, which open July 15. Other rivers are permanently closed to fishing, including a 6-mile stretch of the Yellowstone River in the Hayden Valley; some may close during the season due to bear activity. The useful *Fishing Regulations* pamphlet details the park's complex rules and regulations.

A Yellowstone Park fishing permit is required for anglers aged 16 and older (state licenses are not required). Permits cost $15 for three days, $20 for seven days or $35 for the season; nonfee permits are required for unsupervised anglers aged 15 and under. Permits are available from ranger stations, visitor centers and Yellowstone general stores. A boating permit is required for float tubes, which are allowed only on the Lewis River between Lewis and Shoshone Lakes.

YELLOWSTONE LAKE

Yellowstone Lake is stocked with cutthroat trout, longnose dace, redside shiners, longnose suckers and lake chub. Popular shore or float-fishing spots include Gull Point, Sand Point Picnic Area, Sedge Bay, Mary Bay and Steamboat Point.

Fishing is not allowed on Pelican Creek from its outlet to 2 miles upstream or on the Yellowstone River from 0.25 miles upstream of Fishing Bridge to its outflow from Yellowstone Lake. Hayden Valley is closed to fishing except for two short catch-and-release stretches. All lake trout caught in Yellowstone Lake should be killed.

Detailed fishing information can be found at www.nps.gov/yell/planyourvisit/fishing.htm.

Bridge Bay Marina   MARINA
(☑307-344-7311; fishing trips per 2/4½ hr $160/360; ⊙mid-Jun–mid-Sep) Reserve with the marina for guided Yellowstone Lake fishing trips. Prices are for up to six people, and include three rods and reels. The marina also has a tackle shop and offers good fishing information. The marina area itself is closed to fishing.

GEYSER COUNTRY

The Madison and Gibbon Rivers offer some of the park's best and most scenic fly-fishing. The Firehole (between Biscuit and Midway Geyser Basins), Madison and Gibbon (downstream from Gibbon Falls) Rivers are open for fly-fishing only and lots of pullouts offer access. During hot summers the Firehole is often closed completely to fishing because of the high water temperatures.

The pullout beneath Mt Haynes on the Madison River between Madison Junction and West Yellowstone offers a good, wheelchair-accessible, riverside fishing spot.

ROOSEVELT COUNTRY

Slough Creek is the sweetest fishing spot in the northeast (closely followed by Pebble Creek and Soda Butte Creek), which is one reason why the park's Slough Creek Campground is regularly the first to fill up. Ensure that you make your backcountry reservations early if you want to overnight in any of the Slough Creek backcountry campsites. Other good places include the Black Canyon of the Yellowstone and the Lamar River.

Cross-Country Skiing & Snowshoeing

All backcountry trails are marked with orange markers, so you can theoretically ski or snowshoe most of the backcountry trails described in this chapter.

Once in the park, use skier shuttles to get to and from trailheads, where you can take a trail or just ski back. Shuttles operate from Mammoth to Bunsen Peak Rd and Indian Creek ($15 round-trip, five per day) and from Old Faithful Snow Lodge to Fairy Falls or Divide Trailheads ($15 one way; you must ski back).

Combined snowcoach and ski tours run from Mammoth and Old Faithful to Canyon ($140) once or twice a week. You can ice skate in Mammoth and Old Faithful (free skate rental).

Cross-country ski ($18.50 per day, includes equipment) and snowshoe ($15) rentals are available, as are snowmobile tours ($275 per day) and ski instruction ($23 for two hours, $35 with equipment).

MAMMOTH & ROOSEVELT COUNTRY

The north of the park remains logistically easier to visit in winter because the road between Mammoth and Cooke City remains open year-round

Around the Mammoth region it's possible to ski from Indian Creek Campground to Sheepeater Cliffs and then along a backcountry trail to Bunsen Peak Trail and left to the Mammoth–Norris road (5 miles) or right down the Bunsen Peak Rd to Mammoth. There are also marked loops around Indian Creek (2.2 miles) and part way along the Bighorn Trail (5.5 miles). Bunsen Peak Rd also offers an enjoyable downhill route from the Bunsen Peak trailhead down to the upper Mammoth terraces

The groomed 1.5-mile Upper Terrace Loop Trail follows the Upper Terrace road and is a good place to test out your Nordic legs. A side trail from here follows an old wagon track uphill to Snow Pass and then along Glen Creek back to the Bunsen Peak Trailhead (4.2 miles).

In the park's northeast corner a popular ski trail parallels the Northeast Entrance road below Barronette Peak (10,404ft) between the Soda Butte Creek bridges (3.5 miles). The nearby 2-mile Bannock Trail runs east out of the park from the Warm Creek picnic area along an old mining road to Silver Gate.

Around Tower-Roosevelt, the 8-mile Blacktail Plateau Trail follows the unplowed road of the same name and is a popular shuttle option. The trail climbs gently to the Cut and then descends for 2 miles to the main Mammoth–Cooke City road.

Rangers lead free guided snowshoe walks around Mammoth Hot Springs at 2pm on Monday and Wednesday late December to the end of February (check the park newspaper).

GEYSER COUNTRY

The area around Old Faithful has the most trails and facilities in winter. Three-hour guided snowshoe tours ($25, with shoe rental $32) depart from Old Faithful on Thursday and Sunday. Half-day guided ski tours ($45) leave Old Faithful on Sunday to either Fairy Falls or DeLacy Creek.

Upper and Midway Geyser Basins both make for some fine ski trips. You can ski or snowshoe from Old Faithful to Black Sand Basin via Daisy Geyser (4 miles) or to Biscuit Basin via Morning Glory and Atomizer Geyser (5 miles, with a possible extension to Mystic Falls). The Frozen Fairy Falls hike (p102) is a popular ski day trip – get dropped off at the southern end of Fountain Freight Rd, visit the falls and ski back to Old Faithful (11 miles).

The 9-mile return Lone Star Geyser Trail takes you from Old Faithful Snow Lodge along the Mallard Lake Trail and parallel to the main road, to cross it at Kepler Cascades. The trail then follows the same route as the hike to Lone Star Geyser. A ski shuttle will allow you to take the 8-mile Spring Creek Trail (a former stagecoach road) to Lone Star Geyser.

SLEEPING

Although competition for campsites and lodging may be fierce, there's nothing quite like falling asleep to the eerie sounds of bugling elk and howling wolves and waking to the sulfur smell of the earth erupting and bubbling in the area.

You can make reservations for park accommodations and five of the park's 12 campgrounds through the park concessionaire Xanterra (☎866-GEYSERLAND, 307-344-7311; www.yellowstonenationalparklodges.com; ☺Jun-Aug 7am-6pm, other months 8am-5pm). Online bookings are now possible for both hotels and campgrounds.

YELLOWSTONE'S WINTER WONDERLAND

Winter is a magical time to visit Yellowstone. The falls turn to frozen curtains of ice, the geysers spurt taller and steamier than normal and surrounding 'ghost trees' turn into surreal frozen steam sculptures. The warm thermal areas around Old Faithful, Norris and Mammoth become winter refuges for elk and bison, and the thermally heated (and thus still flowing) rivers attract plenty of waterfowl.

The winter season runs from late December to mid-March, and activity centers on Mammoth Hot Springs Hotel and Old Faithful Snow Lodge, the only two accommodations open in the park. Independent travel is more difficult in winter, and most people sign up for a lodging and activity package, which often works out cheaper than arranging things yourself. The **Yellowstone Institute** (☎307-344-2294; www.yellowstone association.org/institute) runs some particularly good winter programs.

Accessing the park is an adventure in itself. The only road open year-round is the northern Mammoth–Cooke City road via Tower-Roosevelt Junction, plus an extension to Mammoth's Upper Terraces. The long-term future of Yellowstone winter use lies in mass-transit snowcoaches. During the season, **Xanterra** (☎307-344-7311) operates one-way snowcoach tours once daily between Old Faithful and Mammoth ($70), West Yellowstone ($57) and Flagg Ranch ($70). There are also three express runs a day between Old Faithful and West Yellowstone ($55). Most other snowcoach companies offer only return day trips from West Yellowstone.

Trips inside the park include day snowcoach tours to Canyon from Old Faithful ($130) and Mammoth ($125), half-day tours to Norris from Mammoth ($57) and three-hour tours from Old Faithful to the Firehole Basin ($32.75).

Winter Facilities

Mammoth Hot Springs Hotel and Old Faithful Snow Lodge and their restaurants are the only places open, though there is limited (and cold!) winter camping at Mammoth Campground. In theory, you can snow camp anywhere in the park (including in the vicinity of Old Faithful) with a backcountry permit, but winter camping conditions are for specialists only.

Both hotels rent snowshoes, cross-country skis and winter attire, and they also offer skiing instruction and snowmobile tours. After a day on a snowmobile you'll need a dip in Mammoth Hotel's hot tubs or a massage from the Old Faithful Snow Lodge.

There are no public accommodations in Canyon, but **Yellowstone Expeditions** (☎800-728-9333; www.yellowstoneexpeditions.com) runs a winter yurt camp there for its cross-country ski and snowshoe tours. Four-day tours from West Yellowstone cost around $950 per person, including transportation, heated accommodations, food and a guide.

Visitor centers at Old Faithful and Mammoth are open during the winter season. There are winter warming huts at Mammoth, Indian Creek, Old Faithful (in yurts), West Thumb, Fishing Bridge, Madison and Canyon; the latter two have fast food. All except Mammoth and Old Faithful are open 24 hours. Snowmobile fuel is available at Canyon, Fishing Bridge, Old Faithful and Mammoth. Mammoth Clinic is open weekdays and Old Faithful Clinic is open periodically.

Snowmobile Regulations

The park service enforces a daily cap of snowmobiles into the park, proposed at a total of 325 for 2012, and snowmobilers must be accompanied by a commercial guide, in a maximum group size of 10. Regulations are once again under review so it would be wise to check current regulations before heading out on a snowmobile vacation.

Snowmobiles are banned from all the park's side roads, including the Lake Butte Overlook, Firehole Canyon Dr and a section of the Grand Loop Rd from Canyon to Tower. All other roads are groomed for oversnow travel. The Canyon to Washburn Hot Springs Overlook section of the Grand Loop Rd is open to Nordic skiers. Snowmobile operators must carry a valid state driver's license. The speed limit between the West Entrance and Old Faithful is 35mph; elsewhere it is 45mph. Roads are only open 7am to 9pm and off-road snowmobiling is prohibited. See the boxed text, p40, for snowmobiling safety tips.

Camping in the Park

Most of Yellowstone's campsites are in natural junctions, areas once frequented by Native Americans as well as early trappers, explorers and the US Army. There are around 2200 formal campsites in the park, plus well over 100 backcountry sites.

Aside from backcountry campsites (which require a hike to reach), camping inside the park is allowed only in 12 designated campgrounds and it is limited to 14 consecutive days from July 1 to Labor Day, and 30 days for the rest of the year. Check-out time is 11am. See p105 for details on backcountry camping.

The National Park Service has seven campgrounds available on a first-come, first-served basis only. Call ☏307-344-2114 for recorded NPS campsite information.

Xanterra runs five of the park's 12 campgrounds (Canyon, Madison, Fishing Bridge, Bridge Bay and Grant Village) and these are a few dollars pricier than the national park campgrounds. They feature flush toilets, cold running water and vending machines, and a couple have pay showers.

A few campsites are reserved for backpackers and cyclists at all campgrounds except Slough Creek and Canyon. Slough Creek fills early due to popularity with anglers and wolf watchers. Canyon is popular because of its central location. Boaters favor Grant Village and Bridge Bay; canoeists and anglers often base themselves at Lewis Lake. The Madison Campground is closest to Old Faithful, though Grant Village isn't far off. Fishing Bridge is always full of RVs in midsummer, and reservations are essential.

Lodging in the Park

Today's cabins and campgrounds are direct descendents of classy turn-of-the-century hotels and Wylie tent camps, the latter an affordable early option that opened up the park to budget-minded auto tours. Of the cabin options, rustic Lake Lodge is the most peaceful, and Roosevelt Lodge offers the most authentic Western experience. Lake Yellowstone Hotel and Old Faithful Inn provide the park's most atmospheric and upscale accommodations. For reservations and information call Xanterra.

Rooms are priced here at double occupancy, but most lodges have rooms that sleep up to six for an extra $10 per person. All Yellowstone hotel rooms are nonsmoking and none have televisions or internet access.

Mammoth Country

Camping

Mammoth Campground CAMPGROUND $
(Map p58; sites $14) The park's most exposed campground, this is a barren, sagebrush-covered area with sparse shade. On a hairpin bend in the road below Mammoth Hot Springs, it gets road noise – the inner road sites are quietest – but its relatively low elevation makes it the warmest campground and a good choice for early- or late-season visits. Showers and other facilities are in Mammoth, just to the south, or Gardiner, 5 miles north by the North Entrance. When staffed, the registration office assigns sites, accepts credit cards and offers change. There are several wheelchair-accessible and hiker/cyclist sites, and firewood for sale between 6pm and 8:30pm. Join one of the ranger talks at the amphitheater at 9pm or 9:30pm, depending on the month.

Indian Creek Campground CAMPGROUND $
(Map p58; sites $12; ⊙Jun–mid-Sep) This low-key spot is probably the park's most underused campground – most people speed by between Mammoth and Old Faithful – which is one reason we like it. Plus, it's often the last in the park to fill up. It's set in open forest on a low rise and surrounded by moose territory, and there are several hiking trails nearby – to Indian Creek, along the former stagecoach road, or part way along the Bighorn Pass Trail (look for a handout detailing campground trails). Generators are not allowed, but firewood is sold. The site is 8 miles south of Mammoth Junction.

Lodging

Mammoth Hot Springs Hotel HOTEL, CABINS $$
(Map p58; cabins with/without bath $81/112, r with/without bath $87/120, ste $449; ⊙early May–mid-Oct & mid-Dec–early Mar) A classy vibe, a good variety of accommodations (112 rooms) and a useful location make this one of the park's most popular accommodations. The main choice is between the hotel rooms in the main building or cabins out back. The cheaper options come with a sink and communal bathrooms, either down the hall in the hotel block or in a separate block out back by the budget cabins.

The main en suite hotel rooms echo the historic feel of the hotel with antique-style bathroom fittings, clawfoot tubs and old black-and-white photos on the walls. The cabins (closed in winter) are mostly duplex units, with a porch to sit on, but if you value your privacy you can request a detached cabin. The cabins are a bit cheaper than the hotel rooms but don't come with a phone.

Frontier cabins come with a private bathroom, shower and two double beds. Some come with a queen bed and private outdoor hot tub, enclosed in a privacy fence, for $217. The hotel suites have a living room and bedroom, the only cable TV in the park, and can sleep four in two queen beds.

Roosevelt Country

Camping

Pebble Creek Campground   CAMPGROUND $
(Map p63; sites $12; ☺late May-late Sep) The park's remotest ground is surrounded on three sides by the rugged cliffs of the Absaroka Range. It's along the banks of a creek in grizzly habitat and is popular with hikers and wolf-watchers, though the sites are a bit cramped. The Pebble Creek hiking trail starts nearby. Generators are not allowed. Most sites are pull-through. The site is 10 miles from the Northeast Entrance at the lower end of Icebox Canyon. The nearest showers and supplies are at Tower-Roosevelt Junction and there's good fishing at nearby Soda Butte Creek.

Slough Creek Campground   CAMPGROUND $
(Map p63; sites $12; ☺late May-Oct) This remote, peaceful site, 2.2 miles up an unpaved road, is in grizzly habitat along a prime fishing stream. A couple of walk-in sites are available, and there's easy access to the Slough Creek Trail. Generators are not allowed. The campsite is 10 miles northeast of Tower-Roosevelt Junction. An anglers' paradise, this ground fills up by 11am in high season.

Tower Fall Campground   CAMPGROUND $
(Map p63; sites $12; ☺mid-May–late Sep) This small single loop of 32 sites is high above Tower Creek in an open pine forest. There are hiking trails nearby up Tower Creek and groceries at nearby Tower Falls. It's 3 miles southeast of Tower-Roosevelt Junction. There are hiker/cyclist sites. Generators are not allowed.

Lodging

Roosevelt Lodge   CABINS $
(Map p63; Roughrider/Frontier cabins $65/110; ☺early Jun-early Sep) Founded in 1906 as a tented camp, present-day Roosevelt Lodge was built in 1919 and retains an Old West feel, offering 80 rustic cabins, horseback rides and a Wild West cookout in the heart of sagebrush country.

For groups, families or couples traveling together, the Roughrider cabins are among the park's greatest bargains, because the price is the same for cabins with one, two or three beds, meaning you can shoehorn six people in here for around $10 a head! The simple but pleasant wooden cabins come with a log-burning stove, though the one-bed (and some two-bed) cabins are cramped (because it's the same price, book a larger cabin). All beds are doubles rather than queens so can be small for couples. There are no en suite bathrooms and not even running water in the room, but the three communal wash blocks have hot water, showers and ice.

Frontier cabins are nicely decorated and come with private bathroom, electric heating and two or three double beds. There are two wheelchair-accessible cabins with private bathroom.

The Frontier cabins should be booked several months in advance in high season since numbers are limited; the Roughriders should be booked at least a month or two in advance, though you might find a room free on the off-chance. There are a limited number of outdoor grills if you want to cook your own food.

There's good hiking nearby. The hike to Lost Lake starts from just behind the lodge – see p93.

Canyon Country

Camping

Canyon Campground   CAMPGROUND $
(Map p68; sites $20; ☺early Jun-early Sep) The huge Canyon Campground is the most densely forested in the park, but it's also the largest (11 loops!) and one of the most cramped, which makes staying here feel a bit like being churned through a Pink Floyd–style tourism meat grinder. Still, thanks to its central location as a good base for day trips to other parts of park, it's a very popular ground, so book at least a couple of days ahead in summer. Snow can linger here well into early summer.

There are pay showers and laundry on site, and the restaurants and supplies of Canyon Village are nearby. Canyon also

YELLOWSTONE NATIONAL PARK CAMPGROUNDS

CAMPGROUND	LOCATION	DESCRIPTION	NO OF SITES	ELEVATION
Canyon	Canyon Country	A huge 11-loop site slap-bang in the center of the park	272	7734ft
Madison	Geyser Country	Lovely riverside location and the closest campground to Old Faithful	280	6806ft
Bridge Bay	Lake Country	A multiple-loop megacomplex appealing to boaters and anglers	425	7800ft
Fishing Bridge RV Park	Lake Country	A reservations-essential, RV-only spot, well located	112	7800ft
Grant Village	Lake Country	A spacious and shady multiloop complex with conveniences and the lake nearby	425	7800ft
Lewis Lake	Lake Country	A shady, quiet campground close to backcountry trails and lake	85	7800ft
Indian Creek	Mammoth Country	Quiet, small, secluded and woodsy	75	7300ft
Mammoth	Mammoth Country	Fairly barren spot near the North Entrance but the warmest site in spring and fall	85	6239ft
Norris	Norris	Quiet site with a walking trail to the nearby geyser basin	116	7484ft
Pebble Creek	Roosevelt Country	Fairly cramped site popular with wolf-watchers in the nearby Lamar Valley	36	6800ft
Slough Creek	Roosevelt Country	A favorite with anglers, this site fills up the earliest in high season	29	6400ft
Tower Fall	Roosevelt Country	Small site that fills up quickly, with several hiking trails	32	6650ft

*Reservations possible through Xanterra (☎866-439-7375, 307-344-7311)

 Drinking Water

 Flush Toilets

 Ranger Station Nearby

 Wheelchair Accessible

offers the most tent-only sites (four out of 11 loops) of any campground. Head to the amphitheater at 9pm or 9:30pm for the nightly campfire programs.

Lodging

Canyon Lodge LODGE, CABINS **$$**
(Map p68; ☎307-242-3900; lodge d $170, Frontier/Western cabins $96/179; ⊘rooms Jun–mid-Sep, cabins close earlier) This enormous complex has 609 rooms and is set in thick forest. It dates from the opening of the park to mass tourism in the 1950s and 1960s – a drive around the multiple low-rise and potholed loops is like a drive back in time to a classic Middle American suburb.

The cabins date from the 1950s and are laid out barracks-style, grouped into blocks of four, six or eight. The Frontiers have simple bathrooms but are fine. Newly renovated Western cabins come with two queen beds, a coffeemaker and tub/shower, and some are wheelchair accessible. These cabins are slowly being renovated. Cabins can sleep up to four for an extra $10 per person. Loop 'P' generally has the most secluded locations and has a half-mile walking trail that leads to the canyon.

The modern Dunraven Lodge and Cascade Lodge both offer modern hotel rooms that were built in the 1990s, some with forest views. Both have coffeemakers and some wheelchair-accessible rooms but no telephone.

OPEN	RESERVATION POSSIBLE?	DAILY FEE	FACILITIES	PAGE
early Jun-early Sep	yes*	$20		p123
early May-late Oct	yes*	$20		p126
late May-mid-Sep	yes*	$20		p125
mid-May-late Sep	yes*	$28-37		p125
late May-late Sep	yes*	$20		p126
mid-Jun-early Nov	no	$12		p126
Jun-mid-Sep	no	$12		p122
year-round	no	$14		p122
mid-May-late Sep	no	$14		p126
end May-late Sep	no	$12		p123
late May-end Oct	no	$12		p123
mid-May-late Sep	no	$12		p123

 Grocery Store Nearby   *Payphone*   *Summertime Campfire Program*   *RV Dump Station*

Lake Country

Camping

The following campgrounds all feature dump stations, but only Fishing Bridge has full sewer and electrical hookups.

Bridge Bay Campground   CAMPGROUND $
(Map p72; sites $20; ☉late May–mid-Sep) This megacomplex adjacent to the marina, 3 miles southwest of Lake Village, appeals to fishing and boating enthusiasts. Tent campers will appreciate the more desirable forested tent-only loops (I and J). Some lower sites offer lake views, but the more private ones are in the upper section. There are a few hiker and biker sites. Showers and laundry facilities are 4 miles away at Fishing Bridge. There are campfire programs at 6pm and 9:30, the former aimed at young families.

Fishing Bridge RV Park   RV SITES $
(Map p72; RV sites with/without electricity $37/28; ☉mid-May–late Sep) Along the north shore of Yellowstone Lake, 1 mile east of Fishing Bridge Junction, this place only allows hard-shelled RVs because of heavy bear activity. Rates are for up to four people and include water and sewerage hookups; all sites are back-ins, with a 40ft maximum length. Reservations are essential in July and August. Public facilities here include a pay laundry and showers. Stroll over to the nearby visitor center at 9pm or 9:30pm for a ranger talk.

Grant Village Campground   CAMPGROUND $
(Map p72; sites $20; ⊘late May-late Sep) Along the west shore of Yellowstone Lake, 22 miles north of the South Entrance, this is the park's biggest campground. It's an enormous forested site that has a nearby boat launch, an RV dump station and three loops of tent-only sites. Nearby facilities include showers, laundry and groceries. You'll find lovely spots for lakeshore strolls nearby. The campground only opens when bears have stopped fishing the nearby spawning streams, which can be as late as June.

Lewis Lake Campground   CAMPGROUND $
(Map p72; sites $12; ⊘mid-Jun–early Nov) This forested campground is at the south end of Lewis Lake, about 10 miles north of the South Entrance. A nearby boat launch provides easy access to Lewis Lake and the Lewis River channel. Snow often remains here through June because of its high elevation and shaded location, so it may not be the best early-season campground. Bring repellent. A few walk-in and tent-only sites are available and generators are not allowed.

Lodging

TOP
CHOICE **Lake Yellowstone
Hotel**   HISTORIC HOTEL $$
(Map p72; hotel d $207-223, standard annex d $149, Frontier cabins $130; ⊘mid-May–Sep) Right on the lake shore, this is a buttercup behemoth that sets romantics aflutter. It harks back to a bygone era, though the 296 rooms that cost $4 in 1895 have appreciated somewhat. The spacious main building rooms feature wicker and floral designs, some sleeping up to six in three queen beds. Main lodge lakeside rooms cost extra and sell out first, but don't guarantee lake views. The comfortable Frontier cabins are boxed in neat suburban rows. The modern motel-style annex offers limited wheelchair-accessible accommodations.

Lake Lodge   CABINS $$
(Map p72; Pioneer/Frontier/Western cabins $69/106/179; ⊘early Jun-late Sep) The 186 rooms here offer a lackluster budget alternative. The Western cabins are spacious and modern, ideal for families, either in forested back loops or (in the A loop) with French windows and outdoor seating. Cramped Pioneer cabins recall the 1920s, with propane heaters and rustic decor that was last updated when Yogi Bear last wandered into the park. Frontier cabins are a good compromise, recently updated in 2010. The best feature is the rustic main lodge with rockers creaking on the porch, roaring fires inside, a dining hall and a laundromat.

Grant Village   MOTEL $$
(Map p72; r $152; ⊘late May-Sep) The 300 condo-like boxes with standard hotel interiors at Grant Village were once dismissed by author Alston Chase as 'an inner-city project in the heart of primitive America, a wilderness ghetto.' They do happen to be the closest lodging to the Tetons for those getting an early start.

Norris

Norris Campground   CAMPGROUND $
(Map p58; sites $14; ⊘mid-May–late Sep) Nestled in scenic open forest on an idyllic, sunny hill overlooking the Gibbon River and bordering meadows, this is one of the park's nicest sites. There are fishing and wildlife-viewing opportunities nearby, Solfatara Creek Trailhead is in the campground and there's a 1-mile trail from near the campground (just over the bridge) to Norris Geyser Basin. The few riverside sites in Loop A get snapped up very quickly. Bring water, as the stuff in the campground spigots is putrid. Campfire talks are held at 7:30pm and firewood is sold between 7pm and 8:30pm.

Geyser Country

Camping

Madison Campground   CAMPGROUND $
(Map p80; sites $20; ⊘early May-late Oct) The nearest campground to Old Faithful and the West Entrance occupies a sunny, open forest in a broad meadow above the banks of the Madison River. Bison herds and the park's largest elk herd frequent the meadows to its west, making for great wildlife-watching, and it's a fine base for fly-fishing the Madison. Tent-only sites are ideally placed along the river. A junior ranger station and campground amphitheater lie just a short walk away and offer nightly ranger talks. The campground is just west of Madison Junction, 14 miles east of the West Entrance and 16 miles north of Old Faithful. Vending machines offer ice, soft drinks and newspapers but the nearest food and showers are at Old Faithful.

Lodging

TOP CHOICE **Old Faithful Inn** LODGE $$

(Map p82; ste $399-499, d $126-236, without bath $96; ☺early May-early Oct) The lobby of this historic place is a bit of a zoo during the day, but the day-trippers quickly disappear with the sun. The building is full of charm, with 327 rooms, a lovely balcony, library-style desks and century-old furniture, and a pianist and singer at lunch and dinner. A stay here is a quintessential Yellowstone experience, but book well in advance or you'll find there's no room at the inn.

The hotel has a vast variety of rooms, including some wheelchair-accessible rooms. The cheapest 'Old House' rooms pack the most atmosphere, with historically correct wash basins, but the bathrooms are down the hall. Beware also that you can hear every footstep through the creaking wooden ceiling, and the radiator heat can be noisy early and late in the season. Easily the best rooms of this kind are the two- and three-bed 'dormers' off the 3rd-floor lobby.

Families might like the two connecting rooms that can sleep five, either with private bathroom ($213) or with bathroom down the hall (around $30 less). Rates for these rooms are per room, regardless of the number of people.

The only rooms that have a view of Old Faithful are a couple of 'premium' rooms on the front side of the east wing; these get snapped up a year in advance. Back rooms in the east wing cost $25 less and have no view. Even if you face Old Faithful, you'll find that the pine trees block most of the view.

The west wing has comfortable 'frontside' rooms ($220) – those on the upper floor have decent views of the geyser basin. The standard 'high-range' rooms ($150) vary considerably for the same price (rooms with two beds are noticeably larger). Both have bathrooms and can sleep up to four.

The only bum rooms in the hotel are the high-range rooms in the 1000 room number series, as these are below the ground floor. Staff refer to these affectionately as the 'dungeon rooms.' Request a higher floor.

Old Faithful Snow Lodge LODGE, CABINS $$

(Map p82; lodge r $206, Frontier/Western cabins $96/149; ☺May-late Oct & mid-Dec–early Mar) The park's most recent accommodation, this place was built in 1999 in a 'New Western' style and offers the only winter accommo-

YELLOWSTONE STARGAZING

The excellent *Stars Over Yellowstone* interpretive program runs for two weekends in June and July at Madison Campground's amphitheater and is a must for budding astronomers. Astronomers from Museum of the Rockies offer a guided tour of the night sky and there are all kinds of telescopes on site to play with, courtesy of the Southwestern Montana Astronomical Society.

dations available at Old Faithful. The main lodge has a stylish lobby decorated in bear and elk motifs and 134 comfortable, cozy but bland modern hotel rooms, with two double beds, a hair dryer and a coffeemaker. The pine-walled Frontier cabins are fairly simple but come with bathrooms and a coffeemaker. The modern Western cabins are more spacious, with two double beds, and are warmer in winter.

Old Faithful Lodge CABINS $

(Map p82; budget/frontier cabins $67/110; ☺mid-May–mid-Sep) Glummer than its glamorous cousins, the 132-cabin lodge was built in 1923 and has its historical roots in Yellowstone's turn-of-the century tent camps. It's definitely a notch down in atmosphere, though the rooms themselves are fine. The remodeled Frontier cabins come with a private bathroom but no telephone and vary in size; some are very small. Budget cabins have sinks with hot water, but the toilets and showers are in outside blocks. Most cabins are in blocks of twos or fours, though a few are detached. Some north-facing cabins on the north side have priceless views of Old Faithful from the back porch.

Bechler Region

Cave Falls Forest Service Campground CAMPGROUND $

(☎208-524-7500; www.fs.usda.gov/caribou; sites $10; ☺Jun–mid-Sep) Situated in the Caribou-Targhee National Forest, just 2 miles from the southwestern park border, Bechler's trailheads and Cave Falls, the 23 pleasant woodsy sites line a river cliff offering a slight breeze to ward off mosquitoes. Sites feature picnic tables, fire rings and grills. Vault toilets, bear boxes and water are available.

EATING & DRINKING

Food in the park is split between campfire cuisine, cafeteria food, a couple of fast-food choices and the more pleasant dining rooms of the park's historic inns. The park concessionaire, Xanterra, runs most dining options, so don't be surprised if you get a serious dose of déjà vu every time you open a menu. Most places are pretty good value, considering the prime real estate. You can get a sneak preview of park menus at the Xanterra website (www.yellowstonenational parklodges.com).

The park's cafeterias are bland but convenient, and reasonably economical for families. All places serve breakfast and most offer an all-you-can-eat buffet that can quickly wipe out even the best-laid hiking plans. Kids' menus are available almost everywhere. Almost all offer sandwiches for lunch and heavier, pricier fare for dinner.

There's also fast food at major junctions, plus snack shops and grocery supplies in the Yellowstone General Stores. Most places offer reasonably priced sandwiches for lunch. Dinners are considerably more expensive but offer rather more culinary adventure. The Grant Village, Old Faithful Inn and Lake Hotel dining rooms all require dinner reservations (307-344-7311).

Mammoth Country

TOP CHOICE ‣ **Mammoth Hot Springs Dining Room** AMERICAN $-$$
(Map p58; dinner mains $12-26; ☉6:30am-10am, 11:30am-2:30pm, 5-10pm early May–mid-Oct & mid-Dec–early Mar) There are a few surprises in this elegant place, including our favorite, the delicious Thai curry mussels starter. Dinner is a more serious affair, with pistachio and parmesan-crusted trout, bison meatballs and mashed potato, or linguine with crimini and shitake mushrooms – the latter a rare vegetarian find. The huckleberry Brie chicken is another favorite. Try a 'Yellowstone caldera' for dessert – a warm chocolate truffle torte with a suitably molten center. Reservations are only necessary in winter.

The attached bar has nice fireside seating in winter and serves restaurant starters if you just fancy a light dinner.

The hotel lobby's **Espresso Cart** (☉7-9am & 4-9pm) will help you kick-start the day and sells beer and wine in the evening.

Mammoth Terrace Grill FAST FOOD $
(Map p58; mains $4-8; ☉7:30am-9pm; ⊞) Line up for MacYellowstone-style ¼lb burgers, chili cheese fries and ice cream, along with some breakfast foods.

Roosevelt Country

Roosevelt Lodge Dining Room WESTERN $$
(Map p63; lunch & breakfast $10, dinner $10-20; ☉7-10am, 11:30am-3pm & 4:30-9:30pm early Jun-early Sep) Popular for its BBQ Western-style ribs and Wyoming cheese steak, served with cornbread muffins; the meaty menu stretches to elk burgers and bison chili but has glaringly little for vegetarians. Take a post-lunch or pre-dinner stroll up to the Lost Creek Falls, a 10-minute walk behind the lodge. The porch rockers are a fine place for a nightcap.

Old West Cookout WESTERN $$$
(dinner & wagon ride adult/child $57/46; ☉depart 5pm early Jun-Labor Day;⊞) The Roosevelt Lodge activities center offers this fun cookout, with steak, beans and the kind of cowboy coffee you have to filter through your teeth. Kids will love it. Reservations are required, preferably months in advance.

Limited groceries (as well as bear spray) are available at the small **Yellowstone General Store** (☉8am-9:30pm).

Canyon Country

Don't expect too much from Canyon's restaurants; a single kitchen prepares all meals – up to 5000 per day!

Canyon Lodge Dining Room AMERICAN $$
(Map p68; dinner mains $10-17; ☉7-10am, 11:30am-2:30pm & 5-10pm Jun-late Sep) This eatery has a dated casino/steakhouse lounge feel to it, the kind of place you might spot a 1970s-era Joe Pesci in a perm and a leisure suit, but it will do. Lunch features epic build-your-own burgers (including salmon burgers), but the restaurant only truly spreads its chicken wings for dinner, with bison asada and a famed prime rib au jus. The $10 all-you-can-eat soup and salad-bar option is low-grade but refreshing. The good wine and beer list is shared with the bar (open 3:30pm to 11pm). The breakfast menu has some lighter

options, such as yogurt with fresh fruit, as well as a full breakfast buffet ($12).

Canyon Lodge Cafeteria
CAFETERIA **$**

(Map p68; meals $7-10; ⏱6:30-11am & 11:30am-9:30pm Jun-early Sep) There are no surprises at this huge and echoing cafeteria, but it's cheap and easy, serving up salads, lasagna, rice bowls, hot dogs and a mean bison sausage sandwich, with the same menu as the Old Faithful Lodge Cafeteria. Oatmeal and fruit salads are among the lighter options.

Yellowstone General Store
DINER **$**

(Map p68; www.visityellowstonepark.com; mains $8; ⏱7:30am-8:30pm) The old-fashioned soda-fountain counter here churns out burgers, chili dogs and root-beer floats, plus there's ice cream and coffee. Breakfasts include blueberry flapjacks with sausage. Hours are shorter out of season.

Canyon Deli
SANDWICHES **$**

(Map p68; sandwiches $7; ⏱11am-7pm Jun-late Sep) Has prepackaged deli sandwiches, yogurt with granola, salads and ice cream, with a couple of outdoor seats in the sun.

Geyser Country

All of the food options in Geyser Country are clustered around Old Faithful.

TOP
CHOICE **Old Faithful Inn**
Dining Room
AMERICAN **$$**

(Map p82; ☏307-545-4999, 866-439-7375; dinner mains $13-22; ⏱6:30-10:30am, 11:30am-2:30pm & 4:30-10pm early May-early Oct) This buzzing dining room serves good-value steaks, salads and pasta, as well as breakfast, lunch and dinner buffets ($12/14/26). Interesting starters include trout cakes and antelope sausage, while dinner mains are heavier fare, with bison ravioli and the staff-recommended pork osso bucco (pork shank in red wine). Top it off with a Yellowstone sundae – huckleberry ice cream on cake topped with berries. The huge fireplace and wagon-wheel chandelier add to the rustic atmosphere. Make dinner reservations in the morning or, better, the day before (up to 60 days in advance) or you'll end up eating dinner after 9:30pm.

Obsidian Dining Room
AMERICAN **$$**

(Map p82; ☏307-344-7311; mains $13-30; ⏱6:30-10:30am & 5-10:30pm May-mid-Oct, mid-Dec-early Mar, lunch winter only) A quieter affair, the

dining room at the Old Faithful Snow Lodge serves up a few unexpected dishes (such as the house-made butternut squash bisque and the warm goat-cheese salad with maple pecans), alongside bison ribs braised in Moose Drool Ale (the bison are farmed outside the Yellowstone ecosystem). A breakfast buffet is available.

Old Faithful Lodge Cafeteria
CAFETERIA **$**

(Map p82; mains $8-12; ⏱11am-9pm mid-May–late Sep) It's factory-style functionality rather than fine cuisine, but this is a good-value place, churning out solid standards like meatloaf and prime rib alongside lighter fare like the chicken pesto wrap. Try to get here early before the buffet-style food gets too stewed. Most noteworthy are the views of Old Faithful from the side window. The cafeteria does not serve breakfast.

Geyser Grill
FAST FOOD **$**

(Map p82; sandwiches $4-7; ⏱8am-9pm mid-Apr–early Nov & mid-Dec–mid-Mar) Attached to the Snow Lodge, this is a fast-food place with burgers, breakfasts, fish and chips, bagels and beer. It closes early in shoulder season.

Bake Shop
FAST FOOD **$**

(Map p82; snacks $6; ⏱6:30am-10pm) For quick eats visit the Bake Shop in the lobby of the Old Faithful Lodge. It offers fried chicken, chili, pretzels and cinnamon rolls, and there's an ice-cream stand.

Bear Paw Deli
DELI **$**

(Map p82; snacks $7; ⏱10:30am-7:30pm) Just off the lobby of the Old Faithful Inn, the Bear Paw sells unappetizing prewrapped sandwiches, plus salads and ice cream. Look for the original etched cartoon murals on the wall, which date from 1936, when this room housed the hotel bar.

Yellowstone General Stores
FAST FOOD **$**

(Map p82; www.visityellowstonepark.com; mains $8; ⏱7:30am-8:30pm) The two general stores serve up snacks. The original knotted-pine Hamilton's Store near Old Faithful has a '50s-style diner counter, complete with original fountain stools, that serves up burgers, malts and sandwiches. The modern store near the Snow Lodge offers individual pizzas, paninis, salads, breakfast biscuits and prepackaged sandwiches in a cafeteria-style setting.

For postgeyser or après-ski cocktails, try the **Bear Pit Bar** (⏱from 11:30am) in the Old Faithful Inn or the **Firehole Lounge**

(❄winter) in the Old Faithful Snow Lodge, where the cozy fireside seats get snapped up quickly in winter.

Old Faithful **espresso cart** (⊙6:30am-10pm) serves the best coffee in the park.

Lake Country

TOP CHOICE Lake Yellowstone
Hotel Dining Room   AMERICAN **$$$**
(Map p72; ☑307-344-7311; breakfast buffet $14, mains $13-33; ⊙6:30-10am, 11:30am-2:30pm & 5pm-10pm late May-late Sep) Save your one un-wrinkled outfit to dine in style at the dining room of the Lake Yellowstone Hotel. Lunch options include Idaho trout, a fig and pro-scuitto salad and sandwiches. Dinner ups the ante with starters of steamed clams and mains of bison tenderloin and rack of lamb from Paradise Valley's Wolf Ridge estate. Al-ternatively, horrify the vegan wildlife-lovers in your family by ordering the bison, antelope and elk sliders. Dinner reservations are rec-ommended. The hotel's **deli** (sandwiches $6-9; ⊙6:30am-9pm mid-May–late Sep) offers break-fast pastries, wrapped sandwiches and soup.

Lake Lodge Cafeteria   CAFETERIA **$$**
(Map p72; dinner mains $11-15; ⊙6:30am-2:30pm & 4:30-10pm early Jun-early Oct) The nearby af-fordable rustic option offers hearty break-fasts and a limited range of pre-cooked family fare like prime rib, stuffed turkey and pastas, plus lighter wraps and salads.

Grant Village Dining Room   AMERICAN **$$**
(Map p72; ☑307-344-7311; breakfast buffet $12, dinner $17-27; ⊙6:30-10am, 11:30am-2:30pm & 5pm-10pm late May-early Oct) The smoky BBQ aroma emanating from this place could draw a band of grizzlies, who would doubt-less enjoy the house pecan-encrusted trout (but probably turn down the vegetarian qui-noa cakes). Lunch offers deli fare, including a bison meatloaf sandwich; dinners includes prime rib and a fancy mac 'n' cheese with four cheeses and add-on bacon and lobster. Dinner reservations are required; grab a stool at the tiny Seven Stool Saloon for a cold brew while you wait.

Lake House   CAFETERIA **$$**
(Map p72; mains $8-15; ⊙6:30-10:30am & 5-10:30pm mid-Jun–late Sep) This lakeshore spot offers build-a-burger combos, dinner salads and the best lake views in the park in a casual pub-style environment. Walk down

from the main parking area or marina to the lakeshore. It's closed for lunch.

Fishing Bridge Yellowstone
General Store   SNACK BAR **$**
(Map p72; mains $8; ⊙7:30am-8:30pm) This branch of the parkwide general stores has coffee, blueberry pancakes, fish sandwiches and root-beer floats served up at a fun retro soda-fountain counter.

Lake Yellowstone
General Store   SNACK BAR **$**
(Map p72; mains $8; ⊙7:30am-8:30pm) The branch behind the Yellowstone Lake Hotel dates back 90 years and has a similarly fun soda-fountain feel, down to the period 1938 counter stools. The simple food includes paninis, chili and nachos.

Grab a pre-dinner microbrew or glass of wine in the Lake Hotel lobby while lis-tening to the piano or snuggling up by the fireside. Sipping something from the lobby bar of Lake Lodge while watching the lake from on the porchside rockers is another highlight.

SHOPPING

The nonprofit **Yellowstone Association** (www.yellowstoneassociation.org) operates book-stores at the park's visitor centers and infor-mation stations, and at Norris Geyser Basin. Hiking maps and guidebooks are usually available. Members get a 15% discount.

INFORMATION

Medical Services

There are clinics at Mammoth, Old Faithful and Lake Village – see p271.

Money

There are 24-hour ATMs at Canyon Lodge, Can-yon General Store, Fishing Bridge General Store, Grant Village General Store, Lake Yellowstone Hotel, Old Faithful Inn, Old Faithful General Store, Old Faithful Snow Lodge, Mammoth Gen-eral Store and Mammoth Hot Springs Hotel.

Post Offices

The only year-round post office is at Mammoth. Seasonal post offices operate at Canyon, Lake Village, Grant Village and Old Faithful.

Showers & Laundry

Canyon Village, Fishing Bridge RV Park and Grant Village provide laundry (7am to 10pm; $1.50 per load) and showers (7am to 1:30pm and 3pm to 10pm; $3.25, plus $1 for a towel). Old Faithful Lodge, Mammoth Hot Springs Hotel and Roosevelt Lodge offer showers only, and Lake Lodge and Old Faithful Snow Lodge have laundry only. All facilities close in winter.

Tourist Information

Yellowstone's visitor centers and information stations are usually open 9am to 6pm, with extended hours from 8am to 7pm in summer. Most are closed or open reduced hours Labor Day to Memorial Day; the Albright Visitor Center in Mammoth is open year-round, and the Old Faithful Visitor Center is open in winter. Check the park newspaper for current hours of operation.

The park produces a series of informative pamphlets (50¢) on Yellowstone's main attractions; these are available at visitor centers and in weatherproof boxes at the sites.

Albright Visitor Center (Map p58; ☎307-344-2263) Open year-round, with videos and displays on park history.

Canyon Visitor Center (Map p68; ☎307-242-2550; ☺8am-8pm late May–mid-Oct) Has a backcountry office and displays on Yellowstone geology.

Fishing Bridge Visitor Center (Map p72; ☎307-242-2450; ☺8am-7pm late May-late Sep) Has bird exhibits.

Grant Village Visitor Center (Map p72; ☎307-242-2650; ☺8am-7pm late May-late Sep) Has exhibits on wildfires.

Madison Junior Ranger Station (Map p80; ☺early Jun-late Sep)

Old Faithful Visitor Center (Map p80; ☎307-545-2750; ☺8am-8pm late Apr-early Nov & mid-Dec–mid-Mar) New LEED-certified center opened in 2011. Videos and geyser predictions.

Ranger Stations (☺8am-4:30pm) At Grant Village, Lake Village, Lewis Lake, Bechler, Canyon, Mammoth, Bridge Bay, Tower Junction, Old Faithful, Madison, Lamar Valley, and the West and South Entrances.

West Thumb Information Station (Map p72; ☎9am-5pm late May-late Sep)

West Yellowstone Visitor Information Center (Map p168; ☺mid-Apr-early Nov & mid-Dec–mid-Mar) In the Chamber of Commerce in West Yellowstone.

Yellowstone National Park headquarters (☎307-344-7381; www.nps.gov/yell; ☺9am-6pm) At Fort Yellowstone in Mammoth Hot Springs. Most of the park's brochures are downloadable from its website.

GETTING AROUND

Unless you're part of a guided bus tour, the only way to get around is to drive. There is no public transportation within Yellowstone National Park, except for a few ski-drop services during winter.

Driving

The speed limit in most of the park is 45mph, dropping to 25mph at busy turnouts or junctions. In the words of writer Tim Cahill, anything faster than this is 'both illegal and silly.'

Gas and diesel are available at most junctions. Stations at Old Faithful and Canyon are open whenever the park is open to vehicles. The Roosevelt station closes at the beginning of September, Fishing Bridge in mid-September, Grant Village in late September and Mammoth in early October. Stations are manned from around 8am to 7pm and offer 24-hour credit-card service at the pump.

Towing and repair services and basic car parts are available at Conoco stations in **Old Faithful** (☺mid-Apr–early Nov), **Grant Village** (☺late May–mid-Sep), **Fishing Bridge** (☺late May-early Sep) and **Canyon** (☎breakdown service 307-242-7644; ☺May-early Oct).

Dial ☎307-344-2114 to check road and weather conditions prior to your visit, as road construction, rock or mudslides and snow can close park entrances and roads at any time.

Organized Tours

Xanterra (☎307-344-7311; www.yellowstone nationalparklodges.com) runs a slew of daily tours, all of which offer discounts for children aged 12 to 16 and are free for kids under 12:

Across the Northern Range (☺Jun–mid-Sep) Full-day trip departs Bridge Bay Campground, Lake Yellowstone Hotel and Fishing Bridge RV Park (adult/child 12 to 16 years $60/30) or Canyon Lodge ($54/27) and takes in the upper loop, including Mammoth and Norris.

Circle of Fire (adult/12-16yr $66/33; ☺mid-May–mid-Sep) Eight-hour tour departs Old Faithful Inn, Grant Village, Lake Yellowstone Hotel, Fishing Bridge RV Park, Canyon Lodge and Bridge Bay Campground and takes in the lower loop, including the geyser basins and Canyon.

Lamar Valley wildlife excursions (☺mid-Jun–mid-Aug) A less grueling half-day trip departs in the afternoon from Mammoth Hot Springs Hotel and Canyon Lodge (four hours, adult/child 12 to 16 years $63/31.50) and early in the morning from Canyon, Mammoth and Roosevelt (five hours, $78.50/39.25).

Photo safaris ($85) Early-morning trips depart daily from Lake Hotel and Old Faithful Inn.

Sunset tours (adult/12-16yr $34/17; ☺Jun-late Sep) Daily two-hour tour from Lake Yellowstone Hotel and Fishing Bridge RV Park along Lake Yellowstone's north shore to the Lake Butte Overlook.

Yellowstone in a Day (☺Jun–mid-Sep) Ambitious eight-hour trip departs from Gardiner (adult/12 to 16 years $73/36.50), Mammoth Hot Springs and Old Faithful ($71/35.50) twice a week.

There are dozens of other tours, ranging from daily tours of the Tetons to hour-long local tours that don't require reservations. Most of these tours are on the wonderful Old Yellow Buses, a refurbished fleet of classic convertible 19-seater touring cars that plied the park's roads between 1936 and 1956, only to return to the park in 2007. They are guaranteed to add a touch of class to your sightseeing. See the 'Things to Do' section of www.yellowstonenationalparklodges.com for details on all Xanterra tours.

Around Yellowstone

Best Places to Stay

» The Murray Hotel (p151)
» Chamberlin Inn (p147)
» Rainbow Ranch Lodge (p165)
» Chico Hot Springs (p152)
» 320 Ranch (p164)

Best Places to Eat

» Paradise Valley Grill (p154)
» John Bozeman's Bistro (p160)
» 2nd St Bistro (p151)
» Sydney's Mountain Bistro (p171)
» Log Cabin Café (p144)

Why Go?

The 43,750-sq-mile Greater Yellowstone Ecosystem doesn't suddenly end at the park fence. Enveloping the park kernel is a protective cushion of national forests and wilderness areas that offer almost as much scenic splendor as the parks themselves, but without the crowds and the pesky permits. Try to allocate at least a few days to explore this exceptional area.

Latched onto Yellowstone Park's northern boundaries, the three gateway towns of Gardiner, West Yellowstone and Cooke City serve as acceptable visitor hubs, good for a bed and a bite to eat, but it's the four corridors that radiate out from the park that offer the real scenic draws. Plan your itinerary to combine the stunning Beartooth and Gallatin routes, or the Beartooth, Wapiti and Chief Joseph Scenic Hwy via the Wild West town of Cody, and you have the ultimate add-on to a classic Yellowstone trip.

When to Go
West Yellowstone, MT

September
Warm days, clear skies and no crowds; hikers should watch for hunters

July & August
Great for hiking, rafting and rodeo; blistering temperatures in Billings and Cody

December–March
Fantastic skiing in Big Sky and snowmobiling in West Yellowstone

BEARTOOTH ROUTE

Billings

🎵 406 / POP 105,000 / ELEV 3300FT

Montana's largest city has far more in common with the dusty plains of eastern Montana than the much-celebrated Rocky Mountain scenery out to the west of the state. It shouldn't be a priority stop off on your Yellowstone itinerary, but it is not such a bad place to stay for a night before heading out to the park or catching your flight back home.

Around Yellowstone Highlights

① Grip the steering wheel extra tight as you climb the spaghetti loops of the **Beartooth Highway** (p139), America's most scenic road

② Blow off some steam at the night rodeo after exploring the Wild West at the Buffalo Bill Historical Center in **Cody** (p144)

③ Suck down an extra-large chocolate malt at the

Red Box Car after a hike in the mountains around **Red Lodge** (p136)

④ Stare open-mouthed into the open jaws of a T Rex at Bozeman's **Museum of the Rockies** (p158)

⑤ Hit the slopes at stylish **Big Sky** (p162), site of the region's biggest downhill runs

⑥ Mosey through the lovely **Paradise Valley** (p151), home to ranchers, movie stars and plenty of hungry trout

⑦ Enjoy some of the best cross-country skiing and snowmobiling in the country in **West Yellowstone** (p167)

⑧ Hit the hiking trails, take on some white-water rafting or ride horses at a ranch stay in the **Gallatin Valley** (p162)

CUSTER'S LAST STAND

The best Billings day trip is to **Little Bighorn Battlefield** (☏406-638-3204; www.nps.gov/libi; per vehicle $10; ⊗8am-9pm, earlier closing outside of summer), the site of Custer's Last Stand, just an hour's drive (65 miles) east of town. You can drive around the battle sites or, better, take a short local tour in the company of a Crow guide with **Absalooke Tours** (☏406-38-3114).

If you're here for the last weekend of June, visit for the **Custer's Last Stand Re-enactment** (☏406-665-3577; www.custerslaststand.org; adult/child $20/8), 6 miles west of Hardin. Pack your handlebar moustache and you can even attend the weekend ball; only those dressed in 1876 attire are allowed in!

On the way back history buffs can pop into **Pompey's Pillar National Monument** (www.pompeyspillar.org; per vehicle $7; ⊗8am-8pm), home to the engraved 1806 signature of William Clark and the only physical evidence remaining of Lewis and Clark's famed transcontinental journey.

Ernest Hemingway brought some excitement to Billings in November 1930 when he crashed his car on the way home from Yellowstone National Park. Hemingway broke his right arm and had to spend seven weeks in the town's St Vincent's Hospital.

Sights

Western Heritage Center　　　MUSEUM
(☏406-256-6809; www.ywhc.org; 2822 Montana Ave; adult/senior & child $5/3; ⊗10am-5pm Tue-Sat) If you have time in Billings, explore the changing exhibits and excellent artifact collection here, representing the various cultural traditions of Yellowstone Valley.

Yellowstone Art Museum　　　GALLERY
(☏406-256-6804; www.artmuseum.org; 401 N 27th St; adult/child $5/3; ⊗10am-5pm Tue, Wed & Sat, 10am-8pm Thu & Fri, 11am-4pm Sun) Combining a collection of Western art with visiting exhibitions, this museum is on the site of the 1916 Yellowstone County Jail.

The Rims　　　SCENIC DRIVE
Drive up Otters Dr from near the Heights to near the airport, for a fine overview of the city and as far as the distant Beartooth Mountains, and to visit the grave of Yellowstone Kelly, an early scout and guide.

Sleeping

Billings KOA　　　CAMPGROUND $
(☏406-252-3104; www.billingskoa.com; tent/RV sites from $36/40, cabins from $75; ⊗mid-Apr–mid-Oct; ❄✹❄) America's first KOA campground is in a scenic spot by the Yellowstone River, 0.5 miles south of I-90, not far from downtown.

Dude Rancher Lodge　　　MOTEL $
(☏800-221-3302; www.duderancherlodge.com; 415 N 29th St; d from $85; ❄) Groovy ranch oak furniture dating back to the 1940s makes this a character-filled choice if you prefer nostalgia over new-car-smell cleanliness.

Riversage Billings Inn　　　MOTEL $
(☏800-231-7782; www.billingsinn.com; 880 N 29th St; r $75-80; ❄✹) Most rooms here are well run and updated to include a microwave, refrigerator and breakfast.

Josephine's Bed & Breakfast　　　B&B $$
(☏406-248-5898; www.thejosephine.com; 514 N 29th St; r incl breakfast $95-115, ste $135-170; @❄) For those who prefer a more convivial experience, this B&B is down-home and attentive. All five rooms come with private bathroom.

Crowne Plaza　　　HOTEL $$
(☏406-252-7400; www.crowneplaza.com; 27 N 27th St; d from $152; ❄) The city's prime address and tallest building is right in the heart of downtown, built with two million bricks.

Cherry Tree Inn　　　MOTEL $
(☏800-237-5882; www.billingscherrytreeinn.com; 823 N Broadway; r $55; ❄✹) A good-value place to stay.

Rimview Inn　　　MOTEL $
(☏406-248-2622; www.rimviewinn.com; 1025 N 27th St; r $69-84; @❄✹) Quiet, with free airport shuttle.

Eating & Drinking

Some locals claim that **The Rex** (www.therexbillings.com; 2401 Montana Ave; mains $14-32) serves the best steak in town, while others only eat beef at Jake's (www.jakesbillings.com; 2701 1st Ave N; mains $14-32).

For information on Billings' microbreweries see the boxed text p161.

TOP CHOICE **Walkers Grill** AMERICAN $$
(☑406-245-9291; www.walkersgrill.com; 2700 1st Ave N; tapas $8-14, mains $17-33; ☺5-10pm) The classiest place in town offers grill and tapas menus, Sunday jazz and sophisticated Western decor.

McCormick Café BREAKFAST, SANDWICHES $
(www.mccormickcafe.com; 2419 Montana Ave; mains $8; ☺7am-3pm Mon-Fri, 8am-3pm Sat, 8am-1pm Sun; @🛜) For espresso, granola breakfasts, French-style crepes, good sandwiches and a lively atmosphere, stop by this downtown favorite.

Café De Camp AMERICAN $
(☑406-256-7285; www.cafedecamp.com; 1404 6th Ave N; mains $6-14; ☺11am-2pm & 5.30-9pm Tue-Sat) There's a strong focus on fresh locally sourced food at this tiny hard-to-find little cafe. The lamb and bison dishes are particularly good, and there's a fine selection of crepes. It's about 10 blocks northeast of downtown in an industrial area.

Caramel Cookie Waffles EUROPEAN $
(www.caramelcookiewaffles.com; 1707 17th St W; mains $5; ☺7am-5pm Tue-Sat; 🛜) Better known as the Dutch Brothers, this place bustles at lunch with superb soups, European pastries and the eponymous *stroopwafels*. It's worth arranging your entire Yellowstone itinerary around the weekly seafood bisque.

Entertainment

Alberta Bair Theater THEATER
(www.albertabairtheater.org; 2801 3rd Ave N) A magnet for all of eastern Montana, this is Billings' cultural jewel, with productions ranging from world music to symphony concerts.

Information

Base Camp (www.thebasecamp.com; 1730 Grand Ave) The place for last-minute outdoor gear, topo maps and that lost widget for your stove.

Billings Visitor Center (☑406-245-4111, 800-735-2635; www.itsinbillings.com, http://billing scvb.visitmt.com; 815 S 27th St) Can help with hotel reservations. See also www.downtownbill ings.com and www.billingsguide.com.

Custer National Forest (☑406-657-6200; www.fs.fed.us/r1/custer; 1310 Main St) Information on the Beartooth Mountains.

Red Lodge
☑406 / POP 2280 / ELEV 5555FT

A charming historic mining town lined with fun bars, restaurants, interesting shops and art galleries, and with great hiking, camping and skiing nearby, Red Lodge is the kickoff point for the scenic Beartooth Hwy and well worth a stop in its own right. The town gets its name from the painted red tepees of local Crow (Absaroka) Indians.

The early town grew up so quickly around the coal mines that by 1910 the town's largely immigrant population was twice the size it is today. The hard-drinking, fist-fighting, bootlegging town must have been pretty rough-edged to have required one Jeremiah 'Liver-Eating' Johnson as its first constable, but this was perhaps spurred more by the 1897 attempted robbery of the central bank by Butch Cassidy's partner, the Sundance Kid. Most of the mines were closed by 1932, after years of depression and mine disasters, but the Beartooth Hwy opened four years later, just in time.

Red Lodge celebrates its cosmopolitan early Scottish, Scandinavian and Slavic mining population in the annual **Festival of Nationals** (www.festivalofnations.us) in August.

On the west bank of Rock Creek, Red Lodge is 60 miles south of Billings and 65 miles northeast of Cooke City and the north entrance to Yellowstone National Park. US 212 runs north–south through town as Broadway Ave, the main street, and becomes the Beartooth Hwy south of town.

Sights

Carbon County Museum MUSEUM
(☑406-446-3667; www.carboncountyhistory.com; 224 N Broadway; adult/student $5/3; ☺10am-6pm Mon-Sat, 11am-3pm Sun, closed Sun & Mon winter) Antique guns and mining disasters dominate the exhibits here, but it's the 1912 Model T Ford, Yellowstone stagecoach and horrifying early electroshock machine that really grab the attention. Check out the antique Yellowstone buses in the garage a couple of blocks north.

Beartooth Nature Center ZOO
(☑406-446-1133; www.beartoothnaturecenter.org; 615 2nd St E; adult/child $6/2.50; ☺10am-5pm May-Sep, 10am-2pm Oct-Apr; 🎫) Families will

love this nonprofit refuge for 71 animals that can't be returned to the wild, including bears, cougars, wolves, eagles, a lynx and a very vocal sandhill crane (called Niles).

FREE **Carbon County Arts**
Guild Gallery GALLERY
(✏406-446-1370; www.carboncountydepotgallery. org; 11 West 8th St; ◷10am-5pm Tue-Sat) The old railroad depot on Eighth St, one block west of Broadway Ave, is where local artists exhibit painting, sculpture and mixed media.

Montana Candy Emporium HISTORIC BUILDING
(7 S Broadway; ♿) If you are old enough to remember cowtails and bubblegum cigarettes, or simply have a sweet tooth for taffy and chocolate truffles, you'll love this old-style candy store. It's worth setting aside a few hours for browsing the other shops and galleries along Broadway Ave.

Activities

Hiking
A mile south of Red Lodge, just north of the Beartooth Ranger District Office, West Fork Rd turns southwest off US 212 and continues for a bumpy 12 miles up West Fork Creek. Trailheads along the road offer good hikes, including the **Timberline Lake Trail**, (4½ miles, elevation gain 2000ft) and **Basin Lakes National Recreation Trail** (trail 61, 7.4 miles return, elevation gain 2000ft). Much of the upper valley was scarred by wildfires in 2008. Nearby **Wild Bill Lake** is a wheelchair-accessible trail to a lake with accessible fishing. The valley has two USFS campgrounds: Basin and Cascade.

A rugged option further south is the short but strenuous 3.2-mile return trail to **Glacier Lake**, hidden high up in a glacial valley. Hikers have the option of continuing another mile to Little Glacier and Emerald Lakes. Glacier Lake is clearly visible from the Beartooth Hwy. The trailhead is 8 miles southwest of Limber Pine Campground on rough gravel Rock Creek Rd (Forestry Rd No 421). You need fairly high clearage to attempt this road.

The **Lake Fork Trail** accessed from the end of Lake Fork Rd (turn off right about 2 miles before Parkside Campground) offers excellent longer day hikes to Lost Lake (5 miles one way) and 1.5 miles further to Keyser Brown Lake.

For a rugged overnighter or three-day trek, continue over the 11,037 ft **Sundance Pass** into the upper West Fork Valley (21 miles). The pass is only open from mid-July and you'll need to arrange a car shuttle between the two valleys.

Winter Sports
Red Lodge Mountain SNOW SPORTS
(✏800-444-8977, ski reports 406-446-2610; www. redlodgemountain.com; lifts adult $49, child $19-42; ◷end Nov-early Apr) Six miles southwest of downtown, Red Lodge Mountain has a 2400ft vertical drop, serviced by eight lifts. A higher base elevation (7400ft) than any other Montana ski hill, it has some of the state's best spring skiing, particularly during the higher temperatures and longer days of February and March. Full rentals and instruction packages are available, as are guided snowshoe trips.

Red Lodge Nordic Center NORDIC SKIING
(✏406-425-1070; www.beartoothtrails.org; trail fee adult/child $5/3) Two miles northwest of Red Lodge on Hwy 78, this is Red Lodge's top cross-country resource and a good place for beginners. See the website for other local trails.

Sleeping
South of Red Lodge on US 212 are 10 USFS **campgrounds** (sites $15, plus $8 for 2nd vehicle), open May to September. The nearest are small **Sheridan** and **Rattin**, 6 miles and 8 miles from Red Lodge and on the east side of the road. A little further, and with shady creekside locations, are the nicer **Parkside**, **Limber Pine** and **Greenough Lake** campgrounds. All are run by the concessionaire Gallatin Canyon Campgrounds and are reservable through **Recreation.gov** (✏877-444-6777; www.recreation.gov). There's also lots of primitive camping nearby.

Yodeler Motel MOTEL $$
(✏406-446-1435; www.yodelermotel.com; 601 S Broadway Ave; d $89-135; ✆✉) A retro Swiss lodge theme livens up this friendly '60s-era hotel, down to the in-room wet steam showers and ski waxing room. The spacious upper-level rooms with porches are roomier and brighter than the cheaper basement options, with discounts common outside July and August. It's on the corner of 17th St.

Pollard HISTORIC HOTEL $$
(✏406-446-0001; www.thepollard.net; 2 N Broadway Ave; d incl breakfast $95-200, ste $270-295; ✆) Red Lodge's first brick building, dating from 1893, makes for a fun and elegant place to stay, even if you're paying more for the history than the

WACKY RACES

Southeast Montana is a proud home to some of the state's more surreal sports. In March Red Lodge hosts the national **ski-joring finals**, a not-quite-yet Olympic sport that involves a horse towing a skier around an oval speed track. It's like water skiing. On snow. Except with a horse.

Equally silly is the annual **Running of the Sheep** at nearby Reed Point. Inspired by Pamplona's much more impressive Running of the Bulls, the significantly less dangerous herd of sheep thunder down six blocks of Main St every year during the first weekend in September.

Finally, summer weekend evenings (Thursday to Sunday) see hi-octane **pig racing** at the Bear Creek Saloon (☑406-446-3481), 7 miles east of Red Lodge on Hwy 308. Make a bet, urge your porker over the finish line and round off the evening with a bacon sandwich. Proceeds go to charity.

quality of room. The cozy lobby and restaurant are hubs of local activity.

Rock Creek Resort RESORT $$
(☑406-446-1111; www.rockcreekresort.com; d $125-185, ste $210-290; @☏≋) Red Lodge's most upscale accommodation has rooms, condos, suites and a decent restaurant at a quiet creekside location, 4.5 miles south of town off US 212.

Eating

TOP CHOICE Red Box Car BURGERS $
(1300 S Broadway; burgers $4; ☺May-Sep; ☝) Without doubt the Yellowstone region's best fast food is served out of a century-old railroad car at the south end of town. The malts and homemade onion rings are unbeatable.

Bridge Creek Backcountry
Kitchen & Wine Bar AMERICAN $$
(☑406-446-9900; www.eatfooddrinkwine.com; 116 S Broadway; lunch mains $7-14, dinner $17-33; ☺closed Sun & Mon Labor Day-Memorial Day) Fresh mountain cuisine complements the modern bistro vibe here. Daily specials and a huckleberry salad join the three esses for lunch (soup, salad and sandwiches) and dinner is heavier fare, with wine suggestions tailored to each dish.

Café Regis BREAKFAST $
(www.caferegis.com; cnr 16th & Word; mains $7; ☺6am-2pm Tue-Sun) Locals know this as the best breakfast in town, with good-value blue-plate lunch specials and very pleasant garden seating.

Pollard Dining Room AMERICAN $$$
(☑406-446-0001; mains $21-32) This romantic restaurant at the Pollard Hotel has won na-

tional acclaim for its wine list, fresh fish and bison rib eye, and is the place to splash out.

Drinking

Natali's Front Bar BAR
(www.thepizzaco.com; 115 S Broadway; ☺until 11pm) Grab a pail of peanuts and choose from the many local microbrews on tap at this cool wooden bar. You can order in pizza rolls from next-door Red Lodge Pizza or steaks and mussels from the top-quality Carbon County Steakhouse.

Red Lodge Ales BREWERY
(☑406-446-4607; www.redlodgeales.net; 1445 N Broadway Ave; ☺11am-9pm; ☝) Sam's Tap Room lost some of its funkiness when it relocated to roomier, more family friendly digs north of town, but at least there's outdoor seating now. Order the beer sampler ($3.75) to taste the six most popular brews, including our favorite, the grapefruit-infused Bent Nail IPA. Call in advance for a free brewery tour.

Information

Coffee Factory Roasters (☑406-446-3200; 6-1/2 S Broadway; ☝) Free wi-fi with your latte.
Red Lodge Area Chamber of Commerce/ Visitor Center (☑888-281-0625; www.red lodge.com; 601 N Broadway Ave; ☺8am-6pm Mon-Fri, 9am-5pm Sat & Sun) On the north edge of town, with an RV dump station and road condition information for the Beartooth Hwy. Check out 'Liver-Eating' Johnston's former cabin just outside.
Red Lodge Books (☑406-446-2742; www. redlodgebooks.com; 11 N Broadway) Stocks USGS topo maps, and has a tea bar.
Sylvan Peak (☑406-446-1770; 9 S Broadway) Topo maps, outdoor gear and winter rentals.

Beartooth Highway

The breathtaking Beartooth Hwy (US 212) connects Red Lodge to Cooke City and Yellowstone's northeast entrance along a soaring 68-mile road built in 1932. An engineering feat, and the 'most beautiful drive in America' according to the late journalist Charles Kuralt, this 'all-American' road is a destination in its own right and easily the most dramatic route into Yellowstone National Park. Motorbikers in particular love the road, arriving en masse for the Sturgis-like Beartooth Rally in July.

Covering 1474 sq miles, the Absaroka-Beartooth Wilderness stretches along Montana's border with Wyoming (a small section on its east side lies inside Wyoming) and crosses through Gallatin, Custer and Shoshone National Forests, taking in two distinct mountain ranges: the Absarokas and the Beartooth Plateau (the Beartooths). Steep, forested valleys and craggy peaks characterize the Absarokas, while the Beartooths are essentially a high plateau of uplifted three-billion-year-old granite (some of the oldest rock in North America) dotted with more than 1000 lakes and tarns. Together they constitute the most visited wilderness area in the nation.

Most of the wilderness consists of high plateau above 10,000ft. Alpine tundra vegetation is the only thing that grows up here (where snow can last from October to mid-July), lending the landscape a desolate, otherworldly look. In fact, unless you are an outdoorsy type who makes frequent forays above 10,000ft, it probably *is* another world – you can't usually reach this kind of terrain by car. To really experience the surroundings, you must get out of the car, even if it's just for a few minutes, to suck in the thin, cold air.

The highway has a short driving season and is usually closed between mid-October and late May. For information on weather conditions, hikes and bear sightings pull into the **Beartooth Ranger District office** (406-446-2103), just south of Red Lodge on Hwy 212. There's gas at Red Lodge, Cooke City and, less reliably, along the highway at the Top of the World store. For more details see www.beartoothhighway.com and www.beartoothhighway.net.

The political landscape of the highway is as convoluted as the landscape. The highway starts and ends in Montana but dips into Wyoming en route. If you are fishing, you'll need to know exactly where you are so that you have the correct state fishing license.

If you fancy cycling down the Beartooth Hwy, **Beartooth Bike Tours** (406-426-0787; www.beartoothbiketours.com) in Red Lodge will drive you to the top of the Beartooth Plateau and let you coast the 14 miles back to Red Lodge, soaking in the stunning scenery as you roll. The $50 fee includes transfer, bike and helmet.

🚗 Beartooth Highway Drive

Route Red Lodge to Cooke City

Distance 68 miles (3 hours)

Speed Limit Officially 70 mph, but more like 35mph

Summary From its starting point at Red Lodge, the highway climbs Rock Creek Canyon's glaciated valley before dramatically ascending the valley wall via a series of spaghetti-loop switchbacks, gaining an amazing 5000ft in elevation in just a few miles.

A parking area at **Rock Creek Vista Point Overlook** (9160ft), 20 miles from Red Lodge, has toilets and a short walk (wheelchair accessible) to superb views. The road continues up onto the high plateau, past 'Mae West Curve' and into Wyoming.

In another 7 miles the road passes **Twin Lakes**, where a parking area offers good views of the cirque and the ski lift that carries the daring to an extreme spring ski run, established by Austrians in the 1960s. Another 1.3 miles further below the road is **Gardner Lake**. After 0.7 miles, at the start of a series of switchbacks, look northwest across Rock Creek for views of the Hellroaring Plateau and the jagged **Bear's Tooth** (11,612ft; 'Na Piet Say' in the local Crow language), which lends the range its name. A mile later you'll crest the **Beartooth Pass West Summit**, the highest point at 10,947ft. You'll likely pass 15ft-deep snowbanks here as late as June (even July some years).

From this halfway point the road descends past Frozen Lake, Long Lake, Little Bear Lake (the last two with excellent fishing) and then the Chain Lakes (on the left) to the Island Lake and Beartooth Lake Campgrounds. Both offer excellent opportunities for a picnic, day hike or a canoe paddle. Between the campgrounds is the **Top of the World Store** (www.topoftheworldresort.com),

AROUND YELLOWSTONE BEARTOOTH ROUTE

Beartooth Highway

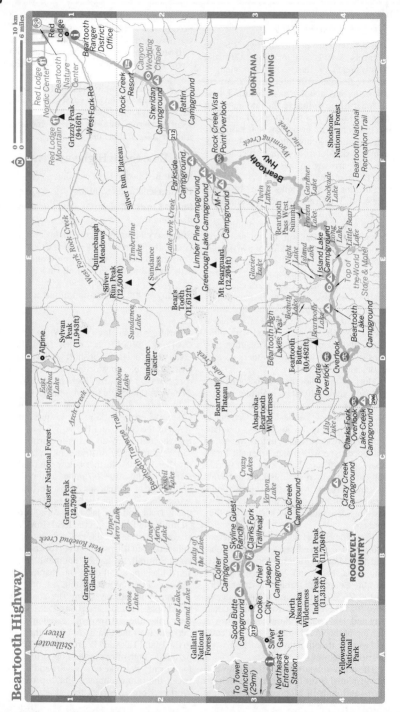

Red Lodge

Red Lodge Nordic Center

Beartooth Nature Center

Red Lodge Mountain

Grizzly Peak (9416ft)

West Fork Rd

Beartooth Ranger District Office

Canyon Wedding Chapel

Rock Creek Resort

Sheridan Campground

Rattin Campground

Rock Creek Vista Point Overlook

Silver Run Plateau

Parkside Campground

M-K Campground

Quinnebaugh Meadows

Limber Pine Campground

Greenough Lake Campground

Mt Rearguard (12,204ft)

Beartooth Hwy

MONTANA

WYOMING

Wyoming Creek

Line Creek

Shoshone National Forest

Beartooth National Recreation Trail

Gardner Lake

Stockade Lake

Beartooth Pass West Summit

Twin Lakes

Frozen Lake

Long Lake

Timberline Lake

Silver Run Peak (12,500ft)

Sundance Pass

Bear's Tooth (11,612ft)

Glacier Lake

Night Lake

Island Lake

Island Lake Campground

Top of theWorld Store & Motel

Sylvan Peak (11,943ft)

Alpine

Sundance Lake

Sundance Glacier

Beartooth Plateau

Beartooth High Lakes Trail

Beauty Lakes

Beartooth Lake

Beartooth Lake Campground

Little Bear Lake

Lake Fork Creek

West Fork Rock Creek

Custer National Forest

Granite Peak (12,799ft)

Grasshopper Glacier

West Rosebud Creek

Upper Aero Lake

Lower Aero Lake

Beartooth Traverse Trail

Fossil Lake

Arch Creek

Rainbow Lake

Lake Creek

Absaroka-Beartooth Wilderness

Beartooth Butte (10,482ft)

Clay Butte Overlook

Beartooth Overlook

Clarks Fork Overlook

Lake Creek Campground

East Rosebud Lake

Crazy Lakes

Vernon Lake

Lily Lake

Crazy Creek Campground

Gallatin National Forest

Stillwater River

Goose Lake

Long Lake

Round Lake

Lady of the Lake

Colter Campground

Skyline Guest Ranch

Clarks Fork Trailhead

Fox Creek Campground

Chief Joseph Campground

Pilot Peak (11,708ft)

Index Peak (11,313ft)

ROOSEVELT COUNTRY

Soda Butte Campground

Cooke City

Silver Gate

North Absaroka Wilderness

Cooke Campground

Northeast Entrance Station

To Tower Junction (29mi)

Yellowstone National Park

which offers a reviving coffee (and a fishing license if you need one).

As the road descends, you'll see **Beartooth Butte**, a huge lump of the sedimentary rock that once covered the Beartooths. Two miles beyond Beartooth Lake Campground, 42 miles from Red Lodge, turn right up a 2.5-mile dirt road to the former fire watchtower at **Clay Butte Overlook** (open July and August; no RVs or trailers). The views from here are fantastic: look for the effects of the 1988 Clover Mist fire and the 'Reef', a snaking line of sedimentary rock that follows the entire valley, prooving that this lofty region was once underwater.

Back on the main road a mile further on is an **overlook** offering views of Index Peak (11,313ft) and jagged Pilot Peak (11,708ft). Next up is the **Clarks Fork Overlook** (with toilets) and then a small turnout by Lake Creek Falls. Less than a mile from here, forestry road 130-1 leads 2 miles north to secluded **Lily Lake**, where you'll find a canoe ramp, good fishing and several free primitive campsites.

The turnoff left is for Chief Joseph Scenic Hwy, which leads 62 miles to Cody and accesses Yellowstone's east entrance via the Wapiti Valley. The Beartooth Hwy descends to several excellent fishing areas on the Clarks Fork and reenters Montana. Opposite Chief Joseph Campground is **Clarks Fork Trailhead**, a fine place for a picnic, a day hike and a look at the flume of the former mining power station. From here it's 4 miles to Cooke City, via the almost imperceptible Colter Pass (8066ft).

Hiking & Backpacking

You can gain about 4000ft of elevation by car and begin your hike right from the Beartooth Hwy, but it's important to allow some time to acclimatize. Also be aware that the barren terrain offers little shade, shelter or wood. In order to protect the fragile alpine vegetation, hikers should not light campfires above the tree line. Grizzly and black bears are not that common in the higher elevations; hikers have a better chance of seeing bighorn sheep, mountain goats or elk.

August is the best month to hike the Beartooths. Snow remains in many places above tree line at least until the end of July and starts to accumulate again after mid-September. Localized afternoon thunderstorms, with hail, are common in the Beartooths during June (the wettest month) and July.

During early summer, you'll also need lots of bug repellent and waterproof shoes to cope with swampy trails. Don't be put off; just be forewarned. With proper preparation, the plateau offers some of Greater Yellowstone's very best hiking.

From Island Lake Campground you can take a wonderful and easy hour-long stroll along the **Beartooth High Lakes Trail** (trail 620) to Island Lake and beyond to Night Lake and Flake Lake. All lakes are popular fishing areas. If you can arrange a shuttle, continue downhill to Beauty Lake and then left (south) to Beartooth Lake for a fine half-day hike.

From Beartooth Lake Campground you can make a wonderful half-day 8-mile loop via **Beauty Lake**. Head up Beartooth Creek (trail 619) and then bear right, passing five lakes, including Claw Lake (trail 620), to the junction with the Beartooth High Lakes Trail. From here descend right past Beauty Lake (trail No 621) back to Beartooth Lake. Parking is limited at the trailhead.

A longer, preferably overnight, option is the 11-mile **Beartooth National Recreation Trail** (trail 613) loop hike accessed from the highway at Gardner Lake. The trail drops from the lake and loops around Tibbs Butte, initially along Little Rock Creek, past turnoffs to Deep Lake, Camp Sawtooth and Dollar Lake to arrive at Stockade Lake, a fine campsite. From here, continue around the loop past Losecamp Lake back to Gardner Lake, or cut east from Losecamp Lake for 3 miles past Hauser Lake to the Beartooth Hwy by a pullout overlooking Long Lake (this requires a shuttle).

Another easy day hike is the 6-mile return ramble to **Rock Island Lake**, which begins from the Clarks Fork Trailhead, about 4 miles east of Cooke City and across from the Chief Joseph Campground. After about 15 minutes be careful to continue along Russell Creek Trail (trail 567) and *not* turn left along Broadwater Trail. The trail brushes Kersey Lake and branches right up to Rock Island Lake. An alternative hike branches right 1.3 miles from the trailhead up to Vernon Lake (trail 565).

The Clarks Fork Trailhead is also the start of the exciting multiday **Beartooth Traverse** that runs along Russell Creek Trail to Fossil Lake and then across plateau trail 15 to Rosebud Lake (shuttle required). You need to be fairly experienced for this remote wilderness trek.

The contoured 1:100,000 *Absaroka Beartooth Wilderness* map by Beartooth Publishing and the USFS 1:63,360 *Absaroka Beartooth Wilderness* map are both excellent. *Hiking the Absaroka-Beartooth Wilderness* and *Easy Day Hikes in the Beartooths,* both published by Falcon Press and written by Bill Schneider, are also useful resources.

Sleeping

There are 13 basic USFS campgrounds along the Beartooth Hwy between Red Lodge and Cooke City. **Island Lake** (20 sites, $10) and **Beartooth Lake** (21 sites, $15) – both open July to mid-September – are up on the high plateau, the latter has a boat launch. Further west are **Crazy Creek** (16 sites, $10) and **Fox Creek** (34 sites, $20 with electricity), the former with a small cascade nearby. These sites come under the **Clarks Fork Ranger district** (☎307-527-6921) of the Shoshone National Forest.

Closer to Cooke City, **Chief Joseph** (6 sites, $8), **Colter** (18 sites, $9) and **Soda Butte** (27 sites, $9) campgrounds are 4 miles, 2 miles and 1.5 miles east of town, respectively. All are open mid-July to September. Only hardsided vehicles are accepted following a fatal grizzly attack at Soda Butte in July 2010 that killed one camper and injured several others. Contact the **Gallatin National Forest Gardiner District Office** (☎406-848-7375; www.fs.fed.us/r1/gallatin) for details.

Skyline Guest Ranch   LODGE $
(☎406-838-2380; www.flyfishyellowstone.com; 31 Kersey Lake Rd; d incl breakfast $88-110; ☁@) The remote Skyline is perfect if you want to get away from it all, experience some Western hospitality and saddle up for some family horse riding. Rooms in a three-story lodge are spacious and modern, with nice outside balconies, and the location – 3 miles outside of Cooke City – is officially the middle of nowhere. The only way to reach here in winter is by snowmobile.

Chief Joseph Scenic Highway

The wild and scenic Clarks Fork of the Yellowstone River runs along much of the Chief Joseph Scenic Hwy (Hwy 296), linking Cody (via Hwy 120 north) with the Beartooth Hwy and Yellowstone National Park's Northeast Entrance, 62 miles away. It's an astoundingly scenic and largely undiscovered corner of the Yellowstone region that links with the Beartooth Hwy to offer several potential loop itineraries. The highway is named for Chief Joseph of the Nez Percé tribe who eluded the US army and escaped through Clarks Fork here in 1877.

The paved highway is open year-round from Cody to the Beartooth Hwy, though not as far as Cooke City. The Beartooth Hwy itself is closed mid-October to late May. Fall colors are particularly lovely here.

The 47-mile Chief Joseph Scenic Hwy starts 16 miles north of Cody, enters the Shoshone National Forest after 8 miles and climbs to a spectacular viewpoint at **Dead Indian Pass** (8048ft). Indians used to ambush game that migrated through the pass between summer mountain pastures and winter ranges down in the plains. The pass is named for a Bannock Indian killed here in skirmishes with the army in 1878.

As you descend from the pass, just 0.3 miles before Dead Indian Campground, a dirt road leads a couple of hundred yards to a trailhead parking lot that offers an excellent short hike to view the 1200ft deep **Clarks Fork Canyon**. The trail leads north for 2 miles to a scenic overlook; watch for cairns marking the spot shortly after you first see the gorge. The views of the 1200ft granite gorge and **Dead Indian Creek waterfall** are breathtaking. The canyon effectively separates the 50-million-year-old volcanic rock of the Absaroka Range from the two-billion-year-old granite of the Beartooth Plateau. The trail continues for another 3 miles right down to the canyon floor, but the 700ft descent and then ascent makes for a considerably more strenuous hike.

Back on the road, USFS Rd 101 branches southwest into the beautiful **Sunlight Basin**, whose upper branches end at a wall of peaks forming the remote eastern boundary of Yellowstone National Park. Writer Ernest Hemingway spent time grizzly hunting here in the 1930s and wrote an article on the subject for *Vogue* magazine.

Where Hwy 296 crosses Sunlight Creek is the terrific **Sunlight Bridge**, the highest in Wyoming. You can park and walk across the bridge for hair-raising views into the gorge (acrophobes beware!), though better overviews can be had 0.5 miles north on the highway.

Just north of Crandall Creek (named after a pioneer miner who was beheaded by American Indians), around Swamp Lake, are six scenic ponds where you might spot sandhill cranes and trumpeter swans.

Hwy 296 continues northwest to the crossbar junction of US 212, where the Beartooth Hwy leads northwest to Cooke City and Yellowstone Park or northeast to Red Lodge and Billings.

Sleeping

Shoshone National Forest has the following three simple campgrounds near the Beartooth Hwy. Contact the **Clarks Fork Ranger District** (☎307-527-6921; www.fs.fed. us/r2/shoshone) in Cody for details. You can reserve Hunter Peak through **Recreation. gov** (☎877-444-6777; www.recreation.gov).

Lake Creek CAMPGROUND $
(6 sites, $10; ☺late Jun-early Sep) Forested but lots of mosquitoes in July; 1 mile from the Beartooth Hwy

Hunter Peak CAMPGROUND $
(9 sites, $15; ☺end May-early Oct) Five miles from the Beartooth Hwy.

Dead Indian Campground CAMPGROUND $
(10 sites, $10; ☺May-Sep) Further south from Hunter Peak, in two loops at a bend in the highway. No water.

7D Ranch RANCH $$$
(☎888-587-9885; www.7dranch.com; weekly rates $1600; ☺Jun–mid-Sep) This guest ranch has a fabulous location 8 miles up Sunlight Valley, with only 10 cabins and excellent horseback riding and fishing opportunities. Early September is kid-free and has discounted rates.

Hunter Peak Ranch RANCH $$
(☎307-587-3711; www.hunterpeakranch.com; cabin/ste from $141/147) Just off Hwy 296, 24 miles from Yellowstone, with plenty of summertime horseback riding and winter skiing.

K Bar Z Guest Ranch RANCH $
(☎307-587-4410; www.agonline.com/kbarz; d cabin $95) Family run and 28 miles from Yellowstone, this ranch offers horseback rides from $25 per hour or $140 per day.

Cooke City

☎406 / POP 85 / ELEV 7800FT
Sandwiched spectacularly between two forested ridges of the Beartooth Mountains, just 4 miles from Yellowstone's Northeast Entrance, this one-street Montana town

(population 85 in winter, 350 in summer) gets a steady flow of summer visitors en route between the scenic splendors of the Beartooth Hwy and the national park. There's not much here in the way of shops, sights or even trailheads, but this isolated town has a backwoods feel that's more laid-back and less commercialized than the park's other gateway towns, and a year-round population that's as rugged as the surrounding peaks.

Cooke City's isolation is due to geography and the lack of a railroad link. Citizens lobbied to bring the railroad to the original mining town of Shoo-Fly, even going so far as to rename the town in 1880 after the Northern Pacific Railroad's Jay Cooke, but even this blatant flattery failed to overcome hard economics. Oddly, this enclave of Montana can only be accessed from Wyoming.

In winter the road from Yellowstone is only plowed as far as Cooke City, so visitors – mostly backcountry skiers and snowmobilers – tend to check in and stay awhile. Gas prices are the highest in the Yellowstone region, but there's not a whole lot you can do about it. There's no cell coverage in town.

Sights & Activities

In winter the network of mining roads northeast of town are favorites of Nordic skiers and snowmobilers. Near Colter Campground, the unpaved Lulu Pass–Goose Lake Rd, the Goose Lake Track (trail 3230) and trails to Aero Lakes are all popular, as is snowmobiling the Beartooth Hwy. Several outfits in town rent snowmobiles ($175 to $225 per day).

Cooke City General Store HISTORIC BUILDING
(www.cookecitystore.com; ☺8am-7pm) This historic 1886 store retains an old-time feel and is a fun browse. It sells fishing permits, topo maps and almost anything else you can think of.

Yellowstone Trading Post MUSEUM
(☺9am-9pm Mon-Sat;⛹) Kids will like the stuffed animal exhibits in this souvenir store next to the Beartooth Café. It's normally free; if not, the small admission fee can be spent in the store.

Sleeping

Soda Butte, Colter and Chief Joseph campgrounds are just 1.5 miles, 2 miles and 4 miles from town respectively; see p142.

Alpine Motel
MOTEL $

(📞406-838-2262; www.cookecityalpine.com; d $78-98, apt $120-175; 🛜) Well-maintained and spacious rooms are the hallmark of this good-value motel, with laundry facilities, family suites and discounted winter rates.

Elkhorn Lodge
CABINS $

(📞406-838-2332; www.elkhornlodgemt.com; s/d $89/99, cabin $120; 🛜) Choose between the six rooms in the main building – with pleasant sitting area, coffee maker and fridge – or the two pricier cabins with kitchenette. All are fresh and spacious.

Antlers Lodge
CABINS $$

(📞406-838-2432; www.cookecityantlerslodge.com; cabins $75-155; 🐾) This ramshackle collection of 17 old-style pine cabins has quarters in all shapes and sizes (some with kitchenettes) and also offers several fresh and spacious motel rooms. The antler-horn chandeliers in the main lodge are a bit too *Psycho* for us.

High Country Motel
MOTEL $

(📞406-838-2272; www.cookecityhighcountry.com; d $80-110; 🐾) A good mix of cabins and motel-style rooms, some with kitchenettes and open year-round.

Pine Edge Cabins
CABINS $$

(📞406-838-2371; www.pineedgecabins.com; cabins $99-198; 🐾) If sleepy Cooke City is too urban for you, try this collection of cozy cabins at the nearly comatose community of Silver Gate (year-round population: 10), 2 miles west of Cooke City and just 2 miles from the park. Enquire at the general store.

Eating

The best place for an espresso is the **Loving Cup** (🕐7am-6pm; 🛜), which also serves up light lunches and a mean breakfast burrito. If you plan to a make an early start into the park, the **Bearclaw Bakery** offers early-morning pastries from 5am and breakfasts from 6am.

⌜TOP⌝ CHOICE Beartooth Café
AMERICAN $$

(www.beartoothcafe.com; lunch $10, dinner mains $16-25; 🕐11am-10pm late May-late Sep) A bright place for lunch sandwiches (such as a buffalo burger, a 'funk burger' or lighter portobello sandwich) served on the pleasant front deck, washed down by a fine selection of 130 bottled microbrews. Dinner mains like ribs, smoked trout and hand-cut steaks are double the lunchtime prices. Breakfast is served weekends only.

Bistro
EUROPEAN $$

(breakfast & lunch $10, dinner mains $16-23; 🕐7am-10pm) A popular place for breakfast, come nightfall the homey Bistro transforms into a demi-French restaurant with dishes like escargot in garlic butter and seafood cassoulette. There's a nice terrace.

Log Cabin Café
WESTERN $$

(📞406-838-2367; www.thelogcabincafe.com; lunch $8-13, dinner $15-25; 🕐7am-10p, mid-May–late Sep) In sleepy Silver Gate, this is an unexpectedly cool place, serving excellent grilled trout, house-smoked salmon and homemade breakfast pumpkin bread. The cozy cabin dates back to 1937 and there are more cabins for rent out back.

Information

Bearclaw Mountain Recovery (📞406-838-2040) AAA-endorsed and the people to call if you have a breakdown. Montana fishing licenses are available.

Chamber of Commerce (📞406-838-2495; www.cookecitychamber.org; 206 W Main; 🛜) A helpful new visitor center with public restroom and free wi-fi.

Silver Gate General Store (🕐8am-10:30pm) In the nearby town of Silver Gate, this store sells topo maps and rents spotting scopes ($30 per day) that can fit a modified digital camera ($15).

WAPITI ROUTE

Cody

📞307 / POP 9000 / ELEV 5095FT

Arrive in Cody at sundown and you'll find costumed gunslingers midbrawl, flanked by Jezebels toiling under a career in false eyelashes. It's not a town to take too seriously. The spirit of showman Buffalo Bill still thrives in the town that he himself promoted with real-estate speculator George Beck in 1901. Beck and his backers milked Cody's fame to promote settlement, attract the railroad and lobby for a massive dam on the Shoshone River. But it's more than farce. Despite the corny cowboy themes, Cody feels like the real West, where graduation photos adorn shop counters, folks chat in doorways and real cowpokes sip silty cups of joe.

Cody is second only to Jackson as Wyoming's premier summer tourist town. Access to the great outdoors is excellent, as are winter sports such as ice climbing and

Cody

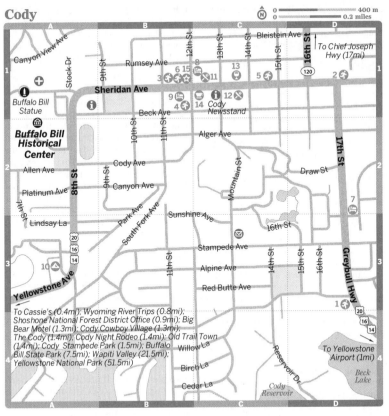

To Chief Joseph Hwy (17mi)

AROUND YELLOWSTONE CODY

To Cassie's (0.4mi); Wyoming River Trips (0.8mi);
Shoshone National Forest District Office (0.9mi); Big
Bear Motel (1.3mi); Cody Cowboy Village (1.3mi);
The Cody (1.4mi); Cody Night Rodeo (1.4mi); Old Trail Town
(1.4mi); Cody Stampede Park (1.5mi); Buffalo
Bill State Park (7.5mi); Wapiti Valley (21.5mi);
Yellowstone National Park (51.5mi)

To Yellowstone
Airport (1mi)

Cody

◎ Top Sights
Buffalo Bill Historical Center A2

◔ Activities, Courses & Tours
1 Absaroka Bicycles D3
2 Gradient Mountain Sports D1
3 North Fork Anglers B1
4 Red Canyon River Trips B1
  Red Canyon Wild Mustang Tours.. (see 4)
5 River Runners C1
6 Sunlight Sports B1

◉ Sleeping
7 Carter Mountain Motel D2
8 Chamberlin Inn C1
9 Irma Hotel B1

10 Ponderosa Campground A3

◼ Eating
Irma .... (see 9)
11 Peter's Café Bakery C1
12 Zapata's C1

◉ Drinking
13 Silver Dollar Bar C1
14 The Beta C1

◉ Entertainment
15 Dan Miller's Cowboy Music
   Revue B1
   Silver Saddle Saloon .... (see 9)

cross-country skiing. But the town's ultimate blessing is its proximity to Yellowstone National Park, 51 miles to the west and connected by the scenic Wapiti Valley.

Sights

Buffalo Bill Historical Center   MUSEUM
(☑307-587-4771; www.bbhc.org; 720 Sheridan Ave; adult/over 6yr/student/senior $18/10/13/16; ⊗8am-6pm, closed Mon-Wed Dec-Feb) While the nickname 'Smithsonian of the West' exaggerates a wee bit, this five-museum complex is still a must-see. Entry is valid for two consecutive days.

The original collection began in 1927 with the **Buffalo Bill Museum**, which presents a wealth of fascinating, if uncritical, information on the life of William F Cody and his Wild West shows. The **Plains Indian Museum** explores Native American culture and history through its artistry. Displays detail Native American ceremonies such as the Sun Dance (which honors the buffalo spirit) and explains the symbolism of tepee designs. Accounts of life on the reservation are conspicuously absent.

With a powerhouse collection including Remington, Russell and NC Wyeth, the **Whitney Gallery of Western Art** introduces Western art through the powerful and energetic landscapes and wildlife scenes from the masters. Most who are not gun fanatics politely rush through the **Cody Firearms Museum**. The newest addition, the **Draper Museum of Natural History**, gives visitors an excellent interactive overview of Greater Yellowstone ecology.

Old Trail Town   MUSEUM
(☑307-587-5302; www.museumoftheoldwest.org, www.oldtrailtown.org; 1831 DeMaris Dr; adult/over 12yr $8/4;⊗8am-7pm mid-May-Sep) The hideouts of Butch Cassidy, Kid Curry and the Sundance Kid comprise this unique museum, a collection of late-19th-century wooden buildings relocated here from all over Wyoming. Look for the bullet holes in the door of the Rivers Saloon and the grave of mountain man Jeremiah 'Liver-Eating' Johnson, reburied here in 1974 with Robert Redford as one of the pallbearers.

Cody Nite Rodeo   RODEO
(www.codynightrodeo.com; Cody Stampede Park, 519 West Yellowstone Ave; adult/7-12yr $18/8; ⊗8pm Jun-Aug; ⚑) The self-proclaimed 'Rodeo Capital of the World' draws crowds summerlong to its nightly displays. Roping, bronc riding and barrel racing are all part of the fun, while the kids can get their faces painted by a rodeo clown and join in the sheep chase. Pay $2 more and you'll get a prime seat in the Buzzard's Roost, just behind the chutes.

Buffalo Bill State Park   PARK
(☑307-527-6076; www.bbdvc.org, day use $6; visitor center ⊗8am-7pm Mon-Fri & 9am-5pm Sat & Sun May-Sep) This scenic state park, 6 miles west of Cody, centers on the Buffalo Bill Reservoir and Dam, unveiled in 1910 as the world's highest dam to provide the irrigation that Cody needed to prosper. Now the reservoir is a hot spot for fishing, windsurfing and boating, and boat launches dot the north and southeast shores. The visitor center just west of the dramatic Shoshone Canyon offers interpretive exhibits on the dam, Bill and local wildlife.

Activities

No longer just for cowboys, Cody is an excellent base for outdoor pursuits. Apart from the activities mentioned here, Cody also offers some of the best winter **ice climbing** in the United States. See www.codyice.com, www.coldfear.com and www.southforkice. com, or enquire at Sunlight Sports.

Just outside of town, the North Fork of the Shoshone River has scenic float trips and excellent class II to class IV white-water, with best conditions in mid-June. Bighorn sheep hang out on the cliffs, and eagles and moose are sometimes spotted. Prices range from $37 for family-oriented lower canyon trips to $70 for a half-day on the North Fork. Reputable companies include **Red Canyon River Trips** (☑800-293-0148; 1119 12th St), **River Runners** (☑307-527-7238, 800-535-RAFT; www.riverrunnersofwyoming.com; 1491 Sheridan Ave) and **Wyoming River Trips** (☑800-586-6661; www.wyomingrivertrips.com; 233 Yellowstone Ave), which also runs inflatable kayak trips.

Gradient Mountain Sports   KAYAKING
(☑307-587-4659; www.gradientmountainsports. net; 1723 Sheridan Ave) If kayaking is more your thing, head here for rentals, shuttles and run information, plus instruction and guided trips.

North Fork Anglers   FLY FISHING
(☑307-527-7274; www.northforkanglers.com; 1107 Sheridan Ave) Anglers should visit Tim Wade's place for local information, flies and guided trips. The website lists current fishing conditions.

HEARTLAND SECURITY

Following the Japanese bombing of Pearl Harbor, over 110,000 Japanese-Americans were interned in 10 camps across the US. Of these, nearly 11,000 were interned in **Heart Mountain Relocation Center** (☑307-250-5542; www.heartmountain.org; Rd 19 off Hwy 14A; admission free), 14 miles northeast of Cody, creating Wyoming's third-largest city. Taking only what they could carry, Japanese-Americans relocated from West Coast homes to these flimsy tar-paper rooms and made the best of three years of confinement there, setting up a newspaper, two theaters and a high school. Only the former hospital and chimney remain from the original buildings but a memorial and new barracks-style interpretive center tells the still relevant story of how – temporarily seized by xenophobia – the US failed its own citizens 60 years ago.

Absaroka Bicycles BIKES
(☑307-527-5566; 2201 17th St, Kmart Plaza; ◎10am-6pmMon-Sat) Ground central for mountain-bike rentals ($45 per day), repairs, tours and info on local fat-tire trails, including to Cedar Mountain, where many locals believe Buffalo Bill to be buried.

Sunlight Sports OUTDOOR GEAR
(☑307-587-9517; www.sunlightsports.com; 1131 Sheridan Ave) Cody's best gear shop offers backpacking gear rentals, bear spray, topo maps and local trail information. Jackson Hole Mountain Guides has a local office here.

Red Canyon Wild Mustang Trips TOURS
(☑800-293-0148; 1119 12th St; ◎mid-May–mid-Oct) For something different take a morning or afternoon van tour (adult/child $29/27) out to the desert badlands of the McCullough Peaks Wild Horse Range, a refuge designated for 142 wild mustangs. For more information on the horses, check out the nonprofit **FOAL** (www.friendsofalegacy.org). Photo safaris are also possible.

Festivals & Events

See p24 for details of the July 4 **Cody Stampede Rodeo** (www.codystampederodeo.com; admission $24; ◎July 1-4) and the **Plains Indians Powwow** (Buffalo Bill Historical Center; adult/7-17yr $7/3) in mid-June.

The **Cowboy Poetry & Range Ballads Festival** takes place the second week of April.

Sleeping

Cody's accommodations are not great value in summer, when rates are 50% higher than in the shoulder season (summer rates are listed here).

For the nicest camping, skip town for more scenic options along the banks of the Buffalo Bill Reservoir. The roadside **North Shore Bay** and **North Fork Campgrounds** (☑307-587-9227; http://wyoparks.state.wy.us; sites $6-12; ◎May-Sep), 6 miles west of Cody, are exposed and shadeless but the former in particular offers lovely sunsets over the lake. A few sites can be reserved online. Nonresidents will have to add on the state park entry fee.

TOP CHOICE **Chamberlin Inn** HISTORIC HOTEL **$$$**
(☑307-587-0202; www.chamberlininn.com; 1032 12th St; r/ste from $185/295; @☎) Recently restored and stunning, Chamberlin Inn conjures up the mystique of the original 1904 boarding house, with French tile paintings, embossed tin ceilings, clawfoot tubs and crushed-satin bedcovers. The old register claims Hemingway crashed in room 18 ($265) on a 1932 fishing trip.

Ponderosa Campground DEVELOPED CAMPGROUND **$**
(☑307-587-9203; www.codyponderosa.com; 1815 Yellowstone Ave; tent/RV sites from $21/31; ◎mid-Apr–mid-Oct; ☎☀) Ponderosa edges out the competition with immaculate showers, laundry and friendly service. Families can overnight in fun tepees ($25).

Irma Hotel HISTORIC HOTEL **$$**
(☑800-745-4762; www.irmahotel.com; 1192 Sheridan Ave; r $112-162) Built in 1902, this atmospheric period saloon offers charming original historical suites with big windows and clunky dressers, home to such past guests as Annie Oakley and Calamity Jane. Less inspiring options are in the dowdy modern annex. Some say it's a better place to visit than stay.

Buffalo Bill built and named the hotel for his youngest daughter Irma, calling it 'just the swellest hotel that ever was.' He kept two suites and an office for his personal use, and his ghost is said to still frequent the creaking corridors. The original front lobby has since been converted into the Silver Saddle Lounge.

The hotel's most famous feature (and the best place to grab a beer or dinner) is the 50ft-long imported French cherrywood bar, in what is now the dining room. Presented to Bill by Queen Victoria, it was transported by stagecoach from Red Lodge and, at $100,000, cost more than the hotel itself.

The Cody
HOTEL $$$

(☑307-587-5915; www.thecody.com; 232 West Yellowstone Ave; incl breakfast d $189-209, ste $229-239; ☎☒) Cody's most luxurious hotel combines New Western chic with green credentials, incorporating paneling made with recycled wood from park facilities and offering free bicycles to guests. Request a balcony room away from the road.

Cody Cowboy Village
CABINS $$

(☑307-587-7555; www.thecodycowboyvillage.com; 203 West Yellowstone Ave; cabin $145-159) Popular and well-run modern and stylish duplex cabins with small porch, or suites for six, plus a large outdoor hot tub.

Carter Mountain Motel
MOTEL $$

(☑307-587-4295; www.cartermountainmotel.com; 1701 Central Ave; d $90-110, ste $148-249; ☎) An unpretentious breezeblock place, but well looked after and decent value, with cheery flowerpots, an upper-floor balcony and kitchenette suites.

Big Bear Motel
MOTEL $

(☑307-587-3117; www.bigbearmotel.com; 139 W Yellowstone Ave; r $109-114; @☒♿☎) Despite the desolate parking lot this is a friendly place and good value off-season. Ask for one of the clean and fresh new-block rooms. Kids will enjoy the pool and miniature pony rides.

Eating & Drinking

Peter's Café Bakery
CAFE $

(www.peters-cafe.com;1191 Sheridan Ave; mains $5-10; ☺6.45am-10pm) Look hard enough and you can find almost anything at Peter's self-service counter, from buffalo burgers and overstuffed sandwiches to ice-cream floats at the soda fountain. The popular all-day low-carb breakfast consist of two eggs and two bacon strips, as well as two sausage patties.

Zapata's
MEXICAN $$

(1362 Sheridan Ave; mains $10-18; ☺closed Sun) serves up spinach enchiladas, green chili and chips with fantastic homemade salsa in comfy booths. The margaritas are a highlight.

Irma
WESTERN $$

(☑307-587-4221; 1192 Sheridan Ave; buffet breakfast & lunch/dinner $9.50/23) Slow-roasted prime rib and meatloaf are the signature dishes in the atmospheric dining room of the Irma Hotel, though the buffets are generally the most popular option. Score a seat at the cherrywood bar.

The Beta
COFFEE

(1132 12th St; ☺6am-8pm Mon-Thu, 6am-10pm Fri & Sat; ☎) Join the locals on their daily chai or espresso hit at this hip coffee shop opposite the Irma.

Silver Dollar Bar
BAR

(1313 Sheridan Ave; ☺to 2am) Try the deck for monster burgers ($7 to $12), microbrews on tap and live music, as the locals shimmy to rock and roll. Penny-pinchers show up in throngs for quarter beer night, held Thursdays.

Entertainment

Cassie's
BAR

(☑307-527-5500; www.cassies.com; 214 Yellowstone Ave) This classic roadhouse and former house of ill repute hosts heavy swilling, swingin' country-and-western tunes and the occasional bar fight. The attached supper club is one of the best places for a steak or walleye dinner, while out-of-towners can try the Rocky Mountain Oysters.

Dan Miller's Cowboy Music Revue
LIVE MUSIC

(☑307-272-7855; www.cowboymusicrevue.com; 1171 Sheridan Ave; admission $15; ☺Mon-Sat May-Sep) The historic Cody Theater hosts this Branson-style family show, serving up folk music and cowboy poetry alongside thick slices of Old West nostalgia. Imagine Hannah Montana in cowboy boots, with a fiddle. A combo ticket including a dinner buffet at the Irma (opposite) will save you a couple of bucks.

Silver Saddle Saloon
BAR

Squeeze among real wranglers and faux-cowboys in 10-gallon hats for the Irma Hotel's Silver Saddle Saloon happy hour – a blast after the gunslingers' mock **shoot-out** on the porch at 6pm daily except Sunday (June to mid-September). The shoot-out itself manages to be both hammy and cheesy (sounds delicious) but kids will enjoy watching costumed characters that include Wild Bill Hickok, Buffalo Bill and Wyatt Earp.

Information

Cody Newsstand (1121 13th St) Stocks maps, newspapers and local guides.

Shoshone National Forest Wapiti Ranger District Office (307-527-6921; www.fs.fed. us/r2/shoshone; 203A Yellowstone Ave; 8am-4:30pm Mon-Fri) Ask for the useful recreation guide.

Visitor Center (307-587-2777; www.cody chamber.org; 836 Sheridan Ave; 8am-6pm Mon-Fri, 9am-5pm Sat, 10am-3pm Sun May-Sep, shorter hours Oct-Apr) The helpful folks in this 1927 lodgepole cabin can solve most problems and sell tickets to the rodeo and other events. See also www.yellowstonecountry.org.

Wapiti Valley

Deemed the 'most scenic 52 miles in the United States' by Teddy Roosevelt, **Buffalo Bill Scenic Byway** (US 14/16/20) traces Wapiti Valley and the North Fork of the Shoshone River from Cody to the East Entrance of Yellowstone National Park. You will find yourself twisting to gape at the volcanic Absaroka Range, a rugged canyon of eroded badlands that gradually gives way to alpine splendor.

The name Wapiti Valley translates as 'pale white rump' from Algonquin Indian. Rather than being a jab at homesteaders' wives, the term distinguishes the lighter-colored elk, or wapiti, from darker-colored moose. The North Absaroka Wilderness Area sits to the north and the Washakie Wilderness Area (named after a revered Shoshone warrior and peacemaker) to the south. This vast wilderness is home to grizzlies, black bears, deer, elk, moose, bighorn sheep and a few bison. The extensive network of trails, easy access to Yellowstone National Park's lake region and a selection of the region's best dude ranches make the valley an excellent wild route into or out of the park.

Six miles west of Cody, US 14/16/20 emerges from the dramatic **Shoshone Canyon** and tunnel to views of the **Buffalo Bill Reservoir**. Past the settlement of Wapiti, Wyoming's high-desert landscape and open ranchland closes in as the road enters Shoshone National Forest and becomes Buffalo Bill Cody Scenic Hwy. The information station at the **Wapiti Ranger Station** (307-587-3925) has a 3D map of the region, as well as information on grizzly sightings. The national forest here was the USA's first and the nearby 1903 ranger station is its oldest.

From here on, the Wapiti Valley is lined with eerie buttes and hoodoos with over-imaginative names, such as the Four Bobsledders and Holy City. National Forest campgrounds, trailheads and guest ranches crop up every few miles as the scenery becomes increasingly rugged.

Two miles before the east entrance to Yellowstone is the gas station, store, restaurant and corrals of **Pahaska Tepee** resort, a good place to refuel. Staff lead free tours of the original lodge, built by Buffalo Bill in 1904 as a hunting lodge, and there are local trail rides (two hours, $50). Pahaska was Bill's Indian name and means 'Longhair' in the Sioux language, a reference to Cody's long white hair and extravagant goatee.

Activities

Most of the valley's guest ranches offer **horseback riding** (per hr from $25), horsepacking trips and cookouts to nonguests in addition to guests. Outstanding **fly-fishing** is easily accessed via the national forest and wilderness areas and campgrounds.

The North Fork Shoshone River is a favorite of **white-water rafting** aficionados. Elk, bighorn sheep and moose are often seen from the river. The rafting season is mid-May to mid-September in the Red Rock and Lower Canyons, and Memorial Day (last Monday in May) to late July for the North Fork. See p146 for details.

North Fork Nordic Trails (307-527-7701; www.nordicskiclub.com) offers 12 miles of groomed cross-country trails behind the Pahaska Tepee resort.

Sleeping

Camping

Nine USFS campgrounds line the Wapiti Valley, starting from 29 miles west of Cody. Overflow from Yellowstone fills up the grounds in July and August, so try to arrive before late afternoon. All campgrounds border the river, offering easy access to trout fishing. Most are open June to early September but can close any time due to grizzly activity. Call the **Shoshone**

National Forest North Zone (☑307-527-6921; htto://fs.usda.gov/shoshone) for details. Four of the campgrounds are reservable at www.recreation.gov.

The following campgrounds are listed from east to west and all have bear-resistant food storage:

Big Game Campground (sites $10) Small but spacious and private, no water. It's reservable.

Wapiti Campground (sites without/with electricity $15/20) More sites but less space. Reservable and the first to open in May.

Elk Fork Campground (sites $10) Cramped and without potable water but popular for hiking and horse-packing trips and open year-round.

Clearwater Campground ($10) Unreliable water supply but some reservable group sites.

Rex Hale Campground (sites without/with electricity $15/20) More exposed but has six sites with electrical hookups. Reservable.

Newton Creek Campground (sites $15) Woodsy and pleasant, with 31 campsites.

Eagle Creek Campground (sites $15) Hard-sided campers only, due to grizzly activity.

Threemile Campground (sites $15) Hard-sided campers only; closest to the park.

Lodging

Wapiti Valley's lodges and guest ranches make a great base for exploring Yellowstone or Cody. Most offer fishing, hiking, rock climbing and guided horseback rides. Luxury in proximity to the park doesn't come cheap, but discounted rates are the norm before May and after September.

Lodges East of Yellowstone Valley (☑307-587-9595; www.yellowstone-lodging.com) provides information on the valley's numerous family-owned member dude ranches and lodges.

Pahaska Tepee CABINS $$
(☑307-527-7701; www.pahaska.com; 183 Yellowstone Hwy; cabins $130-195; ☺May–mid-Oct) The historic lodge is closest to the park and one of the best deals in the shoulder season, as well as a popular place for lunch before entering the park. The cheapest A-frame cabins wouldn't fit a grizzly, but considering the location that might just be a good thing.

PARADISE VALLEY ROUTE

Livingston

☑406 / POP 6800 / ELEV 4503FT

In the late 1880s the Northern Pacific Railroad laid tracks across the Yellowstone River and began building Livingston as the main jumping-off point for Yellowstone National Park. Visited by Clark (of Lewis and Clark fame) and at one point a temporary home to one whip-crackin' Martha Canary (otherwise known as Calamity Jane), Livingston is an excellent departure point for rafting and fly-fishing trips on the Yellowstone River.

Bozeman's overflow has brought upscale restaurants, antique shops and art galleries to Livingston's picturesque old buildings, as well as a growing community of writers and artists, but generally it retains its small-town feel.

Livingston is at the north end of Paradise Valley, where I-90 meets US 89; the latter heads south to Gardiner and Yellowstone National Park, 53 miles away.

Sights & Activities

Livingston is home to over a dozen galleries ('13 galleries; 3 stop lights'), including that of famed local lithographer Russell Chatham. For details see www.livingstongalleries.com.

Depot Center MUSEUM
(☑406-222-2300; www.livingstondepot.org; 200 W Park St; ☺9am-5pm Mon-Sat, 1-5pm Sun late May-early Sep) The original Northern Pacific Railroad Depot, built in 1902 by the architects who designed New York's Grand Central Station, is now home to a railroad history and arts museum. Don't miss the collection of Montana movie trivia upstairs. It's free for now, but admission fees may be introduced.

Yellowstone Gateway Museum MUSEUM
(☑406-222-4184; www.livingstonmuseums.org; 118 W Chinook St; adult/child $6/4.50; ☺10am-5pm May-Sep) Livingston's collection of historical and archaeological treasures is housed in a century-old schoolhouse. The recently revamped exhibits include an early Yellowstone stagecoach.

Dan Bailey's Fly Shop FLY FISHING
(☑800-356-4052; www.dan-bailey.com; 209 W Park St) Built on a legacy of Goofus Bugs, Humpy Flies, Trudes, Green Drakes and Hair Wing Rubber Legs (to name but a few),

Dan Bailey's is one of the world's best fly-fishing shops. It's opposite the Depot Center.

George Anderson's Yellowstone Angler
FLY FISHING

(☑406-222-7130; www.yellowstoneangler.com; Hwy 89) Another good fly-fishing store, with equipment rental and guide service, 1 mile south of town.

Rubber Ducky River Rentals
BOAT RENTAL

(☑406-222-3746; www.riverservices.com; 15 Mt Baldy Dr) For some fun on the Yellowstone River, rent a canoe, raft or kayak here, just north of I-90.

Sleeping

The nearest Forestry Service campground is Pine Creek (p153), 15 miles south in the Paradise Valley. Consider also the excellent options in the Paradise Valley.

TOP CHOICE Murray Hotel
HISTORIC HOTEL $$

(☑406-222-1350; www.murrayhotel.com; 201 W Park St; r $89-169; ☎) Central to Livingston's history since 1904, the Murray is the place to bed down with the ghosts of gunslinger Calamity Jane and director Sam Peckinpah (who lived in a suite for over a year, occasionally shooting holes in the ceiling). The ancient hand-crank lift and creaky wood floors set the tone, but the 25 rooms are fresh and modern, and most are mini-suites with galley kitchens and clawfoot tubs. The Peckinpah suite ($339) is a six-sleeper treat but avoid the cheapest 2nd-floor rooms ($79 to $89), as they pulsate with noise from the bar below until 2am.

Osen's RV Park & Campground
RV PARK $

(☑406-222-0591; www.montanarvpark.com; 20 Merrill Lane; RV/camping sites $29/20; ☎☎) Just south of I-90, this place has laundry and showers and is open year-round

Eating & Drinking

TOP CHOICE 2nd St Bistro
BISTRO $$

(☑406-222-9463; 123 N 2nd St; www.secondstreet bistro.com; dinner mains $15-26; ☎from 5pm Tue-Sat) Our personal favorite, located in the historic Murray Hotel, with a superb range of appetizers, cocktails and draft beers, this is a classy but relaxed bistro with an emphasis on quality local food. From the pear-and-pumpkin-seed salad to the European-style mussels and fries ($14), you simply can't go wrong, and there's more vegetarian fare than the average Montanan restaurant.

Mark's In and Out
DRIVE-IN $

(cnr Park & 8th Sts; ☎11am-10pm Mar-Nov) If your tastes are less merlot and more chocolate milk, Mark's has been churning out quality never-frozen burgers and malts since 1954, the latter made with Livingston's very own Wilcoxson's ice cream. Rollerskating carhops lay on an extra scoop of nostalgia on summer Friday and Saturday evenings.

The Sport
BAR $$

(www.thesportbarandgrill.com; 114 S Main St; dinner mains $16-27; ☎Wed-Sun) This classy wooden bar has been running since 1909 and still has lots of historic touches amid the stuffed game heads. It's a relaxed place for a drink and bar snacks, or move to the next-door restaurant for a formal dinner or Sunday brunch.

Mustang Catering
SELF-CATERING $

(www.mustangcatering.com; 215 W Lewis St; mains $7.50; ☎11am-5pm Mon-Fri, 10:30am-2:30pm Sat; ☎) For a top-shelf picnic, combine a fabulous ciabatta sandwich, gourmet salad or hot daily special from this top-notch cafe with a wine-and-cheese grab from the **Gourmet Cellar** (next to Livingston Depot) and dine al fresco at the picnic tables by Depot Center. Or, even better, picnic in the Paradise Valley en route to the park.

Chadz
COFFEEHOUSE $

(104 N Main; ☎6am-2:30pm, to 9pm Fri; ☎) Lose yourself in the comfy sofas for a light lunchtime panini and reviving espresso at this funky coffeehouse.

Information

Chamber of Commerce (☑406-222-0850; www.livingston-chamber.com; 303 E Park St) Has a very useful website. Try also www.livingstonmontana.com.

Gallatin National Forest Livingston Ranger District (☑406-222-1892; 5242 Hwy 89 S) One mile south of town on I-90, next to Yellowstone Angler.

Timber Trails (☑406-222-9550; 309 W Park St) For maps and outdoor gear, including mountain bikes, skis and snowshoe rentals.

Paradise Valley

With Livingston as a railroad stop, Paradise Valley became the first travel corridor to Yellowstone National Park. Gardiner, 50 miles south of Livingston and just north of the Mammoth Hot Springs entrance to

WORTH A TRIP

TOM MINER BASIN

To get off the beaten track, head west of US 89 on Tom Miner Rd, 17 miles north of Gardiner and 35 miles south of Livingston, into one of the prettiest pockets of land in the area. The washboard road ends 12 miles west of the highway at secluded 16-site **Tom Miner Campground** (sites $7; ⊙Jun-Oct), which has potable water and toilets.

Several trails start at the campground, including a 3-mile loop (trail 286) through the **Gallatin Petrified Forest**, where remnants of 35- to 55-million-year-old petrified wood are scattered among the Absaroka's volcanic rocks. A 0.5-mile interpretive trail winds around volcanic bluffs of fused ash (bear right where a sign says 'Hiker Trail Only') and peters out by a remarkable piece of petrified wood that is lodged in the roof of a small cave. Visitors are allowed to keep one small piece of petrified wood (maximum 20 cubic inches) with a free permit available at the Gardiner, Bozeman or Livingston ranger offices.

Yellowstone, is still one of the park's most popular entry points. The valley is mostly ranchland but has also included at various times such famous residents as Peter Fonda, Jeff Bridges, Dennis Quaid, Tom Brokaw and the Church Universal & Triumphant (CUT), which borders on Yellowstone National Park. And yes, a river, the Yellowstone, does run through it.

US 89 follows the Yellowstone River through this broad valley, flanked by the Gallatin Range to the west and the jagged Absaroka Range to the east. If you have time, the scenic East River Rd offers a parallel and quieter alternative to busy US 89. Amazingly, in retrospect, plans were afoot in the 1960s to dam the Yellowstone River and flood much of the lovely valley.

For a rundown on the valley's various accommodations, restaurants and support services visit www.paradisevalleymontana .com.

CHICO HOT SPRINGS

Thirty miles from Yellowstone National Park, in Pray at the mouth of Emigrant Canyon, **Chico Hot Springs** (☎406-333-4933; www.chicohotsprings.com; r $83-199, cabins $83-215; 🐾) was established in 1900 as a luxurious getaway for local cattle barons. The Victorian elegance has been restored with great attention to rustic detail. It's worth a visit just to poke around and take a plunge in the large outdoor **pool** (adult/7-12yr $6.50/4.50; ⊙8am-11pm), fed from hot springs and a toasty 103°F.

Smallish and creaking rooms in the main lodge with shared bath are the cheapest options ($55 to $69), with motel-style fishermen's cabins and modern high-ceilinged rooms with a porch around double these rates. Chalets up the hill have mountain views and mostly sleep four to six. Suites with private Jacuzzi are a great luxury.

Chico's activity center offers **horseback riding** (1hr/half-day rides $35/85) and **raft trips** ($40) down the Yellowstone. It also rents mountain bikes and cross-country skis, and there's a full spa attached to help you recover. Dogsled tours are operated from Thanksgiving to March through **Absaroka Dogsled Treks** (☎406-333-4933; www. extrememontana.com; per person $120-320).

TOP CHOICE **Chico Inn Restaurant** (dinner mains $25-32, Sun brunch $16) is renowned throughout the region, though there's slim pickings for vegetarians. The beef Wellington ($60 for two) gets rave reviews, as does the Sunday brunch, between 8:30am and 11:30am.

The **Poolside Grill** is cheaper and more casual, with sandwiches, pizza and ribs. The rollicking saloon has live music on Friday and Saturday nights.

SOUTHERN PARADISE VALLEY

South of the Tom Miner turnoff, US 89 winds through Yankee Jim Canyon, a narrow gorge cut through folded bands of extremely old rock (mostly gneiss) that look a bit like marble cake. Yankee Jim George hacked out a toll road through the canyon in the 19th century and made a living from Yellowstone-bound stagecoaches until the railroad put him out of business. This stretch of the Yellowstone River is the valley's hottest white-water spot.

A couple of miles further toward Yellowstone look for the roadside hot springs, which were once channeled into an elegant, turn-of-the-century resort at nearby Corwin

Springs. Across the river is the headquarters of the Church Universal & Triumphant (CUT), which built a huge underground nuclear shelter here in the 1980s after their leader Elizabeth Prophet predicted the end of the world.

Further south, a pullout offers fine views of the Devil's Slide, a superbly named salmon-pink landslide area consisting of 200-million-year-old rock. Keep an eye out for bighorn sheep here.

Activities

Hiking & Backpacking

Paradise Valley's most popular trail is the 10-mile round-trip hike to Pine Creek Lake. The trail starts from the Pine Creek Campground parking area and leads 1.2 miles to Pine Creek Falls and then another 3.8 miles to Pine Creek Lake, gaining around 3000ft en route. Budget at least four hours for the return hike.

Further south, down Mill Creek Rd, is the trailhead for Elbow Lake, 3500ft above the trailhead at the base of 11,206ft Mt Cowen, the highest peak in the Absaroka Range. The strenuous 18-mile, round-trip hike (along trails 51 and 48) is possible as a long day hike, but it's better to overnight at the lake. From the lake you can continue northeast to a second lake and ascend the ridge on the left for views of Mt Cowen.

Further south, there are more hiking opportunities on the east side of the Gallatin Range. A popular day hike from Tom Miner Campground takes you 2.5 miles up Trail Creek to meadows at Buffalo Horn Pass. A viewpoint five minutes' walk offers excellent views of the Gallatin Valley; Ramshorn Peak (10,289ft) beckons to the north.

The USFS *Gallatin Forest East Half* map (scaled 1:126,720) provides a good overview of the valley's routes but lacks contours.

Other Activities

The Yellowstone River winds past 19 fishing access sites along Paradise Valley, most of which have boat ramps. Experienced anglers can pit themselves against challenging private spring creeks such as Nelson's, Armstrong's and Depuy's. For bookings, fees and conditions contact Livingston's fishing shops (p150).

The Montana Department of Fishing, Wildlife & Parks runs basic campgrounds (www.fwp.mt.gov; sites $7, without a Montana fishing license $12) at the Mallard's Rest, Loch Leven and Dailey Lake fishing access sites.

Simple overnight camping is permitted free of charge at the BLM Carbella and Paradise fishing access areas, but the limited and primitive sites get snapped up quickly. All other access areas are day-use only.

Paradise Valley has some of the best cycling in the Yellowstone region. The paved East River Rd from the junction with Hwy 89 to Chico Rd and Chico Hot Springs is a scenic and smooth ride of 24 miles. For something more suited to fat tires, try the 17-mile gravel Gardiner Back Rd between Gardiner and Tom Miner Rd. This route starts from just behind the Yellowstone Heritage and Research Center and follows the old railroad bed and stagecoach road to take you past the Devil's Slide, the narrows of Yankee Jim Canyon and several primitive camping spots. To shorten the ride, turn off at Corwin Springs after 8 miles. Combine these routes, and you'll get a complete traverse of the valley.

Bearpaw Outfitters HORSE TRIPS
(☏406-222-6642; www.bearpawoutfittersmt.com; 136 Deep Creek Rd) This operation, 8 miles south of Livingston, organizes horse-pack trips in the Absaroka-Beartooth Wilderness (half day $90) and day rides in Yellowstone Park (from $160), plus fly-fishing in Yellowstone's Slough Creek.

Sleeping

There are several campgrounds (sites $14) in the Paradise Valley. About 4 miles south of Livingston on East River Rd, Luccock Park Rd heads 3 miles east to 25-site Pine Creek Campground, with pit toilets, water and hiker/cyclist sites. Both this and the 10-site Snowbank Campground, 17 miles south down Mill Creek Rd, serve as springboards to local hikes and are open May to September. (Snowbank closes first, early in September.) Call the Livingston Ranger District (☏406-222-1892; www.fs.fed.us/r1/gallatin) for information. Both are reservable through Recreation.gov (☏877-444-6777; www.recreation.gov).

The roadside, 18-site Canyon Campground (sites $7) in Yankee Jim Canyon, 16 miles from Yellowstone, is waterless but does have picnic tables, fire rings and an accessible toilet. It's open year-round

For a cheaper, less-known option than the pricier ranches, the USFS operates the year-round Big Creek Cabin (cabin $50). The cabin sleeps 10 and is set a half-mile from the ranch in the Gallatin National Forest.

There's also **Mill Creek Cabin** (cabin $45), which sleeps four, on the east side of the valley 12 miles up E Mill Creek Rd, near Snowbank Campground. It has an electric stove and lights but no mattresses. Reserve either from six months to three days in advance at **Recreation.gov** (☑877-444-6777; www.recreation.gov).

KOA CAMPGROUND **$**
(☑406-222-0992; www.livingstonkoa.com; Pine Creek Rd; tent/RV sites from $28/41, cabins $68-158; ⊙May-Oct; 🛜♨🐾) Nicely situated by Pine Creek between US 89 and the East River Rd, 10 miles south of Livingston, this peaceful spot offers an indoor heated pool, cabins and laundry room.

Mountain Sky Guest Ranch RANCH **$$$**
(☑406-333-4911, 800-548-3392; www.mtnsky.com; daily/weekly rates per person from $325/3365; ♨) The western flanks of the valley hide this professionally run dude ranch, 4.5 miles up Big Creek Rd and 30 miles from Yellowstone. Rates include food and everything from fly-fishing to the sauna, hot tub and good kids' programs. The dawn horseback rides to catch sunrise over Emigrant Peak are a highlight. There's a one-week minimum stay June to August.

Eating

TOP CHOICE / **Paradise Valley**
Grill CONTEMPORARY AMERICAN **$$**
(☑406-222-4815; www.paradisevalleygrill.com; 3840 Hwy 89 S; mains $25; ⊙5:30-9pm Tue-Sun) Sustainable local ingredients, fresh Napa Valley cuisine and fine views of the Yellowstone River combine to make this the valley's most popular restaurant. Reservations are recommended, and try a table outside on summer evenings. The restaurant is 14 miles south of Livingston, just below the **Yellowstone Valley Lodge** (www.yellowstonevalleylodge.com), which offers good accommodation in modern duplex cabins ($119 to $159).

Paradise Valley Pop Stand DINER **$**
(www.thepopstand.com; 5060 Hwy 89; mains $6-11; ⊙6:30am-10pm; 🛜) Just 2.5 miles south of Livingston is this 1950s-style joint serving up hand-dipped malts, burgers and homemade pies. After a few days in the park, you deserve it.

Pine Creek Cafe CAFE **$$**
(www.pinecreeklodgemontana.com; dinner mains $15; ⊙11am-3pm & 5:30-9pm Tue-Fri, 8am-1pm & 5:30-9pm Sat & Sun) Near the KOA on East River Rd, this cozy cafe-restaurant is a bit inconsistent but when it's on form it's a great local spot, with patio seating and weekend live music jams on an outdoor stage. Food ranges from trout tacos to elk burritos and even lobster tail.

Gardiner
☑406 / POP 800 / ELEV 5134FT

A quintessential gateway town founded and fed on tourism, Gardiner, Montana, is the only entrance to Yellowstone National Park open to automobile traffic year-round. The park starts just where the souvenir stores peter out at the south end of town. Mammoth Hot Springs is only 5 miles away.

The town is named after Johnson Gardner, an 'illiterate and brutal trapper' who worked the area in the 1830s. Gardiner only made it onto the map, misspelled, in the 1880s when the Northern Pacific Railroad unveiled its Park Branch Line from Livingston to nearby Cinnabar. Stagecoaches ferried passengers on the last leg of the journey to the park, and Gardiner grew as a transit stop. By 1883 the town's 200 thirsty residents could stagger between 21 saloons.

These days the friendly and unpretentious town sticks to its ranching, mining and outfitting roots. The rodeo still pulls into town five times during the summer, and the plaid shirts and pickups haven't yet given way to microbrews and art galleries.

Sights

Roosevelt Arch LANDMARK
Gardiner's most photographed sight is the park's northwestern entry gate, dedicated by Teddy Roosevelt himself on April 25, 1903, and inscribed with Congress' words: 'for the benefit and enjoyment of the people.'

FREE **Yellowstone Heritage**
& Research Center MUSEUM
(☑307-344-2664; www.nps.gov/yell/historyculture/collections.htm; ⊙library 9am-4pm Tue-Fri) The park's abundant archives (over 5 million items and growing) moved from Mammoth to this research facility in 2004. Visitors can peruse the lobby displays and library. Interesting hour-long tours operate at 10am on Tuesday and Thursday (Memorial Day to Labor Day) and take you into the museum and rare book archives. The tour is limited to 10 people, so reserve ahead of time.

Activities

Several outfitters run fishing trips, horseback riding and pack trips into Yellowstone and other nearby mountain areas, though all are primarily hunting operations. Rides start at around $95/160 per half/full day. Outfitters include **Rendezvous Outfitters** (✆406-223-3924; www.yellowstoneroughriders.com) and **Hell's A-Roarin' Outfitters** (✆406-848-7578; www.hellsaroarinoutfitters.com; Jardine), which also does cabin rentals, luxury tent accommodation and steak cookouts, courtesy of the Johnson family.

For back-road biking routes north of Gardiner, see Paradise Valley (p150). For the backdoor route out of Yellowstone Park to Gardiner see p114.

Parks' Fly Shop   FISHING
(✆406-848-7314; www.parksflyshop.com; 202 S 2nd St) Old-school owner Richard Parks sells flies (specifically designed for park waters), rents gear and offers float trips, and is the author of the much-respected *Fly Fishing Yellowstone National Park* (Falcon Press). In winter the action switches to cross-country ski ($15 per day) and snowshoe rental.

Rafting

Half a dozen companies operate family-friendly rafting trips on the Yellowstone River through the Class II to III rapids of Yankee Jim Canyon, one of Montana's more famous white-water spots. Half-day rafting trips start from $40/28 for adults/children, or $77/55 for a full day, and most companies also offer half-day 'paddle and saddle' combos for around $100/90.

Yellowstone Raft Company (✆800-858-7781; www.yellowstoneraft.com; 111 2nd St) With over 30 years of local experience, also has half-day kayaking lessons on the river and offers helmet video cams.

Wild West Whitewater Rafting (✆406-848-2252; www.wildwestrafting.com; Scott St W) Also runs gentler scenic floats in the upper Paradise Valley and inflatable kayak trips.

Montana Whitewater (✆406-848-7398; www.montanawhitewater.com; 603 Scott St W) Rents canoes, kayaks and float tubes, in addition to horseback-riding combo trips in the park.

Flying Pig Adventures (✆406-848-7510; www.flyingpigrafting.com, www.horsebackyellowstone.com; 511 Scott St W) Rafting shop that also offers horseback rides, cowboy cookouts, Yellowstone nature safaris and an outdoor gear shop that stocks bear spray.

River Source (✆888-406-2214; www.riversourcerafting.com; Hwy 89) Eight miles north of Gardiner, with canoe trips and wintertime dog sledding.

Tours

The park concessionaire, **Xanterra** (✆307-344-7901; www.yellowstonenationalparklodges.com) runs its **Yellowstone in a Day** (adult/3-11yr $73/36.50) tour three times a week from Gardiner from June to late September, taking in all the major park sights in an exhausting 11 hours.

Sleeping

Camping

Gallatin National Forest offers the following three first-come, first-served primitive campgrounds just northeast of Gardiner:

Eagle Creek Campground   CAMPGROUND $
($7) Open year-round, with 16 woodsy sites and pit toilets but no water; 2 miles northeast of Gardiner on unpaved Jardine Rd.

Timber Camp Campground   CAMPGROUND $
(FR493; ⊘mid-Jun–Oct) Further along the Bear Creek dirt road from Eagle Creek, 10 miles from Gardiner and 4 miles past Jardine. Free dispersed camping with a toilet but no water.

Bear Creek Campground   CAMPGROUND $
(⊘mid-Jun–Oct) Two miles further, free dispersed camping with a toilet but no water. There are hiking options from Bear Creek Trailhead.

Rocky Mountain RV Park   RV PARK $
(✆877-534-6931; www.rockymountaincampground.com; 14 Jardine Rd; RV sites from $51.50, cabins $50-125; ⊘mid-Apr–mid-Oct; ☎🐾) This friendly place overlooking the river offers showers, laundry, full hookups and fine panoramas of Yellowstone, but little shade. Ask about the simple one- or two-room cabins that can sleep up to six.

Yellowstone RV Park   RV PARK $
(✆406-848-7496; www.ventureswestinc.com; 117 Hwy 89; tent/RV sites $27/48; ☎🐾) At the northwest end of town, this RV park has 46 fairly cramped riverside sites with full hookups, plus showers and a laundry.

Gardiner

Gardiner

Lodging

About half of Gardiner's accommodation closes between October and May and those that remain cut their rates by around 50%.

In addition to the following, other chain places (all with free breakfast) include **Comfort Inn** (☎406-848-7536; www.yellowstone comfortinn.com; d $150;🐾), **Super 8 Motel** (☎406-848-7401; www.yellowstonesuper8.com; d $130; 🐾🏊🐾) and the recently remodeled **Travelodge** (☎406-848-7520; www.yellowstone rooms.com; 1102 Scott St, d $139-279;🐾).

Absaroka Lodge   HOTEL **$$**
(☎800-755-7414; www.yellowstonemotel.com; S 2nd St; r $110-125; 🐾) Modern, but surprisingly

To Eagle Creek Campground (2mi); Jardine (6mi)

Jardine Rd · Scott St E · S 2nd St · W Stone St · S 3rd St · W Main St · S 1st St · E Park St · W Park St · Chamber of Commerce · North Entrance Station · To Mammoth (5mi)

AROUND YELLOWSTONE GARDINER

200; 🛜@) For a more personal touch, this riverside B&B, 3 miles north of town, offers rooms in the main house or more private self-contained cabins, all with fine views of Electric Peak. For insider advice on your park itinerary chat to the owners; a Yellowstone ranger and his knowledgeable wife. Evening cookies and the option of early-morning breakfasts to go are all part of the thoughtful service.

Hillcrest Cottages
MOTEL $
(📞800-970-7353; www.hillcrestcottages.com; 200 Scott St W; d $78-94, 2-room cottages $120; ⊙May-Sep; 🛜) This slightly cramped mini-village features a variety of pleasant if old-fashioned cottages, most with kitchenettes, that sleep two to seven.

Yellowstone River Motel
MOTEL $
(📞406-848-7303; www.yellowstonerivermotel.com; 14 E Park St; d $89-110, ste $145; ⊙May-Oct; 🛜) This is one of the better-run motels, clean and friendly with picnic tables and a BBQ area overlooking the river. The renovated new-block rooms are freshest, with a fridge and microwave.

Yellowstone Village Inn
MOTEL $$
(📞800-228-8158; www.yellowstoneinn.com; 1102 Scott St W; d/ste from $129/199; 🛜🏊) Standing alone at the entrance to Gardiner, this locally owned motel is pretty good value, with a few family suites featuring a private porch.

Best Western by Mammoth Hot Springs
HOTEL $$
(📞406-848-7311; www.bestwestern.com/mammoth hotsprings; 905 Scott St W; d $180; 🏊) It's not 'by Mammoth Hot Springs' (they're 5 miles away), but once you get past that tiny fib this is a solid choice, with spacious modern rooms. Pay $10 more for a mountain-view room, $20 for a riverside view or $30 for a hot tub in your room. After a hard day in the park, the kids can attack the indoor pool while the adults relax in the sauna.

Eating

For a lighter meal try the fresh tacos and quesadillas at the funky **Silvertip Restaurant** (www.the-silvertip.com; 505 Scott St W; ⊙11am-8pm; @), served with homemade salsa on the back deck. Alternatively, browse the selection of Yellowstone books over a fresh wrap, salad or espresso at the **Tumbleweed Bookstore & Cafe** (501 Scott St W; wraps $8.50; ⊙9am-6pm; 🛜).

unobtrusive, this place offers excellent-value doubles, some with kitchenette and all with a fine balcony overlooking the rushing Yellowstone River. Book this one early.

Yellowstone Suites
B&B $$
(📞406-848-7937; www.yellowstonesuites.com; 506 S 4th St; d without/with bath $120/150; @🛜) There's plenty of privacy in this well-appointed, four-room 100-year-old B&B, which makes a nice antidote to motel overload. There are cozy sitting spaces and views of Electric Peak, but only two rooms have attached bathrooms. Get a deal by renting an entire floor (two rooms).

Gardiner Guesthouse
B&B $$
(📞406-848-9414; www.gardinerguesthouse.com; 112 E Main St; d incl breakfast $95-125; 🏊🛜) Kid-friendly, pet-friendly and pretty much everyone-friendly, this homey B&B offers two rooms with shared bath and one suite available in the main house, as well as a rustic cabin ($145) in the back – perfect for anglers hooking up with owner Richard Parks at the next-door fly-fishing shop.

Headwaters of the Yellowstone B&B
B&B $$
(📞406-848-7073; www.headwatersbandb.com; 9 Olson Lake Rd; r incl breakfast $140, cabins $175-

Fill up on park supplies at the **Food Farm** (701 Scott St W; ⏰7am-9pm Mon-Sat, 8am-8pm Sun), across from the Super 8 Motel.

Rosie's Grill   AMERICAN $$
(www.redsbluegoosesaloon.com; 206 Park St; mains $16-24; ⏰5-9:30pm) Dining out in Gardiner is generally a disappointment. That said, Rosie's is probably the best option in town, with good pastas, salmon and trout dinners. The Big Sky pasta is popular.

The Corral Drive-In   DRIVE-IN $
(711 Scott St W; burgers $8-12; ⏰11am-11pm Apr-Oct) This old-style malt-and-greasy-burger stand has been proudly clogging arteries since 1960. It's neither gourmet nor even all that cheap but really, where else are you going to dive into a half-pound elk burger followed by a huckleberry shake?

Sawtooth Deli   SANDWICHES $
(220 W Park St; mains $8, ⏰8am-9:30pm Tue-Sat) For a quick meal join the locals at this friendly place, which serves hot and cold subs, barbeque specials and decent breakfasts.

Drinking

Grab your morning espresso at either **Hi Country Trading** (W Park St; ⏰7:30am-9pm), which has some outdoor seating, or **Yellowstone Perk** (208 W Park St; ⏰from 7am), which also offers ice cream and a pharmacy.

Easily the nicest place for a beer is the rooftop deck above Rosie's, part of **Red's Blue Goose Saloon** (www.redsbluegoose saloon.com; 206 Park St). Kick back on the sun chairs and spot elk the easy way, from the rim of your pint glass.

Information

Chamber of Commerce (☎406-848-7971; www.gardinerchamber.com; 220 W Park St; ⏰9am-6pm Mon-Fri, 9am-5pm Sat, 1-5pm Sun) Tourist information and a public bathroom.

Gallatin National Forest Gardiner District Office (☎406-848-7375; www.fs.fed.us/r1/gallatin; 805 Scott St W; ⏰8am-5pm Mon-Fri) Campground and hiking information.

Sinclair Gas Station (Scott St W) Sells Montana state fishing licenses.

Yellowstone Association (W Park St; ⏰8am-8pm) Impressive restored old general store that houses a bookstore and information office with a map of recent wildlife sightings in the park. For Yellowstone Institute courses see p259; course info and some classes can be found here.

GALLATIN ROUTE

Bozeman

🗺️406 / POP 37,000 / ELEV 4700FT

The hip college town of Bozeman, only an hour's drive north of Yellowstone, is regularly voted one of America's best outdoor towns, and with good reason. With excellent restaurants and shops, one of the region's best museums and outdoor opportunities that beckon from every corner, the town is well worth a stop en route to the more rustic delights of the parks. The town is named after John Bozeman, who guided settlers here along his namesake Bozeman Trail, a spur of the Oregon, from 1864.

To plug into the local scene pick up the free local paper *The Bozone* (www.bozone. com). Highlights of the cultural year include the independent film and arts festival **Hatchfest** (www.hatchfest.org) in October and the artsy **Sweetpea Festival** (www.sweet peafestival.org), with lots of food, art and live music in August.

Sights

TOP CHOICE **Museum of the Rockies**   MUSEUM
(☎406-994-3466; www.museumoftherockies.org; cnr S 7th Ave & Kagy Blvd; adult/child $13/9; ⏰8am-8pm Memorial Day-Labor Day, 9am-5pm Mon-Sat & 12:30-5pm Sun rest of year; 🖪) Arguably Montana's most entertaining museum, MOR offers some of the most jaw-dropping dinosaur displays you'll ever see, alongside displays on native cultures of the Northern Rockies (look for the fabulous 1904 photo of Geronimo driving a Cadillac), hourly planetarium shows and costumed homesteaders reenacting 1880s life at the next-door **Living History Farm** (summer only). The **Kids Explore Yellowstone** exhibit, where kids can play camping in a tent or dangle a line from Fishing Bridge, is particularly good interactive fun for families. Count on at least half a day here; the entry fee gives admission for two days. The museum is in the south of town, next to Montana State University (MSU). You'll be greeted at the door by 'Big Mike,' a life-sized bronze T Rex.

FREE **Emerson Cultural Center**   ARTS CENTER
(☎406-587-9797; www.theemerson.org; 111 S Grand Ave; ⏰most galleries closed Mon) Known around town as 'the Emerson,' the nonprofit is the place to plug into Bozeman's art scene,

MONTANASAURUS REX

It's amazing how much drama you can find in a single 50-million-year-old slab of rock at Bozeman's Museum of the Rockies (MOR). From the group of teenage diplodocus who suffocated when their legs became stuck in river mud, or the dinosaur skeleton surrounded by the teeth of the pack of predators that devoured it, these are fossils that come alive before your eyes. We challenge you to stare at the terrifying claws of a deinonychus without feeling a slight shiver run down your spine.

Like all good museums, MOR also shatters preconceptions, reminding you that many dinosaurs were in fact clad in feathers and that sharks once swam the tropical seas covering current-day Montana. This is mind-boggling stuff. Then there's the scale of the beasts – 9ft-long rib bones stand in the corner near huge 20ft-tall reconstructions of horned torosaurus and Montanaceratops (we kid you not).

Even the curator is larger than life; paleontologist Jack Horner is widely believed to have been the model for the character Dr Alan Grant in the book *Jurassic Park* and served as technical adviser to the film. And yes, they *are* extracting soft tissue from tyrannosaur thigh bones, right here in Bozeman.

---

with retail galleries, exhibits, studios and a fine cafe/restaurant.

Pioneer Museum MUSEUM
(☑406-522-8122; www.pioneermuseum.org; 317 W Main St; adult/under 12yr $5/free; ☉10am-5pm Mon-Sat Memorial Day-Labor Day, 11am-4pm Tue-Sat rest of year) The former town jail does a good job presenting local history and famous residents (including one Gary Cooper).

Activities

Spire Climbing Center CLIMBING GYM
(☑406-586-0706; www.spireclimbingcenter.com; 13 Enterprise Blvd; day pass $15; ☉noon-10pm Mon-Thu, noon-9pm Fri, 10am-6pm Sat & Sun) Hone your climbing skills on the indoor wall here before heading off to tackle Grand Teton. Good-value private lessons and weekly classes are offered.

Bozeman is well served with outdoor gear shops, such as the following:

Bangtail Bikes (☑406-587-4905; www.bangtailbikes; 137 E Main St) Bozeman's best for buying and renting bikes and cross-country skis, in a new location.

Barrel Mountaineering (☑406-582-1335; www.barrelmountaineering.com; 240 E Main St) For all-purpose information, maps, and climbing and skiing gear.

Northern Lights (☑866-586-2225; www.northernlightstrading.com; 1716 West Babcock) Good but pricey gear store, offering demos and rentals.

REI (☑406-587-1938; www.rei.com/bozeman; 2220 Tschache St) Yellowstone topo maps, backpacking rentals and popular weekly talks/workshops.

Sleeping

Camping

There are three USFS campsites (all sites $14) southeast of town near the Hyalite Reservoir: **Langhor** (10 sites, 11 miles from Bozeman), **Hood Creek** (18 sites, 17 miles) and **Chisholm** (10 sites, 18 miles). Take Forestry Rd No 62 from south Bozeman. All sites can be reserved through **Recreation.gov** (☑877-444-6777; www.recreation.gov).

Bozeman KOA CAMPGROUND $
(☑406-587-3030; tent/RV sites from $31/39, cabins $63-73; ▩☏☂☂) Off I-90, 8 miles west of Bozeman in the Gallatin Valley and next to Bozeman Hot Springs, this is the only campground in the area open year-round.

Bear Canyon Campground CAMPGROUND $
(☑800-438-1575; www.bearcanyoncampground.com; tent sites $20, RV sites $28-33; ☉May–mid-Oct; ☂▩) Three miles east of Bozeman, just off I-90 (exit 313), this has a heated outdoor pool, laundry facilities and a store.

Lodging

Lewis & Clark Motel MOTEL $$
(☑800-332-7666; www.lewisandclarkmotel.net; 824 W Main St; r $109-119; ◉☏) For a drop of Vegas in your Montana, stay at this fun locally owned motel. The large rooms have floor-to-ceiling front windows and there are neat touches, from the file case of information on local hikes to the candied pecans at check-in. The piped '50s music just adds to the retro Ratpack vibe. Weekday and off-season discounts help things along.

Lehrkind Mansion Bed & Breakfast   B&B $$

(☎406-585-6932; www.bozemanbedandbreak fast.com; 719 N Wallace Ave; d incl breakfast $159-229;🕏) This sophisticated Victorian B&B of nine rooms was built by a Swiss-German master brewer and is steeped in period furniture and history (the bricks were actually soaked in beer before construction). The 7ft Regina music box (one of only 25) is a highlight, as are the organic breakfasts and clawfoot bathtubs. If they are around, the owners can fill you in on all the park's hidden spots; they are former Yellowstone Park rangers.

Howlers Inn   B&B $$

(☎406-586-0304; www.howlersinn.com; 3185 Jackson Creek Rd; d incl breakfast $115-145; 🕏🐾) Wolf-watchers will love this tranquil spot, in a beautiful valley 15 minutes outside Bozeman. Two captive-born wolf packs live onsite in fenced compounds, supported by profits from the B&B. The three spacious rooms in the main lodge come with a DVD player, or choose the separate two-bedroom cabin ($195) with kitchen. With luck you'll drift off to sleep listening to the howling of the wolves. Take exit 319 off I-90.

Royal 7 Motel   MOTEL $

(☎800-587-3103; www.royal7inn.com; 310 N 7th Ave; d $60-80; @🕏) This little inn really tries. It's dated (squint and it's almost retro cool) but spacious rooms offer large TVs, microwave, fridge, continental breakfast, laundry service and a handful of DVDs for rent. Swings are set up in a grassy space for the kiddies.

Eating

Only Jackson can compete with Bozeman's range of excellent restaurants. The Ale Works and Plonk (see p171) both offer good food.

John Bozeman's
Bistro   CONTEMPORARY AMERICAN $$$

(☎406-587-4100; www.johnbozemansbistro.com; 125 W Main St; mains $14-30; ⊙Tue-Sat; 🍴) Simply put, this is Bozeman's best restaurant. Thai, Creole and pan-Asian slants liven the cowboy-dinner steak, as do fine starters like lobster chowder and cambazola pastry. The weekly 'superfood' specials focus on especially fresh, healthy, seasonal vegetarian food – perfect after a week in the park eating chili out of a can. The back bar is a fine place for a drink.

Community Co-Op   SUPERMARKET $

(www.bozo.coop; 908 W Main; mains $5-10; ⊙7am-10pm Mon-Sat, 8am-10pm Sun; 🕏🍴) The beloved local Co-op is the best place to stock up on a park picnic, from organic trail mix to superb salads and soups. Both the main market and a downtown branch (44 E Main) offer hot meals to eat in or take away and the main branch has great organic coffee and pastries at the upstairs Flying C Café.

La Parrilla   CALIFORNIA WRAPS $

(1624 W Babcock St; wraps $7-9; ⊙11am-9pm) Join the local MSU students for a top lunch of gourmet California-style fish tacos, burritos and exotic wraps, strong on the cilantro and wasabi, served by bright and hip staff.

Cateye Café   BREAKFAST $

(www.cateyecafe.com; 23 N Tracy; mains $8-10; ⊙7am-2pm) The banana-bread French toast and daily specials make the hip and quirky Cateye our favorite Bozeman breakfast. Expect to queue on weekends but at least you can sip on a coffee while you wait.

La Tinga   MEXICAN $

(12 E Main St; mains $1.50-7; ⊙9:30am-2pm Mon-Sat) Simple, cheap and authentic, La Tinga is no-frills cantina dining at its tastiest. The tiny order-at-the-counter taco joint makes a delicious version of the Mexican pork dish it is named after, plus lots of freshly made tacos and lunch specials for around $7. Cash only.

Dave's Sushi   SUSHI $

(www.davessushi.com; 115 N. Bozeman Ave; sushi $6-10; ⊙11am-9:30pm Mon-Sat) Unpretentious converted wooden house, offering the best rolls and freshest fish for miles around, 1½ blocks north of Main St.

Starky's Authentic Americana   DELI $$

(www.starkysonline.com; 24 N Tracy; mains $10-20; ⊙11am-4pm Mon, 5-9pm Tue-Sat, 9am-3pm Sun) Rebuilt from the ashes but still offering great New York–style deli lunches, including matzoh-ball soup and pastrami sandwiches, plus a good Sunday brunch, live music and a nice patio.

Drinking & Entertainment

College dive hangouts include the pumping Haufbrau (22 S 8th Ave), with frequent live music, and the smaller next-door Molly Brown (www.mollybrownbozeman.com; 703 W Babcock). For a rundown of what's playing where visit www.bozemanevents.net or

ROCKY MOUNTAIN BREWS

The Yellowstone states of Wyoming and Montana are fast developing a reputation among beer hounds for hosting some of the country's best microbreweries.

Snake River Brewing Co (p218; www.snakeriverbrewing.com) in Jackson is the region's most popular brewpub. Flagship beers include the Austrian-style Snake River Lager, the crisp Snake River Pale Ale, the dark and creamy Snake River Zonker Stout, and numerous other brews.

Teton Valley's **Grand Teton Brewing Company** (www.grandtetonbrewing.com) uses local spring water to produce its Old Faithful Ale, Teton Ale and Moose Juice Stout. Its Teton Huckleberry Wheat is one of several popular regional fruit beers.

Missoula's **Bayern Brewing** (www.bayernbrewery.com) is the only German microbrewery in the Rockies, serving up amber, pilsner, Killarney and Hefeweizen beers. **Big Sky Brewing** (www.bigskybrew.com), also of Missoula, produces Montana's best-selling microbrew, Moose Drool, a creamy brown ale with hints of coffee. The English-style Scape Goat pale ale is also excellent.

Actually from Big Sky, **Lone Peak Brewery** (www.lonepeakbrewery.com; Meadow Village; ⊙11am-10pm) is a kid-friendly brewpub equipped with a fine shuffleboard and light food menu. The Lone Peak IPA and Nordic Blond are the most popular, or try a range of 4oz samples for $1.25 each.

Yellowstone Valley Brewing (www.yellowstonevalleybrew.com) in Billings names all its beers after fishing flies, including the amber-colored Wild Fly Ale, the dark, malty Renegade Red Ale, the clear Grizzly Wulff Wheat and the full-flavored Black Widow Oatmeal Stout. Pop into the **Brewhouse Garage Pub** (2123 1st Ave N; ⊙4-8pm Mon-Sat) in Billings for a sample, before heading to nearby **Angry Hank's** (2405 1st Ave N) for more excellent Billings brews (the Head Trauma India Pale Ale is recommended).

If you are headed along the Beartooth Hwy, drop into **Red Lodge Ales** (p138) en route for a brewery tour (phone ahead) and sample their refreshing German-style Glacier Ale or grapefruit-infused Bent Nail.

In Bozeman, head for the excellent **Montana Ale Works** (p161) to try the region's best brews, including the local Bozone brews. Or drink from the source at **Bozeman Brewing** (www.bozemanbrewing.com; 504 N Broadway; taproom; ⊙4-8pm Mon-Sun, 12:30-8pm Fri), which has a bustling taproom and offers a four-glass sampler served on a downhill ski. Nearby Livingston offers the small **Neptune's Brewery** (www.neptunesdock.com; 119 N L St; ⊙4-8pm), though the Belgian-style ales here can be a little weak.

The so-called 'Yellowstone Ale' for sale in the park's Yellowstone General Stores is actually a repackaged variety of German-style Dead Man Ale, brewed in Portland, Oregon, but other genuine Yellowstone beers worth tracking down, if only to say their names out loud ('a pint of Old Stinky's, please'), are Monkey's Dunkel, Powder Hound, Trout Slayer, Custer's Last Ale and, yes, Old Stinky's.

www.bozone.com. **Cactus Records** (29 W Main St), the region's best music store, has the lowdown on musical happenings.

TOP CHOICE **Montana Ale Works**   BREWPUB
(www.montanaaleworks.com; 611 E Main St; mains $11-24; ⊙4-11pm Sun-Thu, 4pm-midnight Fri & Sat) Bozeman's former rail warehouse adds some industrial chic to its excellent food, pool tables and people-watching. Staff are happy to let you taste any of the 30 microbrews on tap, including the local Bozones, and if you find a favorite, you can take some home.

Plonk   WINE BAR
(www.plonkwine.com; 29 E Main St; dinner mains $13-26; ⊙11:30am-midnight) You'll need your last unwrinkled shirt and a date to take full advantage of the classy spot, featuring 35 wines by the glass and a discerning selection of imported cheeses or dinner dishes like seared scallops and foie gras. The front and back patios are hard to leave on a summer's day, while the great vinyl collection adds a club vibe to the back lounge on Friday nights.

Zebra Lounge   LIVE MUSIC
(www.zebracocktaillounge.com; 321 E Main St) Most nights bring live music (strong on club

and hip-hop) to this lounge bar, half a block north of Main on Rouse Ave S. Shows start around 8pm.

Information

Country Bookshelf (www.countrybookshelf. com; 28 W Main St) This community institution hosts readings by local authors like Tim Cahill and Jim Harrison.

Downtown Bozeman Visitor Information (☑406-586-4008; 224 E Main St; www.down townbozeman.org) See also www.bozeman chamber.com.

Gallatin National Forest Bozeman Ranger District (☑406-522-2520; www.fs.usda.gov/ gallatin; 3710 Fallon, Suite C) Located to the west of town.

Gallatin Valley

A broad ribbon snaking through big valleys, the Gallatin River leaves its headwaters in the northwest corner of Yellowstone National Park to cascade through the narrow, craggy Gallatin Valley. US 191 traces its path, eventually meeting the Madison, Jefferson and Missouri Rivers at Three Forks. Sandwiched between the scenic Madison and Gallatin Ranges, the route – first forged by Lewis and Clark – is peppered with enough trailheads to make return hikers and skiers arthritic. The commercial heart of the valley is the broad opening connecting Big Sky Ski Resort.

On a clear day, look for a distinct cluster of summits exceeding 10,000ft rising sharply out of the silhouette of the Gallatin Range, west of US 191. These are the Spanish Peaks, the valley's premier hiking and backcountry ski destination and part of the Lee Metcalf Wilderness.

BIG SKY

Commercial development hits hyperdrive near the turnoff to Big Sky, the Gallatin Valley's main attraction, 18 miles north of Yellowstone and 36 miles south of Bozeman. This world-class winter and summer resort attracts a cosmopolitan crowd more partial to an organic Pinot Noir than a can of Bud Lite, and multimillion-dollar homes continue to sprout up like milkweed.

Big Sky spreads from US 191 to the base of Lone Mountain in four areas: Gallatin Canyon, West Fork Meadows, Meadow Village and Mountain Village. Meadow Village and West Fork Meadows offer the bulk of the services, including a dozen restaurants;

all are connected by a bike trail and a free shuttle service.

Activities

Big Sky Resort (www.bigskyresort.com) is comprised of Andesite Mountain (8800ft) and Lone Mountain (11,166ft), with a 4350ft vertical drop and 3800 acres of skiable terrain, a 15-passenger tram, a gondola and multiple high-speed lifts. Tickets are $81/61 for adults/juniors; children under 10 ski free.

A fantastic skiing or snowboarding alternative is **Moonlight Basin** (www.moonlight basin.com), 1.2 miles past Big Sky Mountain Village. Powder is plentiful on Lone Mountain's northern slopes; experts covet its double-diamond chutes and bowls. Terrain includes 2000 skiable acres with 4500ft of vertical drop. Tickets are $58/49 full/half day; children under 10 ski free. Combination tickets with Big Sky (the 'Biggest Skiing in America') now allow you to connect both slopes for an awesome 5500 acres of terrain ($95 for a full day).

From June to September the Ramcharger lift shuttles people and bikes to 10,000ft (10:30am to 3:30pm) for $19 ($30 for unlimited use), from where mountain bikers can choose from a dozen great downhill rides. Thrillseekers will love the new bungee trampoline ($11) and guided ziplines ($63).

Lone Mountain Ranch   RESORT
(☑406-995-4644; www.lmranch.com) Tucked into the sagebrush meadows, this is one of the country's top Nordic resorts, with 47 miles of groomed cross-country trails and a full-service, high-end lodge. Day trail ski/ snowshoe passes cost $20/15; it's free for kids 12 and under. The 'first-timer' package ($53) is a particular bargain, including group lesson, trail fee and gear rental. Other standouts include the prime-rib dinner sleigh rides ($85) and ski and snowshoe tours of the Yellowstone Park's northwest ($85 per person). Summer brings fly-fishing and horseback riding.

East Slope Outdoors   SKI RENTAL
(☑406-995-4369; www.eastslopeoutdoors.com) Among the many rental shops around Big Sky, this place 100 yards south of the Big Sky turnoff on US 191 tends to have the best prices, with downhill/cross-country ski rentals from $21/12 per day.

Sleeping & Eating

Inquire about condo, cabin or house rentals in Big Sky through **East West Resorts**

(☎877-527-1817; www.eastwestresorts.com) or **Big Sky Central Reservations** (☎800-548-4486; www.bigskyresort.com); ski packages are available throughout the winter season.

Hungry Moose Market   GROCERY $
(www.hungrymoose.com; West Fork Meadows; ⊙6:30am-10pm; ☎✍) If a good cabernet and hot made-to-order panini would spice up the picnic, check out Big Sky's favorite post-ride or pre-ski stop. There are also hot breakfasts, espresso, smoothies, bulk food and groceries leaning toward the organic and natural. Take your order to go or use the wi-fi on the patio.

Information
Big Sky Chamber of Commerce (☎800-943-4111; www.bigskychamber.com; West Fort Meadows) For a calendar of events or hiking handouts.
Big Sky Resort (☎800-548-4486; www.bigskyresort.com) Also has information.

BIG SKY TO WEST YELLOWSTONE
After passing the Gallatin Canyon, Hwy 191 briefly enters the far northwestern corner of Yellowstone National Park (there is no entry booth here). The paved route makes for a great bike ride; it's less traveled and notably less crowded than the main park loops.

Several remote park trails offer quiet day hikes and ambitious multiday backpacking trips across the Gallatin range to the Mammoth region. **Specimen Creek Trailhead** leads to Gallatin's petrified forest, created 50 million years ago when lava, ash and mudflows swallowed trees and other vegetation. The **Bighorn Pass** and **Fawn Pass Trailheads** beckon with more good hiking and hot-springs soaks and then the road leaves the headwaters of the Gallatin River at Divide Lake. The Madison Range and Taylor Peaks of the Lee Metcalf Wilderness lie to the west.

About 12 miles before reaching West Yellowstone you'll see the turn-off to Hebgen Lake (Hwy 287).

Activities
Hiking & Backpacking
Hiking trails – all open to mountain biking – head into the mountains along numerous creek drainages from both sides of US 191. Trails are marked on Beartooth Publishing's *Bozeman & Big Sky's Essential Dayhikes* map, available at local sports stores, and they also produce a mountain-bike version.

A favorite dining and hiking combo is to hike up to the fire lookout at the top of the **Cinnamon Creek Trail** (6.6 miles return, gaining 2675ft), then have lunch or dinner at the Cinnamon Lodge, opposite the trailhead across US 191.

The most well-trodden hikes are in the north half of the valley. The popular 6-mile round-trip hike to **Lava Lake** offers decent trout fishing. The trailhead is at tight turnoff at a dangerous curve in Hwy 191. The trail climbs about 1600ft, crossing Cascade Creek several times to meadows and then continues up more switchbacks. Good campsites flank Lava Lake's northeast shore, but fires are banned within 0.5 miles of the lake.

A trailhead on Squaw Creek Rd accesses several trails. The 2.5-mile climb to the top of the **Storm Castle Trail** (trail 92) offers great views, but the 1900 ft climb is unrelenting, with the last quarter-mile, across loose scree, especially strenuous and tricky.

The equally demanding 8-mile round-trip **Garnet Lookout Trail** (trail 85) leads off in the opposite direction, gaining 2850ft to the top of Garnet Peak, where there is a USFS lookout tower that can be rented as a cabin.

One of the best backpacking destinations is the **Spanish Peaks** area, accessed at the end of USFS Rd 982, about 22 miles south of Bozeman. Camping is allowed at the trailhead, and there's a USFS cabin nearby. Most routes are overnighters or multiday loops. A popular loop leads up Falls Creek to the Jerome Rock Lakes (8 miles) and then back down the South Fork. Longer loops take in the Spanish Lakes (8.5 miles from the trailhead) or Mirror Lake (7.5 miles) and return via Indian Ridge and Little Hellroaring Creek.

Other Activities
Scenes from the film *A River Runs Through It* were filmed on the beautiful Gallatin River, where local anglers swear that the sweet spot is anywhere you cast a line. You will also find fishing access sites at Greek Creek, Moose Creek Flat and Red Cliff Campgrounds.

East Slope Outdoors (☎406-995-4369; www.eastslopoutdoors.com), 100 yards south of the Big Sky turnoff, has an Orvis store full of equipment for rent or sale and offers guided fly-fishing trips with instruction, as does **Gallatin Riverguides** (☎406-995-2290; www.montanaflyfishing.com), 0.5 miles south of the Big Sky turnoff, which also offers women-only fishing trips.

Cinnamon Lodge Adventures (☎406-995-4253; www.mountainayresadventures.com)

offers guided mountain-biking and backpacking adventures. Adventure couple Ryan and Morgan do it all – from half-day vehicle-assisted trips to multiday adventures in remote areas as well as Yellowstone National Park.

Gallatin Valley offers the best white-water rafting around Yellowstone – most exciting during June's high water. For inspiration, check out the 'mad mile' of white-water visible from the main road after the Cascade Creek bridge.

Geyser Whitewater Expeditions (☏406-995-4989; www.raftmontana.com) on US 191, 1 mile south of the Big Sky turnoff, offers white-water rafting (full/half day $84/48) and kayaking (half-day $61). **Montana Whitewater** (☏406-995-4613; www.montanawhitewater.com; Hwy 191 mile marker 64; full/half day $79/47) runs similar trips and a half-day introduction to fly fishing for $55 per person in a group.

A number of outfitters offer horseback-riding trips, for about $34 per hour, $80 for a half day and $136 for a full day:

Big Sky Stables (☏406-995-2972)

Diamond K Outfitters (☏406-580-0928)

Jake's Horses (☏406-995-4630; www.jakeshorses.com; Beaver Creek Rd)

Sleeping

Camping

Numerous USFS campgrounds (sites $14, open mid-May to mid-September) snuggle up to the base of the Gallatin Range along US 191. All have potable water and vault toilets. The following are listed from north to south:

Spire Rock Campground (17 sites, $10) Secluded and away from the road; 26 miles south of Bozeman, then 2 miles east on Squaw Creek Rd No 1321.

Greek Creek Campground Doubles as a fishing access site, 31 miles south of Bozeman, with sites on both sides of the highway. Western riverside sites fill early.

Swan Creek Campground Secluded and popular, with 13 sites backing onto Swan Creek; 32 miles south of Bozeman and 1 mile east on paved Rd No 481.

Moose Creek Flat Campground Riverside with good fishing but very close to the road; 9 miles north of Big Sky.

Red Cliff Campground Ample availability with 63 sites, some with electricity ($16); 48 miles south of Bozeman.

The USFS operates four sweet but simple little cabins in the valley: **Little Bear**, **Spanish Creek**, mountaintop **Garnet Mountain** and **Windy Pass**. The last three are accessible by hiking, skiing or snowmobile only. Great value for self-sufficient groups, most cabins are available year-round for $30 per night, sleep four and are equipped with stoves, firewood, cooking supplies and blankets. Contact the **Bozeman district office** (☏406-522-2520) for information. Cabins and campgrounds can be reserved at **Recreation.gov** (☏877-444-6777; www.recreation.gov).

Lodging

Cinnamon Lodge CABINS $
(☏406-995-4253; www.cinnamonlodgeandadventures.com; dm $15, cabins $50-120, cottage $250) This budget roadside establishment attracts a hodgepodge of RVers, families and fly-fishers. The tidy cabins are perhaps the best value in the valley. It is on the Gallatin River 11 miles south of the Big Sky turnoff.

320 Ranch RANCH $$
(☏406-995-4283; www.320ranch.com; cabins incl breakfast from $172) This historic 19th-century ranch occupies a beautiful swathe of the Gallatin, 12 miles south of Big Sky by the Buffalo Horn Creek Trailhead. Guests stay in spacious duplex log cabins with access to a fishing pond (casting lessons cost just $35), outdoor hot tub and trail rides (activities are open to nonguests). Couples should splash out on the historic McGill cabin ($250).

Covered Wagon Ranch RANCH $$$
(☏406-995-4237; www.coveredwagonranch.com; 34035 Gallatin Rd; room & board per night per person $200) Three miles from Yellowstone, near Taylors Fork, this 1925 ranch feels more rugged than some of the rhinestone-cowboy ranches around. With a strong emphasis on riding, a top offer is the small pack trips into Yellowstone.

Gallatin Gateway Inn LODGE $$
(☏406-763-4672; www.gallatingatewayinn.com; r $149-189; ✦✦) At the north end of the valley, 12 miles from Bozeman, the Spanish-style Gallatin Gateway is an elegant retreat built by the Milwaukee Railroad in 1927 as the Yellowstone line terminus. Despite later incarnations as an antique-cars showroom and even a women's mud-wrestling arena, the inn is once again a quiet and classy place to stay. After dinner in the Porter House restaurant retire to the great main hall, with its huge fireplace and Baby Grand.

Rainbow Ranch Lodge   DELUXE LODGE **$$$**
(☎800-937-4132; www.rainbowranchbigsky.com; r $295-400) Rustic and ultra-chic, Rainbow Ranch offers a select group of pondside or riverside rooms, all with roaring stone fireplaces, balconies and access to the romantic outdoor hot tub. The Pondside Luxury rooms are easily the most stylish. The lodge is 5 miles south of the Big Sky turnoff and 12 miles north of Yellowstone.

Eating

Cinnamon Lodge   MEXICAN **$**
(www.cinnamonlodgeandadventures.com; mains $15-20; ⊙dinner) The Western bar and Mexican steakhouse at the Cinnamon Lodge serves excellent food, including good chile rellenos and bacon-wrapped cream-cheese jalapenos, plus there's a nice sun deck to sample Lone Peak brews from Big Sky.

Rainbow Ranch
Lodge   CONTEMPORARY AMERICAN **$$$**
(www.rainbowranchbigsky.com; mains $35; ⊙dinner Tue-Sun) The gourmet restaurant attached to its upscale lodge is the best in the valley and the place for a blowout. The cozy fireside bar boasts Montana's largest wine list.

320 Ranch   WESTERN **$$**
(www.320ranch.com; mains $24-36, saloon mains $10-16; ▣) This rustic ranchhouse restaurant and saloon is heavy on game (go all out for the bison, elk and boar mixed grill) but the real draw is the fun weekly specials. Mondays bring a good-value pig roasts ($10), while the popular Wednesday chuckwagon dinners start off with a two-hour horseback ride (adult/child $85/75) or 20-minute haywagon ride ($55/35); book the latter in advance. Winter activities include fun dessert and appetizer sleigh rides.

Hebgen & Quake Lakes

If the Yellowstone park boundary had been drawn differently, this broad lake valley surrounded by snowcapped peaks would be mobbed with tourists. As it is, visitors with a mind to meander will find wild and beautiful backcountry and a slew of recreational opportunities with a fraction of Yellowstone's crowds.

Connected to Quake Lake by a scenic stretch of the Madison River, Hebgen Lake easily merits a few lazy days of hiking, angling and boating. Motorboats are permitted, and are available for rent at the **Madison Arm Resort & Marina** (www.madisonarmresort.com) on the south shore and the **Yellowstone Holiday** (www.yellowstoneholiday.com) and **Kirkwood Resort** (www.kirkwoodresort.com) marinas on the north shore.

Hiking

Between the Quake Lake visitor center and the dam, Beaver Creek Rd turns north off the highway through an area notorious for grizzly sightings, 3 miles to the **Avalanche Lake/Blue Danube Lake Trailhead** (trail 222/152). Both Avalanche (11-mile round-trip) and Blue Danube (12.5-mile round-trip) lakes make excellent day-hike destinations from July onwards; the trail splits 4.5 miles from the trailhead.

Further along Beaver Creek the road finishes at Potamogeton Park, the trailhead for an excellent mid-summer overnight trip up Sentinel Creek to the dozen or so alpine lakes of the **Hilgard Basin** (trail 202/201, 7 miles, 2700ft elevation gain) of the Lee Metcalf Wilderness.

Along the western shore of Hebgen Lake, a couple of miles past Spring Creek Campground, is the trailhead for Watkins Creek and the 10-mile round-trip day or overnight hike to **Coffin Lakes** (trail 215/209). You can take mountain bikes on this trail, which gains 1700ft in elevation.

The useful 1:63,360 USFS *Lee Metcalf Wilderness and West Yellowstone Vicinity* map marks these and many other trails, as does Beartooth Publishing's *Bozeman & Big Sky's Essential Dayhikes* map.

Sleeping & Eating

On the southwest side of Hebgen Lake, three remote **USFS campgrounds** (late May–mid-Oct) serve boaters and anglers. Four miles down a tarmac road, **Lonesomehurst** (27 sites, sites with/without electricity $16/$24) is the most accessible, with lovely lake views, potable water and a boat ramp. Another 2 miles and 6 miles, respectively, down a dirt road that turns to rough washboard are lakeshore **Cherry Creek** and **Spring Creek** (no fee), both primitive sites with pit toilets but no drinking water. Reach these by turning north off Hwy 20 about halfway between Targhee Pass and West Yellowstone on Denny Creek Rd (USFS Rd 176).

On the southeast shore of the lake is **Rainbow Point Campground** (sites without/with electricity $16/22), 10 miles from West Yellowstone and reservable at www.recreation.gov.

QUAKE LAKE: THE NIGHT THE MOUNTAINS MOVED

Just before midnight on August 17, 1959, an earthquake measuring 7.5 on the Richter scale ripped the landscape of the Upper Madison Valley. As two huge fault blocks tilted and dropped, a massive 80-million-ton landslide suddenly pulverized two campgrounds, before rising halfway up the opposite valley wall.

The slip caused Hebgen Lake's north shore to drop 18ft, flooding lakeshore houses and lodges. Gaps opened up in highways, and cars crashed into the gaping holes in classic disaster-movie style.

Hurricane-force winds caused by the slide then rushed down the valley, tearing off campers' clothes and creating a huge wave on the lake. Mini tsunamis sloshed up and down the lake for the next 12 hours, pouring over the Hebgen Lake Dam, which, amazingly, held firm.

The slide blocked the Madison River, and the waters of newborn Quake Lake soon started to fill, rising 9ft a day as engineers worked around the clock to cut a spillway and avoid a second catastrophic flood. In a final fanfare, several hundred of Yellowstone's thermal features simultaneously erupted.

After the dust settled, it was discovered that 28 people had been killed, mostly in the Rock Creek campsite. Nineteen bodies were never found, presumably entombed under the slide. The quake had been felt in California, and water tables were affected as far away as Hawaii.

Viewing the Site

The best way these days to get to grips with the enormity of the quake, the largest ever to hit the Rockies, is to visit the **Madison River Canyon Earthquake Area Visitors Center** (Quake Lake visitor center; ☎406-682-7620; admission $3; ☺8:30am-6pm Memorial Day-Labor Day), at the end of Quake Lake. Drive up to the interpretive trail for a vista of the dramatic slide area and a memorial boulder inscribed with the names of 28 campers killed in the slide. A dock at the eastern end of Quake Lake allows boaters to glide past the surreal submerged treetops.

The following sites, listed west–east, can be seen on the drive back to West Yellowstone:

» **Cabin Creek Scarp Area** Highlights a 21ft-tall scarp that opened up along the Hebgen Lake fault line. One campsite actually straddled the fault, with the picnic table left above the scarp and the fire ring 21ft below.

» **Refuge Point** Rangers lead a 1.5-mile guided walk from here to view Ghost Village Thursdays at 10am (mid-July to mid-September). Call the visitor center for details. The ski loop here makes for a great 2.3-mile hike in summer but the trail is faint so you need to keep a close eye on the blue diamond tree markers.

» **Ghost Village** A half-dozen cabins lie stranded in the plain here, deposited by the post-earthquake flood. To get here turn off the highway toward Campfire Lodge and then branch right down a dirt road. The cabins are on the other side of the river.

» **Submerged Cabins** Ten miles further east along Hwy 287 a road leads off to a parking area and a short trail to Hebgen Lake, where you can see three partly submerged cabins destroyed by the slide.

Closer to Quake Lake are two scenic concession-run USFS campgrounds: **Cabin Creek** (sites $14; ☺mid-May–mid-Sep), 23 miles from West Yellowstone, and the larger, nearby **Beaver Creek** (reserve at www.recreation. gov; sites $14; ☺early Jun-early Sep).

Call the **Hebgen Lake Ranger District** (☎406-823-6961) in West Yellowstone for information on all of these.

Parade Rest Ranch   CABINS $$
(☎800-753-5934; www.paraderestranch.com; 7979 Grayling Creek Rd; per person per day $178) Ten miles from Yellowstone, northeast of Hebgen Lake, this historic 1935 ranch offers 15 cabins and plenty of activities (see p168). Daily rates include lodging, meals, horseback riding and fly-fishing on Graying Creek. Discounted and room-only rates are available in spring and fall.

Happy Hour Bar & Restaurant   AMERICAN $$
(www.happyhourbar.com; Mile 4, Hwy 287; meals $8-18; ☺11am-midnight) It's hard to think of a better end to the day than grabbing some nachos or a basket of shrimp and watching the sunset sink over Hebgen Lake from the boat-shaped deck. Drawing locals, fly-fishers, bikers and campers, it's a colorful slice of rural Montana, down to the collection of baseball caps and eyebrow-raising boob shots on the walls.

Campfire Lodge Resort   CAMPGROUND, CABINS $
(☑406-646-7258;   www.campfirelodgwestyellow stone.com; RV sites $29-32, cabin $80-200) Just across from Cabin Creek Campground, near Quake Lake, the riverside cabins here sleep up to seven, and there are RV and tent sites, a fly shop and showers ($6). The popular riverside cafe is worth a visit for breakfast or lunch.

Beaver Creek Cabin   CABIN $
(reserve at www.recreation.gov; cabin $30; ☺year-round) A superb base for hiking north of Hebgen Lake, this simple forestry cabin offers bunk beds sleeping four, a stove, utensils, firewood and an ax.

West Yellowstone

☑406 / POP 1500 / ELEV 6600FT

Seated a scant quarter-mile from Yellowstone National Park, the old rail terminus of West Yellowstone is the most popular gateway to Yellowstone Park. It's tiny as towns go but offers its own brand of diversity, from endless variations on the burger joint and souvenir shop to live wolves and grizzlies, RV villages, taxidermy clinics and snowmobile shops. Stop for a quality bison burger, double licks of tart huckleberry ice cream and enough diversions to fill a day's sightseeing.

West Yellowstone is the regional hub for snowmobiling, as well as a launch pad for snowcoach tours into the park. Most locals battled the National Park Service's proposed ban on snowmobiling in Yellowstone National Park, and some are still not happy with the limits imposed. Outside the park, unrestricted snowmobiling continues and is big winter business.

'West' bustles with park traffic in the high seasons (June to September and mid-December to mid-March) but even then the surrounding wilderness remains lightly used. Ride a bike, paddle a canoe, fly-fish or click on skis – even at the height of tourist season, you can have the waterways, lakes and trails mostly to yourself.

History

In the early 1900s the Union Pacific Railroad built a rail line to the western edge of the park, then a fledgling community called Riverside. In 1908, Eagle's General Store (still on Yellowstone Ave today) was established, soon joined by the Madison Hotel in 1912, when its owners arrived after a difficult trek. The frontier-style town, soon rechristened Yellowstone, became a hub of activity fuelled by the railroad, until the rise of automobile travel put the line out of business in 1960. The entrepreneurial spirit ruled even during prohibition, when the town exported potent 'Yellowstone Spring Water.'

In 1920 the community changed its name to West Yellowstone after pressure from Yellowstone's other gateway towns.

Sights

Newcomers can attend a free **orientation talk** (☺9:30am) at the chamber of commerce. Ranger talks are given daily at 1pm at the Yellowstone Historic Center and at 2pm in the Grizzly & Wolf Discovery Center. There are also three weekly ranger-led slide shows at 7pm in the Chamber of Commerce Information Center. Rail buffs should not miss the wonderfully-preserved 1903 **Oregon Short Line Rail Car**, beside the Branch restaurant at the Holiday Inn.

Grizzly & Wolf Discovery Center   ZOO
(☑406-646-7001; www.grizzlydiscoveryctr.org; 201 S Canyon; adult/5-12yr $10.50/5.50; ☺8am-dusk; ♿) Offering an afterlife to 'pest' grizzlies facing extermination, this nonprofit center grants a chance to see captive wolves and bears if you failed to see any in the park. The indoor bear exhibit is good, and there is an information wall with clippings of recent bear encounters, as well as the latest wolf-pack locations. The daily programs on hiking safely in bear country and using bear spray are excellent primers for the park. The twice-daily 'Keeper Kids' program even allows kids to hide food in the enclosures and then watch the bears sniff them out – fun! Admission is good for two days. Here's an interesting fact: faced with a regular supply of food, the bears here don't hibernate.

Yellowstone Historic Center   MUSEUM
(☑406-646-1100;   www.yellowstonehistoriccenter. org; 104 Yellowstone Ave; adult/child $5/3; ☺9am-

West Yellowstone

9pm mid-May–mid-Oct) Housed in the 1909 Union Pacific depot, this small museum explores early stagecoach and rail travel. There are also displays on the 1988 fires and 1959 Hebgen quake, as well as good rotating exhibits.

Yellowstone IMAX Theater CINEMA
(☑406-646-4100; www.yellowstoneimax.com; 101 S Canyon; adult/child $9/6.50; ⊙hourly showings 9am-9pm May-Sep, 1-9pm Oct-Apr) If it's raining head indoors for *Yellowstone, Lewis & Clark* and other films on a screen six stories high.

Eagle's Store HISTORIC BUILDING
(☑406-646-9300; www.eagles-store.com; 3 Canyon St) Grab an old-fashioned soda at the antique 1910 fountain while stocking up on motley collection of fishing supplies at this century-old stalwart.

Activities

West Yellowstone hosts a range of cultural and sporting events, from summer **rodeo** (www.yellowstonerodeo.com; adult/child $12/6) and mountain-man rendezvous to the Spam Cup, a series of ski races in which the lucky winner receives a free can of preserved pork products.

Summer
Both the Rendezvous and Riverside trail systems offer great **mountain biking** and **trail running** when the snow melts. The chamber of commerce sponsors a fall **cycle tour** (www.cycleyellowstone.com; fee $55) to Old Faithful with part of the proceeds going to charity. These fully supported trips (with a van and repair assistance) are a lot of fun and are geared toward a range of abilities.

West Yellowstone has some of the best fishing shops in the Rockies. Top places for information, equipment, rentals and guides include the following:

Arrick's Fly Shop (☑406-646-7290; www. arricks.com; 37 Canyon St)

West Yellowstone

Bud Lilly's Trout Shop (☎406-646-7801; www.budlillys.com; 39 Madison Ave) Rents fishing equipment and offers one-day float and walk trips from $230 per person.

Jacklins Fly Shop (☎406-646-7336; www.jacklinsflyshop.com; 105 Yellowstone Ave) Offers a free weekly casting clinic on Sundays at 7:30pm.

Madison River Outfitters (☎406-646-9644; www.madisonriveroutfitters.com; 117 Canyon St)

Free Heel & Wheel ADVENTURE SPORTS (☎406-646-7744; www.freeheelandwheel.com; 40 Yellowstone Ave; ◎9am-7pm Sun-Thu, 9am-8pm Fri & Sat) The place for maps, gear and advice on cycling and skiing conditions. In addition to renting mountain bikes ($25 per day), skis and snowshoes ($20), it offers touring and skate-ski lessons and organizes free women's rides.

Parade Rest Ranch HORSEBACK RIDING (☎406-646-7217; www.paraderestranch.com) Nine miles from West Yellowstone, this dude ranch offers horseback rides from one to four hours

($35 to $60 per personMonday to Saturday), including sunset rides and corral rides for kids under seven. There are also fun Western cookouts on a section of the old Bannock Trail overlooking Hebgen Lake on Monday and Friday evenings (adult/child $35/15).

Lava Creek Adventures KAYAKING (☎406-646-5145; www.lavacreekadventures.com; 433 Hwy 20) Local expert offers single or double kayak rental (from $49 per day) and wonderful guided sunset glides on Hebgen Lake ($65 per person) that can be combined with park sightseeing trips.

Winter

In November the world-class **Rendezvous Trail System** (www.rendezvousskitrails.com; day pass $8) becomes the training ground for US Olympic cross-country ski teams, with 30 miles of groomed skiing and skating trails. Grooming goes through March, when the Rendezvous Marathon Ski Race draws hundreds of skiers. There are also special kids' loops. For more information, visit Free Heel & Wheel.

Less developed but incredibly scenic, the **Riverside Trails** cut through 1.5 miles of fir and pine to emerge on old National Park Service roads and other trails alongside the Madison River. Catch a link to the trail on the east side of Boundary St between Madison Ave and Firehole Ave.

Rangers lead free **snowshoe walks** from West Yellowstone's Chamber of Commerce Information Center (1:30pm weekends).

Many of the hotels rent snowmobiles and offer good-value winter lodging and rental packages. Guided snowmobile day tours to the park cost around $180 per person. Several agencies rent snowmobiles for outside the park for $114 to $169 per day, including **Rendezvous Snowmobile Rentals** (✆406-646-9564; www.yellowstonevacations.com; 415 Yellowstone Ave) and **Two Top Snowmobile Rentals** (✆800-522-7802; www.twotopsnowmobile.com; 645 Gibbon Ave).

Hellroaring Ski Adventures SNOW SPORTS
(✆406-570-4025; www.skihellroaring.com) Powder hounds keen to get off the grid should try the Centennial Mountains, 25 miles from West Yellowstone. From $200 per person (in a group of up to four), you get a shuttle, guide, meals (take off $50 if you supply your own food), avalanche rescue equipment, climbing skins, hut accommodations and excellent backcountry terrain. Hut rental, for a minimum of four experienced people, costs $250 per night.

Tours

Buffalo Bus Touring Company BUS TOUR
(✆800-426-7669; www.yellowstonevacations.com; 415 Yellowstone Ave; adult/child $65/49) Summertime tours pick up from local campgrounds and motels for a full day of park highlights. In winter they also run full-day guided snowcoach tours to Old Faithful (adult/child $109/90) or Canyon ($119/99) in the park.

Yellowstone Alpen Guides TOUR
(✆800-858-3502; www.yellowstoneguides.com; 555 Yellowstone Ave; adult/child $110/90) Runs 10-person snowcoach tours to Old Faithful, departing daily from mid-December through mid-March. Guided or independent skiing, snowshoeing and kayaking options are also available, as are summer van tours of the park and multiday tours.

Sleeping

Considering the number of motel signs, there is precious little variety in accommo-dations. Expect hefty discounts during the off-season (October, November, and mid-March-June).

Camping

Tent camping in town means cramming between rows of powered-up RVs. For more breathing space, don't forget the national forest campsites on Hebgen Lake.

Bakers Hole Campground CAMPGROUND $
(sites without/with electricity $16/22; ☽mid-May–mid-Sep) The nearest Forestry Service campground has 73 pleasant sites on the banks of the meandering Madison River, just 3 miles north of West Yellowstone.

Yellowstone Grizzly RV Park RV PARK $
(✆406-646-4466; www.grizzlyrv.com; 210 S Electric St; RV site $50-65, cabins $89-125; ☽end May–mid-Oct; ✿) This RV metropolis is pricey but professional and the friendly service includes help with tours and rentals. Facilities include showers, laundry, cable TV and a recreation room.

Lodging

Three Bear Lodge LODGE $$
(✆800-646-7353; 217 Yellowstone Ave; www.threebearlodge.com; main lodge d $219, motel d $159; ✿✪✺) Rebuilt with reclaimed original wood after a 2008 fire, this friendly lodge once again offers spacious, stylish hotel rooms, as well as a cheaper motel option. Kids will go nuts over the themed 'Goldilocks and the Three Bears' suites ($249 to $279).

Stage Coach Inn HOTEL $$
(✆800-842-2882; www.yellowstoneinn.com; 209 Madison Ave; r $189-209) A longtime hub, the Stage Coach has eye-catching stuffed wildlife in the lobby, indoor hot tubs and a Mexican restaurant. Deluxe rooms are bigger and fresher than the historic rooms.

Madison Hotel HOSTEL $
(✆406-646-7745; www.madisonhotelmotel.com; 139 Yellowstone Ave; dm $33, r $79-109, without bathroom $49-62; ☽late May–mid-Oct; ✿) It's hard to picture President Hardy or Clark Gable snuggled in one of the basic timber rooms here but it's this sense of history that might just draw you to this creaky 1912 hostel. Rooms are simple but clean and most share a bathroom down the hall. The lobby hides behind a labyrinth of souvenir crap; detour to find the lounge with retro armchairs and bear skins on the wall. Nonguests are free to poke around unoccupied rooms before 6pm. Give the motel rooms a miss.

Alpine Motel   HOTEL $$
(406-646-7544; 120 Madison Ave; www.alpine
motelwestyellowstone.com; r $80-125, ste $159;)
The friendly and well-tended Alpine has a
rather cramped courtyard but remains one
of the best-value places in town. The suites
come with a kitchen and can sleep six.

Moose Creek Cabins   CABINS $$
(406-646-9646;   www.moosecreekcabin.com;
220 Firehole Ave; r $119-185) This friendly mix
of 1950s-era wooden cabins and modern
rooms is a good choice, with winter discounts of 50% and coffee and muffins in the
lobby. They also run a nearby motel with the
same name.

Lazy G Motel   MOTEL $
(406-646-7586; www.lazygmotel.com; 123 Hay-
den St; r $76-98, ste $141;) Nothing flash here
but good-value motel rooms with fridges,
some with kitchenettes.

One Horse Motel   MOTEL $$
(406-646-7677;   www.onehorsemotel.com,   216
Dunraven St; s $79, d $119-139) Friendly, fresh
and family-run.

Kelly Inn   HOTEL $$
(800-635-3559;   www.yellowstonekellyinn.com;
104 Canyon St; r from $169;) Generic but
immaculate, with a pool, spa and free breakfast, plus deep discounts in low season.

Gray Wolf Inn & Suites   HOTEL $$
(800-852-8602; www.visityellowstonepark.com;
250 Canyon St; r from $137;) The same
standards and facilities as the Kelly Inn.

Holiday Inn   HOTEL $$$
(406-646-7365; www.holdayinn.com; 315 Yel-
lowstone Ave; d from $200;) Considered the
best lodging in town, with a good bar and
the Branch restaurant.

Eating

Pick up groceries at the **Food Roundup**
(cnr Madison Ave & Dunraven St; 7am-9pm)
supermarket.

**Sydney's Mountain
Bistro**   CONTEMPORARY AMERICAN $$
(406-646-7660;   www.sydneysbistro.com;   38
Canyon St; mains $17-26; 5-10pm Mon-Sun) An
island of modern upscale cuisine in a sea of
chicken-fried steak and gravy, sophisticated
Sydney's is the place to turn to for a pear-
and-walnut salad or orange Thai curry. The
dining area is small and intimate so reserve
a table.

Kiwi's   BURGERS $
(cnr Hwy 20 & Electric St; mains $6-10; 11am-
3:30pm & 5-7pm Mon-Fri) The best burgers in
town aren't made by an American but a
Kiwi, and they're served up in this simple
counter-style cafe. From the tilapia fish and
chips to the New Zealand green mussels, all
the food is made fresh on the spot. Grab one
of the bison meat pies before they run out
and do it soon because there are tentative
plans to move in 2014. No credit cards.

Ernie's   SANDWICHES $
(www.erniesbakery.com; 406 Hwy 20; sandwich $8;
6:30am-4pm) An unpretentious sandwich
maker on the highway between Geyser and
Hayden Sts, Ernie's is popular and cheap
and does good breakfasts, though service
can be chaotic at rush hour. Check the wall
for the full menu.

Old Town Café   WESTERN $$
(128 Madison Ave; dinner mains $14-20; 7am-
10pm) Grab a stool or a booth at this laid-
back local diner-bar and feast on authentic
down-home beef and trout dinners.

Running Bear Pancake House   BREAKFAST $
(cnr Madison Ave & Hayden St; mains $6-9; 7am-
2pm;) Serves up small and large stacks,
eggs and sausage links – a family favorite.

Drinking

For a strong shot of that other kind of brew,
hit the **Morning Glory** (129 Dunraven; 6am-
3pm) coffee roasters or **Mocha Mamas** at
Free Heel & Wheel.

Wild West Saloon   BAR
(14 Madison Ave; 10am-late) Live honkytonk
rock packs this divey but fun place on summer weekends, plus you can order in the
best pies in town from the attached pizzeria.

Wolf Pack Brewing Co   BAR
(139 Canyon St; noon-10pm) Sadly no longer
brews its own pints, but still pours the town's
biggest range of local microbrews on tap.

Entertainment

Playmill Theater   THEATER
(406-646-7757; www.playmill.com; 29 Madison
Ave; tickets $17.50; Mon-Sat Memorial Day-
Labor Day;) Churning out light musicals,
melodramas and comedies for 40 years, the
Playmill is a local institution. Reserve your
tickets in advance. It also offers a summer
theater camp for children aged 12 to 18.

Shopping

Bookworm Books
BOOKSTORE

(14 Canyon St; ⏾9am-11pm summer) Rummage through the stacks for the region's best selection of out-of-print and hard-to-find regional titles.

Book Peddler
BOOKSTORE

(106 Canyon St; ⏾8am-10pm summer) A good general selection and fine espresso.

Information

Canyon Street Laundry (312 Canyon St; ⏾7am-10pm) Has slightly rundown public showers ($3.25 for six minutes).

Chamber of Commerce Information Center (☎406-646-7701; www.westyellowstone chamber.com; Canyon St; ⏾8am-8pm; 🛜) Friendly traveler assistance, convenient parking and free wi-fi. There's also a ranger-staffed park desk and backcountry office, where you can buy entry permits to the park.

Gallatin National Forest Service Headquarters (☎406-646-7369; Canyon St) Two blocks north of Firehole Ave, for information on Hebgen Lake campgrounds and trails.

Getting There & Away

Budget (☎406-646-7882; www.budget -yellowstone.com; 131 Dunraven St & Yellow stone Airport) and **Big Sky Car Rentals** (☎800- 426-7669; 415 Yellowstone Ave) offer car rentals from $50 a day.

Karst Stage (☎406-556-3540; www.karst stage.com) runs buses daily, December to April, from the airport to Big Sky ($51, one hour) and West Yellowstone (around $63.50, two hours); summer service is by reservation only.

Grand Teton National Park

Best Hikes

» Hidden Falls (p190)

» Phelps Lake (p193)

» Lake Solitude (p190)

Best Places to Stay & Eat

» Jenny Lake Lodge (p205)

» Triangle X Ranch (p204)

» Climbers' Ranch (p205)

» Jenny Lake Lodge Dining Room (p207)

» Pizza Pasta Company (p207)

Why Go?

Rough-cut summits rising sharply from a lush valley floor, the Tetons are a sight to behold. Simply put, it's sublime and crazy terrain, crowned by the dagger-edged Grand (13,770ft), a giant in the history of American mountaineering. But there's much more, from sagebrush flats and wildflower meadows to the hundreds of alpine lakes and fragrant forests trodden by bear, moose, grouse and marmot.

While the park is dwarfed by Yellowstone, it can offer visitors a more immediate intimacy with the landscape and more varied and scenic hiking. In addition, climbers, boaters, anglers and other outdoor enthusiasts find plenty to do. For lovers of alpine scenery, the Tetons' visual impact far exceeds that of Yellowstone. Whichever way you wander, these rock spires exercise a magnetic attraction on your gaze.

When to Go
Teton Village, WY

June & July Meadows blaze with wildflowers, rivers rush and days are long

September Cool blue skies, rutting elk and fall foliage

April Milder days for ski touring the snowbound park

GATEWAY TOWNS

» Jackson (p210), near the South Entrance;

» Teton Village (p219), near the Southwest Entrance.

Fast Facts

» Area: 484 sq miles

» Highest elevation: 13,770ft

» Lowest elevation: 6109ft

Reservations

Lodging should be reserved as far in advance as possible, especially for peak-season dates. Grand Teton Lodge Company accepts reservations for the following season starting November 1. Most campgrounds are first-come, first-served but some allow a limited number of reservations. Check websites for more details.

Grand Teton Lodge Company (www.gltc.com)

Spur Ranch Log Cabins (www.dornans.com)

Signal Mountain Lodge (www.signalmountainlodge.com)

Flagg Ranch Resort (www.flaggranch.com)

Resources

» Official park website: www.nps.gov/grte

» Official park blog with current updates: www.gtnpnews.blogspot.com

» Official online ranger station: www.tetonclimbing.blogspot.com

Entrances

The park begins 4.5 miles north of Jackson. There are three entrance stations. If you are in Jackson, the closest is the South Entrance at Moose on Teton Park Rd west of Moose Junction. If you are coming from Teton Village, the Southwest Entrance is a mile or so north via the Moose–Wilson rd. If you are driving south from Yellowstone, take the North Entrance 3 miles inside the park on US 89/191/287 north of Moran Junction.

The 14-mile section between the Taggart Lake Trailhead and Jenny Lake is closed to vehicles during winter months (dates depend on snowfall). For other seasonal road closures, consult with the park before travel.

DON'T MISS

Don't miss sunrise from the deck of a canoe. **Leigh Lake**, our favorite, requires some effort but it's well worth a short haul in first light to see Mt Moran hulking in these still, clear waters. More visitors arrive with each hour of the day but this one is yours. First paddle String Lake, entering just off the trailhead. There is a short canoe portage and then you're on Leigh. Either come early with headlamps or reserve a paddle-in backcountry campsite to make a night of it – though it's only a short trip, the off-trail setting feels marvelously rugged and wild. Bring binoculars to spot wildlife.

Canoes can be rented from Dornan's in Moose, along with life jackets and straps or racks for transporting. You can obtain both your canoe and backcountry permits (required) from the Craig Thomas Discovery & Visitor Center.

When You Arrive

» To drive on Teton Park Rd, park entrance permits are required. They are valid for seven days for entry into both Grand Teton and Yellowstone National Parks; the fee is $25 per vehicle, $20 per motorcyclist and $12 for cyclists or hikers on foot. Winter day use costs $5. An annual pass to both parks costs $50.

» Keep your receipt to be able to leave and re-enter the park.

» There is no charge to transit the park on Hwy 26/89/191 from Jackson to Moran and out the East Entrance to the Togwotee Pass. This area encompasses the access road to Jackson Hole Airport.

» Visitors receive a free orientation map and copy of the park newspaper, *Grand Teton Guide,* which details the extensive program of ranger-led activities, road closures and park news.

Orientation

Just south of Yellowstone National Park, Grand Teton National Park stretches 40 miles along the compact, 15-mile-wide range. Its western boundary merges with the Jedediah Smith Wilderness within Targhee National Forest. The Bridger-Teton National Forest sits east. The steep eastern flank overlooks Jackson Hole valley, where Jackson Lake catches the Snake River flowing south from its source in Yellowstone National Park. On the western side of the range, Idaho's Teton Valley features more gradual slopes.

MAIN REGIONS

Jackson Lake dominates the northern half of the park with the Tetons to the west. The popular central Teton peaks, ringed by alpine lakes, are concentrated in the southwest. The most remote and least visited area of the park is the northwest region, accessible only by multiday backpacking. This is the Tetons' prime grizzly habitat, although sightings have extended south and east through other parts of the park.

Before crossing into Idaho, the Snake River winds through flat glacial deposits on the south side of the park. The quieter, less visited east side is bordered by the forested hills of the Bridger-Teton National Forest and the remote trails of the Teton Wilderness.

MAJOR ROADS

The main north–south route through the park is US 26/89/191, contiguous with the east bank of the Snake River between Jackson and Moran Junction. At Moran Junction US 89/191 joins US 287 heading north along Jackson Lake to the Rockefeller Memorial Parkway; US 26 joins US 287 heading east to Dubois via Togwotee Pass.

Teton Park Rd links Moose Junction to Jackson Lake Junction and US 89/191/287 via Jenny and Jackson Lakes. The 5-mile Jenny Lake Scenic Dr connects North Jenny Lake and South Jenny Lake Junctions; the road is two way to Jenny Lake Lodge and one way south of it. Gros Ventre Rd heads east from US 26/89/191 at the south end of the park to Kelly and out of the park into the Gros Ventre Valley. Antelope Flats Rd is 1 mile north of Moose Junction, east of US 26/89/191.

The narrow Moose–Wilson Rd connects Teton Village to Moose; no RVs or trailers are allowed.

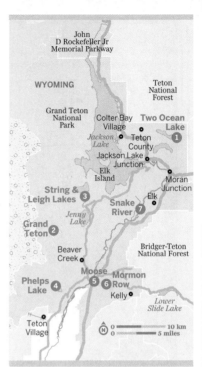

GRAND TETON NATIONAL PARK

Grand Teton National Park Highlights

1 Hike and hunt huckleberries in the wilds around **Two Ocean Lake** (p189)

2 Climb to the coveted summit of the **Grand Teton** (p198) with a local outfitter

3 Explore the islands and inlets of **String and Leigh Lakes** (p182) in a canoe

4 Brave the brisk green waters of **Phelps Lake** (p193) from Jump Rock

5 Join foot-tapping locals at a Monday-night **hootenanny** (p207) in Moose

6 Pedal past pronghorn on the back roads of historic **Mormon Row** (p197)

7 Float **Snake River** (boxed text, p184) at sunset in search of moose

VISITOR SERVICE HUBS

The southern hub is Moose, with a new visitor center, a gas station, accommodations, restaurants, groceries and equipment rental. The nearby Laurance S Rockefeller Preserve Center is south on the Moose-Wilson Rd.

Further north on Teton Park Rd, Signal Mountain has accommodations, a grocery

Grand Teton National Park

177

GRAND TETON NATIONAL PARK

Grand Teton National Park

store, a gas station and a restaurant. Jackson Lake Lodge has shops and restaurants.

Colter Bay hosts the highest concentration of visitor services, with a visitor center, gas station, grocery store, restaurants, laundromat, showers, campground, RV park and marina.

Park Policies & Regulations

Backcountry permits are required for all overnight backcountry trips in Grand Teton; see p194 for details.

Permits are required for boating (p199) and fishing (p200).

Dangers & Annoyances

Though people are the greater nuisance, black bears and a growing population of grizzlies live in the park. For advice on encounters (and their prevention), see p273.

Mid-October to early December is elk-hunting season in areas east of US 26/89/191, west of US 26/89/191 along the Snake River between Moose and Moran Junctions, and the Rockefeller Memorial Parkway. If you must venture into these areas during hunting season, exercise caution: don a bright-orange vest and avoid elk-like behavior.

FRIEND THE PARK

» Share photos and thoughts or get updates by friending Grand Teton National Park on **Facebook** (www.facebook.com/pages/Grand-Teton-National-Park-Official-Page/130250293656242)

» Follow GTNP on **Twitter** (twitter.com/GrandTetonNPS)

» To help plan your visit get the **Teton app** (http://tetonapp.com)

The National Park Service (NPS) *Elk Ecology & Management* pamphlet offers more details and a map.

SIGHTS

John D Rockefeller Jr Memorial Parkway

This NPS-managed parkway is a 7.5-mile corridor linking Yellowstone and Grand Teton National Parks. Congress recognized Rockefeller's contribution to the creation of Grand Teton National Park by designating this 24,000-acre parkway in his honor in 1972. Here, the Tetons taper to a gentle slope, and rocks from volcanic flows in Yellowstone line the Snake River. A transitional zone between the two national parks, the area combines characteristics of both, though it's less spectacular than either. Activities focus around historic Flagg Ranch, which was established as a US Cavalry post in 1872.

North–south US 89/191/287 is the main road through the parkway. The turnoff to Flagg Ranch Rd is 2 miles south of Yellowstone's South Entrance Station and 15 miles north of Colter Bay Village. The turnoff to Grassy Lake Rd, which leads west to Ashton, Idaho, is just north of Flagg Ranch.

The **Flagg Ranch Information Station** (☑307-543-2401; ⊗9am-6pm Jun-Sep) is near the Grassy Lake Rd turnoff. Flagg Ranch Resort (p202) offers parkway accommodations, dining, gas and activities. Once a popular winter launch pad into Yellowstone National Park, the resort now closes in winter since stricter snowmobiling regulations have been put in place. Winter trails can still be accessed here.

GRASSY LAKE ROAD

The 52-mile, east–west Grassy Lake Rd links US 89/191/287 to US 20 at Ashton, Idaho, offering an infrequently used 'back way' into the national parks. This bumpy gravel road, also a good mountain-biking route, follows an old Native American trade and hunting route. The road is open until snow conditions warrant its closure in late fall, when snowmobiles take over.

Heading west from US 89, Flagg Ranch is the first landmark on the road. Shortly after crossing the Polecat Creek Bridge, the pavement ends and the graded gravel road parallels the north bank of the Snake River. Camping is restricted to designated sites, and is popular with anglers, hunters and folks headed west along the rough Reclamation Rd (USFS Rd 261) to the Cascade Corner in Yellowstone's lush Bechler region.

Sandwiched between the Winegar Hole and Jedediah Smith Wildernesses, this region is peppered with lakes with great fishing options. The most accessible are the roadside **Indian Lake** and **Loon Lake**, 1 mile down a bumpy track off Reclamation Rd. Further east is the turnoff for the rough road down to stunning **Lake of the Woods**, site of the Boy Scouts' Loll Camp. A mile further east is the 0.5-mile detour south to Tilley Lake. Beyond here is the expansive and popular **Grassy Reservoir**, with boating, fishing and dispersed campsites. Just after the reservoir the road enters the Rockefeller Parkway. For details of the eight free campsites further along Grassy Lake Rd (USFS Rd 261), see the boxed text on p203.

For information on hikes from Grassy Reservoir into Yellowstone's Bechler region, see p104.

Colter Bay Region

The road south from Yellowstone drops off the Yellowstone plateau at the end of the Rockefeller Parkway, where a startling view of the Tetons soaring above Jackson Lake comes into play. Past Lizard Creek Campground several beaches tucked into nooks offer some of the park's best picnic areas.

Jackson Lake is a natural glacial lake that has been dammed, so water levels fluctuate, dropping considerably toward the end of the summer. Mt Moran (12,605ft), named after landscape painter Thomas Moran, dominates the north end of the park. After Moran first traveled this way with Hayden's geo-logical survey in 1871 his grand depictions forever became synonymous with the area.

Two Ocean and Emma Matilda Lakes sit east of Jackson Lake, tucked into the hills. Visitor services are concentrated at Colter Bay Village.

COLTER BAY

At Colter Bay Visitor Center, the **Indian Arts Museum** (admission free; ☉8am-5pm May & Sep, 8am-8pm Jun-Aug) displays artifacts from the collection of David T Vernon, including beautiful beadwork, bags and photographs. At the time of research, the center was planning a remodel for 2012. It's well worth browsing; pick up a spiral-bound museum guide for a self-guided tour, or take a daily guided tour. The visitor center offers books on Native American history and lore. There are frequent craft demonstrations, and videos are shown all day on subjects ranging from wildlife to Native American art.

South of the visitor center is the marina and trailhead for hikes to Swan Lake and Hermitage Point. A popular picnic and **swimming area** sits just north of the visitor center, though there's countless other secluded swimming and sunbathing spots dotted around Jackson Lake.

For a nice evening or early-morning stroll, try the 45-minute **Lakeshore Trail**, which traces a figure eight across a causeway onto a small island. Take the forest trail that dips onto the beach or just walk along the shore. The trail starts on a paved road beside Colter Bay Marina, or you can access it from the amphitheater next to the visitor center. Finish the hike at the amphitheater by 7pm or 9pm to catch the evening ranger talk.

Regular fishing boats depart from Colter Bay Marina. **Grand Teton Lodge Company** (GTLC; ☎307-543-3111) offers guided fishing trips on Jackson Lake for $80 per hour for two people, plus full-day, guided fly-fishing trips ($475 for two people) on the Snake River. GTLC also offers scenic lake cruises (see p199) – make bookings at the activity desks in Colter Bay or Jackson Lake Lodge.

Ranger Activities

Ask at the visitor center about early-morning birdwatching walks. Rangers also lead a daily 8am morning walk from Colter Bay Visitor Center to Swan Lake (3 miles, three hours) and campfire programs in the evening.

GRAND TETON NATIONAL PARK SIGHTS

Colter Bay Region

0 2 miles
0 4 km

To Yellowstone National Park (18mi)

COLTER BAY VILLAGE

Indian Arts Museum

Lakeshore Trail

Colter Bay

Swan Lake

Heron Pond

Half Moon Bay

Little Mackinaw Bay

Little Mackinaw Bay Backcountry Campsite

Sheffield Island

Badger Island

Dollar Island

Elk Island

Marie Island

Hermitage Point

Hermitage Point Backcountry Campsite

Donoho Point

Jackson Lake

Signal Mountain Marina

Third Creek

Second Creek

Pilgrim CK

Cygnet Pond

North Park Rd

Pilgrim Creek Rd

Christian Creek

Two Ocean Lake Trail

Two Ocean Lake

Two Ocean Lake Rd

Emma Matilda Lake

Grand View Point (7586ft)

Grand Teton National Park

Lozier Hill (7655ft)

Pacific Creek

Three Rivers Rd

Pacific Creek Rd

Moran

Moran Junction

Moran Entrance Station

Pacific Creek Boat Launch

North Park Rd

Buffalo Meadow

Oxbow Bend

Snake River

Signal Mountain (7953ft)

Signal Mountain Summit Rd

Teton Park Rd

Jackson Lake Dam

Jackson Lake Jr Rd

Jackson Lake Junction

Christian Pond

Wagon Rd

Spring Creek

North Park Rd

To Jenny Lake (10.5mi)

Colter Bay Region

AROUND JACKSON LAKE LODGE

The elegant Jackson Lake Lodge is worth a stop, if only to gape at the stupendous views through its 60ft-tall windows. In cold weather the cozy fireplaces in the upper lobby are blazing. In summer you can drink in fine Teton views and a cold Snake River Lager while sitting outdoors.

Rangers answer questions on the back deck of Jackson Lake Lodge daily from 6:30pm to 8pm, and there is a free talk on the history of the valley every Sunday at 8pm.

The willow flats below the hotel balcony are a top spot to catch a glimpse of moose, which flock to willow as a critical food source, particularly in winter. Since the area has become popular with calving elk and bears, it now has a seasonal closure between mid-May and mid-July. You can still enjoy the nearby **Willow Flats turnout**, with views of Mt Moran, Bivouac Peak, Rolling Thunder Mountain, Eagles Rest Peak and Ranger Peak.

A short walk from the lodge, **Christian Pond** is a good place to spot riparian birdlife. The trail to the pond crosses the main road by a bridge just south of the lodge.

About a mile north of Jackson Lake Lodge a rough dirt road branches east off the main road to a trailhead, from which it's a 1-mile walk one way (with a steep climb at the end) to **Grand View Point** (7586ft), which offers fine views of both the Tetons and Two Ocean Lake. You can also visit the viewpoint as part of the Two Ocean Lake hike (p189).

One of the most famous scenic spots for wildlife-watching is **Oxbow Bend**, 2 miles east of Jackson Lake Junction, with the reflection of Mt Moran as a stunning backdrop. Early morning and dusk are the best times to spot moose, elk, sandhill cranes, ospreys, bald eagles, trumpeter swans, Canada geese, blue herons and white pelicans. The oxbow was created as the river's faster water eroded the outer bank while the slower inner flow deposited sediment.

Heading south on Teton Park Rd, you'll find interpretive displays along the west shoulder near **Jackson Lake Dam**. Built in 1916, the dam raises the lake level by 39ft and was paid for by Idaho farmers who still own the irrigation rights to the top 39ft of water. The dam was reinforced between 1986 and 1989 to withstand earthquakes.

South of here is the **Log Chapel of the Sacred Heart**. Open to visitors, it's also a pleasant picnic area.

SIGNAL MOUNTAIN SUMMIT ROAD

This 5-mile paved road (no RVs) east of Teton Park Rd winds up to the top of **Signal Mountain** for dramatic panoramas from 800ft above Jackson Hole's valley floor. Below, the Snake River, the valley's only drainage, runs a twisted course through cottonwood and spruce. Abandoned dry channels demonstrate the changing landscape.

Views are superb at sunrise, but the best vistas are actually from three-quarters of the way up at **Jackson Point Overlook**, a short walk south from a parking area. William Jackson took a famous photograph from this point in 1878, when preparing a single image could take a full hour, using heavy glass plates and a portable studio.

The mountain's name dates from 1891, when Robert Ray Hamilton was reported lost on a hunting trip. Search parties lit a fire atop Signal Mountain after he was found a week later, floating in Jackson Lake. A 6-mile round-trip hiking trail leads to the summit from Signal Mountain Campground, through groves of scrumptious huckleberries.

In winter Signal Mountain Rd offers a great Nordic skiing route, with stunning views and a fun 5-mile downhill return run. To get to the turnoff, ski 1 mile south from Signal Mountain along a snowmobiling trail.

The Eastern Slopes

Highway 26/89/191 traverses the park's eastern flank for about 25 miles from the Moran Junction to the park's southern gate past sagebrush flats and the occasional ranch – always with the Tetons' sharp spires diverting your gaze westward. The hardscrabble lives of Jackson Hole's early homesteaders are reflected in the valley's characteristic lodgepole buck and pole fences.

MORAN TO BLACKTAIL BUTTE

Ranchers Pierce and Margaret Cunninghams, early major supporters of Grand Teton National Park, cultivated a cattle ranch at **Cunningham Cabin** in 1890, 6 miles south of Moran Junction. The property is one of the best surviving examples of a homestead cabin; a short trail elucidates local homesteading.

Four miles south, the **Snake River Overlook** offers good panoramas of the Tetons and opportunities for wildlife-watching, though forest growth means the photo ops aren't quite as good as when Ansel Adams immortalized the shot.

A better place for photos is **Schwabacher's Landing**, a popular rafting put-in 4 miles further south. The jagged Tetons reflected in the meandering river ranks as some of the park's most sublime scenery. Access the landing via a short dirt road.

East of Blacktail Butte, an unpaved road great for cycling (p197) connects Antelope Flats Rd to the north with Gros Ventre Rd to the south (when not washed out). Its scenic collection of ranches with pioneer barns and cabins is known as **Mormon Row**, where 10 settlers took up residence in the 1890s. A resident bison herd, gorgeous post-dawn light and superb Teton views make this area exceptionally popular with photographers. Two barns sit north of the junction and two south, including one that has evolved into a photogenic state of near-collapse.

Gros Ventre Rd leads east to the Gros Ventre Slide (p222).

Central Tetons

South of Signal Mountain, Teton Park Rd passes the Potholes, sagebrush flats pockmarked with craterlike depressions called kettles. The kettles were formed slowly by blocks of orphaned glacial ice that were stranded under the soil, left by receding glaciers. Just south is the Mt Moran turnout.

JENNY LAKE SCENIC DRIVE

Seven miles south of Signal Mountain, the Jenny Lake Scenic Dr branches west to offer the park's most picturesque drive.

The **Cathedral Group turnout** boasts views of the central Teton spires, known as the Cathedral Group. Interpretive boards illustrate the tectonic slippage visible at the foot of Rockchuck Peak, named for its resident yellow-bellied marmots. **String Lake** is the most popular picnic spot, with dramatic views of the north face of Teewinot Mountain and Grand Teton from sandy beaches along its east side. The road becomes one way beyond String Lake, just before exclusive Jenny Lake Lodge.

Perched on the lake's glacial moraine, **Jenny Lake Overlook** offers good views of the Tetons, tall Ribbon Cascade to the right of Cascade Canyon, and shuttle boats headed for Inspiration Point. Be careful not to miss the turnout, as you can't back up on this one-way road.

TOP FIVE SPOTS TO SPY WILDLIFE

Hunker down at dusk or dawn with a spotting scope or binoculars to feast your eyes at the following sites:

» **Oxbow Bend** (p181) A scenic river bend populated with moose, elk, sandhill cranes, ospreys, bald eagles, trumpeter swans, Canada geese, blue herons, white pelicans and...oh, yeah, abundant mosquitoes.

» **Willow Flats Turnout** (p181) Views of a freshwater marsh that's home to birds, moose, elk and beavers.

» **Blacktail Ponds** (p185) Features ospreys, eagles and moose.

» **Antelope Flats** (p185) Bison and pronghorns at home on the range.

» **Swan Lake** (p188) The spot to see beavers, trumpeter swans and geese.

JENNY LAKE

The scenic heart of the Grand Tetons and the epicenter of Teton's crowds, Jenny Lake was named for the Shoshone wife of early guide and mountain man Beaver Dick Leigh. Jenny died of smallpox in 1876 along with her children.

The **Jenny Lake Visitor Center** is worth a visit for its geological displays and 3D map of Jackson Hole. The cabin was once in a different location as the Crandall photo studio.

From the visitor center a network of trails leads clockwise around the lake for 2.5 miles to Hidden Falls and then continues for a short uphill run to fine views at **Inspiration Point**. Once you're here, it's worth continuing up **Cascade Canyon** for as long as you can, as you've already finished most of the hard climb. From here you can return via the way you came or continue clockwise to the String Lake Trailhead to make a 6-mile circle around the lake. If you're on the Jenny Lake Trail in the early morning or late afternoon, detour approximately 15 minutes (about 0.5 miles) from the visitor center to **Moose Ponds** for a good chance of spotting moose.

Alternatively, **Jenny Lake Boating** ([☎]307-734-9227; www.jennylakeboating.com) runs **shuttles** (adult/7-12yr round-trip $9/5, one way $5/4; ⊙8am-6pm Jun-late Sep) across Jenny Lake between the east-shore boat dock near Jenny Lake Visitor Center and the west shore boat dock near Hidden Falls, offering quick (12-minute) access to Inspiration Point and the Cascade Canyon Trail. Shuttles run every 15 minutes, but expect long waits for return shuttles between 4pm and 6pm.

Rangers lead hikes from Jenny Lake Visitor Center at 8:30am to Inspiration Point (2 miles, 2½ hours) via the Jenny Lake ferry. Numbers are limited to 25, and places are first-come, first-served; arrive at the visitor center by 8am to secure a spot.

Canoes, kayaks and boats with motors less than 8HP are allowed on Jenny Lake. The put-in is by the east-shore boat dock and is accessed by a separate road that branches off the Lupine Meadows Trailhead road. Jenny Lake Boating rents kayaks and canoes ($12/60 per hour/day). It also offers hour-long scenic Jenny Lake cruises ($14/7) throughout the day. Inquire at the dock or call to reserve.

Jenny Lake also offers good fishing and is stocked with lake, brown, brook and Snake River cutthroat trout.

DIAL-A-TOUR

The mass return of the holster to the West doesn't herald gunfights. Grand Teton is tapping into technology addictions by offering cell-phone tours. The two- to three-minute messages cover subjects such as park history, geology and the homesteading lore of Menor's Ferry. There's no charge except for the minutes used. Look for the tour map with the details at any visitor center or at Menor's Ferry.

SOUTH OF JENNY LAKE

Just south of Jenny Lake, Teton Park Rd passes the turnoff to the Lupine Meadows Trailhead, for hikes to Surprise Lake and Garnet Canyon. On the east side of the road watch for **Timbered Island**, an enclave of forested glacial soils stacked atop poorly drained sedimentary soils.

Two miles south of here, Teton Glacier turnout offers some of the best views of **Teton Glacier**, the largest in the park. The Taggart Lake Trailhead is 1.5 miles further on.

A short trail and the homestead cabin of William Menor sit half a mile north of Moose Village, off a paved road. Menor was alone on the west bank of the Snake River for 10 years, building a pontoon raft that provided a vital crossing for mule teams and riders who hunted, picked mushrooms and berries, and cut lumber on the Teton side. In 1910 he sold the property to entrepreneur Maude Noble, who started charging a then-brazen $1 to locals and $2 for those with out-of-state plates to cross. Today you can cross in a replica of **Menor's Ferry** (early July to August). Old photographs, restored buggies and the original settlers' wagon offer insight into the lives of early settlers. Stop by the obligatory old-fashioned period **store** (⊙9am-4:30pm).

The nearby **Chapel of the Transfiguration** (1924) has aspen pews and views of the Tetons through the altar window. In summer Episcopal services are held on Sundays.

Just beyond is Moose Entrance Station and the **Craig Thomas Discovery & Visitor Center**, offering interpretive displays, an auditorium hosting excellent speakers and events, and the largest selection of books in the park. The park's southern hub, Moose also offers accommodations, restaurants and shops, and serves as the jumping-off point

WORTH A TRIP

THE SNAKE RIVER

Ansel Adams immortalized the Snake as a luminous ribbon retreating from sharp snow-bound peaks. With outstanding wildlife-watching, this iconic river is a prime spot for boating. For white-water rafting options, see p214.

Commercial trips

Float trips (averaging adult/child $60/40) start after Jackson Lake Dam and meander through park wilderness; the wildest white-water flows south of the town of Jackson. Usually kids must be six years or older to participate.

Barker-Ewing Float Trips (☑307-733-1800; www.barker-ewing.com; Moose) Offers float trips from Deadman's Bar to Moose, free for four- and five-year-olds.

Solitude Float Trips (☑888-704-2800, 307-733-2871; www.solitudefloattrips.com; Moose) Recommended, runs Deadman's Bar-to-Moose trips and sunrise trips, plus shorter 5-mile floats.

Triangle X Float Trips (☑888-860-0005; www.jackson-hole-river-rafting.com) Offers dawn, daytime and sunset floats, plus a four-hour early-evening float and cookout.

Do it Yourself

The easiest do-it-yourself float is the 5 miles from just below Jackson Lake Dam to Pacific Creek Boat Launch. Pacific Creek to Deadman's Bar and Flagg Ranch to Lizard Creek are considered intermediate floats. Anything south of Deadman's Bar is considered advanced. Deadman's Bar to the Moose landing is the most commonly offered commercial white-water trip and is considered Class II. Southgate (at Yellowstone's South Entrance) to Flagg Ranch via Flagg Canyon is considered advanced Class III white-water. You'll find boat put-ins near Oxbow Bend, at Pacific Creek, Deadman's Bar, Schwabacher's Landing and Moose.

Early trappers didn't name the Snake the 'Mad River' for nothing! The highest water levels are in spring. Independent floaters should have all the required safety equipment (including life jackets and throw bag) and know how to use it. For information on Snake River flows call ☑800-658-571.

Save your inner tubes and air mattresses for the lake – they are explicitly banned on the river.

for many park activities. It also serves as the center for wintertime park activity.

Moose–Wilson Road

Moose–Wilson Rd is a partially paved 15-mile route (its southernmost 3 miles are gravel) that connects Teton Village to Moose. RVs and trailers are not allowed on this road inside the park, which is quite narrow in sections.

LAURANCE S ROCKEFELLER PRESERVE

For solitude coupled with the most stunning views that don't include the Grand, visitors should definitely check out this newer section of Grand Teton National Park. Once the JY Ranch, an exclusive Rockefeller family retreat, these 3100 acres around Phelps

Lake were donated in full in 2001 by Laurance S Rockefeller. His grandfather John D Rockefeller had been an early park advocate, purchasing the first tracts of land to donate in 1927. Despite strong local opposition, by 1949 he had donated some 33,000 acres of former ranchland to Grand Teton National Park.

With this sector, Laurance Rockefeller's vision was to create a space of refuge and renewal. In contrast to other visitor centers, the beautiful **Laurance S Rockefeller Preserve Center** (☑307-739-3654; ⊙9am-6pm May 22-Jun 4, 8am-6pm Jun 5-Sep 5) is a meditative experience. Sparely furnished and LEED-certified, it features quotes from naturalists and writers etched into walls, giant picture windows to admire the views and a library with leather armchairs and books on conservation and nature to browse.

The center also hosts a full range of ranger programs.

Little trace is left of the ranch. Homes and cabins have been torn down, roads left to revegetate and an 8-mile network of nature trails were created. By design, the preserve promotes an intimate experience. To prevent overcrowding, there is no parking allowed nearby on the shoulder of the Moose–Wilson road and the parking lot only accommodates 40 vehicles – come before 10am or after 3pm in summer to insure a spot. It's 4 miles south of Moose Junction.

DRIVING

It's sweeping views, park history and wildlife aplenty on these four-wheeled sojourns.

Hole in One

Duration One hour plus stops

Distance 40-mile loop

Start/Finish Jackson

Nearest Town Jackson

Speed Limit 15–45mph

Summary A scenic drive through sagebrush flats and forest with picturesque barns and Teton panoramas.

You could say **Gros Ventre Butte** ruined it for Jackson – there are no Teton views from the park's main hub due to the blockage created by this oversized hump. But this driving tour, not suitable for RVs or other oversized vehicles, is just the remedy.

Head out of Jackson on Hwy 191. First stop: the **National Museum of Wildlife Art** (p211). You may ask, why do this when you have the real thing? Just look. The way these masters envisioned this landscape will change the way you see it yourself.

Continue north on Hwy 191. At the Gros Ventre Junction, take a right and drive along Gros Ventre Rd, skirting the **Gros Ventre River**, which is lined with cottonwoods, juniper, spruce and willows. The river ecology contrasts sharply with the dry sagebrush flats north of it, where pronghorn can often be seen, bounding at speeds up to 60mph (officially, that's faster than you should be going here). At the next junction, take a left to drive north on **Mormon Row**, a picturesque strip that includes a much-photographed rambling barn, left from the hard days of the Mormon settlement. At the

end of the row loop left on **Antelope Flats Rd**, from which you may be able to see bison and more pronghorn. It soon meets Hwy 191 again. Go left, then right at Moose Junction.

Before the park entrance gate, take a left on the small **Moose-Wilson Rd**. Squeeze to the side when you face oncoming traffic: this is why oversized vehicles are explicitly banned. Mind the blind curves, twisting through dense foliage. You will pass a dirt road to Death Canyon Trailhead and later the Granite Canyon Trailhead, both on your right. If you're keen on a swim, detour to the latter, which will take you to **Phelps Lake** (but it will take a few hours). This short section of the road is unpaved but even.

The road spills out near **Teton Village**, where you can take a gondola to the top for views or grab lunch at Mangy Moose Saloon (p222). Follow the Moose–Wilson rd south to Hwy 22. Go left to return back to Jackson.

Plains & Panoramas

Duration 1.5 hours

Distance 45-mile loop

Start/Finish Moose Junction Map p186

Nearest Town Moose

Speed Limit 30–45mph

Summary A loop with long views of the Tetons and prolific wildlife.

This scenic loop offers fantastic views of the Teton Range from the flats of Jackson Hole Valley. With some luck, you will spot pronghorn, deer or moose. Each year animals are killed on this road, so drive cautiously and watch for animals bounding across the road.

Begin the tour 8 miles north of Jackson at Moose Junction. Follow Hwy 191 north past **Blacktail Ponds Overlook** and Glacier View Turnout. Seven miles after Moose Junction, **Snake River Overlook** has views of the braided channels of the Snake. Dense cottonwoods, willows and Engelmann Spruce provide an excellent habitat for moose and deer. Spotted sandpipers should be easy to pick out.

Make a stop at **Cunningham Cabin**, the site of an 1892 shootout when a band of self-deputized locals sought to root out rumored horse thieves.

At Moran Junction bear left (continuing on 191). The hulking peak of **Mt Moran** looms to the west, bearing five glaciers. Stop about 3.5 miles later at **Oxbow Bend** to look for fishing eagles and ospreys, and trumpeter

Central Tetons

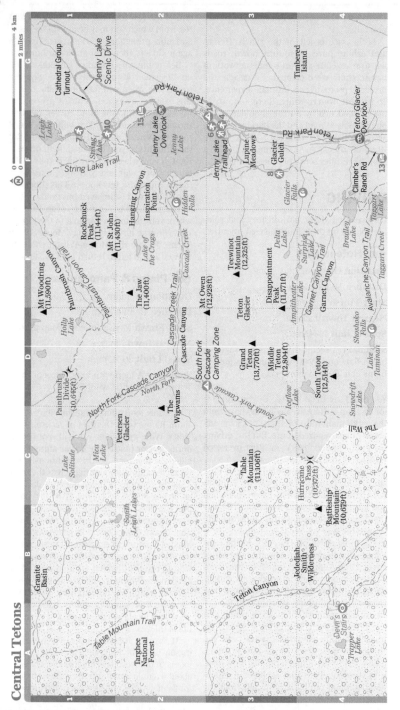

0 2 miles
0 4 km

G

Cathedral Group Turnout
Jenny Lake Scenic Drive
Teton Park Rd
Leigh Lake
String Lake
7
10
15
Jenny Lake Overlook
Jenny Lake
6
14
4
Jenny Lake Trailhead
Lupine Meadows
8
Glacier Gulch
Timbered Island
Teton Glacier Overlook
Teton Park Rd
Climber's Ranch Rd
13
Teton Glacier Overlook

F

String Lake Trail
Paintbrush Canyon Trail
Mt Woodring (11,590ft)
Rockchuck Peak (11,144ft)
Mt St John (11,430ft)
Hanging Canyon
Inspiration Point
Lake of the Crags
Hidden Falls
Cascade Creek
Teewinot Mountain (12,325ft)
Disappointment Peak (11,571ft)
Delta Lake
Surprise Lake
Amphitheater Lake
Garnet Canyon Trail
Garnet Canyon
Glacier Falls
Bradley Lake
Taggart Lake
Taggart Creek
Avalanche Canyon Trail

E

Holly Lake
The Jaw (11,400ft)
Cascade Creek Trail
Cascade Canyon
Mt Owen (12,928ft)
Teton Glacier
South Fork
Shoshoko Falls
Lake Taminah

D

Paintbrush Divide (10,645ft)
North Fork–Cascade Canyon
North Fork
Lake Solitude
Petersen Glacier
The Wigwams
South Fork Cascade Camping Zone
South Fork Cascade
Grand Teton (13,770ft)
Middle Teton (12,804ft)
Iceflow Lake
South Teton (12,514ft)
Snowdrift Lake
The Wall

C

Mica Lake
South Leigh Lakes
Table Mountain (11,106ft)
Hurricane Pass (10,372ft)
Battleship Mountain (10,679ft)

B

Granite Basin
Jedediah Smith Wilderness
Teton Canyon

A

Targhee National Forest
Table Mountain Trail
Devil's Stairs
Trapper Lake

GRAND TETON NATIONAL PARK DRIVING

Central Tetons

swans. Long-legged great blue herons stalk the shallows. Head south along Teton Park Rd at Jackson Lake Junction. The **Log Chapel of the Sacred Heart** follows. On your left you will see a sign for **Signal Mountain Rd**, a 5-mile climb. You can detour here or continue on.

Turn on the one-way **Jenny Lake Scenic Dr**, twisting through a forested area with the spires of the Tetons just above you. It will deposit you again on Teton Park Rd. On your left you will see **Menor's Ferry** historic area. The brainchild of Bill Menor, the ferry provided the only transportation across the river. In late summer, when tourists crossed the river to pick berries, Menor charged them 'Huckleberry Rates.' The log **Chapel of the Transfiguration**, built in 1914, still holds church services. Detour slightly for these. Return to the main road and follow it until it exits the park at Moose Junction.

DAY HIKES

The Tetons' extreme verticality means the hikes in this park follow a different standard; with the steep terrain, flat and easy rambles are few. The easy-to-moderate day hikes following are suitable for families and most walkers. Hikers should adjust the distance they walk to their satisfaction. For more information on hike classifications, see p30.

Paved wheelchair-accessible trails include the Jenny Lake shoreline, String Lake shoreline and Colter Bay Lakeshore Trail (next to the marina) and the southern edge of Jackson Lake Dam.

Colter Bay Region

Birds, animals and wildflowers all feature in this popular section of the park.

🏃 Hermitage Point

Duration 4 hours (shorter loop 1¾ hours)

Distance 9.2 miles (shorter loop 3 miles)

Difficulty Easy–moderate

Elevation Change Negligible

Start/Finish Hermitage Point Trailhead (Map p180)

Nearest Town/Junction Colter Bay Village

Summary A wild and windswept point with outstanding views of the multifanged Mt Moran.

From the Colter Bay Visitor Center follow the parking lot to the southern end. At first the trail's signage may seem a little unclear, but throughout the hike the junctions are well marked. The trail itself starts by a sign that reads 'Foot Trail Only, No Road.' The trail follows a former road for less than 10 minutes, turns right, and then turns right again to climb up to the **Jackson Lake Overlook**.

The trail descends and passes along the left (eastern) side of lily-filled **Heron Pond**, where you can look for moose, trumpeter swans and cranes. It branches right then right again for 2.2 miles to the cairn marking **Hermitage Point** (4.4 miles, 1¾ hours).

TETON NAMES

Impressions are everything... French Canadian fur trappers named the three Tetons – South, Middle and Grand – 'les Trois Tetons' (the three breasts), most likely in a lonely moment of Western wandering and reflection. Trapper Osborne Russell claimed their Shoshone moniker was 'Hoary Headed Fathers.' Teewinot means 'Many Pinnacles' in Shoshone – it now describes the range as well as Teewinot Mountain. The Snake River gets its name from the local Shoshone, or Snake, Native American tribe, though the name Snake was mistakenly given to the Shoshone when the weaving sign for the Shoshone (who called themselves the people of the woven grass huts) was confused with the sign for a snake.

This lesser-hiked leg is densely forested and without views. Be sure to announce your presence approaching blind corners in case of bears. The return leg (4.8 miles, two hours) loops back, taking a right to **Third Creek** and then a left past **Swan Lake**. Keep a watchful eye out for beavers munching on lily pads.

If you don't have the time to tackle the entire Hermitage Point loop, then turn left at the southeast end of Heron Pond to Swan Lake and back for a 3-mile, 1¾-hour loop, which is commonly used by horseback riders and ideal for families with small children.

It's also an easy and enjoyable destination for overnight backpacking. Reserve ahead backcountry campsite No 9 at Hermitage Point.

Two Ocean Lake & Grand View Point

Duration 4 hours

Distance 6.4 miles

Difficulty Easy–moderate

Elevation Change 400ft

Start/Finish Two Ocean Lake Trailhead (Map p180)

Nearest Town/Junction Jackson Lake Junction

Summary On this unique hike views take a backseat to the beauty of Two Ocean Lake and the lush surrounding forest.

The park's wildflowers peak in July, when abundant huckleberries and chokeberries make the area prime black bear territory. The tall grass makes long trousers a good idea. Set out by 8am to take advantage of a calm lake and great birdwatching opportunities. Grizzlies frequent this area, so be bear aware.

To reach the trailhead turn north onto the smooth, gravel Pacific Creek Rd around 1 mile west of Moran Junction. After 2 miles turn left onto the rougher Two Ocean Lake Rd and follow it for 2.5 miles to the parking area.

Follow a clear trail counterclockwise around **Two Ocean Lake** through lovely wildflower meadows with aspens and Teton views. At the west end of the lake (1¼ hours from the trailhead) the trail branches off to the right; at the next junction, turn left to continue around the lake. Another option is to take the right branch and then a left branch for 1.3 miles uphill to **Grand View Point** (7586ft).

The second hill boasts the best views of Mt Moran, as well as Two Ocean and Emma Matilda Lakes. Return to the main lake trail via the same route.

From the lake junction take a right turn and continue around Two Ocean Lake. Sometimes the trail follows the lakeshore and sometimes it's through conifer forest and open meadow. It's about an hour to the trailhead.

Central Tetons

There's something for everyone here: lakes, waterfalls, glaciers, canyons and viewpoints.

Leigh & Bearpaw Lakes

Duration 3½ hours

Distance 7.4 miles

Difficulty Easy–moderate

Elevation Change Negligible

Start/Finish Leigh Lake Trailhead (Map p186)

Nearest Junction North Jenny Lake Junction

Summary A fun, flat family outing skirting forest-clad, crystal-clear swimming holes.

The Leigh Lake Trailhead is at the end of the side road off Jenny Lake Dr; don't confuse it with the String Lake Trailhead. Try to get an early start on this trail, as it's very popular, particularly with young families. Canoeing these lakes (with short portages) is an excellent option on a hot summer's day. Always keep track of your picnic food, since bears are frequently spotted here.

The trail quickly joins **String Lake**. After around 20 minutes a trail branches left across the outlet to Paintbrush Canyon (and a possible loop of String Lake). Instead, take the right branch and then turn right again up to **Leigh Lake**. You may see people carrying their canoes over this portage area.

As you continue north along Leigh Lake, your surroundings open up to fine views of Mt Moran and its Falling Ice and Skillet Glaciers. The dark central stripes in both Mt Moran and Middle Teton consist of 1.5-billion-year-old lava-injected rock called diabase, which extends 7 miles west into Idaho.

Continue past the lovely lakeside campsites 12A (group site), 12B and 12C, which make easy camping destinations for families with small children. Ten minutes further along the trail you'll pass a picturesque beach, with views of Mystic Island and, from left to right, Rockchuck Peak, Mt Woodring, Mt Moran and Bivouac Peak.

After an hour (about 2 miles) of Leigh Lake views, the trail heads into forest to a meadow junction; take the central path to the west side of **Bearpaw Lake** and campsites 17A and 17C. The trail then veers away from the lake for 0.5 miles to **Trapper Lake**. Before you descend too far on the trail back to Bearpaw Lake, watch for a faint path that veers off to the left. This drops through forest and over a log bridge to campsite 17B, looping back to join the earlier junction. Return to String Lake the way you came.

Several backcountry campsites are outstanding. On Leigh Lake the most popular sites are 12B and 12C – you'll need to reserve these well in advance. Remoter sites 13 and 15 are accessible by foot on an unmaintained trail that leads north from the bridge over Leigh Lake outlet. The nicest site at Bearpaw Lake is 17B, which has fine views of Rockchuck Peak. Site 17A is on the lakeshore below the path; 17C is more private but a bit uphill. Trapper Lake offers the quietest site (18A). These sites are among the few in Teton where campfires are allowed (in fire grates only).

Lake Solitude

Duration 6–7 hours

Distance 14.4 miles with boat shuttle, 18.4 miles without

Difficulty Moderate–difficult

Elevation Change 2240ft

Start/Finish Jenny Lake Boat Shuttle (Map p186)

Nearest Junction South Jenny Lake Junction

Summary This ultra-popular hike scales to a mountain lake via a gradual climb.

Thanks to wide patronage, this rewarding trail (particularly its beginning) lacks its namesake solitude, but still provides a rewarding challenge. Though a long hike with an elevation gain of 2240ft, it is not especially tough since the grade is quite gradual. Gear up for steep sections at the beginning near Inspiration Point and just before Solitude Lake. Moose and bear frequent the area.

Taking the boat shuttle will shave 4 miles off. The Cascade Canyon (west) dock meets a network of trails. Head left to pass **Hidden Falls** after 0.2 miles and ascend to **Inspiration Point** in another 0.5 miles. Climbers complete the scenery – Exum Guides uses this area for training. Soon afterward, the horse trail from String Lake joins from the right.

The Cascade Canyon Trail continues straight, past a lovely beach and a high cascade, with fine views. About two hours (4.5 miles) from the dock the valley splits. The left branch leads to South Fork and Hurricane Pass. Turn right and climb gently for 30 minutes to enter the **Cascade Camping Zone** (12 sites), which stretches for the next 30 minutes. From the zone's end it's 10 minutes up to the lake, past a small cascade and a hitch rail marking the end of the line for horses. It's about three hours (7.2 miles) from here back to the dock.

Rimmed by fir and pines and sporting ice until midsummer, **Lake Solitude** (9035ft) is a great spot to loll around (but probably not to swim). To the northeast, the diagonal slash leading up the hillside leads to **Paintbrush Divide**. Camping is prohibited at the lake.

Return to the boat dock the way you came. The terrain, shaded most of the afternoon, is all downhill, affording full views of Mt Owen and Grand Teton.

🏃 Surprise & Amphitheater Lakes

Duration 5–6 hours

Distance 9.6 miles (10.2 miles with Glacier Overlook extension) round-trip

Difficulty Difficult

Elevation Change 3000ft

Start/Finish Lupine Meadows Trailhead (Map p186)

Nearest Junction South Jenny Lake Junction

Summary One of the park's oldest, this trail is a classic leg-burner. Expect company: great views make it very popular.

Even before cubicle fever existed, two 1920s businessmen built this trail. The route should be free of snow by late June. Bring plenty of water since none is available between the trailhead and the two lakes near the top of the climb.

There are three designated campsites at Surprise Lake for those who want to stay overnight, though due to heavy use, some areas are off-limits for regeneration.

The well-worn trail gently winds through pine forest until it mounts a shoulder and the ascent begins in earnest. A junction with the Taggart and Bradley Lakes Trail lies atop the shoulder, 1.7 miles (40 minutes) from the start. Keep right and tackle the series of switchbacks up the flank of **Disappointment Peak**. The route offers views over Taggart Lake and Jackson Hole. About 1½ hours (3 miles) from the trailhead there is a signed junction with the Garnet Canyon trail (p191).

The switchbacks ease shortly before the lakes, and after 2¼ hours of solid climbing, you'll finally reach the inviting, gemstone waters of **Surprise Lake**. Set in a hollow beneath jagged white rocks and cliffs, it is a resplendent payoff for your efforts. The slightly bigger and starker **Amphitheater Lake** lies just 0.2 miles further along the trail. Return the way you came.

SIDE TRIP: EXTENSION TO TETON GLACIER OVERLOOK

To reach the **Teton Glacier Overlook**, follow the trail around the northeast shore of Amphitheater Lake, staying right at several indistinct forks. Climb between the rocks to the top of a shoulder for breathtaking views into the valley, sweeping down from the Grand Teton. A shattered ridgeline between the razor-sharp spires of Teewinot and Mt Owen to the north contrast with the flatlands visible between sheer valley walls south. Vertigo sufferers beware!

Retrace your steps to the trailhead.

🏃 Garnet Canyon

Duration 9 hours

Distance 12 miles

Difficulty difficult

Elevation Change 4800ft

Start/Finish Lupine Meadows Trailhead (Map p186)

Nearest Junction South Jenny Lake Junction (Map p186)

Summary This climbers' route hauls hikers into the world of rock and ice. You must be fit and well acclimatized.

It's possible to hike this trail in a day, but it's best done as an overnighter, camping at either the Meadows or South Fork sites. Set off at first light since afternoon weather is notoriously fickle up here.

For the first 3 miles follow the Sunrise & Amphitheater Lakes hike description (p191). At the trail junction branch left instead of right. From this junction the trail curves around the hillside to dramatic views of Garnet Canyon and Middle Teton (12,804ft). Just over a mile from the junction the maintained trail stops and the sometimes indistinct **climbers' path** continues over boulder fields for 20 minutes to the Meadows campsite. If you aren't confident with bouldering and trail finding, this spot makes a good terminus (8.4 miles round-trip, five hours).

The path splits right to Spalding Falls and the base camp for **Grand Teton** and left through indistinct boulder fields to switchback up to a small saddle, where you'll find a couple of campsites. From here the trail traverses a small snowfield (present until August) and heads up the valley over a series of false saddles.

With several indistinct trails at your disposal, finding the right one involves some guesswork and bouldering. About 2 miles from the meadows you'll finally reach the **saddle** between Middle and South Teton, with fabulous views down to Iceflow Lake and across to the Wall and Hurricane Pass. You will likely meet groups of climbers heading to Middle Teton.

From the saddle it's a 3½- to four-hour return the way you came. Take great care on the rocks and snowfields as you return, as you'll be tired; this is no place to sprain an ankle or worse.

🚶 Taggart & Bradley Lakes

Duration 3 hours

Distance 5.9 miles

Difficulty Easy–moderate

Elevation Change 560ft

Start/Finish Taggart Lake Trailhead (Map p186)

Nearest Town/Junction Moose Junction

Summary An easy amble; this pair of glacial lakes sits at the base of the Tetons, surrounded by grassy areas thick with summer wildflowers or fragrant pine forest.

These lakes were named after surveyors of the 1872 Hayden Expedition. The terrain is open from earlier fires, so it's a bit easier to spot wildlife, particularly moose. The trails here offer several easy loop options ranging from 3 to 5 miles total. Plan an early start in summer since much of the trail lacks shade. Don't forget the bathing suit.

The Taggart Lake Trailhead is just off Teton Park Rd, 5 miles north of Moose. Follow the trail northwest, past horse corrals, and take the first left at a marked signpost after 0.2 miles. Although this trail is only slightly longer, it receives far less traffic than the other option. After another 1.4 miles, turn right and climb open slopes to a point on the moraine wall overlooking the beautiful rusty-green Taggart Lake. Descend the short distance to the lakeshore and use a wooden footbridge to cross the outlet creek. A small, rocky outcropping makes a fine point to swim. The views of the Tetons are fantastic.

The trail winds around the east shore of Taggart Lake, passing a signposted trail junction for the parking area (a shortcut back if you're tired) to your right. Climb steadily away from Taggart Lake and crest the moraine wall separating Taggart and Bradley Lakes. Descend through the trees to reach the thickly forested shores of Bradley Lake. You'll reach a junction just before the trail reaches the shores of Bradley Lake. Turn right to begin the trip back to the parking area or forge ahead to explore the perimeter of Bradley Lake before returning to this junction. The campsite at Bradley Lake is reserved for hikers on multiday loops of the Valley Trail.

If it's still early and you're brimming with energy, consider forging on to Avalanche Canyon and Lake Taminah (p192). You might want to combine your hike with the ranger-led wildflower and naturalist walks that depart every morning from the Taggart Lake Trailhead.

🚶 Avalanche Canyon & Lake Taminah

Duration 6–7 hours

Distance 11 miles

Difficulty Difficult

Elevation Change 2300ft

Start/Finish Taggart Lake Trailhead (Map p186)

Nearest Junction Moose Junction

Summary This challenging hike runs the gamut of good stuff: lake swims, waterfalls and killer views.

Park at the Taggart Lake Trailhead, where there's a convenient toilet. Take the shortest route to Taggart Lake, branching right initially then left after 1.1 miles. At Taggart Lake branch right toward Bradley Lake.

Curving around the north side of Taggart Lake, you'll lose sight of the lake shortly before the faint left-hand turnoff to Avalanche Canyon – if you start to climb the moraine hill to Bradley Lake, you've gone too far.

The trail heads up Avalanche Canyon, past steep fern-thick inclines, with views ahead to 11,490ft Mt Wister. As the trail becomes increasingly wet, you'll first hear and then see Taggart Creek. There's a good chance of spotting moose here. At the head of the valley, about 2½ hours from the trailhead, look for the waterfalls up both branches of the valley – you are headed right for Shoshoko Falls.

The trail winds up a steep talus slope to the right of the falls and, once you have gained most of the elevation, swings left up a small gully to meet remote Lake Taminah. Approach the falls to get great views down the valley. The ascent takes about 3½ hours.

Return the way you came. At the junction with the main Taggart-Bradley Lake Trail, you can head back to the trailhead, though it's worth detouring to Bradley Lake on the

Bradley Lake Trail – this only adds an extra 0.7 miles (30 minutes) and it provides more secluded swim spots. From Bradley Lake it's 2 miles back to the trailhead.

Moose–Wilson Road

At the southern extreme of the park, these hikes are more likely to offer solitude.

🚶 Death Canyon

Duration 5 hours

Distance 8–10 miles

Difficulty Moderate

Elevation Change 1360ft

Start/Finish Death Canyon Trailhead (Map p186)

Nearest Junction Moose Junction

Summary Lesser-known Death Canyon offers moderate hiking up an ethereal river valley flanked by granite climbing walls.

To reach the Death Canyon Trailhead, take the turnoff 3 miles south of Moose on Moose–Wilson Rd. Go right 1.6 miles down a narrow dirt track, which is in poor condition. The small parking area is often crowded with climbers' and backpackers' vehicles. Nearby, the **White Grass Ranger Station** was once an outfitters' cabin.

The trail climbs 0.9 miles to **Phelps Lake Overlook** (7200ft) and then descends 0.7 miles through lovely aspen forest to a junction; go right here. As you enter the towering gorge, the ascent kicks in – a relentless uphill over rocky switchbacks that quickly joins the river, which cascades over large boulders. After a hard slog of about 1.5 miles the path flattens out. Devoid of the river's roar, the valley seems impressively serene.

The trail hits a junction by an old patrol cabin, 3.7 miles from the trailhead. The right branch climbs steeply to **Static Divide**; if you have the energy, switchback up the trail to the treeline for great views of the peaks and plains (a two-hour detour). Or continue straight on the main trail up **Death Canyon**, through riverside willows in prime moose habitat. The trail crosses a log bridge and enters a lush forest filled with berries, which indicate bear territory. The campsites of the Death Canyon Camping Area pop up occasionally, as do views of the **Death Canyon Shelf**, an impressive layer of sedimentary rock atop harder granites and gneiss. You can continue along this trail as long as you wish, perhaps using one of the campsites as a picnic spot, though a good turnaround point comes where the trail crosses the stream.

To exit, retrace your steps. Consider descending to the pine-rimmed **Phelps Lake** for a dip before the final grind, a 1.6-mile hike back up the moraine hill, which somehow seems a lot longer at the day's end.

🚶 Phelps Lake Trail

Duration 3½ hours

Distance 7-mile loop

Difficulty Easy–moderate

Elevation Change negligible

Start/Finish Phelps Lake Trailhead (Map p186)

Nearest Town/Junction Moose

Summary A lovely and flat forested amble around a beautiful lake.

The trail leaves the Laurance S Rockefeller Preserve Center and splits. If you go left over the bridge, you will be on the **Lake Creek Trail**. Go right for the **Woodland Trail**. Before long it crosses the main road and continues in a gentle, winding ascent through pine forest and aspens, hitting the junction of the **Boulder Ridge Trail** at 0.7 miles. Continue straight; soon after, views open up and you get a glimpse of Static Peak and Buck Mountain on its right. It should take 30 or 45 minutes total to reach Phelps Lake. Go the extra 20yd to the lake viewpoint for gorgeous views of the headwall across the lake; there's benches here for resting.

Start the **Phelps Lake Trail** loop counterclockwise. The trail intersects again with the longer Boulder Ridge Trail; continue on the lake loop, going through forested and sometimes bouldery terrain with lake views on the left. After about an hour of hiking, you'll reach **Jump Rock**, an immense boulder used for launching swimmers into the lake. It's a fine spot to rest or picnic. The rock itself has a 23ft drop and the water is about 30ft deep here, so it's perfect for jumping in.

Ten minutes on, there are campsites 2 and 1 (respectively) to the right side of the trail. If you want to stay here, obtain a backcountry permit ahead of time. Shortly you will reach the opposite side of the lake from where you started. It's in this area that hikers can get turned around, since a nearby avalanche created some trail detours. However, if you pay attention it is easy to follow the route. Briefly turn onto **Valley Trail**, which ascends a humid aspen grove with a waterfall within earshot.

Two short paths veer toward the lake; keep right and continue rounding the lake, looking up to your right to see the waterfall. This area is popular with moose, so keep an eye out for them. A muddy section has round log stepping stones. Ascend away from the lake to a trail sign that marks the halfway point. Go left here and cross a bridge over the stream. The trail ascends, surrounded by ferns, and on the left you will have a view of the creek feeding the lake. Keep ascending and reach the trail's highest point, the intersection of Valley Trail with Phelps Lake Trail. Veer left here, and it's 3 miles to the Laurance S Rockefeller Preserve Center.

The trail has views across the lake to Jackson Peak. A mile on, consider taking the short lefthand trail to lakeside **Huckleberry Point** if it's berry season – this spot will be loaded with them. Rejoin the trail, which passes over marshlands on a steel boardwalk. Continue straight at another intersection with the Boulder Ridge Trail. Soon after you will reach the road: cross carefully as it's a blind curve. The trail crosses the river before ending at the Visitor Center.

Other Moose-Wilson Road Hikes

Another day-hike loop starts from the top of the tram down the South Fork into **Granite Canyon** and back to Teton Village (13 miles). For more area hikes from Jackson and the Idaho side, check out p211 and p224.

John D Rockefeller Jr Memorial Parkway

Polecat Creek offers a pleasant stroll if you're staying overnight at Flagg Ranch. The trail leads across Grassy Lake Rd from the main parking lot, passing two turnoffs to the right and an employee-housing loop before branching right to peaceful Oxbow Meadows. From here you can take a left at the next junction over a small creek to **Huckleberry Hot Springs**. The NPS advises against bathing here due to high radiation levels in the water (caused by naturally occurring radon), but this hardly deters locals who come here for post-work alfresco soaks. You can also get to the springs from a parking lot 1 mile west of Flagg Ranch, though you need to ford Polecat Creek on this route, so bring waterproof shoes. This former road led to a hot-springs resort that was torn down in 1983.

A fairly interesting hiking trail also runs beside the volcanic walls of **Flagg Canyon**, northeast of Flagg Ranch. Get the brochure *Flagg Ranch Area Trails* from the Flagg Ranch information station.

Along Grassy Lane Rd, 2.2 miles west of Flagg Ranch, is the **Glade Creek Trailhead**, which accesses the rarely visited northwest corner of the park and its Berry Creek and Moose Creek Trails.

OVERNIGHT HIKES

Hikes are roughly organized by starting points, from north to south.

Backcountry Permits

Backcountry permits are required for all overnight backcountry trips in Grand Teton. Permits are free and given on a first-come,

---

DITCH THE CROWDS

Parking lots at popular trailheads and areas such as Jenny Lake, String Lake, Lupine Meadows and Granite Canyon are often packed before 11am. The Death Canyon Trailhead parking stays full since overnight backpackers leave cars for multiple days. Cascade Canyon hums with day-trippers to Solitude Lake in August. Get an alpine start on your hike (leave before most of your neighbors think of breakfast) to beat the crowds. It's a good way to see more wildlife too.

Jenny Lake Campground is perennially full, and Signal Mountain Campground fills up early in the day. You can avoid the campground crowds by choosing less-popular campgrounds like Lizard Creek or Gros Ventre. Two Ocean and Emma Matilda Lakes, in the northeast section of the park, offer excellent hiking without the crowds.

first-served basis, 24 hours in advance, from the backcountry offices at Craig Thomas and Colter Bay Visitor Centers or Jenny Lake Ranger Station. For best results, apply early in the morning the day before your intended departure. A notice board at Craig Thomas Discovery & Visitor Center indicates which backcountry sites are full each day.

About a third of the backcountry sites can be reserved from January 1 to May 15 by mail (Grand Teton National Park, PO Box 170, Moose, WY 83012), fax (📠307-739-3438) or in person at Craig Thomas Discovery & Visitor Center, for a nonrefundable $25 fee.

Backcountry camping is restricted to camping zones. Hikers (with backcountry permits) can choose their own sites inside many of these areas, but in the most heavily used zones all sites are designated (indicated by marker posts). Fires are prohibited, except at some lakeshore sites, so bring a camp stove. Campsites must be at least 200ft from waterways.

No permits are required for backcountry camping in the John D Rockefeller Jr Memorial Parkway, though campers must keep a minimum of 1 mile from roads and 100ft from water sources. Fires are generally allowed, but check current regulations at the information station. No bikes or pets are permitted on trails.

Central Tetons

🏃 Paintbrush Divide

Duration 2–3 days

Distance 17.8-mile loop

Difficulty Moderate

Elevation Change 3775ft

Start/Finish String Lake Trailhead (Map p195)

Nearest Town/Junction North Jenny Lake Junction

Summary This pretty grind lifts you up into the alpine scenery above tree level.

This is the Teton's most popular backpacking trip. If you like some social atmosphere with your backcountry, make sure you reserve a campsite in advance or keep an open itinerary. Uber-athletes could zip through on an epic day hike.

DAY 1: STRING LAKE TRAILHEAD TO HOLLY LAKE
4 HOURS, 6.2 MILES, 2540FT ASCENT

From the String Lake parking lot take the trail that curves south around String Lake. It climbs gently until the left-hand junction with **Paintbrush Canyon**, 1.6 miles in. This steeper

GRAND TETON NATIONAL PARK OVERNIGHT HIKES

Paintbrush Divide Loop

but moderate trail borders a stream flowing over granite boulders, passing through the Lower Paintbrush Camping Zone and some stock campsites. It reaches an upper basin surrounded by snowy peaks. The first lake isn't Holly; continue right of it to reach **Holly Lake**. There are two shady designated campsites at the lake's southeast corner. If these sites are booked, camp in the Upper Paintbrush Canyon Camping Zone.

DAY 2: HOLLY LAKE TO NORTH FORK CASCADE CAMPING ZONE
3 HOURS, 3.2 MILES, 1235FT ASCENT

Ascend steeply to join the main trail; it's one hour to **Paintbrush Divide** (10,645ft). The pass may be snowy into early July – consult a ranger before going. An ice tool could come in handy here. Enjoy the outstanding views before descending along broad switchbacks to reach **Lake Solitude** after another hour or so. Camp in the nearby North Fork Cascade Camping Zone or continue down Cascade Canyon to either the String Lake Trailhead or to Jenny Lake via the shuttle boat (details in the Lake Solitude hike, p190).

🏃 Marion Lake & Death Canyon

Duration 2 days

Distance 18 miles (or 23.5-mile loop)

Difficulty Moderate

Elevation Change 3850ft descent (from top of tram to Death Canyon Trailhead)

Start Teton Village (Map p186)

Finish Death Canyon Trailhead

Nearest Town Teton Village

Summary Downhill but not a downer, this hike gets you steeped in the backcountry quickly by the tram shortcut.

DAY 1: JACKSON HOLE AERIAL TRAM TO MARION LAKE
4 HOURS, 6.6 MILES, 1400FT DESCENT

This hike starts with a considerable boost: after reopening in 2008, the Jackson Hole Aerial Tram to the top of Rendezvous Mountain gains 0.8 miles of elevation. From the tram, descend to a junction at the park boundary and turn right to descend into the South Fork of Granite Canyon. Take a left at the next junction and then a right at the next two junctions to descend into the North Fork of **Granite Canyon**. From here it's a short climb to lovely **Marion Lake**, 6.6

miles from the trailhead, where you'll find three designated campsites.

DAY 2: MARION LAKE TO DEATH CANYON TRAILHEAD
6 HOURS, 11.3 MILES, 2450FT DESCENT

Today it's 2.3 miles up to **Fox Creek Pass**, then it's all downhill for 9 miles through the forests of Death Canyon to Phelps Lake Overlook (p193). To avoid a car shuttle, hike south at the junction before Phelps Lake along the Valley Trail to Teton Village (5.5 miles).

By choosing to hike in the opposite direction you can save a few bucks (the downhill tram ride is free of charge), but you'll gain much more elevation.

🏃 Teton Crest Trail

Duration 4 or 5 days

Distance 31.4 or 39.9 miles

Difficulty Moderate–difficult

Elevation Change 6000ft

Start String Lake (Map p186)

Finish Granite Creek Trailhead or Teton Village

Nearest Junction North Jenny Lake Junction

Summary This epic takes hikers rambling over the lofty spine of the Tetons for jaw-dropping views and a fair share of high exposure.

This classic route is one to remember. Dipping in and out of the neighboring Jedediah Smith Wilderness, the route has numerous outs – the canyons and passes that access the trail on either side. The following is only a suggested itinerary. Hikers must arrange for a shuttle here or have two cars to leave at the start and end points. Bring plenty of sunscreen – there is almost no shade.

DAYS 1 & 2

Day one is the same as the Paintbrush Divide loop (p195). Day two continues to follow this route until the junction between the North and South Forks of Cascade Canyon, where the trail branches up the South Fork to the **South Fork Cascade Camping Zone** (19 campsites). You can start the hike from Jenny Lake and spend night one at the South Fork Camping Zone after hiking up Cascade Canyon Trail; this shaves off a day.

DAY 3: SOUTH FORK CASCADE CAMPING ZONE TO ALASKA BASIN
3-3½ HOURS, 6.1 MILES, 1992FT ASCENT

The trail climbs up to **Avalanche Divide** junction: head right (southwest) to **Hurricane Pass** (10,372ft), which has unsurpassed views of Grand, South and Middle Tetons. (An excursion from the Avalanche Divide junction leads 1.6 miles to the divide, a scenic overlook above Snowdrift Lake.) From the pass the trail descends into the Jedediah Smith Wilderness, past Sunset Lake, into the **Basin Lakes** of the Alaska Basin, where you'll find several popular campsites. No permits are needed here since you're outside the park, but you must camp at least 300ft from lakes and 50ft from streams.

DAY 4: ALASKA BASIN TO MARION LAKE
4½ HOURS, 8.2 MILES

The trail crosses South Fork Teton Creek on stepping stones and switchbacks up the Sheep Steps to the wide saddle of **Mt Meek Pass** (9718ft) to re-enter the park. The trail dips for the next 3 miles into the stunning plateau of **Death Canyon Shelf** and camping zone. Past the turnoff to Death Canyon, the it climbs to **Fox Creek Pass** (9560ft) and continues southwest over a vague saddle to **Marion Lake** and its designated campsites.

DAY 5: MARION LAKE TO TETON VILLAGE
5 HOURS, 9.7 MILES

The trail descends into the Upper Granite Canyon Camping Zone and continues past the Upper Granite Canyon patrol cabin to the junction with the Valley Trail. From here continue south to the Granite Canyon Trailhead or straight on to Teton Village.

OTHER COMBINATIONS

The Teton Crest Trail can be accessed from the east by several steep canyons. Trailheads (south to north) are: Granite Canyon, Death Canyon, Taggart Lake, Lupine Meadows, Jenny Lake and String Lake/Leigh Lake. Hike canyon-to-canyon to make a combination hike of any length. Options include the following:

Open Canyon to Granite Canyon One-night 19.3-mile loop from the Granite Creek Trailhead.

Granite Canyon to Death Canyon A two- to three-night 25.7-mile loop via the Teton Crest Trail.

Death Canyon to Open Canyon A 24.7-mile loop from the Death Canyon Trailhead.

Other Central Tetons Hikes

Other good options for overnighting include camping at **Marion Lake** (13-mile round-trip) from the Jackson Hole Aerial Tram. For an easy overnighter, check out the Hermitage Point hike (p188) or the Leigh & Bearpaw Lakes hike (p189). Also check out Alaska Basin from the Idaho side (p224).

CYCLING

Cyclists are in less danger from motorists in the Tetons than in Yellowstone because the roads are wider and more open, but it is still best to venture out early to avoid traffic. Grand Teton National Park gets little traffic from September to early October, and the cool temperatures make for pleasant pedaling. In April, Teton Park Rd is open only to cyclists and pedestrian traffic. This is a great time to bike if the snow has cleared. For tips on cycling with traffic and wildlife, see p31.

The best spot for cycling in the park, the new **multi-use pathway** borders the Teton Park Rd between Moose and Jenny Lake (a 7.6-mile stretch). Riders can park at the lot just after the Moose Entrance Station. Construction is underway to extend the path south all the way to Jackson and north through the park, but should take several years.

For a mellow, scenic ride, try **Mormon Row**, a 16-mile loop including terrain beyond Mormon Row, which starts and finishes in Gros Ventre Junction. While part of this ride is paved, the 3-mile Mormon Row section, bumpy and unpaved, is not great for road bikes. This trail follows an abbreviated version of the Hole in One driving loop (p185). Start at Gros River Junction. Go right at the turnoff, heading northeast with Blacktail Butte to your north. Take a left at Mormon Row, another left at Antelope Flats Rd. It ends at Hwy 191; take the highway south to return to the start.

If you are on a road bike, check out the various driving-route options (p185). The biking tours listed following require mountain-bike treads, but only Shadow Mountain is steep and may require suspension.

Snake River Road

Duration 2–3 hours

Distance 15 miles one way

Difficulty Easy–moderate

Elevation Change Negligible

Start Riverside Rd at Cottonwood Creek (Map p176)

Finish Signal Mountain Summit Rd

Nearest Junction Moose Junction

Summary Explore the incredible riparian landscape on a short mountain-bike ride.

The gravel River (RKO) Rd parallels the west side of the **Snake River** between Signal Mountain and Cottonwood Creek. Those doing the ride one way can park at the turn-out near **Cottonwood Creek**. There is no shade here and it gets quite hot in summer, so bring plenty of water or bike early. Wildlife is prolific, especially bison. Maintain a safe distance of 300ft and never pass through them. Wait until they move away or bike around.

Be prepared for a bumpy, uneven ride. The road parallels braided channels of the scenic Snake River, one of the most heavily used rivers in the west. Binoculars would be useful here: the river is critical habitat for beaver and river otter. Osprey and eagle are here too, fishing for cutthroat trout, and moose and deer frequent the willows. The track rejoins **Teton Park Rd** just south of the Signal Mountain Rd turnoff. Arrange a vehicle shuttle or be prepared to cycle the 12 miles south on the paved Teton Park Rd back to Cottonwood Creek.

Shadow Mountain

Duration 2½–3 hours

Distance 6-mile loop

Difficulty Difficult

Elevation Change 1300ft

Start/Finish Antelope Flats Rd (Map p176)

Nearest Junction Moose Junction

Summary Challenge yourself with this strenuous but quick ascent and descent.

Just east of the park in Bridger-Teton National Forest, the forested **Shadow Mountain** offers a strenuous 6-mile round-trip loop. Set off along a gravel road from the parking lot at the end of paved Antelope Flats Rd. A steady climb, the road is rutted and rocky at points. Open sections offer excellent Teton views. Just over 0.5 miles past the summit there's a single-track path to the left. It splits, but your best option is to stay left, although all trails do lead to the bottom. Be alert as fallen logs cross the path in places. After this exciting downhill run join the fire road. Watch for muddy conditions, which make this section a lot trickier. A webbed network of trails here means it is easy to get turned around. For topographical maps, visit Hoback Sports (p214) in Jackson.

Hole in One

Duration 5 hours

Distance 33-mile loop

Difficulty Moderate

Elevation Change 340ft

Start/Finish Jackson, Wyoming

Nearest Town Jackson

Summary Scoot past Jackson Hole highlights on this fun loop with long, flat stretches.

This trail follows an abbreviated version of the Hole in One driving loop; for a more detailed description, see p185. Start in Jackson and head north on Hwy 191 to **Moose Junction**. Go left here and left again to the narrow and winding Moose-Wilson Rd. While it is paved there are some deep potholes, so stay alert. Horned owls nest along this section. Approaching **Teton Village**, the road becomes smooth and stays that way. Continue on the flats of Moose-Wilson Rd until you hit a juncture with Hwy 22; turn left here. There will be a lot of car traffic on Hwy 22.

An early start will help you avoid traffic on the narrows of Moose-Wilson Rd.

SUMMER ACTIVITIES

Rock Climbing & Mountaineering

Garnet Canyon is the gateway to the most popular scrambles to Middle and South Teton, and the technical ascent of Grand Teton. These nontechnical climbs can be handled as day hikes from bases at the Meadows, South Fork, Caves or Moraine campsites, but you need to know what you're doing and be with someone familiar with the routes.

The Grand Teton is cherished by climbers as a classic climb. It starts with a strenuous hike up Garnet Canyon (4000ft-plus) and making camp. Day two requires an alpine start. The Owen-Spaulding route is the most popular, but there are lots of variants to choose from. The climb itself consists of 2700ft of elevation gain, fun scrambling, three easy 5th-class pitches and an exciting rappel from high on the mountain. Views from above are unparalleled. Ah, and then there's getting down… Very fit nonclimbers can complete the climb with an outfitter and some training beforehand.

Day climbers don't need to register, but those staying overnight need a backcountry use permit (see p194). Call ☑307-739-3604 for recorded climbing information.

Ground zero for climbing information, **Jenny Lake Ranger Station** (☑307-739-3343; ☺8am-6pm Jun-Sep) sells climbing guidebooks and provides information. A board shows campsite availability in Garnet Canyon.

An excellent resource and the spot to meet outdoor partners in crime, the American Alpine Club's **Climbers' Ranch** (Map p186; ☑307-733-7271; www.americanalpineclub .org; Teton Park Rd; ☺summer only) has been a climbing institution since opening. It also runs an inexpensive summer dormitory (see p205) and rents some gear. The ranch is just south of the Teton Glacier turnout.

The region's oldest climbing school, the excellent **Exum Mountain Guides** (Map p186; ☑307-733-2297; www.exumguides.com; Lupine Meadows) runs climbing schools at Hidden Falls on Jenny Lake's west shore and has a base camp at Grand Teton's Lower Saddle (11,600ft).

Horseback Riding

Colter Bay corral offers 1½- and 2½-hour trail rides around Swan Lake for $33/48. Children are charged the same rates and must be at least eight years old. Families with small children can check out the breakfast wagon rides (adult/child $37/15). Make reservations at the **activities booth** (☺7am-8pm) next to the Colter Bay grocery store, preferably a couple of days in advance.

Jackson Lake Lodge offers **guided horseback rides** (per 2hr $75) that loop around the local trails, as well as breakfast and dinner rides by horseback or wagon.

Flagg Ranch runs hour-long **horseback riding trips** ($38) hourly from June to September.

Boating

All private craft must obtain a permit, which costs $20/40 per week/year for mo-

torized and $10/20 for nonmotorized craft (rafts, canoes or kayaks). The Craig Thomas and Colter Bay Visitor Centers and Buffalo Fork Ranger Station at Moran Junction issue permits. Display yours on the port (left) side of the vessel at the rear. Permits for Yellowstone are good for Grand Teton (and vice versa) but must be registered at either Moose or Colter Bay Visitor Centers.

The state of Wyoming also requires boaters to purchase an aquatic invasive species decal for watercraft over 10ft long to help fund prevention efforts against invasive quagga and zebra mussels. Cost is $10/5 for motorized/nonmotorized watercraft registered in Wyoming, and $30/15 for motorized/nonmotorized watercraft owned by nonresidents. Decals are sold by Wyoming Fish and Game Department (www.gf.state.wy.us) online and at automated license agents.

Motorized craft (maximum 7.5 horsepower) are allowed only on Jackson, Phelps and Jenny Lakes. On Jenny Lake, crafts with over 10 horsepower (HP) are prohibited. Hand-propelled nonmotorized craft are permitted on Jackson, Two Ocean, Emma Matilda, Bearpaw, Leigh, String, Jenny, Bradley, Taggart and Phelps Lakes, as well as the Snake River 1000ft below Jackson Dam. Sailboats, water skis and sailboards are permitted only on Jackson Lake. Jet skis are not allowed in the park.

Floating is prohibited within 1000ft of Jackson Lake Dam. Only hand-powered rafts, canoes and kayaks are allowed on the Snake River. Watercraft are forbidden on other rivers.

On Jackson Lake, fires are forbidden along the east shore from Spalding Bay to Lizard Creek and otherwise permitted only below the high-water mark.

See the park's *Boating* and *Floating the Snake River* brochures.

COLTER BAY REGION

A fun, mellow activity for families or groups is to rent a motorboat for a day and explore Jackson Lake, stopping to picnic and swim at uncrowded inlets and islands. Though they cover less terrain, canoes and kayaks are similarly great. Next to the lodge, **Signal Mountain Marina** (☑307-543-2831; ☺7am-7:30pm mid-May–early Sep) rents boats, canoes and kayaks. Reservations are accepted for larger boats only and depend on lake levels. Ten-mile **scenic floats** (adult/6-12yr $60/38) on the Snake River offer good wildlife-watching opportunities.

Busy **Colter Bay Marina** (☏307-543-2811; ⏱8am-5pm, no rentals after 3pm) provides fishing gear and licenses, as well as boat rentals. Don't expect anything too adventurous here, as canoes aren't allowed more than 0.25 miles from the shore.

Grand Teton Lodge Company (GTLC) arranges daily scheduled **lake cruises** from Colter Bay (1½ hours adult/child $28/13) as well as breakfast (three hours adult/child $37/22) and dinner (three hours adult/child $57/37) trips. GTLC operates an **activities booth** (⏱7am-8pm) next to the Colter Bay grocery store.

Leek's Marina (☏307-543-2494), north of Colter Bay Junction, is a simpler affair, with a gas dock and overnight buoys.

Canoes and kayaks rented at the marinas are not supposed to be taken beyond Colter Bay or Half Moon Bay (from Colter Bay) or Dornan's Island (from Signal Mountain).

Trip Options

Overnight boaters can use backcountry campsites around Jackson Lake at Deadman Point, Bearpaw Bay, Grassy Island, Little Mackinaw Bay, South Landing, Elk Island and Warm Springs. Book these sites in advance, especially on summer weekends when the lake is chock-a-block with powerboats, sailboards, sailboats and canoes. There is a maximum three-night stay.

Outfitter **OARS** (Outdoor Adventure River Specialists; ☏209-736-4677, 800-346-6277; www.oars.com) guides trips kayaking around Jackson Lake (overnight adult/child $273/222) with instruction for beginners and multiday rafting trips on the Snake River (three days adult/child $659/554).

With dramatic close-ups of the toothy Mt Moran, Moran Bay is the most popular destination from Colter and Spalding Bays. While boating you can stop at Grassy Island en route. The following sample distances start from Signal Mountain: Hermitage Point (2 miles), Elk Island (3 miles) and Grassy Island (6 miles); from Colter Bay to Little Mackinaw Bay is 1.5 miles.

Alternatively, you can paddle from Lizard Creek Campground to remote backcountry trails on the northwest shore. Wilcox Point backcountry campsite (1.25 miles from Lizard Creek) provides backcountry access to Webb Canyon along the Moose Basin Divide Trail (20 miles). For a longer intermediate-level trip, paddle the twists and turns of the Snake River from Flagg Ranch to Wilcox Point or Lizard Creek.

Predominant winds from the southwest can be strong, especially in the afternoon, when waves can swamp canoes. Morning is usually the best time to paddle.

JENNY LAKE SCENIC DRIVE

String Lake is perfect for a family canoe trip or even just a splash about. The canoe-only put-in is at the end of a turnoff just before the Leigh Lake Trailhead parking lot.

Particularly suited to families, **Leigh Lake** offers the most scenic day and overnight paddles. Getting there requires a 120ft portage between paddling sections. Six beautiful backcountry campsites flank the lakeshore, three of which (16, 14A and 14B) are only accessible by boat. It is 3 miles one way from the portage point at the outlet of Leigh Lake to furthest campsite (16). Leigh Lake also offers quality fishing.

JOHN D ROCKEFELLER JR MEMORIAL PARKWAY

At Flagg Ranch Resort, Flagg Ranch Rafting offers three-hour scenic **floats** (adult/6-12yr $60/40) plus a three-hour **white-water trip** (adult/child $58/48) from mid-June to early September.

Fishing

Cutthroat, brown and lake trout cruise the waters of Jackson Lake. For fishing excursions, Signal Mountain Marina guides up to two people ($80/280 per hour/half day) on the lake. Your catch can be cleaned and most fine-dining restaurants within the park will cook it up for you too. Colter Bay Marina charges $80 per hour (minimum two hours) for guided lake fishing, plus fly-fishing day trips for $475 for two people.

Anglers must carry a valid Wyoming fishing license. Fishing licenses are issued at Moose Village store, Signal Mountain Lodge and Colter Bay Marina. Jackson Lake is closed to fishing in October. The Snake, Buffalo Fork and Gros Ventre Rivers are closed November 1 to March 31. In general anglers are limited to six trout per day, with varying size limitations. Get a copy of the park's fishing brochure for details.

WINTER ACTIVITIES

With the crowds gone, bears tucked away in their dens and powdery snow blanketing the pines, the Tetons make a lovely winter destination. Moose is the focus of

TETON WINTER FACILITIES

In Grand Teton National Park the **Craig Thomas Discovery & Visitor Center** (☏307-739-3300; ⊙8am-5pm winter, closed Christmas day) is the winter-activity hub, offering information on weather, road, ski and avalanche conditions. **Spur Ranch Log Cabins** (☏307-733-2522; www.dornans.com) sits close to the center. There is limited tent and RV camping near the **Colter Bay Visitor Center** (☏307-739-3594; ⊙8am-5pm early May–mid-May & Sep-early Oct, 8am-7pm Jun-early Sep). On the eastern edge of the national park, **Triangle X Ranch** (☏307-733-2183; www.trianglex.com) has wood cabins at discount winter rates.

winter activities and the Craig Thomas Discovery & Visitor Center has information on ski trail, weather, road and avalanche conditions. Teton Park Rd is plowed from Jackson Lake Junction to Signal Mountain Lodge and from Moose to the Taggart Lake Trailhead.

Grand Teton National Park brochures for Nordic skiing (appropriate for snowshoeing) and snowmobiling can be downloaded from www.nps.gov/grte/planyourvisit/brochures.htm.

Nordic Skiing

The park grooms 14 miles of track right under the Tetons' highest peaks, between Taggart-Bradley Lakes parking area and Signal Mountain. Lanes are available for ski touring, skate skiing and snowshoeing. The NPS does not always mark every trail: consult at the ranger station to make sure that the trail you plan to use is well tracked and easy to follow.

Remember to yield to passing skiers and those skiing downhill. You can find rentals in Jackson (p218).

Taggart Lake to Beaver Creek NORDIC SKIING
A moderate to difficult trail with some climbing. It's 3 miles round-trip to Taggart Lake or 4 miles round-trip to do the Beaver Creek Loop, climbing through a glacial moraine. Use care on the return descent, the trail may be icy. Park at the Taggart Lake parking area.

Jenny Lake NORDIC SKIING
An easy 8-mile round-trip. Park at the Taggart Lake parking area. Follow the Jenny Lake trail parallel to Cottonwood Creek and return via Teton Park Rd. There are great views of the Tetons throughout.

Moose-Wilson Road NORDIC SKIING
Park at the entrance to Death Canyon Rd. To ski Moose-Wilson Rd, it's an easy 5.8 miles

round-trip, with some climbing. A 2-mile loop detours to the edge of Phelps Lake. You can also approach via Teton Village, parking at Granite Canyon trailhead. Pets are allowed on Moose-Wilson Rd but not on the trails into the park.

Snowshoeing

Snowshoers may use the Nordic skiing trails described previously. For an easy outing, try Teton Park Rd (closed to traffic in winter). Remember to use the hardpack trail and never walk on ski trails – skiers will thank you for preserving the track!

Polecat Creek SNOWSHOEING
Park at the Flagg Ranch Lodge. Traveling clockwise, this easy 2.5-mile loop soon arrives at Polecat Creek and Huckleberry Hot Springs. After crossing power lines, in 0.4 miles another trail intersects. Stay right on the loop, continuing south to the lodge.

Ranger-led Tours TOURS
From late December through to mid-March rangers lead free 1.5-mile (two-hour) snowshoe hikes. It's also a good opportunity to study animal tracks and learn about winter ecology. Snowshoe hikes depart several times a week from the Craig Thomas Discovery & Visitor Center. Snowshoes are provided, and children over eight years old can take part.

Snowmobiling

The Tetons don't exactly cater to snowmobilers, who have more options in Yellowstone (p121) and West Yellowstone (p169). Any person operating a snowmobile must have a valid driver's license. In the park, snowmobiling is only allowed on the frozen surface of Jackson Lake. Vehicles must have Best Available Technology (BAT) and meet other standard requirements, listed on the NPS snowmobiling brochure.

On the John D Rockefeller Jr Memorial Parkway, Grassy Lake Rd is open to snowmobiles without BAT requirements.

Flagg Ranch Resort SNOWMOBILING
(☎307-733-2237; www.flaggranchresort.com; ☺Dec-Mar) Offers guided snowmobile tours to Old Faithful and the Grand Canyon of the Yellowstone, departing at 6:30am. Since the resort is closed to guests, Flagg Ranch offers hotel pickups in Jackson for its snowmobilers. Flagg Ranch information station does stay open in winter for those using the trails.

Backcountry Skiing

There is excellent backcountry skiing here, but skiers should have adequate knowledge of avalanche safety and use a transceiver, or book a guided tour.

Rendezvous Backcountry Tours SNOW SPORTS
(☎877-754-4887; www.skithetetons.com; 2-person downhill/XC tour $325/250) Guides small groups of one to four on backcountry ski and snowboarding tours for all abilities. Day trips and multiday tours available. It also operates the only hut system in the Tetons and runs safety clinics.

SLEEPING

Most campgrounds and accommodations are open from early May to early October, depending on the weather conditions. Camping inside the park is permitted in designated campgrounds only and is limited to 14 days (seven days at popular Jenny Lake). The NPS operates the park's six **campgrounds** (☎800-628-9988) on a first-come, first-served basis.

Demand for campsites is high from early July to Labor Day, and most campgrounds fill by 11am (checkout time). Jenny Lake fills by about 8am, followed by Signal Mountain. Colter Bay is a large site and fills later; Gros Ventre fills last, if at all.

Signal Mountain is probably the easiest place to base yourself because of its central location. Colter Bay and Jenny Lake have tent-only sites reserved for backpackers and cyclists.

Group sites (for up to 75 people) available at Gros Ventre and Colter Bay Campgrounds can be reserved only by calling park concessionaire **Grand Teton Lodge Company** (GTLC; ☎800-628-9988). Reservations are only taken for groups, up to one year in advance.

John D Rockefeller Jr Memorial Parkway

The parkway is a handy place to stay en route between Yellowstone and Grand Teton National Parks. For additional camping options, see the boxed text, p203.

Camping

Flagg Ranch Campground CAMPGROUND, RV SITES $
(Map p176; tent/RV sites $35/64; ☺May-early Oct) Among the most expensive campsites around, it features pull-through sites, propane for sale, 24-hour showers, laundry and a nightly campfire program. Sites are generally available the same day, but RV campers should reserve a week or more in advance.

Lodging

Flagg Ranch Resort CABINS $$
(Map p176; ☎307-543-2861, 800-443-2311; www.flaggranch.com; r $189; ☺mid-May–mid-Sep; ☎☒) Since its occupation by the US Cavalry, this 1910 resort has been gussied up: walkways lead to prim log duplexes featuring rooms with phones, coffeemakers and patio rockers. While less rugged than a mountain hideaway, the grounds still provide solitude for a short break. Pet-friendly ($10 extra), it's popular with families and couples; most stay a night or two between parks. The lodge offers upscale dining, a minimarket and an activities desk. Shuttles go to Jackson and the Jackson Hole Airport.

Colter Bay Region

Camping

At campgrounds run by the Grand Teton Lodge Company (GTLC), walk-in hikers and bicyclists pay only $8 per person, with specific sites reserved for them.

Lizard Creek Campground CAMPGROUND $
(Map p176; ☎800-672-6012; US 89/191/287; sites $21; ☺early Jan-early Sep) Snug in a forested peninsula along Jackson Lake's north shore, about 8 miles north of Colter Bay Junction, these secluded woodsy sites (60 total) are a great option. Register early since it's popular with boaters. Vehicle length limited to 30ft.

Signal Mountain Campground CAMPGROUND $
(Map p180; ☎800-672-6012; Teton Park Rd; sites $21; ☺early May–mid-Oct) This popular cam-

ℹ CAMPING ON THE CHEAP

Some lesser-known, first-come, first-served sites near the park may have fewer amenities, but they also have openings when NPS campgrounds are bursting and charge a third to half of the price.

Hidden **Sheffield Creek Campground** (Map p176; sites $5; ☉late Jun-Nov) is a five-site USFS campground 2.5 miles south of Yellowstone's South Entrance and just south of Flagg Ranch, across the Snake River Bridge, then a half-mile east on a rough dirt road from a subtly signed turnoff.

Eight free, minimally developed, first-come, first-served campgrounds are strung out along the bumpy unpaved **Grassy Lake Rd**, which begins just west of the parking lot at Flagg Ranch. The first (and most popular) campground is 1.6 miles along the road and has four riverside campsites. Each of the next three riverside campgrounds, in the 1.5-mile stretch past Soldiers' Meadow, has two sites. The last four campgrounds, spaced out along the next 3.5 miles, are useful for hikes into Yellowstone's southern reaches. All sites have toilets and trash service but no potable water. Camping is only allowed in designated sites.

Hidden, free eight-site **Pacific Creek Campground** (Map p176; ☉mid–Jun-Dec) is 12 miles up the graveled Pacific Creek Rd (USFS Rd 30090) from Grand Teton's Moran Ranger/Entrance Station. It's generally used as a base for backpacking trips into the Teton Wilderness.

Several free dispersed campsites sit on **Shadow Mountain**, on the east edge of the valley. This spot has a dedicated following, so show up early. Don't expect water or toilets, and there's a two-day maximum stay. It's a rough drive anywhere, but you'll be rewarded with stunning dawn views of the Tetons.

pground with 86 sites looks out on lovely sunsets on Jackson Lake from 5 miles south of Jackson Lake Junction. Sites can be cramped but are convenient: a restaurant, bar, grocery store and marina are nearby. Vehicle size is limited to 30ft. There's a dump station for RVs.

Colter Bay Campground   CAMPGROUND **$**
(Map p180; US 89/191/287; sites $20; ☉mid-May–mid-Sep) The merits and detractions of this large, noisy campground (350 sites) on the east shore of Jackson Lake, 3 miles north of Jackson Lake Junction, relate to its size. It should always have available spots and there's a separate RV park, a grocery store, a laundromat and hot showers available at nearby Colter Village. Propane is available, and there's a dumping station. GTLC-run.

Colter Bay RV Park   RV SITES **$**
(Map p180; ☑reservations 307-543-2811, 800-628-9988; sites $56; ☉mid-May–mid Sep) Sewer, electrical and water connections are perks at these long pull-though sites (112 total). There's a surcharge for vehicles over 38ft. GTLC-run.

Lodging

Colter Bay Village and Jackson Lake Lodge are operated by **Grand Teton Lodge Com-**

pany (GTLC; ☑advance reservations 307-543-3100, 800-628-9988, same-day reservations 307-543-2811; www.gtlc.com).

Jackson Lake Lodge   LODGE, CABINS **$$$**
(Map p180; ☑307-543-2811; r/ste/cottage from $229/625/229; ☉mid-May–early Oct; @🛜🏊) This lodge perches on a bluff overlooking the Tetons and Jackson Lake, 1 mile north of Jackson Lake Junction. Standard rooms have barely changed in 50 years, but aesthetics take the backseat to nature here, and the lodge gets many nostalgic returning guests. Perks include soft sheets, meandering trails and enormous picture windows framing the luminous peaks (though you can save yourself $100 and catch the views off the patio). The 348 cinderblock cottages – lifted straight out of the suburbs – are generally overpriced, though some offer private balconies with a view. The duplex walls can be very thin. Amenities include a business center, a heated outdoor pool and a nearby medical clinic.

Signal Mountain Lodge   CABINS, MOTEL **$$**
(Map p180; ☑307-543-2831; www.signalmtnlodge.com; r $175-228, cabins $132-198; ☉mid-May–mid-Oct; 🏊) While these lakeside lodgings beg for a thorough update, they have one thing clear: location, location, location. Smack in the middle of the park, accommodations

GRAND TETON NATIONAL PARK CAMPGROUNDS

CAMPGROUND	LOCATION	DESCRIPTION	NO OF SITES	ELEVATION
Gros Ventre	Central Tetons	Spacious and shady, with plenty of ample spaces; tent sites are on separate loops	372	6783ft
Jenny Lake	Central Tetons	The most coveted camp spot amid boulders and trails; tenters only	51	6803ft
Colter Bay	Colter Bay	Enormous but wooded, with ready conveniences; buzzing with activity	350	6820ft
Colter Bay RV Park	Colter Bay	RV zones are separate with electrical connections	112	6820ft
Lizard Creek	Colter Bay	A secluded spot with shade and lake access	60	6768ft
Signal Mountain	Colter Bay	Close to shops and restaurants, with lake access and forest shade	86	7593ft
Flagg Ranch	Rockefeller Parkway	Features dining and conveniences nearby but not a haven for tenters	175	6300ft

*Reservations through Flagg Ranch (☑800-443-2311)

 Drinking Water   Flush Toilets   Ranger Station Nearby   Wheelchair Accessible   Dogs Allowed (On Leash)

GRAND TETON NATIONAL PARK SLEEPING

range from motel rooms to cabins, bungalows and lakefront retreats. Extras can include a kitchenette, gas fireplace and lake views. All units have electric heat, while perks include self-service laundry and dryers, and a TV and games room. Pets lodge too with a $10 fee. Look for early-season discounts. Located on Teton Park Rd, 2 miles southwest of Jackson Lake Junction.

Colter Bay Village　　　　　CABINS $
(Map p180; tent cabins $52, cabins without bath $65, with bath $119-165) Half a mile west of Colter Bay Junction, Colter Bay Village offers two types of accommodations. Tent cabins (June to early September) are very basic log-and-canvas structures sporting all the charm of a Siberian gulag. Expect bare bunks, a wood-burning stove, picnic table and outdoor grill. Bathrooms are separate and sleeping bags can be rented. At these prices, you're better off camping. The log cabins, some original, are much more comfortable and a better deal; they're available late May to late September.

Eastern Slopes

Triangle X Ranch　　　　　RANCH $$$
(Map p176; ☑307-733-2183; www.trianglex.com; 2 Triangle X Rd, Moose; weekly all-inclusive per person, double occupancy $1880, winter cabins per person $125) With the gorgeous backdrop of the jagged Tetons, this ranch on the eastern flanks of the park was started in 1926 by the Turner family, who still run it now. Cabins with wood interiors are immaculate, and activity options – from square dancing and trout fishing to Dutch-oven cookouts – keep guests out enjoying the fresh air. Cabins have one to three bedrooms and prices drop with larger groups. Summer visits require a weeklong minimum. Kids get special attention with their own dining hall and a 'Little Wrangler' program, featuring horseback riding, swimming and crafts. Winter rates are a steal.

Moose Head Ranch　　　　　RANCH $$$
(Map p176; ☑307-733-3141; www.moosehead ranch.com; all-inclusive per person double occupancy $375; ☺Jun-Aug) Families rave about this ranch, which has modern log cabins, friendly young staff, a varied and tasty menu and a slew of activities for adults and kids alike. Rides are for all abilities. Visits require a five-night minimum and children get discounted rates. It's located between the Tetons and Yellowstone, 18 miles north of Jackson at 6800ft.

OPEN	RESERVATIONS REQUIRED?	DAILY FEE	FACILITIES	PAGE
late April–mid-Oct	no	$20		p205
mid-May–late Sep	no	$20		p205
mid-May–mid-Sep	no	$20		p202
mid-May–mid-Sep	no	$56		p202
early Jun–early Sep	no	$21		p202
early May–mid-Oct	no	$21		p202
late May-late Sep	yes*	tent/RV $35/64		p202

 Grocery Store Nearby　 Payphone　 Summertime Campfire Program　 RV Dump Station

Central Tetons

Camping

At the following campgrounds, walk-in hikers and bicyclists pay $8 per person, with specific sites reserved for them.

Jenny Lake Campground　CAMPGROUND $
(Map p186; Teton Park Rd; tent sites $20; ☺mid-May–late Sep) This congenial and popular tent-only campground (51 sites) sits among the evergreens and glacial boulders 8 miles north of Moose Junction. Convenient to many trailheads, it is almost always full. Only vehicles less than 14ft long are allowed, and trailers are prohibited.

Gros Ventre Campground　CAMPGROUND $
(Map p176; Gros Ventre Rd; sites $20; ☺late Apr–mid-Oct) This sprawling but secluded 372-site campground sits near the Gros Ventre River, 4.5 miles northeast of US 26/89/191/287 and 11.5 miles from Moose. With the tall cottonwoods for shade and nearby river, it's very attractive. Closer to the Gros Ventre Mountains than to many park attractions, it tends to fill up later in the day. The more private sites west of the loops fill quickly. There's an RV dump but no hookups.

Lodging

TOP CHOICE Jenny Lake Lodge　CABINS $$$
(Map p186; ☎307-733-4647; cabins incl half-board $620; ☺early Jun-early Oct; ☏@) Rife with history, this is the oldest lodge within the whole park system. Worn timbers, down comforters and colorful quilts imbue this elegant lodging off Teton Park Rd with a cozy atmosphere. Outdoor rockers welcome you to your private cabin, furnished with flannel chairs, plush quilts and down comforters. Perks include robes and remodeled baths, but no TVs or radios (phones available on request). Rainy days are for hunkering down at the fireplace in the main lodge with a game or book from the stacks. Rates include breakfast, a five-course dinner, cruiser bicycles and guided horseback riding on nearby trails. The lodge goes above and beyond to create a community feel, with daily activities for guests only, like naturalist talks or croquet on the lawn. Reservation lines open November 1 for the following year. It's run by Grand Teton Lodge Company.

Climbers' Ranch　CABINS $
(Map p186; ☎307-733-7271; www.americanalpineclub.org; Teton Park Rd; dm $22; ☺Jun-Sep) Started as a refuge for serious climbers, this

group of rustic log cabins run by the American Alpine Club is now available to hikers. In a spectacular, in-park location, with a climbers' library and occasional talks and slide shows. Amenities include a bathhouse with showers and sheltered cook station with locking bins for coolers. Bring your own sleeping bag and pad (the bunks are bare), but it's still a great deal. Members of the AAC get a discounted rate and volunteers for June's work week stay the rest of the month for free. The ranch is just south of the Teton Glacier turnout.

Moose

Spur Ranch Log Cabins   CABINS $$$
(Map p186; ☎307-733-2522; www.dornans.com; cabins $175-250) Gravel paths running through a broad wildflower meadow link these tranquil duplex cabins on the Snake River in Moose. Lodgepole pine furniture, Western stylings and down bedding create a homey feel, but the views are what make it. Cabins equipped with a kitchen, a porch and an outdoor grill can sleep up to six. There are only 12, so reserve at least six months in advance. It is an excellent winter base for those interested in Nordic skiing or snowshoeing – you can make tracks right out the door. High-season rates run from the end of May to the end of September (with a three-night minimum); the shoulder season offers deep discounts.

EATING & DRINKING

Visitors dine in the park for the convenience or the stunning views, but generally not for the food. The better restaurants face the challenge of getting chefs on a seasonal basis – the quality of your meal will depend largely on their success. For foodies, it's worth a trip to nearby Jackson.

Other options include taking a Jackson Lake dinner and breakfast cruise (p199) or packing a picnic basket with five-star goodies. Dornan's in Moose offers an impressive selection of wines.

John D Rockefeller Jr Memorial Parkway

Bear's Den   WESTERN $$
(Map p176; ☎800-443-2311; lunch mains $9-12, dinner mains $9-34) Hungry travelers flock to this eatery at Flagg Ranch, the area's sole dining option. Breakfast and lunches are casual at this handsome lodge while dinner goes Western with grilled steaks, meatloaf and chicken potpie. Whiskey and local brews are served at the Burnt Bear Saloon. The adjoining minimart has a deli (open 1:30pm to 5:30pm).

Colter Bay Region

COLTER BAY
For the cheapest nearby picnic fixings, hit the deli counter at the Colter Bay grocery store across the road.

Leek's Pizzeria   PIZZERIA $$
(Map p180; ☎307-733-5470; pizzas $9-21; ⊙11am-10pm) Pizza and draft beer on the patio is a fine way to end an active day. North of Colter Bay Village, this casual but cozy eatery also serves soup, salad and sandwiches. There is a basic kids menu. Open-mic nights are on Monday, and live bands play every two weeks.

John Colter Café Court
Pizza & Deli   CAFETERIA $
(Map p180; mains $5-9; ⊙11am-10pm) An airy, plain cafeteria offering salads, burritos, picnic takeout and grill staples. Kids will like this place. The service is friendly and the grilled free-range chicken tacos are tasty but they get you with pricey canned and bottled drinks.

Ranch House   WESTERN $$
(Map p180; breakfast buffet adult/child $13/7; dinner mains $13-25; ⊙7:30am-9pm May-Sep; ☎) Serving wild game, salmon and flank steak, this Western dining room with a branded bar offers a more formal setting. Vegetarians are appeased (but barely) with veggie burgers or tofu lo mein. The all-you-can-eat breakfast buffet is a pre-hike institution.

JACKSON LAKE LODGE
Mural Room   CONTEMPORARY AMERICAN $$$
(Map p180; ☎307-543-3100; Jackson Lake Lodge; meals $18-28) The ambiance could hardly be heightened: in addition to stirring views of the Tetons and moose ambling in the willow flats, the dining room walls are adorned with the romantic Rendezvous Murals, depictions of 19th-century life by Carl Roters. Gourmet selections include game dishes and imaginative creations like trout wrapped in sushi rice with sesame seeds. Breakfasts are very good; dinner reservations are recommended.

The Blue Heron recaffeination station serves lattes and espressos from 6am and alcohol and appetizers from 11am to midnight; occasionally you'll hit on live music. To fully appreciate the outdoor patio, sip a huckleberry margarita while watching the alpenglow on Mt Moran.

Pioneer Grill DINER **$$**
(Map p180; Jackson Lake Lodge; mains $7-15; ☺6am-10:30pm) A casual classic diner with leatherette stools lined up in a maze, the Pioneer serves up wraps, burgers and salads. A Mt Owen – an oversized profiterole topped with ice cream, hot fudge and whipped cream – takes the burn off hiking Cascade Canyon. Pioneer has a takeout window, boxed lunches (order before 9pm for the next day) and room service pizza for pooped hikers (5pm to 9pm).

Poolside Barbecue BBQ **$$$**
(Map p180; ☏307-543-2811; Jackson Lake Lodge; adult/child $23/12; ☺6-8pm Sun-Fri Jul-Aug) Reservations are required for this all-you-can-eat BBQ buffet (think brisket, burgers, chicken, grilled veggies and lots of sides) with live music.

SIGNAL MOUNTAIN

The Peaks CONTEMPORARY AMERICAN **$$$**
(Map p180; ☏307-543-2831; Signal Mountain Lodge; meals $18-28) At Signal Mountain Lodge, dine on selections of cheese and fruit, local free-range beef and organic polenta cakes. Small plates, like wild game sliders, are also available. While the indoor ambiance is rather drab, the patio seating, starring sunsets over Jackson Lake and top-notch huckleberry margaritas, gets snapped up early.

Trapper Grill CAFE **$$**
(Map p180; ☏307-543-2831; Signal Mountain Lodge; mains $5-16) With an encyclopedic menu, the Trapper Grill should please each picky member of the family, offering a real range of choices from grass-fed burgers and Mexican meals to gourmet sandwiches and ribs. The hot breakfasts, with sides of ham, bacon or buffalo sausage, are gut busters. You could also grab a Philly steak and a pint of Snake River Lager at Deadman's Bar, named after the site of an unsolved murder in 1886.

Central Tetons

TOP CHOICE **Jenny Lake Lodge**
Dining Room CONTEMPORARY AMERICAN **$$$**
(Map p186; ☏307-733-4647; breakfast dishes $19, lunch mains $10-30, dinner mains $60) A five-course meal in the wilderness. Leave your hiking boots in the car; men must wear jackets at the park's premier restaurant. Pasta, an excellent wine list and strip steak in soy glaze are some of the offerings. Dinner reservations are required. If you're on a budget, try the more casual lunch, with affordable lighter meals (try the smoked trout), but reservations are still a good idea.

Moose

Pizza Pasta Company PIZZERIA **$$**
(Map p186; mains $9-16; ☺noon-9pm) Packed with crowds nightly, this unpretentious pizza parlor is simple yet so satisfying. Crusty pizza, pastas and nachos are offered with beer, wine and snappy service. Guests line up and make their orders at a counter. The 2nd-floor terrace serves up a fun evening atmosphere, lovely Teton views and occasional live music.

Dornan's Grocery Store MARKET, DELI
(Map p186; ☏307-733-2415; Moose Village) The park's best-quality selection, with an excellent deli, with imported cheeses, sandwiches, espresso counter and a wildly popular frozen-yogurt machine. The Wine Shoppe offers 1700 selections as well as monthly wine tasting, as per its motto – life is too short to drink cheap wine. Salud!

Dornan's Chuckwagon BBQ **$$**
(Map p186; ☏307-733-2415 ext 213; Moose Village; dinner $17; ☺7:30-11am, 11:30am-3pm & 5-9pm Jun–mid-Sep, closed Fri & Sat evening) Dinner doesn't get any more casual than these picnic tables scattered in the open air, but the views are simply grand. At this family favorite, breakfast means sourdough pancakes and eggs off the griddle while lunchtime means light fare and sandwiches. At dinner time the Dutch ovens are steaming with steak dinners and Mexican dishes, along with a bottomless salad bar. Kids get special rates. The bar boasts zinging margaritas and Snake River Lager on tap.

Locals and travelers flock to the Monday-night Hootenanny, an open-mic event, heavy on the folk tunes and Appalachian jams. Bring your own beer and blanket or sign up early to perform. It can be quite a good time.

GRAND TETON NATIONAL PARK EATING & DRINKING

INFORMATION

Three park concessionaires operate various accommodations, restaurants, marinas and activities:

Dornan's (☑307-733-2522; www.dornans.com)
Grand Teton Lodge Company (GTLC; ☑307-543-3100, 800-628-9988; www.gtlc.com)
Signal Mountain Lodge (☑307-543-2831; www.signalmtnlodge.com)

Media

Grand Teton Natural History Association (☑307-739-3403) This nonprofit organization sells books and maps at all park visitor centers.

Internet Access

Dornan's (☑307-733-2522; www.dornans.com; Moose Village; per hr $5) Provides internet access.

Post

Post office (Moose Village)

Ranger Stations

Visit the following for backcountry information:
Colter Bay Visitor Center (☑307-739-3595)
Craig Thomas Discovery & Visitor Center (☑307-739-3309)
Jenny Lake Ranger Station (☑307-739-3343; ☺summer) Also offers backcountry permits and climbing information.

Tourist Information

Colter Bay Visitor Center (☑307-739-3594; ☺8am-5pm early May–mid-May & Sep-early Oct, 8am-7pm Jun-early Sep) On US 89/191/287, 6 miles north of Jackson Lake Lodge. Issues backcountry permits and offers crafts demonstrations and tours of its Indian Arts Museum (p179). Newcomers can get their bearings at 'Teton Highlights,' a daily 30-minute ranger talk at 11am at the auditorium.

Craig Thomas Discovery & Visitor Center (☑307-739-3300; ☺8am-5pm year-round, 8am-7pm peak summer season, closed Christmas Day) Inaugurated in 2007, this $21-million center on Teton Park Rd, half a mile west of Moose Junction, is open year-round. Backcountry, climbing and boating permits are available here, as is information on weather, road and avalanche conditions. Excellent interactive displays include working models that demonstrate glacial movement and animal migration. An auditorium hosts speakers and events.

Flagg Ranch Information Station (☑307-543-2327; ☺9am-4pm Jun-early Sep, closed for lunch) Provides park information, rest rooms and a small bookstore. Located 2.5 miles from Yellowstone's South Entrance.

Grand Teton National Park Headquarters (☑307-739-3600; www.nps.gov/grte) Shares the building with the Craig Thomas Discovery & Visitor Center. For general visitor information call ☑307-739-3300. For weather information contact the 24-hour recorded message at ☑317-739-3611.

Jenny Lake Visitor Center (☑307-739-3343; ☺8am-4:30pm Sep-May, 8am-7pm Jun-Aug) On Teton Park Rd, 8 miles north of Moose Junction. Facilities include a store, lockers, geology exhibits, a relief model, rest rooms and telephones. With indepth information on backpacking and trails, it's also the meeting place for guided walks and talks, with activity schedules posted.

GETTING AROUND

Driving

The speed limit on US 26/89/191 is 55mph; elsewhere it's generally 45mph. Watch for wildlife at dusk, as well as cyclists crossing sections of the multiuse pathway on Teton Park Rd. Gas stations are open year-round at Moose (24 hours, credit card only 8pm to 8am) and Flagg Ranch Resort, and summers only at Colter Bay, Signal Mountain and Jackson Lodge.

Organized Tours

GTLC runs half-day tours of Grand Teton (adult/three to 11 years $5/18), full-day tours of Yellowstone ($65/40) and a tour combining both parks ($90/50) daily from Jackson Lake Lodge (p206). Make arrangements at the hotel activities desk.

Gray Line (☑307-733-3135, 800-443-6133; www.graylinejh.com) runs all-day tours from Jackson to Grand Teton National Park ($80) or Yellowstone ($95), park entry not included.

Flagg Ranch (☑800-443-2311; www.flaggranch.com) calls its full-day tours of Teton (adult/child $170/150) or Yellowstone ($190/170) 'wildlife safaris.' Entrance fee for the parks isn't included. Also see wildlife tours p35.

Public Transportation

Alltrans Park Shuttle (☑800-443-6133, 307-733-3135; www.alltransparkshuttle.com; daily pass $12; ☺7am-7pm Jun-Sep) Operates several buses a day in summer between Jackson, Moose, Jenny Lake Lodge, Signal Mountain Lodge, Jackson Lake Lodge and Colter Bay. Riders can pay with cash or credit cards. Rides are unlimited on the daily pass. The service is free for guests of GTLC properties. Call for airport shuttle service (one way from Jackson is $16).

Around Grand Teton

Best Hikes

» Table Mountain (p224)

» Devil's Staircase to Alaska Basin (p225)

» Jackson Peak (p211)

Best Places to Stay & Eat

» Spring Creek Ranch (boxed text, p215)

» Alpine House (p215)

» The Hostel (p221)

» Snake River Grill (p217)

» Teton Thai (p221)

Why Go?

Outside the park boundaries, the landscape doesn't turn dull – it continues the rampage of beauty with cold clear rivers, winding single tracks and steep powder runs. One of the best times to visit this region is in winter, when Jackson Hole and Grand Targhee serve up deep, pillowy snow to ride. Lodges light roaring fires and the wilderness becomes a haven for dogsledding, snowshoeing, ski touring and winter fun.

Posh and popular Jackson serves as the regional hub and base camp, where you can browse for Western baubles, down pints of fresh organic lager or wrap yourself in honey and rose petals. The foodie scene is one of the best in the West, with an emphasis on local, farm-raised food. On the Idaho side, rural Teton Valley is another world. If you have come to embrace every scrap of solitude, a trip west across the divide might be in order.

When to Go
Jackson Hole

June-August Farmers' markets, fat-tire adventures and the Grand Teton Music Festival

September Crisp air coincides with the Jackson Hole Fall Arts Festival

January & February Snow-dusted peaks, powdery slopes, après-ski parties deluxe

Jackson

📞307 / POP 9915 / ELEV 6234FT

Beautiful and studiedly rustic, technically this is Wyoming, but with the highest per-capita income in the US. Once a diamond in the rough, now McMansions spread here like brucellosis: it's a haven for millionaires since there's no income tax. This is the new West, a human confluence that includes ranchers, rhinestone cowboys, mountain athletes and an army of service workers. As the community evolves, tensions sometimes flare over wilderness, since 97% of Teton County is, in fact, public land.

Yet Jackson is abuzz with life: trails and outdoor opportunities abound, fresh sushi is flown in daily and generous purse strings support a vigorous cultural life. When it becomes a little much, just skip the souvenir

Around Grand Teton Highlights

① Ride through the wildflower meadows to explore Idaho's **Teton Valley** (p225) on horseback

② Tear down single-track trails on mountain bikes only to catch your breath on the gondola ride up at **Jackson Hole** (p219)

③ Cross streams and crest lofty ridges on the trail to **Table Mountain** (p224)

④ Luxuriate at **Rock Spring Yurt** (p221) in a guided overnight trek to the backcountry

⑤ Soak in **Granite Hot Springs** (p222) pool after a hard day on the hoof

⑥ Shred powder at the legendary **Jackson Hole Mountain Resort** (p219)

⑦ Hit happy hour at one of **Jackson's upscale eateries** (p216)

shops and dwell in the glorious backyard called Grand Teton National Park.

Jackson marks the intersection of Hwy 22 (heading west to Teton Pass) and US 26/89/191. The main drag follows East–West Broadway into the downtown area, where it turns north onto Cache Dr at the town square, the heart of the pedestrian-oriented commercial district. Hwy 390 (Moose–Wilson Rd) leads north 7 miles to Teton Village.

Sights

TOP CHOICE National Museum of
Wildlife Art   MUSEUM
(☑307-733-5771; www.wildlifeart.org; 2820 Rungius Rd; adult $10, child free with adult; ☺9am-5pm; ☻) If you visit only one area museum, make it this one, with major works by Bierstadt, Rungius, Remington and Russell that will make your skin prickle. The discovery gallery has a kids' studio for drawing and print-rubbing that adults plainly envy. Check the website for summer film series and art-class schedules. Under renovation, this Arizona sandstone facility blends into the landscape overlooking the National Elk Refuge, just northeast of town on the west side of US 26/89/191.

FREE **National Elk Refuge**   NATURE RESERVE
(☑307-733-9212; 675 E Broadway; ☺daylight hours Oct-May) About 7000 Rocky Mountain 'welfare' elk (and a few hungry wolves) winter on alfalfa hay pellets here when snow covers the native grasses. Access these 25,000 acres northeast of Jackson via Elk Refuge Rd, an extension of E Broadway. Bundle the kids up for the refuge's one-hour winter **sleigh ride** (adult/5-12yr $16/12), departing from the National Museum of Wildlife Art mid-December through early April. These elk provide the 'raw materials' for the **antler arch** on Jackson Town Sq, celebrated with Elkfest (p23).

FREE **Jackson National
Fish Hatchery**   FISH HATCHERY
(☑307-733-2510; 1500 Fish Hatchery Rd; ☺8am-4pm) Just north of the elk refuge, with daily tours.

Activities

The cowboy myths may have gone to pasture, but Jackson remains paradise for outdoor enthusiasts. Options are only limited by your lack of gear or imagination, so consult the shops listed here for rentals or trip suggestions.

Goodwin Lake & Jackson Peak   HIKING
Popular with locals, this 9-mile round-trip is one of the closest summits to Jackson with cross-valley views of the Tetons.

Drive east on East Broadway until it ends, turning left into the National Elk Refuge. The road switchbacks. Bear right at Curtis Canyon for Goodwin Lake (after 9.2 miles) and drive 2.7 miles to the parking lot. The trail climbs steadily through a field of wildflowers, topping out on a level hilltop, passing through fragrant forests of Douglas fir. Approach the forested shores of **Goodwin Lake** (880ft), a nice spot for a swim or trout fishing.

The bare, pointed summit of **Jackson Peak** (10,741ft) sits directly above the lake. Its most secure approach winds left up a more gradual saddle. Continue past Goodwin Lake heading southeast, crossing an open field. Take a right at a well-worn but narrow trail marked with cairns. The trail climbs steeply to the ridge, crossing snow patches and rocky outcrops to the peak. Return via the same route. Dogs are welcome to hike with their owners.

Mill Iron Ranch   HORSEBACK RIDING
(☑307-733-6390, 888-808-6390; www.milliron ranch.net; 5 US Hwy 89; 2hr ride $50) This fourth-generation operation of a Wyoming ranch family is the real deal. Climbing 2000ft, their two-hour ride in the Bridger-Teton National Forest is rated the number-one trail ride in the US. They also offer dinner rides, sleigh rides and barn dances. To get there, drive south from Jackson on Hwy 89.

Jack Dennis Outdoor Shop   FLY-FISHING
(☑307-734-8103; www.jackdennis.com; 70 S King St) A pro fly shop offering guided fly-fishing and casting instruction. Native whitefish and cutthroat, as well as lake and brown trout, abound in most area waterways. Fishing is subject to Wyoming state regulations (buy licenses at visitor centers).

**Jackson Hole Mountain
Guides**   ROCK CLIMBING
(☑307-733-4979, 800-239-7642; www.jhmg.com; 165 N Glenwood St) With world-class climbing at your nubby fingertips, Jackson is an ideal center for instruction or guided climbs. Offers guided Teton rock climbing and programs for kids.

Jackson

0 ___ 200 m
0 ___ 0.1 miles

To Jackson Hole Airport (9mi);
Grand Teton National Park Entry (13mi);
Yellowstone National Park (60mi)

North Park

Flat Creek

National Elk Refuge

Jackson Hole &
Greater Yellowstone
Visitor Center

Wyoming Game &
Fish Department

Perry St

Rosencrans

USFS Bridger-Teton
National Forest
Headquarters
& Jackson
Ranger District

Mercill Ave

N Cache Dr

Cache Creek

E Gill Ave

W Gill Ave

N Millward St

N Glenwood St

Center St

N King St

Miller Park

Valley Bookstore

E Deloney Ave

W Deloney Ave

Town Square

E Broadway

W Broadway

To Bubba's Bar-B-Que (0.2mi);
Hoback Sports (0.2mi); Barker-Ewing
River Trips (0.9mi); Happy Trails Pet
Resort (1.1mi);
Hwy 22 (1.2mi);
Albertson's (1.3mi)

To Golden Eagle
Motor Inn (0.1mi);
National Elk Refuge
Headquarters (0.4mi)

W Pearl Ave

E Pearl Ave

S Millward St

S Glenwood St

S Cache Dr

S King St

S Willow St

W Simpson Ave

E Simpson Ave

S Jackson St

W Hansen Ave

To Buckrail
Lodge (0.1mi)

To Snow King
Resort (0.2mi)

Jackson

**Continental Divide Dogsled
Adventures** DOGSLEDDING
(☑307-455-3052; www.dogsledadventures.com; half-day $180) Iditarod veteran Billy Snodgrass and his team of Alaskan racing dogs sled through the beautiful winter backcountry. Trips run from half-day to overnight in Grand Teton, the Shoshone National Forests and greater Yellowstone.

**Snake River Kayak &
Canoe School** KAYAKING
(☑307-733-9999, 800-529-2501; www.snakeriver kayak.com; 260 N Cache St) Offers kayak rentals and instruction in addition to multiday paddling trips to Yellowstone Lake.

Snow King Resort SNOWSPORTS
(☑307-733-5200, 800-522-5464; www.snowking .com; 400 E Snow King Ave; adult/child $42/32; ☺Thanksgiving-Mar) Sling the skis over your shoulder and walk to this tiny 400-acre resort from downtown. Three lifts serve ski and snowboard runs with a vertical drop of 1571ft (15% beginner, 25% intermediate, 60% advanced). This north-facing slope catches less snow than other resorts but is convenient and well suited to children and families. Also popular are **night skiing** (adult/child $20/15; ☺4:30-8:30pm Mon-Sat) and **tubing** (adult/child per hr $16/13). The best value is the 'Ski All Three' package, which includes three nights' lodging with breakfast and two full-day lift tickets for Snow King, Jackson Hole Mountain Resort and Grand Targhee, and transfers to and from the airport and between the resorts. See p219 for details on nearby ski areas.

For stunning views of five mountain ranges, take the scenic 20-minute **Snow King Chairlift** (adult/child $12/8) ride up to 7751ft. Follow the nature trail at the top through wildflower fields and aspen groves. The lift operates 9am to 6pm mid-May to early September, with extended summer hours. The resort's meandering 2500ft **Alpine Slide** (☑307-733-7680; per ride $15) is open late May to mid-September. Other diversions include **indoor ice skating** and **minigolf**.

Wyoming Balloon Co BALLOONING
(☑307-739-0900; www.wyomingballoon.com; per person $325; ☺mid-Jun–mid-Sep) The ultimate float trips are these hour-long flights over the Tetons. Flights are weather-dependent.

Enclosure CLIMBING GYM
(☑307-733-2297; Hwy 89; www.enclosureclimbing .com; adult/child $16/11; ☺11am-9pm Mon-Fri, 10am-8pm Sat & Sun) The Rockies' largest indoor climbing center, with rental shoes and harnesses available. It's 3.5 miles south of town on Hwy 89.

Cycling

With excellent mountain biking, popular rides in the area include Cache Creek, southeast of Jackson into the Gros Ventre; Game Creek, along USFS Rd 30455 east off US 26/89/191; and Spring Gulch Rd, west of and parallel to US 26/89/191 between Hwy 22 and Gros Ventre Junction. Hard-core riders can try Old Pass Rd, the old route over Teton Pass, south of Hwy 22.

Hoback Sports   BICYCLE RENTAL
(☑307-733-5335; 520 W Broadway Ave; ⊙9am-7pm) Offers bike rentals ($30 to $40 per day), tours (from $65), repairs and maps of area biking trails.

White-Water Rafting & Floating

A splashy paddle down the class-III **Snake River Canyon**, south of Jackson along US 89/26 between Hoback Junction and Alpine, is a popular summer pastime. Wildlife includes ospreys and eagles nesting along the river. Half-day trips (from $48) put in at West Table Creek and take out at Sheep Gulch (8 miles). Full-day trips (from $80) put in at Pritchard Creek, upstream from West Table Creek, and take out at Sheep Gulch (16 miles). The rafting season runs May to Labor Day, but the best white-water is in June. July and August are crowded, so reserve ahead.

Half-day **scenic float trips** on a 13-mile section of the swift-flowing Snake River put in south of Grand Teton National Park and take out north of Hoback Junction, passing through the Jackson Hole wetlands, which are rich with bird and wildlife-viewing opportunities. For more information on boating the Snake, see p184.

Barker-Ewing River Trips WHITE-WATER RAFTING
(☑307-733-1000, 800-448-4202; www.barker-ewing.com; 45 W Broadway) A reputable outfitter.

Dave Hansen Whitewater WHITE-WATER RAFTING
(☑307-733-6295, 800-732-6295; www.davehansenwhitewater.com; 515 N Cache St) Gets rave reviews from families.

Festivals & Events

For the scoop on Jackson's annual events see local newspaper listings.

If an ungulate rack would provide the finishing touch to your home decor, check out **ElkFest & Antler Auction**, which takes place every May around the town square. Boy Scouts collect and sell the shed antlers during the festival to raise money to buy pellet win-

ter feed for the elk – thus the elk financially support themselves during the winter.

The **Teton County Fair** takes over the Teton County Fairgrounds (Snow King Ave and Flat Creek Rd) in late July. Also held at the fairgrounds, the **JH Rodeo Company** (☑307-733-2805) saddles up at 8pm Wednesdays and Saturdays June through August.

September's **Jackson Hole Fall Arts Festival** features live auctions, artist talks and samples of local chefs' culinary wizardry.

Kids shouldn't dodge what's considered the longest-running **shoot out** (⊙6:15pm Memorial Day-Labor Day) in the country, on Jackson Town Sq, where the good guys and bad guys face off on a daily basis.

Sleeping

Unfortunately, budget lodgings in Jackson have gone the way of the stagecoach. The best deals come during the shoulder seasons (from October 1 until the opening of ski season in late November and after spring snowmelt in early April until Memorial Day, when rooms are as much as 50% less than high-season prices quoted here. Those on a tight budget should plan to camp or stake out the bargain off-season ski lodgings over the pass in Idaho.

Advance reservations are essential during holiday periods. Options are listed below – for more, contact **Jackson Hole Central Reservations** (☑888-838-6806; www.jacksonholewy.com), which has listings for the town of Jackson as well as Teton Village.

Rates quoted here are for doubles with private bathroom, since single rates are often not available. Walk-in rates can be up to 20% lower than rack rates, especially during slow periods when it pays to shop around. Check online for special seasonal package deals.

Camping

For more information on campgrounds in the Jackson Ranger District call ☑1-800-342-CAMP.

Curtis Canyon Campground CAMPGROUND $
(sites $12; ⊙late May-Sep) Conveniently located, this popular 12-site campground, on gravel USFS Rd 30440 (off Elk Refuge Rd), sits 7 miles northeast of Jackson at 6900ft, with splendid views of the Tetons.

Cabin Creek Campground CAMPGROUND $
(sites $10; ⊙late May-Sep) The roadside, 11-site Cabin Creek is 19 miles south of Jackson

SPLURGE: SPRING CREEK RANCH

Embodying every Western fantasy, this rustic **resort** (📞800-443-6139; www.spring creekranch.com; Spring Creek Rd; resort fee $20, r/ste incl breakfast $340/360; @🛜💺) gazes smack at the Tetons from the top of a butte ringed in sagebrush. The views are unreal and the vibe is oh-so-relaxed. Guests can rent sprawling mountain villas or little studios with fireplaces. Trails criss-cross the property, where you can also ride horses. Naturalist programs take visitors on dawn or dusk safaris to see bison, wolves and other wildlife. Then grab a juniper massage or mineral-rich seaweed wrap from the lauded Wilderness Adventure Spa.

If staying is out of your range, consider heading to its gourmet restaurant **Granary** for happy hour (**4–7pm**) or live jazz on Fridays. Lauded by *Wine Spectator* magazine, staff also mix tasty house cocktails at the copper bar with wild mountain panoramas. To get there, take Hwy 22 from Jackson; the Spring Creek Rd is on your right.

and 7 miles west of Hoback Junction off US 26/89 in Snake River Canyon at 5800ft.

Elbow Campground   CAMPGROUND $
(sites $15; ⊘late May-Sep) Three miles further along on the south side of US 26/89 from Cabin Creek Campground is the scenic, nine-site Elbow, 22 miles south of Jackson.

East Table Campground   CAMPGROUND $
(sites $15; ⊘late May-early Sep) Two windy miles further along toward Idaho on the southeast side of US 26/89 is the roadside, 18-site East Table, 24 miles south of Jackson at 5900ft.

Hoback Campground   CAMPGROUND $
(sites $15; ⊘late May–mid-Sep) Along the Hoback River, 8 miles east of Hoback Junction and 22 miles southeast of Jackson (6600ft), is the shady, 13-site Hoback.

Kozy Campground   CAMPGROUND $
(sites $12; ⊘late May-Sep 10) Five miles further along on the east side of US 189/191 is riverside, eight-site Kozy, 30 miles southeast of Jackson at 6500ft.

Granite Creek Campground   CAMPGROUND $
(sites $15; ⊘late May-Sep) The signed turnoff for 52-site Granite Creek is 1 mile north of Kozy Campground. The campground itself is 35 miles from Jackson, since it's 9 miles northwest of US 189/191 up (often washboard) gravel USFS Rd 30500, nestled deep in the Gros Ventre Mountains at 6900ft. With drinking water, flush toilets and shade.

Station Creek Campground   CAMPGROUND $
(sites $15; ⊘late May-Sep) One mile further west along the Snake River from Granite Creek Campground is 16-site Station Creek, 25 miles south of Jackson at 5900ft.

Snake River KOA   CAMPGROUND $
(📞307-733-7078, 800-562-1878; www.srpkoa.com; tent/RV site from $43/70; ⊘late May-Sep) Grassy Snake River is 12 miles south of town off US 26/89/191 near Hoback Junction. Cheaper, recommended public US Forest Service (USFS) campgrounds are outside town.

Lodging

🔝 **Alpine House**   B&B $$$
(📞307-739-1570, 800-753-1421; www.alpinehouse .com; 285 N Glenwood St; d incl breakfast $185-225; @🛜) Two former Olympic skiers infused this eco-certified downtown home with sunny Scandinavian style and personal touches like great service and a cozy mountaineering library. Amenities include brushed-cotton robes, down comforters, a shared Finnish sauna and an outdoor Jacuzzi. Save your appetite for the creative breakfast options like poached eggs over ricotta toast with asparagus or multigrain French toast. Newer cottages down the road are modern-adorable, with cast-iron woodstoves, fully decked kitchens and green lawns. The Little Spa offers massage and mud wraps.

Rusty Parrot Lodge and Spa   LODGE $$$
(📞888-739-1749; www.rustyparrot.com; 175 N Jackson St; r incl breakfast $360-595) With a collection of Remington sculptures and amazing Western art, this elegant lodge is excruciating in its luxury. Service is top-notch and rooms pamper with well-tended bedroom fireplaces and a plush teddy bear posed on the bed. The gourmet restaurant prepares innovative international cuisine. Those who don't ski will get distracted at the spa, where the arnica sports massages and rose and honey wraps are pure hedonism.

Inn on the Creek INN $$$

(☎307-739-1565, 800-669-9534; www.innonthe creek.com; 295 N Millward St; r incl breakfast $179-599; @) Elegant and intimate, this stone inn offers nine handsome rooms. Details include recessed fireplaces, top-quality linens on comfy beds and views of a gurgling creek out back. It's wedged into the edge of town, handy to restaurants and shopping.

Wort Hotel HOTEL $$$

(☎307-733-2190, 800-322-2727; www.worthotel .com; 50 N Glenwood St; r $349-389; ✸@🛜) Western themes run amok, but in a good way, at this historic 1940s English Tudor. It's gussied up with lodgepole pine beds and cowboy-motif sheets, with full-sized baths and Jacuzzis. It has, hands-down, the best concierge service in Jackson, with great outdoor tips. Attached is the popular Silver Dollar bar and restaurant, featuring an antique S bar encrusted with silver dollars and painted bordello scenes.

Buckrail Lodge MOTEL $$

(☎307-733-2079; www.buckraillodge.com; 110 E Karnes Ave; r $143; ✸@🛜) Spacious and charming log cabin–style rooms, this steal is centrally located, with hanging flower baskets and rockers outside each room and an outdoor Jacuzzi. With a sprawling lawn and wooden swing, it's a good bet for families.

Cowboy Village CABINS $$$

(☎307-733-3121, 800-962-4988; www.townsquare inns.com/cowboy-village; 120 S Flat Creek Dr; cabins $158-258; ✸🛜✹✸) Though they're in an urban lot, these cozy log cabins have a spark of yesteryear, snugly furnished with knotted pine, bark beds and animal carvings. It's family friendly, all rooms have kitchenettes and there's a fitness center, outdoor grills and an indoor pool. It's just off W Broadway.

Snow King Resort HOTEL, CONDOS $$

(☎307-733-5200, 800-522-5464; www.snowking .com; 400 E Snow King Ave; r from $140, condos from $195) This expanding resort offers a variety of options ranging from condominiums to luxury suites, with the advantage of being slopeside. Inquire about the attractive seasonal package deals.

Golden Eagle Motor Inn MOTEL $$

(☎307-733-2042; 325 E Broadway; r $148; ✸) Run by a friendly Jackson native and just far enough out of the fray, this refurbished motel is a reliable choice in the center.

Pony Express MOTEL $$

(☎307-733-3835, www.ponyexpresswest.com; 1075 W Broadway; r $149; ✸🛜✹✸) A proud little motel hidden behind the gas station. Fresh and spacious rooms have pine walls and tucked-away bunks. Outdoors there's a plush lawn with tables and a heated pool. Cyclists can make use of the cleaning buckets and rags.

Parkway Inn INN $$$

(☎307-733-3143, 800-247-8390; www.parkwayinn .com; 125 N Jackson St; r $219-389) You may feel like you're spending the weekend at grandma's (except the wolf remains in Yellowstone). This Victorian-themed lodging – really a glorified motor inn – offers ample suites decked in chintz with quilted brass beds. Perks include a well-stocked continental breakfast, indoor lap pool, hot tub and fitness facility.

Sundance Inn MOTEL $$

(☎307-733-3444, 888-478-6326; www.sundanceinn jackson.com; 135 W Broadway; d/ste $139/209; ✸) Simply a well-run motel from 1953, the Sundance distinguishes itself with good service and tidy rooms. Perks include an outdoor Jacuzzi and continental breakfast.

Anvil Motel MOTEL $$

(☎307-733-3368, 800-234-4507; www.anvilmotel .com; 215 N Cache Dr; r $128-192; ✸🛜) Friendly and well scrubbed, the barn-red Anvil offers good value, is centrally located and has one Jacuzzi suite. Passes are available to the local recreation center with pool, sauna and hot tub.

Rawhide Motel MOTEL $$

(☎307-733-1216, 800-835-2999; www.rawhide motel.com; 75 S Millward St; r $159; 🛜✸) New Berber carpets and pine furniture spruce up these typical motel rooms, which also have friendly staff, flatscreen TVs, hair dryers and coffee makers.

Eating

Jackson's fare boasts sophistication – even if that means garnishing your burger with a basil leaf. Those hungry for exotic options won't come away disappointed: all manner of game and international cuisine are present, particularly if you're willing to pony up. Pick up a free *Jackson Hole Dining Guide,* found in shops and hotel lobbies, for menus.

Travelers who plan to pack a cooler can shop at grocery stores **Jackson Whole**

(☎307-733-0450; 974 W Broadway), emphasizing local and organic food, or **Albertson's** (105 Buffalo Way; ◉). Both are at the west end of town off Broadway.

Snake

River Grill   CONTEMPORARY AMERICAN $$$
(☎307-733-0557; 84 E Broadway; mains $21-52; ⊙from 5:30pm) With a roaring stone fireplace, an extensive wine list and snappy white linens, this grill creates notable American haute cuisine (though fan and local Dick Cheney would have you believe it's a populist place). Start with tempura string beans with spicy sriracha dipping sauce. The crispy pork falls off the bone and grilled elk chops show earthy goodness. Splurge – desserts like crème brulee or homemade ice cream easily satisfy two.

Rendezvous Bistro   CONTEMPORARY AMERICAN $$$
(☎307-739-1100; www.rendezvousbistro.net; 380 S Broadway; mains $15-29; ⊙5:30-10pm) A sure bet for sophisticated bistro food. The happy-hour menu hits the mark with well-priced sophisticated small plates, like oyster shooters, foie gras with fig jam and a creamy chipotle corn dish that's out of this world. Mains also show a good variety, from comfort foods like a local steak frites to fish with spicy roasted grits.

Atelier Ortega   BAKERY $
(www.atelierortega.com; 150 Scott Lane; desserts $6; ⊙8am-7pm Mon-Sat, 9am-5pm Sun; ☎) A must, this funny strip mall transports you to Paris with its elaborate, authentic desserts, each well worth its weight in cellulite. There are also wonderful handmade chocolates by Oscar Ortega, crepes and French pastries. Scott Lane is just off W Broadway; the bakery is in a small shopping plaza on the left.

Pica's Mexican Taqueria   MEXICAN $$
(1160 Alpine Lane; mains $7-15; ⊙11:30am-9pm Mon-Fri, 11am-4pm Sat & Sun) Cheap and supremely satisfying, with Baja tacos wrapped in homemade corn tortillas or cochinita pibil (chile-marinated pork), served with Mexican sodas. Locals love this place; it's the best value around. It's just around the corner from Albertson's.

Café Boheme   CAFE $
(☎307-733-5282; www.cafebohemejh.com; 1110 Maple Way, suite B; mains $7-15; ⊙6:30am-4pm Mon-Thu, 6:30am-10:30pm Fri, 7am-3pm Sat & Sun) Locals endure bread lines for these bright breakfasts of crepes and fruit, baguette

sandwiches and hearty soups, often served by the owner herself. Well away from the tourist traps, Cathy's lively French cafe also has live music or salsa dancing on weekends. It's behind the new post office in an office building.

DoG   BREAKFAST $
(25 S Glenwood; burrito $6; ⊙7am-2pm) For bomber breakfast burritos, you would be hard-pressed to beat this tiny shack whose expert eggman serves them up fresh and wrapped in a grilled tortilla, surefire fuel for the slopes.

Blue Lion   CONTEMPORARY AMERICAN $$$
(☎307-733-3912; 160 N Millward St; mains $15-34; ⊙from 6pm) In a precious cornflower-blue house, the Blue Lion offers outdoor dining under grand old trees on the deck. Served in peppercorn-rosemary cream sauce, the renowned rack of lamb may take a while but wins rave reviews. There's also early-bird specials.

JH Roasters   COFFEE $
(145 E Broadway; ⊙6:30am-6pm Mon-Sat, 6:30am-5pm Sun; ☎) With fragrant and robust certified organic roasts, this coffeehouse is a godsend for rough mornings.

The Bunnery Bakery & Restaurant   CAFE $
(☎307-733-5474; 130 N Cache St; mains $10; ⊙7am-3pm & 5-9pm summer) Lunch and breakfast at this buzzing cafe offer an assortment of hearty fare, including all-day eggs and great vegetarian options. The dessert case tempts with mammoth slices of chocolate-cake, pecan pie and caramel cheesecake.

Pearl Street Meat Co   DELI $
(260 W Pearl Ave; www.pearlstreetmeatandfish.com; sandwiches $8; ⊙8am-7pm Mon-Sat, 11am-7pm Sun) Jackson's answer to Dean & Deluca is this busy deli stocked with artisan cheeses, gourmet products, natural local meats and takeout sandwiches.

Bubba's Bar-B-Que   BBQ $$
(☎307-733-2288; 100 Flat Creek Dr; mains $5-15; ⊙7am-10pm) With the biggest, fluffiest breakfast biscuits for miles. Later on, this energetic bring-your-own-bottle (BYOB) eatery serves up a ranch of ribs and racks alongside a decent salad bar.

Drinking
Jackson isn't exactly a wild-night-out kind of town; our guess is that most folks are tuckered from playing all day. But happy hours

FARMERS MARKETS

Get a massage, watch a chef demo and sample some gourmet grub while you're at it. These bustling markets run from late June/early July to mid-September.

People's Market (cnr Gill St & Willow St, Jackson; ☺4-7pm Wed)

Farmer's Market (Main St, Driggs, Idaho; ☺10am-2pm Fri)

Farmer's Market (Jackson Town Sq, Jackson; ☺8-11am Sat)

are exceptionally lively, and a good way to sample the finer restaurants with small plates and cheap prices.

Cadillac Grille BAR
(☎307-733-3279; 55 N Cache) Locals in fleece and Carhartts pile around the island bar for two-for-one happy hours from 5pm to 7pm, complemented by a Billy burger served from next door. Those feeling fancy will appreciate the tantalizing martini menu and calamari and oyster appetizers.

Snake River Brewing Co BREW PUB **$$**
(☎307-739-2337; 265 S Millward St; mains $6-15; ☺11:30am-midnight) With an arsenal of 22 microbrews made onsite, some award-winning, it is no wonder that this is a favorite rendezvous spot. Happy hour is from 4pm to 6pm.

Million Dollar Cowboy Bar BAR
(25 N Cache Dr; cover $5) Most can't wait to plunk their hind quarters on a saddle stool in this dark chop house, an obligatory stop on the Western tour. Weekends get lively when the dance floor sparks up and karaoke drones.

The Rancher BAR
(☎307-733-3886; 20 E Broadway) This pool hall is a local happy-hour favorite.

Entertainment

The free weekly *Jackson Hole Weekend Guide* appears Friday and reviews local entertainment options, as does the *Stepping Out* insert.

Center for the Arts ARTS CENTER
(☎307-734-8956; www.jhcenterforthearts.org; 240 S Glenwood S) One-stop shopping for culture, attracting big-name concert acts and featur-

ing theater performances, classes, art exhibits and events. Check the calendar of events online. Students get discounts on performances.

The Lounge LOUNGE
(☎307-733-5200) Popular nightspot at Snow King Resort that features live acid jazz on Saturday nights.

Jackson Hole Playhouse THEATER
(☎307-733-6994; www.jhplayhouse.com; 145 W Deloney Ave) Local theater troupes stage acclaimed Broadway-style musical comedies and provide dinner.

Teton Theatre CINEMA
(120 N Cache Dr) This 1941 sandstone theater is the best place to catch a flick; ring the Jackson Movieline (☎307-733-4939) for a rundown of current listings.

Shopping

Teton Mountaineering SPORTING GOODS
(☎307-733-3595; 170 N Cache St) Stocks a good range of books and outdoor gear. Singles seeking climbing partners can check the bulletin board.

Alaska Fur Gallery FUR
(☎307-733-4772; 135 N Cache Dr) Among a herd of kitsch and souvenir shops in downtown Jackson, but here you can pick up a toasty beaver-pelt jockstrap (a bestseller) or a fur bra for your sweetie.

Skinny Skis OUTDOOR GEAR
(☎307-733-6094; 65 W Deloney Ave) One of the best backcountry ski shops in the US, with Nordic ski rentals, quality hard goods and a huge selection of the best women's outdoor clothing. Also knowledgeable about trails.

**Boardroom of
Jackson Hole** SNOWBOARD RENTALS
(☎307-733-8327; www.boardroomjacksonhole.com; 225 W Broadway) A handy snowboarding shop.

Information

Tune to 90.3 FM (NPR), 93.3 (KJAX) or 96.9 (KMTN) for the local lowdown. Free newspapers include the *Jackson Hole Daily* (liberal) and the *Daily Guide* (conservative).

Bank of Jackson Hole ATMs (990 W Broadway, cnr E Broadway & S Cache)

Jackson Hole & Greater Yellowstone Visitor Center (☎307-733-3316; www.jacksonhole chamber.com; 532 N Cache St; ☺8am-7pm summer, 8am-5pm winter) Provides information, books, rest rooms, an ATM and a courtesy phone for free local calls.

Jackson Ranger District (☑307-739-5450; www.fs.fed.us/btnf; 25 Rosencranz Lane; ⏱8am-4:30pm Mon-Fri) Side-by-side with the USFS Bridger-Teton National Forest Headquarters.

St John's Medical Center (☑307-733-3636; 625 E Broadway)

Teton County Library (☑307-733-2164; www .tclib.org; 125 Virginian Lane; ⏱10am-9pm Mon-Thu, 10am-5pm Fri & Sat, 1-5pm Sun) Great resource for topo maps and local information, with free internet and wi-fi.

USFS Bridger-Teton National Forest Headquarters (☑307-739-5500; www.fs.fed.us/ btnf; 25 Rosencranz Lane) Office in the Jackson Ranger District; information available at the visitor center.

Wyoming Game & Fish Department (☑307-733-2321; 420 N Cache St; ⏱8am-5pm Mon-Fri) For fishing licenses and required decals on motorcraft.

Getting There & Away

Actually within Grand Teton National Park, **Jackson Hole Airport** (☑307-733-7682; www.jackson holeairport.com; @) is 7 miles north of Jackson off US 26/89/191. Always packed, the airport yearns to expand but is limited by a 50-year agreement with the National Park Service (NPS).

For shuttle service, **Alltrans' Jackson Hole Express** (☑307-733-1719, 800-443-6133; www .jacksonholebus.com) goes daily from Jackson to Salt Lake City (one way $70, 5½ hours) and points in between. Reservations are recommended. Jackson pickup is at Exxon service station, on the corner of Hwy 89 S and S Park Loop Rd. In winter it offers packages with lift tickets to Grand Targhee Ski Resort.

Getting Around

Major car rental agencies have outlets at the airport.

Alltrans (☑307-733-3135, 800-443-6133) Taxi service.

Hertz (☑307-733-2272, 800-654-3131; www .hertz.com) Counter at Jackson airport.

Southern Teton Area Rapid Transit (START; ☑307-733-4521; www.startbus.com) Around-town shuttle and two routes (Red Line and Workers' Special) between Jackson and Teton Village. One-way fares are free within town limits and $1 to $2 outside of town; exact change is required. Check maps and timetables posted at stops for current routes and schedules.

Taxi Tim (☑307-690-4141) For shuttle service to trails.

Thrifty (☑307-739-9300, 800-367-2277; www .jackson.thrifty.com; 1255 W Hwy 22) Car rentals in town.

Jackson Hole

Now that it's clad in faux fur, Stetsons and trophy homes, it's hard to remember that the first settlers to Jackson Hole wrangled with harsh winters and a short growing season, not to mention the horse thieves, poachers and elk tuskers that roamed the rural valley. Dubbed 'hole' by early European visitors, the broad valley is bounded by the Gros Ventre (*grow*-vant: 'big belly' in French) and Teton Ranges to the east and west, respectively, and the Yellowstone lava flows and Hoback and Wyoming Ranges to the north and south. The communities of Jackson, Teton Village, Kelly, Moose and Wilson, as well as much of south Grand Teton National Park, lie within the Hole. (Some of these are inside the Grand Teton National Park and are covered in that chapter.)

This is one of the most breathtaking destinations in the country. Moose, elk and bison roam the valley floor against the rugged backdrop of the Tetons. Eagles and osprey fish the cold, crystalline streams and lakes. Surrounding the valley, the mountainous 3.4-million-acre Bridger-Teton National Forest is the second-largest forest in the lower 48.

Downhill skiing rules winter, but summertime visitors find no shortage of things to do.

TETON VILLAGE & JACKSON HOLE MOUNTAIN RESORT

Long runs, deep powder and a screeching 4139ft vertical drop may have earned it infamy, but Jackson Hole has quickly become the pet resort of a tony, jet-setting crowd. There are real athletes here, though, and those with any interest in playing outdoors can revel in the fair-weather pursuits of hiking, cycling, white-water rafting, fly-fishing, mountain biking and faux cowboying. This modern year-round resort is at the foot of Rendezvous Mountain, 12 miles northwest of Jackson.

Sights

Jackson Hole's lifts provide a high-altitude piggyback to the high-country trails in Grand Teton National Park. Tickets can be purchased from guest services.

Aerial Tram   RESORT LIFT
(☑307-729-2654; adult/child $29/20; ⏱9am-5pm Jun-Sep) The 60-passenger tram travels 2.5 miles in 10 minutes to the top of Rendezvous Mountain (10,450ft), offering great views

of Jackson Hole. Paragliding is done from here too.

FREE **Bridger Gondola** RESORT LIFT
(☉Sun-Fri mid-Jun–Sep) Offers unlimited rides to the headwall (which is 1355ft lower than Rendezvous Mountain) and hiking trails. It's open in the evening to bring diners up to Couloir (p221).

Teewinot Quad RESORT LIFT
(ticket $25; ☉9am-5pm mid-Jun–Aug, Sat & Sun in Sep) This high-speed chairlift provides access to downhill mountain-bike trails. The resort distributes free bike trail guides.

Activities

Hiking and mountain biking are the big summer activities. Resort lifts give a head start into high country. From the Rendezvous summit, hikers can either descend Granite Canyon Trail or choose from a series of shorter trails: the 0.5-mile Summit Nature Loop, 3-mile Cody Bowl Trail or the 4.25-mile Rock Springs Bowl.

Pick up free bike trail guides at guest services and rental bikes at the ski shops. Downhill trails can be accessed via the Teewinot Quad.

Jackson Hole Mountain Resort SNOWSPORTS
(☎307-733-2292, 888-333-7766; www.jacksonhole.com; ☉Dec-Mar) 'The Hole' is all about vertical, boasting a continuous vertical rise of 4139ft – beaten only by Big Sky, by 41ft (we're sure that some front loader is poised to adjust this injustice). Among the world's top ski destinations, the resort has 2500 acres of ski terrain blessed by an average of 380in of snow annually.

The runs (10% beginner, 40% intermediate and 50% advanced) are served by six lifts, an aerial tram, two high-speed quads and the Bridger gondola. Depending on snowfall, the ski season may start early or end late.

**Jackson Hole Mountain
Sports School** COURSES
(☎800-450-0447, 307-733-4505). For downhill or snowboard lessons, check out this school; its top-dollar draw is skiing with Olympic gold medalist Tommy Moe.

Jackson Hole Paragliding PARAGLIDING
(☎307-739-2626, 307-690-7555; www.jhparagliding.com; tandem flight $245) Tandem rides take off from several local peaks (no experience necessary), meeting at the gondola.

**Bill & Scott's Jackson
Hole Trail Rides** HORSEBACK RIDING
(☎307-733-6992; 1/2hr rides $35/50; ☉late May-Sep) Takes would-be cowboys on the trails around the ski area. Early-morning rides offer cool temperatures while late-day rides tend to spot wildlife.

Teton Village AMUSEMENT PARK
(☎307-739-2654; www.jacksonhole.com; tickets $12; ☉10am-5pm late Jun-Labor Day) Kids can bounce on a bungee trampoline, scramble up a climbing wall or fish for free at Crystal Springs Pond (poles for rent at the pond building). Adults may want to join in for disc golf, free to all guests. Purchase tickets from guest services and discs at Jackson Hole Sports.

Jackson Hole Nordic Center NORDIC SKIING
(☎307-739-2629) Offers 20 miles of groomed track and wide skating lanes with rentals and instruction.

High Mountain Heli-Skiing HELI-SKIING
(☎307-733-3274; www.heliskijackson.com; per person $1050) Delivers advanced skiers and snowboarders to ungroomed backcountry powder. Rates are for one day and six heli-skiing runs – about 12,000 vertical feet.

Jackson Hole Sports RENTALS
(☎307-739-2687; Bridger Center; ☉8:30am-6pm) Rents and sells downhill gear. In the summer it tunes and rents mountain bikes and can offer the lowdown on area rides.

Wildernest Sports RENTALS
(☎307-733-4297; www.wildernestsports.com; Village Center) Rents skis and snowboards and mountain bikes in summer. Reservations available (with coupons) online.

Festivals & Events

The **Grand Teton Music Festival** (☎307-733-1128; www.gtmf.org; prices vary) in Teton Village offers nightly symphony concerts in summer, with free Tuesday concerts geared at families. In Teton Valley, a fabulous summer music festival series includes individual artists of renown, as well as the **Targhee Fest** (featuring a range from hip-hop and alt music to funk) in mid-July, and the **Grand Targhee Bluegrass Music Festival** in early August.

Sleeping

Rates vary widely and seasonally; some hotels also levy a resort fee. Rates drop up to 50% in the shoulder seasons (when it is

WILSON

Big barns and open range make this little outpost 13 miles from Jackson feel more like cowboy country, even though the median home price passes a cool million. It's a popular stop before that last push over the pass to Idaho, especially for cyclists and skiers going to Grand Targhee Ski Resort.

A popular mainstay of live music, mingling cowboys with rhinestone cowgirls, hippies and hikers, Wilson's **Stagecoach Bar** (☑307-733-4407; 5755 W Hwy 22) is worth the short drive. 'Mon-day' means reggae, Thursday is disco night and every Sunday the house band croons country and western until 10pm.

Local institution **Nora's Fish Creek Inn** (☑307-733-8288; 5600 W Hwy 22; dinner mains $15-35; ⊗6am-2pm & 5-9:30pm) reels 'em in with heaping country breakfasts. Lunch and dinner feature prime rib, fresh trout prepared five ways and homemade cobbler.

too warm to ski but too muddy to mountain bike). The village has extensive lodging options; see p222 for central reservations.

The Hostel HOSTEL $
(☑307-733-3415; www.thehostel.us; dm/q $32/89; ⊗closed shoulder seasons; @▣) A steal, this central old ski lodge offers narrow four-bunk rooms with newly remodeled bathrooms. The spacious lounge with fireplace is ideal for movies or Scrabble tournaments and there's a playroom for tots. Guests can use a microwave and outdoor grill, coin laundry and a ski-waxing area. Closure dates vary by year and according to snowfall.

Rock Spring Yurt YURT $$$
(☑307-739-2654; up to 8 people half-board $425) If you're craving a wilderness experience without the hassle, come here for a modified Central Asian–style tent equipped with a woodburning stove and gas lamps. An expert guide cooks your food and does the dishes (but you tell the bedtime stories yourself). The hut is reached via a 2.5-mile hike from Teton Village in summer.

Alpenhof Lodge HOTEL $$$
(☑307-733-3242; www.alpenhoflodge.com; r incl breakfast $175-300) The classic Tyrolean Alpenhof has snug gable rooms with thick duvets, hand-painted furniture and cozy wood paneling. The cozy bistro specializes in wild game and schnitzel. The après-ski scene is popular with the older 40s crowd.

Jackson Hole Campground CAMPGROUND $
(☑307-413-0495; www.jacksonholecampground .com; 2780 N Moose-Wilson Rd; tent/RV sites $49/64, cabins $329-429; ⊗May-Oct; ▣▣) Probably the highest-end campground you could find, 2 miles north of Hwy 22 on Hwy 390. Cabins are rustic chic, with luxury bedding,

flatscreen TVs, fireplaces and private outdoor fire pits.

Eating & Drinking

TOP CHOICE **Couloir** CONTEMPORARY AMERICAN $$$
(☑307-739-2675; www.couloirrestaurant.com; 4-course meal $89; ⊗from 5pm) 'Approach love and cooking with reckless abandon,' says the seasonal menu. Dashed with exotic influences and located in the grandest of settings, Couloir does innovative American food well worth the trek (or ride). Greens with sage-roasted cashews and fresh manchego cheese, Wagyu beef with red onion marmalade and truffle-crusted halibut are just some sublime options. In summer, local farms supply free-range meat and organic produce. A lucky few can reserve to dine in-kitchen with Chef Hamilton, a custom menu and wine pairings. It's perched at the summit of Bridger Gondola.

Teton Thai THAI $$
(☑307-733-0022; 7342 Granite Loop Rd; mains $10-18; ⊗noon-10pm) Long a local favorite for fragrant curries with a kick, there's also satisfying soups, Thai street ribs and Crying Tiger (wine-soaked beef in tamarind sauce). The best meal for your dollar in the village, with vegan and vegetarian options.

Calico Italian Restaurant & Bar ITALIAN $$
(☑307-733-2460; Hwy 390; mains $14-26; ⊗from 5pm) Serves original salads, earthy minimalist pizzas, roast chicken and hearty pastas in a renovated 1905 church. Greens come from the organic vegetable garden out back, and there's also lovely porch seating, a good wine list and a $3 kids meals.

Bar J Ranch   WESTERN $$

(☑307-733-3370; Hwy 390; adult/child $18/8; ⊙7pm Memorial Day weekend-Sep) We know it's corny, but all who visit rave about the sing-along chuck-wagon suppers, featuring BBQ beef, biscuits and beans. Dinner is followed by an hour of stories and songs from the wranglers. Lap-sized kids go free. Reservations are recommended.

Mangy Moose Saloon   PUB $$

(☑307-733-4913, music hotline 307-733-9779; www.mangymoose.net; lunch mains $8, dinner mains $14-29; ⊙7am-9pm; ☎) A cavernous pub serving baskets of nachos and buffalo burgers to hungry families. Après-ski gets busy and dinner features pizzas, steaks from local farms and a good salad bar. Check the website for big-name live music.

Cascade Grill House & Spirits   BAR $$

(☑307-732-6932; ⊙7am-10pm) A popular stop for après-ski cocktails in the Teton Mountain Lodge. The menu is upscale Western.

Information

Jackson Hole Central Reservations (☑888-838-6306; www.jacksonholewy.com) Lodging with off-season specials and package deals.
Jackson Hole Guest Services (☑307-739-2753, 888-333-7766; Clock Tower Bldg) Information on activities and tours, located near the tram ticket office in Teton Village. Pick up a free *Jackson Hole Mountain Map & Guide* here.
Jackson Hole Resort Lodging (☑307-733-3990, 800-443-8613; www.jhrl.com; 3200 W McCollister Dr) Property manager with listings ranging from studio condos ($245 per night) to two-bedroom town homes (from $420) as well as multiple-bedroom houses (from $530).

GROS VENTRE SLIDE AREA

On June 23, 1925, a vast slide of 50 million cubic yards of rock, one of the world's largest recent movements of earth, plummeted 2000ft down the side of the Gros Ventre Mountains to form a 225ft-high dam, creating a lake atop the Gros Ventre River. Two years later when the dam suddenly gave way, it created a monster wave that killed six and washed away the downstream town of Kelly.

Today the Gros Ventre Slide Geological Area offers a 0.5-mile interpretive trail with views over the slide. Amazingly, some trees survived the fall, 'surfing' the slide to reroot on the valley floor. The resulting Upper and Lower Slide Lakes attract anglers and boaters. The turnoff to the slide area is 1 mile north of Kelly. Not far from the junction is the Kelly Warm Spring, an undeveloped pool of warm (80°F) water.

The slide sits outside Grand Teton National Park, but is most easily accessed through it by taking Gros Ventre Rd east off Hwy 26/89/191. Three very attractive and economical USFS campgrounds (☑Jackson Ranger District 307-739-5400; sites $15; ⊙early Jun-Sep) are spread out along Gros Ventre Rd beyond the Gros Ventre Slide Geological Area (18 to 23 miles northeast of Jackson). Sites have pit toilets and water but no RV hookups. Twenty-site Atherton Creek campground, 5.5 miles along Gros Ventre Rd at Lower Slide Lake, at the end of the paved road, has a boat dock. If your car can take rough roads, check out the five-site Red Hills Campground, 4.5 miles further east, fronting the Gros Ventre River; the six-site Crystal Creek Campground is 0.5 miles further east. A 7-mile round-trip day hike heads up to Grizzly Lake from near Red Hills Campground.

GRANITE HOT SPRINGS

The signed turnoff for the developed Granite Hot Springs Swimming Pool (☑307-734-7400; www.granitehotsprings.mountainman country.com; adult/child $6/4; ⊙10am-8pm summer, 10am-5pm winter) and Granite Creek Campground (☑Jackson Ranger District 307-739-5400; sites $15; ⊙Jun-Sep) is 35 miles southeast of Jackson on Hwy 189/191. Free camping is allowed along the road to the hot springs, but not within 2 miles of the hot springs. In winter, the springs (a delicious 112°F) are accessible by snowmobile or skiing only. In summer the water temperature drops to 93°F. The route south through Hoback Canyon affords views of the stunning south face of the Gros Ventre Mountains.

The campground bumps up against the Gros Ventre Wilderness and offers good hiking up Granite Creek. Within walking distance of the campground is the undeveloped Granite Falls Hot Springs, accessed from the dirt parking area just below the falls. Reaching the hot springs (on the east bank of the creek) requires an often tricky and always chilly ford, and water levels only allow for soaking from around late May until spring snowmelt submerges the pool, with winter access by snowmobile or cross-country skis. Please respect the place and enjoy one of Wyoming's best natural soaks.

Upper Wind River Valley

Part of the Wyoming Centennial Scenic Byway, US 26/287 climbs east from Grand Teton National Park's Moran Junction up the slopes of Bridger-Teton National Forest to Togwotee Pass (*Toe*-ga-tee; 9658ft), before dropping into the upper Wind River valley. To the north is the 914-sq-mile Teton Wilderness; to the south is the more distant Gros Ventre Wilderness. Dubois is the only town in the upper valley, east of which the landscape yields to the semi-arid red sandstone Dubois badlands.

The Bridger-Teton National Forest **Buffalo Ranger District Blackrock Ranger Station** (☏307-543-2386, 307-739-5600), 8 miles east of Moran Junction, has general information and free maps of the region.

MORAN JUNCTION TO TOGWOTEE PASS

About 3 miles east of Moran Junction, the paved Buffalo Valley Rd forks off the main highway to offer a 4-mile detour northeast up the Buffalo Fork to the Turpin Meadow Recreation Area, a popular launching pad for local outfitters.

There's a USFS campground here and lots of dispersed camping. The road loops south as the unpaved USFS Rd 30050 to rejoin US 26/287.

Three miles from this junction, just past Togwotee Cowboy Village, a short detour to the left leads to a **scenic overlook** with fine views back to the Tetons. A second viewpoint, the **Togwotee Pass Vista View**, is 5 miles further along; the actual pass is another 12 miles from here. The pass, named for a Shoshone medicine man who led the US Army Corps of Engineers here in 1873, marks the Continental Divide. Just by the pass, the lovely **Wind River Lake** makes a perfect picnic spot.

Six miles downhill, the turnoff to Falls Campground offers access to pretty **Brooks Lake Creek Falls**, with fine views up to the breccia (lava and ash) cliffs of the Pinnacle Buttes.

Across from Falls Campground, unpaved Brooks Lake Rd (USFS Rd 515) winds uphill for 5 miles to gorgeous **Brooks Lake**, a popular base for camping, canoeing, fishing and hiking set at the base of dramatic Pinnacle Buttes. The road passes Pinnacle Campground before it descends to **Brooks Lake Campground** (tent/RV sites $10/15), a boat ramp and a trailhead. From the Brooks Lake turnoff it's 23 miles to Dubois, or 31 miles back to Grand Teton. For information about the **campground** (sites $10) call the **Wind River Ranger District** (☏307-455-2466)

Idaho's Teton Valley

The west face of the Teton Range soars above this broad valley, which is warmer, sunnier and more tranquil than its well-known Wyoming neighbor. Most of the valley lies in Teton County, Idaho, though a small portion (up to the Teton crest) is in Teton County, Wyoming. In Jackson it's dubbed the Tetons' backside, while in Idaho it's dubbed the 'sunny side.'

Teton Valley (6200ft) was first frequented by Blackfoot, Bannock, Shoshone, Nez Percé and Crow Indian tribes as a summer hunting ground. Lewis and Clark expedition member John Colter stumbled upon it in 1808 while hunting for beaver, finding them in abundance. The valley soon became known as Pierre's Hole, a favored mountain-man rendezvous, until a violent battle with a band of Blackfoot in 1832 caused the fur company's abandonment. Trade ended when beaver hats fell out of fashion (although some await their return with anticipation).

Mountains surround the valley: the Targhee National Forest and the Teton Range to the west, the Snake River Range to the south and the Big Hole Mountains to the southwest. Farming has been the valley's mainstay since Mormon families settled here in the late 19th century, but these once-sleepy ranching towns are now a year-round mecca for outdoor adventure and summer music festivals, with fabulous skiing, hiking, mountaineering and mountain-biking. North of Driggs, however, the classic Fords and antique grain silos hark back to days of yore.

VICTOR

A friendly feel, the great outdoors and a growing number of good eats make Victor, Idaho a growing draw, especially for those who work in Jackson and can't afford to live there.

Eating & Drinking

Sundogs CAFE $
(5 S Main St; mains $3-9; ☺7-11am Mon-Fri, 7am-noon Sat & Sun) Hit the patio for a relaxed cafe breakfast (think buckwheat cakes or green chile eggs) at a shady table.

Scratch MODERN AMERICAN $$
(☏208-787-5678; 185 W Center St; mains $8-22; ☺5-9pm Wed-Fri, 8am-9pm Sat & Sun) In a

ON THE FARM

It doesn't get more homegrown than the **farm dinners** (☎307-413-3203; onthefarmin idaho@gmail.com; Victor, ID; adult/child $75/35; 🐾) at the Blue Flax family farm in Idaho, where two long tables flank green fields. Preparation is on site (check out the old pickup bed recycled into a grill and the field kitchen erected from train depot walls). Every dinner showcases a different local farm but menus list only ingredients – deciphering each dish becomes part of the lively table conversation for the six-course meals. It's a great way to meet locals. Kids get to run around and are even called upon to pick herbs for the table. Beer from nearby Grand Teton Brewery and organic biodynamic wine from Cinder Vineyards are served. Latecomers can take advantage of spool seating at a discounted rate ($35).

rambling red house, this sustainable eatery serves up jalapeño cornbread, local elk burgers and sweet potato fries with a touch of cinnamon and chipotle spice.

Knotty Pine   LIVE MUSIC, PUB
(☎208-787-2866; 58 S Main St) Cranks out an eclectic summer music line-up that yanks crowds on their feet for frantic fun. It is known for its burgers, microbrews and relaxed local vibe.

Spud Drive-In Theater   DRIVE-IN
(☎208-354-2727; www.spuddrivein.com; 231 S Hwy 33; adult/child $7/3; �)Mon-Sat summer) A classic shot of Americana. Grab a malt and fries and get the kids in their jammies for the full experience. Look for the monstrous potato on the back of the vintage flatbed between Victor and Driggs.

Victor Outdoors Seconds   OUTDOOR GEAR
(☎208-787-2887; �) 10am-6pm Mon-Sat) Outdoor gear, quality used items and seconds.

DRIGGS
Rapidly growing Driggs (population 1439) is the valley's tourist nerve center.

Sights & Activities

TOP CHOICE Table Mountain   HIKING
This outstanding hike offers solitude, wildflowers galore and stunning high-alpine scenery without the crowds on the eastern side. While it is a long haul (12 miles roundtrip), it is straightforward for experienced hikers. If you are inexperienced, the stream crossings and steep sections make it advisable for you to go with someone experienced. The trail is optimal after snow pack has melted (early July through September). The final scramble onto Table Mountain can be slippery – tread carefully.

To get here, heading north through Driggs, take a right at the traffic light (toward Targhee Ski Resort). Take a right onto a gravel road (6.5 miles) when the road forks toward Teton Campground. Just past the campground there are two parking lots. Park in the first and follow the trail for Table Mountain. The Teton Campground next door provides a good base for day hikes.

The hike features significant elevation change and the first section is a thigh-burner. Ascend a steep forested trail to a lovely **wildflower meadow** dotted with aspens and frequented by moose. The next part of the hike is more mellow, with a slow ascent that requires crossing the north fork of **Teton Creek** several times (note: there are plans to reroute the trail by 2013 to avoid these crossings). Meanwhile, you may have to wade once or twice. Hiking poles and sandals are a great help here.

After the last stream crossing, the trail winds through a tall pine forest giving way to the open cirque below Table Mountain. Here you ascend steeply – the trail zigzags with breathtaking views of the valley below and the Jedediah Smith Wilderness. You may have to cross a few patches of snow, so step carefully.

Once you achieve the ridge, the rounded knob of Table Mountain appears so close! But it will take you about an hour and a half to reach its summit, sighting marmots along the way. Follow the trail as it bends left toward Table Mountain. Once there, ascend the steep, crumbly rock with care, using the least steep path.

The flat-top summit of **Table Mountain** (11,106ft) affords great gawping views of the Grand Teton, Alaska Basin and the western slope of the peaks. Make sure you save time to drink it all in. Photographer William H

Jackson took the first photos of the Grand Teton here, during the 1872 Hayden Survey. Head down at a reasonable hour since snowmelt will increase the runoff in the streams and make the crossing more challenging as the day goes on.

Moose and bear frequent this trail.

Devil's Staircase to Alaska Basin   HIKING

Get ready for an epic trek. This one, nine hours and 15.7 miles, is stunning – savor it best by overnighting in Alaska Basin. This moderate-to-difficult loop can be done in either direction, but by hitting it counterclockwise you will encounter fewer people in the early leg of the hike and quickly achieve stunning views after ascending the Devil's Staircase.

To get to the trailhead, follow the driving directions in the Table Mountain hike, but park instead in the second parking lot with pit toilets. Bring water tablets or a purifier, sandals for river crossings and ample sunscreen.

The first 2.7 miles follow an old jeep track at a mellow grade through fir and lodgepole pine. The south fork of Teton Creek parallels the trail. The trail forks for Alaska Basin and Devil's Staircase. Take the right-hand fork, which quickly gets steep. After a few switchbacks, you end up on a gently up-sloping high meadow with views. Heading toward Mt Meek Pass, look for Dall sheep on the cliffs that tower to the right. A gurgling brook parallels most of this section, steeped in wildflowers.

The trail splits, with the right fork heading toward Mt Meek Pass and the left dropping down the Sheep Steps into Alaska Basin. Savor the views of Mt Meek, Buck Mountain (11,938ft) and South Teton (12,514ft). Take the fork to Alaska Basin. This high-alpine area resembles the open tundra of Alaska. There are many good campsites and overnighters have extra time to explore the Basin Lakes.

The rest of the hike follows the valley downhill through switchbacks and stream crossings (either shallow or with stepping stones or a bridge). Polished rock outcrops show evidence of glacial movement. This rocky and sometimes steep forested section can be somewhat tough on the knees. From Alaska Basin to the signed junction with Devil's Staircase it is 5 miles. Continue toward the parking lot via the way you entered. If you're hot and sweaty, there are a couple of great swimming holes off short paths to the creek.

Habitat   BIKE SHOP

(208-787-7669; www.ridethetetons.com; 18 N Main St; bike rental $45; ⊙9am-6pm) A hip full-service bike shop that also rents kid carts. Check out its group rides on Tuesday and Thursday, and Saturday chaperoned rides. Features ski and snowboard gear too.

Sleeping & Eating

Alta Lodge B&B   B&B $$

(307-353-2582; 590 Targhee Towne Rd; d incl breakfast $85-150) Located just minutes from the ski slopes, Dee's friendly B&B offers outstanding views and a cozy atmosphere. Rooms have Berber carpets and quilted beds. To get there take Ski Hill Rd 5 miles east of the main road, then go north on State Line Rd for half a mile.

Forage Bistro   CAFE $$

(208-354-2858; www.forageandlounge.com; 285 Little Ave; mains $10-18; ⊙4pm-late Tue-Sun) A little cafe with a crisp and vibrant atmosphere serving cheese flights and locally farmed meat and vegetables. Dishes like dill trout or bacon and egg salad with fresh greens are simple but standup. There are vegan options too; happy hour is 4pm to 7pm.

Information

Targhee National Forest Teton Basin Ranger District (208-354-2312; 525 S Main St) Information on trails and campgrounds, and offers free travel-planner maps.

Teton Valley Chamber of Commerce (www.tetonvalleychamber.com) For online information.

GRAND TARGHEE SKI & SUMMER RESORT

On the west side of the Teton Range, Grand Targhee Ski & Summer Resort (307-353-2300, 800-827-4433; www.grandtarghee.com) is revered for its incredible powder stashes (more than 500in of snow falls each winter) and its easygoing vibe. Base elevation is 8100ft, and four high-speed lifts to the top of Fred's Mountain (10,200ft) access 1500 acres of runs, with a total vertical drop of 2200ft in 3.2 miles. The runs are suited for families and intermediate-level skiers.

The ski season runs from mid-November to mid-April. Targhee lift tickets (adult/child $69/29) are a bargain compared with the competition. The ski and snowboard schools offer private and group instruction, as well as telemark and skate clinics. Performance demos and rentals are available.

Wilderness snowcat powder skiing (half/full day $349/199) leads intermediate

AROUND GRAND TETON IDAHO'S TETON VALLEY

DON'T MISS

TETON ICE PARK

Ever wanted to climb Spiderman-style up frozen waterfalls? Here's your chance. With 40ft vertical cliffs, this fun new ice park (☎888-864-8029; www.tetonice.com; 3300 E Ski Hill Rd, Alta; half-day private lesson $225, day pass $20) is the ideal spot to learn the sport or hone existing skills with top AMGA-certified guides from Aerial Boundaries. More advanced instruction is available in the Tetons. It's at Grand Targhee Ski & Summer Resort.

and advanced skiers to Peaked Mountain (10,230ft) for breathless powder runs that average 2000 vertical feet. There are 10 miles of groomed Nordic trails (adult/child $15/10) and skating tracks. Other winter activities include snowshoeing, tubing, skating and dogsledding.

When the snow melts, and muddy trails then wildflower fields replace it, the valley becomes a haven for hiking, climbing and biking. The mountain offers scenic chair-lift rides (adult/child $10/6; ⊙late Jun–early Sep) to the summit of Fred's Mountain; horse-back riding (2hr $59) and lift-served mountain biking (day pass/bike rental $20/60). Horseback riding takes advantage of the stunning scenery at Grand Targhee. Riders amble the dusty trails rimmed by wildflowers in the shadow of the Tetons. Pack trips and lessons on Western and English riding are also available. A one-hour hike affords a spectacular vista of Grand Teton itself; ride the lift down for free.

Frisbee fans take note: there's also free disc golf, in addition to a climbing wall ($10). The staff naturalist provides excellent free naturalist outings (⊙10:30am & 1:30pm Thu-Sun) on topics ranging from wolves to botany and geology. Register via the resort activity center.

Amenities include a full spa, kids' programs and day care. A fabulous summer music festival series includes individual artists of renown, as well as the Targhee Fest (featuring a range from hip-hop and alt music to funk) in mid-July, and the Grand Targhee Bluegrass Music Festival in early August.

Sleeping & Eating

Rates vary seasonally; contact Targhee Resort (☎800-827-4433; www.grandtarghee.com) about off-season specials and package deals. Kids under 15 stay for free. All lodgings are ski-in, ski-out.

Teewinot Lodge   LODGE $$$
(d $199; @☎❄❄) Snug and luxurious, with deluxe doubles, flatscreen TV, phone, huge indoor Jacuzzi, outdoor heated pool and ski-in location.

The Tower   HOTEL $$$
(d $399; @☎❄) The newest lodgings at the resort, these spacious VIP residences are decked in hardwoods, with leather arm-chairs, a fireplace and full kitchen.

The Sioux Lodge   CONDOS $$$
(q $429; @❄) A steal in summer, these are recently remodeled, bright, four-person studios and eight-person two-bedroom units with flatscreen TV, microwave, mini-fridge and full bath. Ideal for families and groups.

Targhee Lodge   HOTEL $$
(d $139; @☎❄❄) Standard rooms slopeside with two queen-sized beds, full bath, TV and phone.

Getting There & Away

From Driggs head 4 miles east on USFS Rd 025 (toward Alta) to the Idaho-Wyoming state line and continue east 8 miles to Targhee. From the second switchback en route to the resort you get the first glimpse of Grand Teton and an overlook of the Teton Basin. Sunset colors are wonderful from here.

Resort **shuttles** (☎800-827-4433; 2 passengers $150) between Targhee and airports in Idaho Falls and Jackson, Wyoming, can be booked for two or more people. **Targhee Express** (☎800-443-6133; www.jacksonhole alltrans.com; combo shuttle & lift ticket $91) operates daily winter bus service between Jackson, Teton Village and Targhee. Reservations are required.

Understand Yellowstone & Grand Teton

population per sq mile

| Montana | Wyoming | USA |

≈ 1 person

The Parks Today

Created by the *Yellowstone National Park Act* (1872) as a 'public park or pleasuring-ground for the benefit and enjoyment of the people,' this mother of all national parks straddles a tense line between preservation and recreation, access and excess, encapsulating along the way the very best and worst of the national parks system.

Grand Teton is the only national park in the lower 48 that allows hunting and the only national park with its own commercial airport, receiving 60,000 flights a year.

HUNTING

Loved to Death

Yellowstone and Grand Teton are more popular than ever, each attracting up to 30,000 visitors daily and more than three million visitors annually – a volume that writer Edward Abbey termed 'industrial tourism.' When bison or elk graze by the Grand Loop Rd, the result is close to a mob scene, with traffic backing up for hundreds of yards. Debate rages over how best to manage this influx. While the democratic approach to public access remains the parks' greatest strength, their great appeal ironically threatens to destroy the very features that attract such numbers.

Managing Mother Nature (& Other Controversies)

If you want to start an argument in Yellowstone country, simply start a conversation on any of the following: wolf reintroduction, the park's fire policy, bison hazing, grazing rights, snowmobile access, oil drilling or the health advantages of tofu over Angus steak. Fractured regional politics means that a cloud of legal challenges descends over almost every major wildlife policy decision made in Yellowstone.

The successful reintroduction of the wolf to Yellowstone since 1996 has been wildly popular among park visitors, restoring an ecological balance and integrity to the park, yet opponents of the wolf remain among ranchers and hunters, who believe that wolves are decimating the local elk pop-

Top Books

» **Lost in My Own Backyard** (Tim Cahill) Engaging, funny and our personal favorite.

» **Travels in the Greater Yellowstone** (Jack Turner) Series of essays from fly-fishing to hiking the Beartooth Plateau. See also Turner's elegant *Teewinot*.

» **Walking Down the Wild** (Gary Ferguson) Account of a 500-mile walk through Greater Yellowstone from the Red Lodge resident.

» **Free Fire** (CJ Fox) Yellowstone thriller featuring Mammoth, Bechler, Grand Prismatic Spring and Old Faithful Inn.

Top Documentaries

» **Silence and Solitude** (2003) Follows photographer Tom Murphy into the Yellowstone backcountry in the depths of winter.

» **The National Parks: America's Best Idea** (2009) Ken Burn's engaging visual history of America's national parks.

Yellowstone
(% of landscape)

80 Forest

5 Water

15 Grassland

if 100 people visited Yellowstone, when would they come?

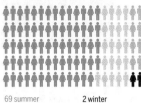

69 summer
21 fall

2 winter
8 spring

ulation. In 2011 the wolf finally lost its federally protected status, to howls and cheers from respective sides, just as park wolf numbers dropped to under 100 in the wake of parvovirus and distemper outbreaks.

The policy of hazing wandering bison back into the park each winter (irritating them with noises, helicopters etc) in an attempt to stop brucellosis entering the Montana cattle industry remains another dicey topic, especially since the bloody winter of 2007/8, when around one-third of Yellowstone's entire bison herd was slaughtered just outside the park boundary.

Nothing goes to the heart of the public access versus preservation debate like snowmobiling access, which the park restricted further in 2012 to limit its environmental impact, much to the anger of businesses in gateway towns like West Yellowstone.

> The number of elk in Yellowstone has dropped 70% since wolves were introduced in 1995

An American Icon

Maintaining good relations with its neighboring communities may ultimately turn out to be a simpler challenge than managing Mother Nature. The park planners' understanding of Yellowstone's complex web of ecological interconnections will be tested like never before over the coming decades, as climate change affects everything from grizzlies dependent on thinning white-bark pines to bison faced with ever-drying meadows. How the park service responds to these changes will define its second century.

Yellowstone is many things to many people: a natural Eden, a paradise lost, an outdoor extreme-sports playground or the world's biggest petting zoo. Despite all the controversies, the traffic jams and the crowds, Yellowstone and Grand Teton still deliver, big time. From Yogi Bear to the Teton skyline, the parks have gone beyond their physical landscapes to become an essential part of the American national consciousness, loved and treasured by millions. Long may they prosper.

Top Maps

» **Yellowstone** (1994) IMAX big-screen movie that shows daily at West Yellowstone.

» **Beartooth Publishing** (www.beartoothpublishing.com) Bozeman company produces a good 1:113,730 *Yellowstone National Park* map.

» **Trails Illustrated** 1:63,360 series of four maps covering *Mammoth Hot Springs, Tower/*

Canyon, Old Faithful and *Yellowstone Lake*, offering more detail to hikers.

» **Trail Illustrated** 1:78,000 *Grand Teton National Park* map is best, with a 1:24,000 inset of the Grand Teton climbing area.

History

As the world's oldest national park, Yellowstone holds a key place in both the historical development of the US National Park Service and the spread of protected wilderness areas across the globe. This is hallowed ground to both environmentalists and tourists, and the tensions between the two form the major theme of the past, present and doubtless the future of Yellowstone and Grand Teton.

First Peoples

To experience Native American culture in the Yellowstone region, attend the Crow Fair or the Plains Indians Powwow in Cody; visit Cody's Plains Indian Museum or Colter Bay Indian Arts Museum; or join a Crow interpreter tour of the Battle of Little Bighorn outside Billings.

Recent archaeological evidence unearthed near Pinedale, Wyoming, and excavations from Osprey Beach on Yellowstone Lake suggest that human inhabitation of the Greater Yellowstone region began soon after the Pinedale Glaciation period ended, between 12,000 and 14,000 years ago. Only a few thousand years before that, the Yellowstone region was almost completely covered in glaciers.

Archaeologists divide Greater Yellowstone's first inhabitants – ice-age hunter-gatherers who chased spectacular megafauna such as bear-sized beavers, enormous camels, gigantic moose, massive mastodons and 20ft-tall bison – into two distinct cultures, Clovis and Folsom, based on the uniquely shaped stone spearheads they fashioned.

The human presence in Greater Yellowstone increased dramatically 1500 to 2000 years ago, coinciding with a more favorable climate, resurgent large mammal populations and development of the bow and arrow, which replaced the *atlatl* (spear-thrower). Sheep traps and *pishkum* (buffalo jumps) were the weapons of choice in the Rockies and Great Plains, respectively. Obsidian from Yellowstone (still visible at Obsidian Mountain on the Mammoth–Norris road) made such durable spear and arrow tips that they were traded for hundreds of miles.

The Tukudika (or Sheepeaters) – a Shoshone-Bannock people who hunted bighorn sheep in the mountains of Yellowstone – were the region's only permanent inhabitants before white settlement, though

TIMELINE	9000 BC–AD 1870	1797	1805–06
	Native American inhabitation of area now known as Greater Yellowstone. Most tribes only entered the high mountains on summer hunting trips to collect food and medicinal plants.	French map makes first reference to the 'R. des Roches Jaunes,' or Yellow Stone River, itself a translation of the Minnetaree word *Mi tsi a-da-zi* that described the yellow bluffs around Billings, Montana.	Lewis and Clark expedition passes north of Yellowstone; Clark carves his name on Pompey's Pillar near Billings – today it is the only surviving physical evidence of the expedition

surrounding tribes such as the Crow/Absaroka (to the northeast), Shoshone (east), Bannock (south and west), Blackfeet/Siksikau (north) and Gros Ventre (south) hunted, traded and traveled seasonally through the region.

The Tukudika never acquired horses or iron tools and are often portrayed as a simple and undeveloped people, but they were proficient tanners whose composite sheep-horn bows were powerful enough to send an arrow straight through a bison (it's thought the Tukudika made the horns more pliable by soaking them in Yellowstone's boiling hot springs). The Tukudika, who never numbered more than about 400, spent the summers in camps of *wikiups* (tepee-like frames of leaning lodgepole branches), using dogs to transport their gear. The last of the Tukudika were hustled off the new park territory into the Wind River Reservation in the early 1870s to come under the control of the Shoshone chief Washakie.

One of the region's most extraordinary modern episodes involving Native Americans was the 1877 flight of the Nez Percé, led by Chief Joseph. The Nez Percé fled their ancestral lands in Oregon to escape persecution by the US Army. Today, the National Park Service recognizes formal affiliations with 25 modern tribes.

For a historical chronicle of the park's original inhabitants, try *Indians in Yellowstone National Park*, a slim volume by Joel C Janetski.

Trappers, Traders & Tourists

The first Europeans to come in contact with Native Americans in Greater Yellowstone were French fur trappers from eastern Canada. They encountered the Crow and Sioux in the late 1700s while exploring the upper Missouri River tributaries in search of beaver. It was these lonesome French-speaking trappers who gave the Tetons their name for their highly tenuous resemblance to female breasts. (As one writer wryly noted, that's what happens when you let French fur trappers name mountains!)

The USA's Louisiana Purchase of present-day Montana, most of Wyoming, and eastern Colorado from the French in 1803 led President Thomas Jefferson to commission the famous Lewis and Clark Corps of Discovery in 1804–06. The Shoshone and Nez Percé told the expedition's leaders about a 'thundering volcano to the south' that made the earth tremble, though the expedition only made it as far south as the lower Gallatin Valley (which they named) and the area along the Yellowstone River, east of Livingston, Montana.

As knowledge of the American West grew, so did interest in its exploitable resources. Most sought after was the beaver, whose 'plews' (pelts) became known among the trappers as 'hairy dollars.' John Colter, a member of the Lewis and Clark expedition, returned to explore the Yellowstone area during the winter of 1807–08 to try his luck as a trapper.

Colter's most famous exploit was when he was captured by Blackfoot, stripped naked and forced to run for his life. He managed to elude the Blackfoot by hiding in a valley and he walked 300 miles back to civilization, living off berries and roots.

HISTORY TRAPPERS, TRADERS & TOURISTS

1807–08	1829	1834	1835-39
John Colter's winter journey into Greater Yellowstone makes him the first 'white man' to travel through the area. Colter's Hell, a series of thermal features along the Shoshone River, are named after him.	Bill Sublette names Jackson Hole ('hole' means valley) after fellow trapper David Jackson; trapper Joe Meek stumbles upon Norris Geyser Basin.	Warren Ferris is the first 'tourist' to Yellowstone and the first person to use the word 'geyser' to describe Yellowstone's thermal features.	Trapper Osborne Russell travels through Yellowstone three times, eventually penning his story in the classic autobiography *Journal of a Trapper*.

Colter headed south from the Bighorn River into the Absaroka Mountains, into Jackson Hole, over the Tetons (in winter!) and then north past Yellowstone Lake. His epic 500-mile loop hike made him the first white man to visit the Yellowstone region, though it's not thought he saw any of the region's geysers.

After the War of 1812, renewed demand for furs propelled another generation of trappers westward. Legendary 'mountain men' like Jedediah Smith, Jim Bridger, David Jackson (after whom Jackson Hole is named), William Sublette, Kit Carson, Jim Beckwourth (a free African American)

THE FLIGHT OF THE NEZ PERCÉ

The discovery of gold in 1877 spurred the United States government (under army General Oliver Howard) to forcibly relocate the Nez Percé (Nimi'ipuu in their language) from Oregon's Wallowa Valley. After an initial skirmish, the Nez Percé (pronounced 'Nez Purse') set off on what would become an epic 1100-mile flight from the US Army. The route of their journey is now a national historic trail. For more information about this, see www.fs.fed.us/npnht.

By August 23, 1877, 700 of the Nez Percé (of whom only 250 were braves), led by Chief Joseph, crossed the Targhee Pass and entered Yellowstone Park along the Madison River, crossing the Firehole River at modern-day Nez Percé Creek. At that time only 25 tourists were visiting the park, and the Nez Percé somehow managed to bump into all of them, taking six hostage, killing one, and releasing the others near Mud Volcano. Just before reaching Pelican Creek, a band of braves diverted General Howard's men up into the Hayden and Lamar Valleys (at one point camping at Indian Pond) while the bulk of the tribe hurried up Pelican Creek and out of the park's northeast corner. You can visit the spot of two of the group's river crossings at Nez Percé Creek (p88) and the Nez Percé Ford (p71).

In September they progressed through Crandall Creek into the Clarks Fork of the Yellowstone, with US forces pressing hard on their heels, and troops led by General Sturgis blocking routes ahead. Sturgis' son had been killed by Native Americans the year before at the Battle of Little Bighorn, and one can only imagine that he was itching for revenge. The Percé once again pulled off a brilliant escape. A group of braves diverted Sturgis' troops while the Nez Percé slipped through the net, passing out of the valley through a gorge thought impassable by the US Army.

Believing they were in Canada, the Nez Percé slowed down just 30 tragic miles before the border, where US troops under General Nelson Miles finally caught up with them at the Battle of Bear Paw. After a 1500-mile, 3½-month chase that included four battles, 87 men, 184 women and 47 children surrendered on October 5, 1877, with Chief Joseph's words: 'From where the sun now stands, I will fight no more forever.' It was the end of a fight they had not sought. Joseph was never allowed to return to his homeland and died in 1904, allegedly of a broken heart.

1869	1870	1871	1872
Folsom, Cook and Peterson's month-long expedition into what would later become Yellowstone National Park takes them as far south as Shoshone and Yellowstone Lakes.	Washburn-Langford-Doane expedition names Old Faithful, Tower Fall and Mt Washburn, and starts the legend of the founding of Yellowstone National Park.	Hayden expedition to Yellowstone, with photographer William Henry Jackson and artist Thomas Moran, whose images are instrumental in the creation of the park the following year.	President Ulysses S Grant signs the *Yellowstone National Park Act* on March 1; Nathaniel Langford claims to have climbed Grand Teton.

and Thomas Fitzpatrick came to know the rugged Rockies' backcountry better than anyone except the Native Americans, with whom many of the men formed beneficial relationships, often learning the languages and taking Native American wives. Annual summer rendezvous – huge trading fairs attended by suppliers, Natives Americans and even tourists – began in 1825 at the headwaters of Wyoming's Green River, only to peter out in 1840, as the fur trade hit the skids.

The romantic image of the mountain man is an exaggeration. Rather than rugged individualists selling their catch to the highest bidder, most of the trappers were salaried company men who were often advanced a year's supplies and ended the year in debt (many a mountain main blew his entire year's income on women and liquor during a two-week-long rendezvous binge). The lasting contribution of the mountain men was their local knowledge of the terrain and the opening up of the routes across the mountains, which paved the way for later immigrants and explorers. After the decline in the beaver trade, many mountain men became army scouts or tourist guides.

Official Explorations

The US defeat of Mexico in the 1846–48 Mexican War yielded a bounty of new Western territory to explore. The US Corps of Topographical Engineers, guided by ex-trapper Jim Bridger, attempted to explore the Yellowstone Plateau from the south in 1860, but snow-covered mountain passes put the kibosh on their journey.

In the fall of 1869, the private three-member Folsom-Cook-Peterson expedition headed south from Bozeman, Montana, for a month to explore the divide between the Gallatin and Yellowstone Rivers. They made it past the Grand Canyon and Yellowstone Lake as far south as Shoshone Lake and returned in fine fettle to write a popular magazine article that refueled interest in exploration among the Eastern establishment. Upon witnessing a 150ft eruption of Great Fountain Geyser in the Firehole Lake region, the team wrote: 'We could not contain our enthusiasm; with one accord we all took off our hats and yelled with all our might!'

With considerable foresight, Cook wrote 'We knew that as soon as the wonderful character of the country was generally known outside there would be plenty of people hurrying in to get possession, unless something was done.'

Folsom, Cook and Peterson gained enough notoriety to be invited along for the landmark 1870 Washburn-Langford-Doane expedition, bankrolled primarily by the Northern Pacific Railroad, which was seeking a route across the Montana Territory and publicity to attract investors and tourists. The 19-man party, led by former Montana tax collector Nathaniel Langford and Montana Surveyor-General Henry Washburn,

HISTORY OFFICIAL EXPLORATIONS

For an overview of the mountain men, try *The Mountain Men* by George Laycock, which provides individual portraits of John Colter, Jim Bridger, Jedediah Smith and others, and gives an insight into the craft of trapping.

MOUNTAIN MEN

1877	1883	1890
Philetus W Norris becomes park superintendent and builds the first roads; the Nez Percé, led by Chief Joseph, flee the US Army through Yellowstone National Park.	Railroad spur line finished to Cinnabar, near north entrance of Yellowstone National Park; Great Plains bison pronounced extinct east of Continental Divide; first bicycle tour of the park.	First tourist guidebook to Yellowstone published; Wyoming becomes the 44th state of the USA, one week after Idaho becomes the 43rd state.

DAVID TOMLINSON / LONELY PLANET IMAGES ©

» Grazing bison (p247)

was given a military escort by Lt Gustavus Doane from Fort Ellis (near present-day Bozeman). They successfully traced the route of the 1869 expedition, named many thermal features (including Old Faithful) and returned to the East Coast 40 days later. They received a hero's welcome from the national media, which finally began to take seriously their reports of a landscape 'so grand as to strain conception and stagger belief.' One of Langford's lectures about Yellowstone caught the attention of Dr Ferdinand Hayden, director of the newly formed US Geological Survey (USGS). Hayden soon persuaded Congress, with substantial lobbying muscle from Northern Pacific supporters, to appropriate $40,000 for the first federally funded scientific expedition to the Greater Yellowstone region.

In 1871 the 34-man Hayden expedition set out from Fort Ellis with a full cavalry escort. Hayden's scientific work was fairly pedestrian, but two members of his party, landscape painter Thomas Moran and photographer William Henry Jackson, produced works of art that offered proof of the region's amazing sights and ultimately led to the designation of Yellowstone as a national park in 1872.

The National Park Idea

Portrait artist George Catlin is credited with originally suggesting the idea of a 'national park' during an 1832 trip through the wild Dakota Territory. The US' first nationally protected area was created a few months later at Hot Springs, Arkansas. For decades the park service promoted the romanticized notion that the idea of a Yellowstone national park was born at Madison junction by the members of the Hayden expedition, though the reality was more complex.

In 1872 President Ulysses S Grant signed the landmark *Yellowstone National Park Act,* setting aside 'the tract of land in the Territories of Montana and Wyoming, lying near the headwaters of the Yellowstone River,' and 'all timber, mineral deposits, natural curiosities, or wonders... in their natural condition.' The proclamation put a box on the map around what was thought to be the extent of the region's thermal areas but neglected to appropriate any management funds. The park's first superintendent, one Nathaniel Langford (he of the 1870 expedition), was unpaid and only visited the park twice in his five-year tenure. This lack of funding led the park to seek private business partners, such as the railroads, to develop infrastructure and promote tourism; a problem that today's park administrators would recognize well.

The most important legacy of the National Park Service (NPS) is much greater than simply preserving a unique ecosystem. That the national park and preservation idea has spread worldwide is a testament to the pioneering thinking of early US conservationists.

Historic Hotels

» Old Faithful Inn, Yellowstone National Park

» Lake Hotel, Yellowstone National Park

» Gallatin Gateway Inn, Gallatin Valley

» The Irma, Cody

» Murray Hotel, Livingston

» Pollard Hotel, Red Lodge

You can see examples of Jackson and Moran's iconic artwork at Mammoth's Albright Visitor Center, alongside a copy of the 1872 act of Congress that created Yellowstone National Park.

1902	1903	1908	1915
Only 25 bison remain in Yellowstone National Park, despite the passing of the *Lacey Act* eight years earlier, which prohibited hunting in the park.	President Theodore Roosevelt dedicates Yellowstone National Park North Entrance Arch; Northern Pacific Railroad line reaches Gardiner; construction starts on Old Faithful Inn and Fort Yellowstone.	Union Pacific Railroad spur line arrives in West Yellowstone; first dude ranch opens in Jackson Hole; Teton National Forest established by Teddy Roosevelt.	The first car (a Model T Ford) is allowed into Yellowstone National Park; car entry fees cost the modern equivalent of $93 per vehicle.

The US Army & Early Stewardship

A decade of rampant squatting, wildlife poaching, wanton vandalism of thermal features and general lawlessness in Yellowstone National Park preceded an 1882 visit by Civil War hero General Philip Sheridan. Sheridan persuaded Congress to appropriate $9000 to hire 10 protective assistants to aid the park's staff-less superintendent. But park regulations still didn't allow for any substantial punishments beyond expelling trespassers. The jurisdiction of Wyoming territorial law was extended into the park in 1884, but poaching remained rampant.

After a series of political scandals in the early 1880s involving land-grab attempts by a string of shady park superintendents (widely perceived to be in the pocket of railroad interests, who wanted a monopoly on lodging and transportation in the park), Congress flatly refused to fund the park's civilian administration in 1886. With no budget forthcoming, the secretary of the interior had little choice but to call in the US cavalry from nearby Fort Custer to provide protection.

In the absence of park rangers, the army patrolled the park from 1886 until the hand over to the newly created National Park Service and first park superintendent Horace Albright in 1918. At first, troops were stationed in a makeshift fort at Mammoth Hot Springs called Camp Sheridan. Construction of nearby Fort Yellowstone (present-day park

Learn more about early park history by taking one of the five daily historic tours of the Old Faithful Inn or a ranger-led historical walk around Fort Yellowstone at Mammoth.

HISTORY THE US ARMY & EARLY STEWARDSHIP

ROCKEFELLER, ROOSEVELT & THE TETONS

Despite the precedent set by Yellowstone, transformation of the Tetons into a national park was no easy matter, as commercial ranching and hunting interests resisted attempts to transfer private and forestry service lands to the National Park Service (NPS). At its creation in 1929, Grand Teton National Park included only the main part of the Teton Range and the lakes immediately below. Distressed at Jackson Hole's commercial development, John D Rockefeller Jr surreptitiously purchased more than 55 sq miles of land to donate to the park (but retained rights to all park concessions), but political bickering prevented the philanthropist's tax write-off until President Franklin D Roosevelt interceded.

Rockefeller's 32,000-acre bequest finally came under NPS jurisdiction when Roosevelt declared Jackson Hole a national monument in 1943. With post-WWII tourism booming in 1950, legislation conferred national park status and expanded the boundaries to include most of Jackson Hole. A final piece of the puzzle slipped into place in 2008 when the Rockefellers' private retreat, the former JY Ranch, was handed over to the park service to become the Laurance S. Rockefeller Preserve.

Today, the Rockefeller-founded Grand Teton Lodge Company remains the park's major concessionaire.

1916–18

In 1916 the National Park Service (NPS) is created under President Wilson. In 1918 the NPS assumes management of Yellowstone from US Army, which had governed the park since 1886.

1923

Meeting at cabin of Maude Noble to try to establish Grand Teton National Park; the last gray wolf den in Yellowstone National Park is destroyed by park rangers.

RICHARD CUMMINS / LONELY PLANET IMAGES ©

» The Museum of the Rockies (p158), Bozeman

headquarters) began in 1891. By the early 1900s, mounted troops were stationed year-round throughout the backcountry. Fighting fires, building roads, protecting desirable wildlife (bison and elk) from poaching and predators, entertaining visitors and preserving the park's natural features were the soldiers' primary duties. Predator control, such as poisoning coyotes, was common, but under the army's rule Yellowstone's environmental status quo was largely maintained. Of the 16 original soldier stations, three remain – at Norris (now a park ranger museum), Tower and Bechler.

Railroads, Automobiles & Mass Tourism

The Northern Pacific Railroad arrived in Livingston, Montana, in 1883, the same year Congress allocated funds to begin construction of the Grand Loop Rd in Yellowstone National Park. Park tourism and the railways were intimate bedfellows and it was the railways that ushered in the era of modern mass tourism in Greater Yellowstone.

MILLION-DOLLAR MICROBES

In 1966 microbiologist Dr Thomas Brock isolated a unique enzyme in a thermophilic micro-organism called *Thermus aquaticus*, or 'Taq,' which he extracted from the 158°F+ Mushroom Pool in Yellowstone's Lower Geyser Basin. Brock's discovery ultimately facilitated the replication of DNA for fingerprinting and genetic engineering, sparking an ongoing debate about 'bioprospecting' and the commercialization of public domain resources.

The National Park Service (NPS) continues to issue around 50 free research permits per year to scientists studying microbes. 'Extremeophiles' harvested for free have generated hundreds of millions of dollars of revenue for patent holders, including over $100 million a year for the Taq enzyme alone. Only recently has the NPS begun to benefit financially from benefit-sharing agreements.

Not all research efforts are strictly commercial. NASA has studied the biogeochemical signature of cyanobacteria found around hot springs in an attempt to match this signature with a similar one on Mars, which would help to decide where to land on the red planet when attempting to confirm the existence of ancient volcanoes and hot springs.

Other startling discoveries include the DNA sequencing analysis of an organism found in a hot spring in the Hayden Valley. This revealed what is considered to be the living entity most closely related to the primordial origin of life.

Researchers estimate there are at least 18,000 active thermal features in Yellowstone National Park, and that as many as 99% of species present in Yellowstone's extreme environments have yet to be identified. And with more thermophiles estimated to live in one square inch of a hot spring than the number of people living on earth, there's plenty of room for research.

1926	1929	1943	1948
Rockefeller travels through the Yellowstone and Teton region, encouraged by the park superintendent, leading to the purchase of millions of acres of land later donated to the nation.	Congress creates Grand Teton National Park; President Hoover extends the east and northwest extents of Yellowstone National Park, adding a further northern chunk three years later.	President Franklin Roosevelt creates the Jackson Hole National Monument, with Forest Service and Rockefeller's land.	Yellowstone National Park receives one million visitors in a single year for the first time, in a post WWII tourist boom.

Early park visitors rode the rails to West Yellowstone (via the Union Pacific Railroad), Livingston and later Cinnabar (Northern Pacific), Cody (Burlington) or Gallatin Gateway (Chicago, Milwaukee, St Paul & Pacific) and then transferred to stagecoaches for a six-day park tour that still mirrors today's overnight stops. The 'dudes' (tourists) would brave dust clouds and holdups to stay in classy hotels attended by 'savages' (concession employees) and beanery girls, entertained at night by string quartets, while generally behaving badly during the day – throwing handkerchiefs into geysers, bathing in hot springs and (later) feeding the bears.

The railroad's grand plans to monopolize public access to the park even went as far as a plan to extend rail tracks through the park itself, though Congress put its foot down at this. Ultimately, it was the arrival of the automobile that would scuttle the railroad's bid for domination of concession and transportation interests. Whereas over 80% of Yellowstone's 52,000 visitors in 1915 arrived via railroad, by 1940 nearly all of Yellowstone's half million visitors entered the park in private automobiles.

In 1905 completion of the skeleton of what is known today as the Grand Loop Rd by the US Army Corps of Engineers established the blueprint of the standardized Yellowstone tourist experience. Lobbying by motoring clubs persuaded the NPS to admit automobiles in 1915. Constant clashes between cars and stagecoaches over right-of-way on the narrow one-way roads led to the banishment of horse-drawn wagons in 1916.

Establishment of the nation's first forestry reserve, the Yellowstone Timber Reserve (part of today's Shoshone and Bridger-Teton National Forest) in 1891, Jackson's National Elk Refuge in 1912 and Grand Teton National Park in 1929 opened up Greater Yellowstone's south flank to public visitation. East Coast philanthropist John D Rockefeller's 200,000-acre land grant in 1949 added the final pieces of Grand Teton National Park and marked the tipping point in Greater Yellowstone's transition from a resource-based region to a tourist-driven economy.

Modern intensive development of a small area (about 1%) of Yellowstone National Park for tourism, however, has not been without controversy. The park is now home to more than 2000 buildings, thousands of employees and tens of thousands of nightly tourists. Historian Richard White has argued that rather than being a vestige of wild America, Yellowstone is 'a petting zoo with a highway running through it.'

Herein lies possibly the biggest challenge facing Greater Yellowstone today – is it possible for swarms of wilderness- and wildlife-seekers to enjoy solitude and appreciate nature en masse?

To get a sense of how important the railways were to the development of the park, visit West Yellowstone's Yellowstone Historic Center, the Depot Center in Livingston or Gallatin Gateway Inn – all three are former railway depots.

Yellowstone Park's Heritage & Research Center in Gardiner is home to the park's archives and boasts 90,000 photographic prints and negatives, 20,000 books and 35,000 archeological artifacts. Behind-the-scenes tours of the archives take place every Tuesday morning.

HISTORY RAILROADS, AUTOMOBILES & MASS TOURISM

1950	1959	1968–77	1970
Jackson Hole National Monument becomes part of Grand Teton National Park; Mission 66 is launched to radically boost the park's tourist infrastructure.	A huge 7.5-scale earthquake hits the Hebgen region, creating Earthquake Lake and causing the eruptions of several Yellowstone geysers.	Signing into law of the *Wild & Scenic Rivers Act* (1968), *National Trails System Act* (1968), *National Environmental Policy Act* (1969), *Endangered Species Act* (1973), *Clean Water Act* (1977) and *Clean Air Act* (1977).	New bear management plan; last of the bear-feeding garbage dumps closed, emphasizing the shift from recreational use to environmental protection.

Managing Natural Resources

During its formative years, the National Park Service in Yellowstone racked up a – shall we say – checkered history. It poisoned predators, shot wolves, stocked fisheries with nonendemic species, destroyed habitat in the name of development and arranged bear-feeding displays, all of which contributed to the development of an artificial and ultimately unsustainable ecology. Modern managers now openly admit that many early park policies were misguided.

Beginning in 1959 with John and Frank Craighead's pioneering studies of Yellowstone's grizzly population, the NPS emphasized scientific study of its natural resources. The landmark *Leopold Report*, published in 1963, suggested that 'a national park should represent a vignette of primitive America.' The report concluded that a more passive 'natural regulation' regime should replace past policies biased toward hands-on resource manipulation.

A major test of that policy, and Yellowstone's most famous recent event, was the summer fire season of 1988, when one-third of the park went up in smoke as 25 fires raged through the park for 3½ months. Over 25,000 firefighters were drafted in to battle the flames at a cost of $120 million and TV anchors proclaimed 'the death of Yellowstone National Park.' The event cast a critical spotlight on the park service's policy of letting natural fires burn. Twenty-five years on, a mosaic of meadows and new-growth forest has rejuvenated the park. Regardless of our instinctive desire to protect the park, fire is in fact essential to replenish the poor soils of the Yellowstone plateau, and Yellowstone is a healthier place for it.

Controversy continues to reign over Yellowstone. Battles over the ever-decreasing numbers of snowmobiles allowed to enter the park and delisting of the grizzly bear's endangered status in 2007 ricocheted through the courts in the first decade of the millennium. Born out of the contradictions inherent in its mandate of both preservation and utilization, Yellowstone's controversies are likely to twist and turn for some time to come.

Jellystone's Yogi Bear, Ranger Smith and Boo-Boo were all inspired by Yellowstone National Park, with a little help from baseball star Yogi Berra.

YOGI
BEAR

1972	1988	1995	2011
50-millionth visitor to Yellowstone National Park in first century of the park – the next 50 million arrive by 1992; John D Rockefeller Jr Memorial Parkway is established, linking the two parks.	Much-publicized wildfires sweep through the Greater Yellowstone region, burning one-third of the park; the entire park closed on August 20 for first time in history.	14 Canadian gray wolves are reintroduced to Yellowstone National Park; Yellowstone joins the list of World Heritage Sites in danger.	Wolf delisted as an endangered species and control is given over to individual states, allowing wolf hunts in Montana, Wyoming and Idaho.

Geology

As a supervolcano sitting on one of the foremost hot spots on earth, Yellowstone hosts some of the premier geothermal features found anywhere on the planet. These geysers, hot springs and steam vents offer geologists and visitors a vivid peek into the center of our world. From acidic soils to waterlogged valleys, the environment on this superheated plateau shapes the lives of the plants and animals that call this park home and this has made it one of the leading wildlife destinations in North America.

The Yellowstone Hot Spot

Stand in the park and you are perched atop a thin piece of crust floating over a huge 125-mile-deep plume of molten rock known as a hot spot. This buoyant molten rock, heated by magma deep under the earth's crust, has risen through the upper mantle close to the earth's surface.

Hot spots may be fixed, but as the earth's crust moves over them, it forms a line of progressively newer volcanoes. The North American plate moves southwest one inch per year. Its contact with the Yellowstone hot spot has burned a chain of volcanoes across the West from southeastern Oregon (where it was active 16 million years ago) to northern Wyoming (where it was last active 600,000 years ago). After a few million years, it will slide over to North Dakota.

The Yellowstone region has been sitting atop this hot spot for about two million years, with massive supervolcanic eruptions occurring roughly every 650,000 years. The last three have been centered on Island Park, Henry's Fork and Yellowstone.

What do these eruptions entail? The most recent explosion formed the 1000-sq-mile Yellowstone caldera at the center of the park 600,000

GEOLOGIC WONDERS

» **Grand Prismatic Spring** The park's most beautiful geothermal feature.

» **Grand Teton** Molten dikes, fault scarps and those peaks!

» **Hebgen Lake** Ponder the awesome result of the 1959 earthquake.

» **Mammoth Hot Springs** Graceful travertine terraces.

» **Mud pots** Head to Mud Volcano south of Canyon; Artist Paint Pots south of Norris; or Fountain Paint Pot in the Lower Geyser Basin.

» **Norris Geyser Basin** The region's hottest geothermal area, featuring Echinus Geyser, the park's largest acidic geyser.

» **Obsidian Cliff** Dark volcanic glass from the interior of a cooled lava flow.

» **Petrified forests** Hike up Specimen Ridge in Yellowstone or take the interpretive walk at Tom Miner Basin in Paradise Valley.

» **Calcite Springs** Hexagonal basalt columns near Tower Falls.

» **Upper Geyser Basin** Old Faithful, Morning Glory Pool and other gems.

VOLCANOES

years ago. The explosion spat out magma and clouds of 1800°F liquid ash at supersonic speeds, vaporizing all in its path and suffocating the land in blisteringly hot ash flows. Billowing ash traveled thousands of square miles in minutes, landing as far away as the Gulf of Mexico. The crater roof and floor then imploded and dropped thousands of feet, creating a smoldering volcanic pit 48 miles by 27 miles wide. Ash circling the globe caused a volcanic winter by reducing the amount of solar heat reaching the earth.

Visitors may be surprised that Yellowstone is not more mountainous; the reason quite simply is that the mountains were either blown away by the explosion or sank into the caldera.

Since the explosion, at least 30 subsequent lava flows, dating from 150,000 to 70,000 years ago, have filled in and obscured the caldera, and forests have reclaimed the area, though you can still make out the caldera in numerous places. Turnouts on the road south of Dunraven Pass provide excellent views of its northern part, and much of the caldera's outline can be seen from the summit of Mt Washburn (p96).

The Yellowstone Volcano Observatory, created in partnership with the United States Geological Survey (USGS), monitors volcanic and earthquake unrest in the park. See their work at http://volcanoes.usgs.gov/yvo.

Yellowstone's Thermal Features

Fueled by its underground furnace, Yellowstone is a bubbling cauldron of over 10,000 geothermal features – more than all other geothermal areas on the planet combined. Maybe it isn't all that surprising. Magma, the earth's molten rock, is just 3 to 5 miles underground, closer to the surface here than anywhere else on earth. The average heat flow from the region is 40 times the global average.

But heat isn't everything. Essential to Yellowstone's thermal features is the addition of water, falling onto the park as rain or, more commonly, snow. This surface water may seep down as deep as 2 miles over long periods of time before it drains through the side channels of geysers, hot springs and underground aquifers. The next time you watch a geyser, remember that the water spurting out may have fallen as snow or rain up to 500 years ago.

With the plumbing of Yellowstone's geothermal features constantly in flux, what seem like permanent features are mere blips on the geologic timescale. Geysers suddenly erupt, or dry up; hot springs gradually appear, or explode so violently that they destroy themselves.

Scientists are only beginning to fathom these complex underground systems, but it's clear that this is a threatened landscape unless the broader region is safeguarded thoughtfully. Through conservation, Yellowstone protects about half of the world's geysers, but in areas like Iceland and New Zealand, where geothermal features have been developed as energy sources, geysers and geothermal activity may be altered or cease altogether.

Geysers

Only a handful of Yellowstone's thermal features are active geysers (from the Icelandic *geysir*, meaning 'to gush or rage'), but these still comprise about 50% of the global total, making the park a globally significant resource.

How do geysers form? First, snowmelt trickles down into hot rock where it is superheated. The heated water begins to rise, creating convection currents. The earth acts like a giant pressure cooker, keeping the water liquid even though it reaches temperatures of over 400°F. As the water rises, it dissolves silica trapped in the surrounding rhyolite rock base. At the surface this silica is deposited as the mineral sinter (geyserite), creating the familiar ash-colored landscape of Yellowstone's thermal basins.

Oil, gas, and groundwater development near the park and drilling in Island Park, Idaho, and Corwin Springs, Montana, have the potential to alter the natural function of geothermal systems in the park.

PSYCHEDELIC SCIENCE

Given that Yellowstone, with its 10,000 geothermal features, is the world's foremost source of heated water, it comes as no surprise that heat-loving (thermophilic) microorganisms were first discovered in the park's boiling hot waters.

A huge variety of microbes and bacteria thrive in these extreme waters, tolerating heat, extremely acidic or alkaline conditions and toxic minerals. One such species has yielded an important enzyme crucial to DNA fingerprinting tests (p236). Other research is revealing important clues about the origins of life on earth and survival of life in outer space.

Much of this activity occurs on a microscopic scale, but visitors can still appreciate the brilliant colors these micro-organisms produce in bodies of water. With species inhabiting a highly specific temperature and chemical zone, each layer produces the rings and patches of vibrant color that gives Yellowstone waters their psychedelic signature.

What gives geysers their 'oomph' is the sinter seal that junks up the escape valves in geyser chambers. This temporary blockage causes an intense buildup of gas until the seal breaks and releases the accumulated pressure. As the superheated water rushes toward the surface, water pressure drops and the water expands more than 1500 times in a violent chain reaction as it flashes into steam and explodes into the sky. Geysers require walls of hard rock like rhyolite, which is part of the reason why Yellowstone's geysers are concentrated in the southwest of the park.

Geysers and hot springs are often connected in complex and delicate underground networks and affect each other in ways we don't yet understand.

The pink to grey rhyolitic lava that dominates park landscapes owes its hue to silica. The same substance is known to clog up narrow steam vents to create powerful geyser explosions.

Hot Springs

Hot springs occur with a gradual release of hot water. Springs may rage like oil in a deep fryer, churn like giant washing machines or remain completely still. Their crazy colors are a combination of mineral content, which affects the absorption and reflection of light, and water temperature, which supports a range of algae communities. Since algae or thermophiles are very temperature-specific, they may create beautiful concentric bands of colors. Blue pools are the hottest, absorbing all color except blue. Green pools result when the blue is mixed with small amounts of yellow sulfur.

Mud Pots

Imagine that the sulfuric acid in groundwater is potent enough to dissolve rock, creating a sort of hot spring of viscous bubbling mud. The mud is known as kaolinite, a form of clay. Mud pots form above the water table, where less water is available. Most derive their water directly from rain, snow and condensation, so their consistency depends on precipitation and the seasons. Are they really boiling? No, the bubbling is actually the release of steam and gas. Sulfur and iron content give rise to the nickname 'paint pots.'

Yellowstone's fascinating geology is laid bare in *Windows into the Earth*, by Robert B Smith and Lee J Siegel.

Fumaroles

Essentially dry geysers, fumaroles' water boils away before reaching the surface, where they burst with heat. These steam vents also give off carbon dioxide and some hydrogen sulfide (that nice 'rotten egg' smell) with a hiss or roaring sound.

Roaring Mountain (p62) on the Mammoth–Norris road is a huge collection of fumaroles.

Travertine Terraces

The limestone rock of the Mammoth region contrasts with the silica-rich rhyolite found elsewhere in the park. Here, carbon dioxide in the hot water forms carbonic acid, which then dissolves the surrounding limestone (calcium carbonate). As this watery solution breaks the surface, some carbon dioxide escapes from the solution and limestone is deposited as travertine, forming beautiful terraces. They can grow up to an inch per day and are in constant flux.

For a unique angle on thermal activity, check out the aerial photographs of Norris Geyser Basin at http:// volcanoes.usgs. gov/yvo/2007/ balloon.html.

Yellowstone Lake

One of the world's largest alpine lakes, Yellowstone Lake was formed by the collapse of the Yellowstone caldera and shaped by glacial erosion. Hydrothermal explosions have further shaped the shoreline, creating the inlets of West Thumb (a smaller caldera within the larger one), Mary Bay and nearby Indian Pond. Robotic cameras have revealed underwater geysers, 20ft-high cones, rows of thermal spires and more than 200 vents and craters, some the size of football fields, on the lake floor. Mary Bay and the lake floor canyon west of Stevenson Island are the hottest parts of the lake, due to numerous hot springs and vents.

Grand Canyon of the Yellowstone

This canyon is one of the park's premier attractions. It was formed as rising magma lifted the land and the Yellowstone River carved through rhyolite weakened by thermal activity. The fledgling canyon was temporarily blocked up to three times by glaciers (18,000 to 14,000 years ago), and the subsequent glacial flooding created a classic V-shaped, river-eroded canyon. It reached its present form only about 10,000 years ago.

Like many of Yellowstone's waterfalls, the Lower Falls of the Yellowstone tumble over the junction of hard lava bedrock and softer rock, in this case rhyolite and thermal areas. The spectacular colors of the canyon walls are created as hot waters percolate through the rhyolite picking up iron oxides that stain the walls many different colors.

The Teton Fault

The Tetons are mere geologic toddlers. Surrounding ranges like the Gallatins and Beartooths were formed 55 to 80 million years ago by volcanic action, as part of the east end of the Basin and Range region that dominates western USA. At this time Jackson Hole was still a high plateau. The Tetons started to rise only 13 million years ago as the earth's crust stretched apart. At that time the current peaks of the Tetons were still some 6 miles underground.

In 1959 a 7.5-scale earthquake occurred in the Hebgen Lake region just west of the park, causing 300 of Yellowstone's geysers to spontaneously erupt and creating Quake Lake.

The key to the Tetons' breathtaking profile is the 40-mile-long Teton Fault, which runs along the base of the range. The range was essentially created by a succession of several thousand major earthquakes and slippages. Land east of the fault has fallen, over millions of years, as the west block has hinged and angled upward. The east block has in fact dropped four times further than the peaks have risen. Several of these scarps are visible near Jenny Lake.

As tall as the Tetons appear, their height is actually only a third of the fault's total displacement. Gradual erosion of the peaks, combined with sedimentation in the Jackson Hole valley, has diminished their scale by up to two-thirds.

The very tops of the Tetons consist of limestone, deposited by an ancient sea 360 million years ago. Time has eroded these relatively soft sedimentary rocks, exposing the more resistant granite. To create today's impressive pinnacles, freezing ice wedged and shattered the rock along its weakest joints.

You can note the Tetons' angled faulting by observing the westward tilt of the entire Jackson Hole valley. The west half of Jackson Lake is three times deeper than the east, due to both tilting and glacial scouring. Oddly, the land west of the Teton peaks is drained to the east, unlike the drainage systems in most other mountain ranges.

Glaciation

As if supervolcanic activity weren't enough, sheets of ice up to 4000ft thick periodically covered Yellowstone and the Tetons, leaving only the tips of the highest mountain peaks visible. The most recent ice sheet, known as the Pinedale Glaciation, covered about 90% of Yellowstone National Park and melted about 13,000 years ago.

Moving glacial ice worked its artistry, sharpening peaks, carving out glacial valleys, scouring walls, and creating ridges of debris (moraines) and lakes. Glaciers shaped the piedmont lakes at the base of the Tetons and the classic U-shaped Cascade Valley, a popular Teton trail. While the Snake River once flowed south out of Jackson Lake, glacial moraines diverted its flow east. South of Jackson Lake, huge blocks of melting glacial ice formed the depressions known as the Potholes.

In Yellowstone's Geyser Basin, ice melted so quickly that large mounds of glacial debris formed low ranges like the Porcupine Hills, while deposits of glacial debris beneath today's thermal features act as water reservoirs for the various geysers and hot springs.

Today's glaciers have largely retreated, their best example are the nearby Wind River Mountains, with the largest glaciers in the Lower 48.

Yellowstone's Future

The Yellowstone region has been geologically stable for about 10,000 years now, but the land remains restless. Continued tension in the earth's crust and earthquakes make this one of the most seismically active areas in the USA, with 1000 to 3000 earthquakes occurring each year.

Although a 6.1-scale earthquake rocked the Norris Geyser Basin in 1975, geologists don't expect large earthquakes in Yellowstone National Park because underground heat softens the bedrock and makes it less likely to fracture.

Yellowstone is rising or falling as much as an inch a year, moving 65ft with each slow motion 'breath,' particularly at Mallard Lake Dome just east of Old Faithful, and Sour Creek Dome, east of the Hayden Valley. These movements in the earth's crust are probably due to the withdrawal of molten rock from twin magma chambers on the rim of the Yellowstone caldera.

No one knows for sure what will happen if (or when) Yellowstone's slumbering giant awakens. The last major Yellowstone eruption dwarfed every other volcanic eruption on the earth's surface for the past several million years, and such an explosion remains beyond human experience. The bulging of magma chambers on the rim of the Yellowstone caldera indicates that another eruption is likely but scientists agree, not for at least another 10,000 years. A major eruption would undoubtedly destroy the park as we know it, and cause major climate change that would affect human activity around the world.

Until then, enjoy the wondrous spectacle of Yellowstone's thermal features, and as you gaze up at Old Faithful or down through a hot spring into the bowels of the earth, remember the awesome forces at work below the grandeur.

Glaciers in the Teton range were formed in the Little Ice Age, a cold period from roughly 1400–1850. Numbering around a dozen, they will likely disappear if climate change continues its current path.

Grasshopper Glacier, outside Cooke City, was named for millions of extinct grasshoppers entombed in its ice. However, most of the grasshoppers have decomposed as the glacier melts due to global warming.

GEOLOGY GLACIATION

Wildlife

The 2.5 million acres of wilderness within Yellowstone and Grand Teton National Parks constitute the biological heart of the Greater Yellowstone Ecosystem – the earth's largest intact temperate ecosystem. Greater Yellowstone radiates out from its untamed core into 18 million acres of surrounding federal lands and private property, forming a vast wilderness that is one of the world's premier wildlife-viewing areas, especially for larger mammals.

Animals and plant communities within Yellowstone are shaped by the region's legacy as a geologic and geothermal 'hot spot.' Not only has uplift made the park a high-elevation landscape, but the leaching of rhyolite volcanic deposits has created acidic soils ideal for the lodgepole pine forests that cover 60% of Yellowstone's main plateau. The park's elevation also led to extensive glaciation during the ice ages, which left behind impermeable deposits that create waterlogged landscapes in places like Hayden Valley.

Charismatic species of Yellowstone include the lynx, bald eagle, grizzly bear, whooping crane and reintroduced gray wolf. Featured below are some species visitors are most likely to see – or would most like to see.

Catch up with cool research happening at the park at www.greateryellowstonescience.org, a portal which lays out the natural and cultural resources of both Yellowstone and Grand Teton.

Animals

Large Mammals

Yellowstone National Park alone harbors 60 resident mammal species, including seven native species of ungulates (hoofed mammals). Much of the wildlife mentioned below also ranges beyond the parks' boundaries into surrounding areas.

Bears

The black bear roams montane and subalpine forests throughout Greater Yellowstone, hibernating in a den over winter. It's an adaptable, primarily vegetarian forager that sporadically hunts smaller animals. Although they are generally more tolerant of humans and less aggressive than grizzlies, black bears should always be respected.

In 2009 the grizzly returned to the endangered species list. The grizzly bear once ranged across the western US. Today its population in the Lower 48 has been reduced to less than 1200, with 600 grizzlies inhabiting the Greater Yellowstone region.

Male grizzlies reach up to 8ft in length (from nose to tail) and 3.5ft in height at the shoulder (when on all fours) and can weigh more than 700lb at maturity. If you find some bear tracks, you might notice that the toe pads of a black bear are widely spaced and form a strong arc, while grizzly bear tracks show closely spaced toes in a fairly straight line, along with impressions from their very long claws. About half of black bears are black in color; the anomalies are brown or cinnamon. Black bears are somewhat smaller than grizzlies and have more tapered muzzles, larger ears and smaller claws.

Omnivorous opportunists and notorious berry eaters, grizzlies have an amazing sense of smell – acute enough to detect food miles away. Their wide range of food sources varies seasonally. After bears emerge from hibernation between early March and late May, they feed mostly on roots and winter-killed carrion, turning to elk calves and then spawning cutthroat trout in late June. A feast of army cutworm moths lures bears to higher elevations in early September. Fall signals the buildup to hibernation, and consumption of whitebark nuts and the raiding of squirrels' pinecone stashes becomes an obsession. Before hibernation, bears can eat up to 100,000 berries in a single day. Scientists are concerned that falling levels of cutthroat trout in Yellowstone Lake and the spread of blister rust fungus, which kills whitebark pines, will have an increasingly detrimental effect on grizzly food supplies in the park.

Male grizzlies generally live alone, require over 800 sq miles of territory, and live for up to 30 years. Females have one to four cubs every three years and are fiercely protective of their young, which stay by their mother's side for two years.

Grizzlies are most active at dawn and dusk in open meadows and grasslands near whitebark and lodgepole pines. They can become extremely agitated and aggressive if approached or surprised, but otherwise they do not normally attack humans. However, they viciously defend carcasses and can outrun a horse when provoked, thus trails are often closed when a grizzly is feeding nearby on a bison, elk or moose. For tips on what to do if you encounter a bear, see p272 and p274.

Pronghorn undertake the longest migration in the Lower 48. Since 2007 Grand Teton National Park has been part of a dedicated migratory pathway called Yellowstone to Yukon (www.y2y.net).

Coyotes, Foxes & Wolves

The cagey coyote (locally pronounced 'kye-oat') is actually a small opportunistic wolf species that devours anything from carrion to berries and insects. Its slender, reddish-gray form and nocturnal yelps soon become familiar to hikers. Coyotes form small packs to hunt larger prey such as

FINDING WILDLIFE

ANIMAL	HABITAT	WHEN & WHERE	PRECAUTIONS
black bear	forest and meadows	in summer at Tower and Mammoth areas	keep minimum distance of 100yd, see p271
grizzly bear	forest and meadows	at dawn and dusk; Hayden and Lamar valleys; Fishing Bridge to East Entrance	keep distance of 100yd, see p271
bison	grasslands	year-round in Hayden and Lamar valleys; in winter at hydrothermals around Madison River	responsible for more human injuries than bears; a lifted tail signals charge, keep a distance, drive slow around herds
moose	marshes, lakeshores and rivers	at lower elevations in summer, like Willow Flats (Grand Teton National Park); migrate to subalpine and forests of Douglas fir in winter	Don't corner or approach calves, adult may kick
pronghorn	sagebrush and grasslands	in summer at Lamar Valley near North Entrance; in winter between North Entrance and Reese Creek	keep distance of 25yd
wolf	forest and meadows	at dawn and dusk in Lamar and Hayden Valleys	don't feed, keep a respectable distance

WOLF POLITICS

Wolves flourished in the West until the late 19th century, when homesteaders' livestock replaced bison herds. Poaching and predator control greatly reduced wolf populations and by the 1920s they had become extinct in Yellowstone. Despite controversy, wolves were reintroduced to restore balance to the ecosystem in the Lamar Valley in 1995 and thrived. Wolves have recently been delisted as an endangered species, making their future uncertain.

Yet, wolf reintroduction has been contentious. Since 1995 thousands of sheep and cattle have been reportedly killed, with many of the ranchers compensated for their losses. At the same time 'wolf watching' now brings in about $35 million a year to the local economy. Wolves have also proven key to keeping coyote populations under control and assisting in the regrowth of key species like aspen and willow.

The return of the wolves has been shown to be key to providing balance to native ecosystems, though their restoration to the west remains precarious. In 2010 there were only around 100 wolves in Yellowstone – down from a peak of 275 a decade earlier – and over 1600 in the surrounding area. Part of the problem is that states have vastly different approaches to management.

Wolves remain protected in the national parks, but parks are unable to keep these populations from roaming outside the park boundaries into unprotected areas. Both Montana and Idaho now allow the licensed seasonal hunting of wolves. In Wyoming, elected officials have created a controversial wolf management plan that deems 88% of the state a predator zone, allowing for the unregulated killing of wolves in all but the northwest corner of the state.

Critics of these plans decry the fact that politicians are deciding on animal management issues rather than wildlife biologists. Regions where tourism is the primary focus, such as Teton County, Wyoming, are concerned about the huge impact these policies may have on visitation. For additional info you might consult Douglas Smith and Gary Ferguson's *Decade of the Wolf: Returning the Wild to Yellowstone* or Hank Fischer's *Wolf Wars*.

elk calves or livestock, for which ranchers detest them. While wide-scale coyote eradication programs have had no lasting impact, the reintroduction of wolves (which fill a similar ecological niche) is estimated to have reduced the region's coyote population by 50%.

The small, nimble red fox grows to 3.5ft, weighs up to 15lb and has a brilliant red coat. Foxes have catlike pupils, whereas wolves and coyotes have round pupils. Foxes favor meadows and forest edges and are primarily nocturnal. Although widely distributed, the red fox is not as abundant as the coyote, perhaps because the latter is such a strong competitor.

Check out the *Yellowstone Journal*, with information on the park, as well as extensive listings useful for trip planning and travel within the Yellowstone region.

The gray wolf (also see the boxed text, p246), aka timber wolf, was once the Rocky Mountains' main predator, but relentless persecution has reduced its territory to a narrow belt stretching from Canada to the northern Rockies. Its successful reintroduction continues to spark much controversy. Wolves roam in close-knit packs of five to eight animals ruled by a dominant 'alpha' male and female pair. The alpha pair are the only members of a pack to breed (normally in February), but the entire pack cares for the pups. Between four and six pups are born in April or May, and denning lasts into August.

Wolves eat meat only and, in Greater Yellowstone, tend to focus their predation on elk. Packs communicate via facial expressions, scent markings and long, mournful howls that can be heard from miles away.

Elk

Greater Yellowstone's most abundant large mammal, elk (aka wapiti or red deer in Europe) can weigh 700lb and stand up to 5ft tall at the shoulder. Their summer coats are golden-brown, and the males (bulls) have a darker throat mane. Each year bulls grow impressive multipoint antlers (up to 5ft long, weighing up to 30lb) for the fall rut (mating season), when they round up harems of up to 60 females (hinds) and unleash resonant, bugling calls to warn off other males. Although elk populations were decimated in the 19th century, their numbers have largely recovered – beyond sustainable levels say some. Elk are cautious and elusive, and prized by trophy hunters who covet the massive rack of antlers that male elk briefly carry each fall.

Elk graze along forest edges; the largest herd in Yellowstone National Park beds down in the meadows west of Madison Campground. September to mid-October is the rutting season. Irresistibly cute calves drop in May to late June. An estimated 10,000 to 20,000 elk from seven to eight different herds summer in Yellowstone National Park, and a further 17,000 summer in Jackson Hole. In winter, large herds migrate south to the National Elk Refuge (p211) in Jackson. Winter counts of elk have dropped 50% since wolves were reintroduced, but scientists can't agree whether these declines are due to wolves, several years of drought or intense pressure from hunters.

Bison

The continent's largest land mammal, the American bison – commonly called 'buffalo' – once roamed the American West in vast numbers (60 million), often migrating to Greater Yellowstone's high plateaus during summer. Greater Yellowstone is the only region where wild bison have lived since primitive times. By 1902 there were only 23 wild bison living in the Yellowstone region. The park's current population, estimated at 3900 in summer, was effectively bred back from the brink of extinction. Today, numerous herds exist throughout the Greater Yellowstone Ecosystem (an increasing number on private ranches), with three distinct herds ranging in Yellowstone National Park and another in Grand Teton National Park.

A truly majestic animal, full-grown male (bull) bison may stand more than 6ft high at the shoulder, have a total length of 12ft and weigh 2000lb. Bison have a thick, shaggy light brown coat and a high, rounded back. Both sexes have short black horns that curve upward.

Despite their docile, hulking appearance and 'aloof' manner, bison are surprisingly agile. They become increasingly uneasy when approached. A raised tail indicates one of two subsequent events: a charge or discharge. Statistically speaking, bison are much more dangerous than bears. Every year several visitors are gored and seriously injured by these animals, and some are even killed.

Bison roam three main park areas: Lamar Valley, Pelican Valley at the north end of Yellowstone Lake, and along the Mary Mountain corridor between Hayden Valley and Lower Geyser Basin beside the Firehole River. August is rutting season – keep your distance to avoid becoming an unwilling rodeo clown.

The bacterial disease brucellosis (p248) is one of the ecosystem's hottest issues. Management plans call for intense monitoring of bison populations, with a goal of reducing the herd and maintaining Montana's 'brucellosis class-free' status.

Moose

The largest of the world's deer species, moose typically stand up 5ft to 7ft at the shoulder, can reach 10ft in length and weigh as much as 1000lb. They have a brownish-black coat and a thick, black horselike muzzle. The male (bull) has massive, cupped antlers, each weighing up to 50lb, which are shed after the fall rut.

Wildlife-watching Protocol

» Animals have the right of way on roads

» Never position yourself between an animal and its young

» Resist feeding animals and never chase a photo

» If you cause an animal to move, you are too close

Moose mainly browse aspen and willows, but also feed on aquatic plants. Superb swimmers, they can dive to depths of 20ft. Moose may become aggressive if cornered or defending calves and may strike out with powerful blows from their front hooves. An estimated 200 moose are found in Yellowstone National Park, favoring marshy meadows like Willow Valley, just south of Mammoth Springs, or on the east side of Lamar Valley.

Bighorn Sheep & Mountain Goats

Bighorn sheep are arguably the animal that best symbolize the Rocky Mountains. They are robust, muscular beasts, colored grayish brown with a white muzzle tip, underbelly and rump patch. Males (rams) grow up to 6ft long, stand almost 4ft at the shoulder and weigh more than 300lb. Their ideal habitat is alpine meadows or subalpine forests fringed by rocky ridges, which allow them to easily escape predators. Rams have thick, curled horns (weighing up to 40lb), which they use during the fall rut (from mid-September to late October) in fierce head-butting bouts with rivals. Discreet hikers can often closely observe bighorn herds around ridges or alpine valleys; try looking for them on rocky crags between Mammoth and Gardiner.

Introduced to Montana for sports-hunting, non-native mountain goats expanded their range into Yellowstone in 1990, raising concerns that they might impact the area's fragile mountains meadows. Surefooted and confident in even the most precipitous terrain, the mountain goat is highly adapted to the harsh environment of the upper subalpine and alpine zones. It has a shaggy, snow-white coat that includes a thin beard and narrow, almost straight, black horns. Mountain goats can reach 5ft, stand 4ft at the shoulder and weigh up to 300lb. Beware where you pee: goats crave salt and will gnaw down vegetation (and anything in their way) in order to satisfy their hankering.

Cats

The solitary, mostly nocturnal, bobcat is a handsome feline (a scaled-up version of the domestic tabby) with a brown-spotted, yellowish-tan coat and a cropped tail. It mainly eats birds and rodents, but when easier prey is scarce it may take small deer or pronghorn. Bobcats are thought to be widespread in the region, and it's not unusual to see one darting across a meadow or into a willow thicket.

Surveys in 2001 confirmed the presence of at least one lynx in Yellowstone. This threatened cat is similar in appearance to the bobcat, but can be recognized by its entirely black tail tip.

BISON & BRUCELLOSIS

A national symbol long revered by Native Americans, Yellowstone's bison are some of the USA's last free-roaming herds. Despite protection within national parks, their existence outside the park is precarious. About half of Yellowstone's 3900 bison test positive for brucellosis, a bacterium that causes domestic cows to abort their calves. Brucellosis spreads from the region's abundant elk population to the bison, who merely carry the bacteria while themselves remaining unaffected.

For many years, bison that strayed outside the park have faced removal, a term which usually meant extermination. In 2000, a long-term management plan was put into place under which 840 bison were shipped or slaughtered. After many lawsuits, public dissatisfaction and controversy, the plan has seen considerable revision. In recent years, bison removal has declined, in part due to some success with a cattle brucellosis vaccine. Management is now looking to remote vaccination as a potential solution. In addition, 80,000 acres in Montana have been opened up as a sanctuary.

North America's largest cat, the mountain lion (aka cougar) prefers remote, forested areas of the park. With a size and shape similar to that of a smallish (African) lioness, the mountain lion may reach 7.5ft from nose to tail and can weigh up to 170lb. Even biologists who study it rarely encounter this solitary and highly elusive creature. It typically preys on mule deer, elk and small mammals, following their summer migrations to higher ground. While curious mountain lions are known to 'stalk' people without harmful intent, they occasionally attack humans.

Birds

Boasting 316 recorded winged species (of which 148 stay to nest), Greater Yellowstone offers a delightful bird-watching experience. The American Bird Conservancy recognizes Yellowstone National Park as a 'globally important bird area.' Noteworthy large birds include common ravens, resurgent peregrine falcons, reclusive sandhill cranes, honking Canadian geese and American white pelicans. Smaller birds like pesky black-billed magpies and yellow-headed blackbirds are common sights.

Birds of Prey

This group of birds (aka raptors) includes eagles, falcons, hawks and harriers. Sweeping across lakes, forests or plains in search of fish or small game, they are some of the most interesting and easily watched birds in the area.

The iconic bald eagle is a large raptor, with a wingspan up to 8ft, brown plumage and a distinctive 'bald' white head. Bald eagle pairs mate for life, building their nest close to water. Nests grow with each breeding season to become truly massive structures up to 12ft in diameter. The bald eagle takes fish (or harasses an osprey until it drops its catch), but also preys on other birds or smaller mammals. Nesting eagles are extremely sensitive to human disturbance.

The true 'King of the Rockies,' the gracious golden eagle is sometimes spotted riding thermals high above craggy ridges. Native Americans fashioned headdresses from its golden-brown plumage. Marginally smaller but heavier than the bald eagle, they typically nest on rocky cliff ledges and can easily spot potential prey and predators. With a varied diet, it will swoop down on anything from fish and rodents to deer fawns.

The great horned owl is mottled gray-brown with prominent, 'horned' ear tufts, a white throat and a deep, resonant hoot. Its camouflage is so effective that few hikers even notice its presence. Asleep during the day, it preys on nocturnal rodents but also feasts on grouse and other birds.

The fish-eating osprey haunts larger lakes and rivers, nesting in shoreline treetops. Its upper wings and body are dark brown, and its underside is white and speckled on the outer wings. This well-adapted hunter has efficient water-shedding feathers and clamplike feet with two pairs of opposing toes to better grasp slippery, wriggling fish.

Waterfowl

A vast number of waterfowl visit the many lakes, marshes and rivers of Greater Yellowstone, but coots, cranes, gulls and some ducks stay to nest.

North America's largest wild fowl, the spectacular trumpeter swan, is hardy enough to winter here in the Henry's Fork and Red Rock Lakes region west of the park. In 1932 only 69 swans remained alive in the Lower 48 states, all of them in Greater Yellowstone. Since then numbers have climbed to around 2500, but are declining again. It has proven difficult to wean them from winter feeding to find their own wild foods, and cantankerous Canadian trumpeter populations continue to crowd them out.

WOLF PACKS

Learn more about wolves and advocacy at www. wolfwatcher.org. Kids can track the activities of individual wolves or wolf packs via www.yellowstone wolves.org.

WILDLIFE-WATCHING

The Lamar Valley is dubbed the 'Serengeti of North America' for its large herds of bison, elk and the occasional grizzly or coyote. It's the best place to spot wolves, particularly in spring. Wolf-watchers can get a copy of the park's wolf observation sheet, which differentiates the various packs and individual members. The best wolf-watching bases are posted at campgrounds at Pebble and Slough Creeks (p125).

The central Hayden Valley is the other main wildlife-watching area, where spotters crowd the pullouts around dusk. It's a good place to view large predators like wolves and grizzlies, especially in spring when thawing winter carcasses offer almost guaranteed sightings. Coyotes, elk and bison are all common. The tree line is a good place to scan for wildlife. The more you know about animals' habitat and habits, the more likely you are to catch a glimpse of them.

In general, spring and fall are the best times to view wildlife, but different seasons each offer their own highlights. Spotted wapiti calves and baby bison are adorable in late spring, while the fall rut brings the call of bugling elk. In summer you need to head out around dawn and dusk, as most animals withdraw to forests to avoid the midday heat.

It is worth having good binoculars or even renting a spotting scope. A good-quality telephoto camera lens can help the observation of wildlife at a safe distance.

Long-legged great blue herons and red-capped sandhill cranes may be seen striding gracefully in wet meadows and along the edges of water, where they use their long bills to capture fish, snakes, frogs and rodents. In the fall and spring, cranes gather into large noisy flocks.

On larger bodies of water the common loon is prevalent, its beautiful mournful wail echoes across tranquil backcountry lakes. Up to 35in long, it has a black-green head with a speckled upper body and white underparts. Its dense body mass enables it to dive to 150ft but also necessitates a long runway for takeoff, which limits it to larger lakes.

Smaller Birds

The boisterous Clark's nutcracker, a member of the crow family, is light gray with black wings and a white tail. It patrols subalpine forests, feeding largely on conifer nuts, which it breaks open with its long, black beak.

The diminutive mountain chickadee is a playful and gregarious year-round resident of subalpine forests. It has a black cap and throat bib, and its onomatopoeic name describes its distinctive call, 'chick-a-dee-dee.'

The red-naped sapsucker is a woodpecker species with a black back, white stripes above and below each eye, and a red chin and forehead. It bores into tree bark (preferably aspen or willow), discharging gooey sap that traps insects, devouring both. Ironically, the bird's activity helps control the even more destructive bark beetle and other noxious insects.

The striking blue Steller's jay has a black crest, head and nape. Its grating 'ack-ack-ack' is unmistakable. Although it consumes pine nuts, berries and insects, it's also an incorrigible scavenger and frequently raids camps for scraps.

Fish

Yellowstone Lake is at the heart of one of North America's most significant aquatic wildernesses, home to 21 gilled species, including nonnatives like rainbow trout, brown trout, brook trout, lake trout, lake chub and a cutthroat-rainbow trout hybrid. Fish provide critical forage for bears, waterfowl, otters and raptors throughout the ecosystem.

Yellowstone has more than 220 lakes and at least a thousand streams. Yet when it became a national park, 40% of its waters were fishless. The stocking of some 310 million fish drastically altered the aquatic environment. Current threats to Yellowstone's near-pristine aquatic ecosystem include the illegal introduction of predatory lake trout (the biggest culprits in the decline of endangered native cutthroat) into Yellowstone Lake, and the invasion of New Zealand mud snails, which have been found in densities of ½ million snails per square yard and crowd out native aquatic insects. Invasive mussel species are also a threat.

Today 40 of the park's lakes are fishable, with native sport fish being catch-and-release. It's worth watching cutthroat trout spawn in spring at the outlet of Yellowstone Lake at Fishing Bridge and LeHardy's Rapids.

Plants of Yellowstone and Grand Teton National Parks, by Richard J Shaw (Wheelwright Press, 2000), is a well-illustrated introduction to the region's rich vegetation.

WILDLIFE PLANTS

Plants

Flora from the surrounding mountains, deserts, montane forests, arctic tundra and Great Plains all converge in Greater Yellowstone, where they are grouped into five distinct vegetation zones – riparian, foothills, montane, subalpine and alpine. Yellowstone National Park's herbarium has inventoried 1717 species, seven percent of which are considered rare.

Trees

Harsher climatic conditions at higher elevations strongly favor hardy conifers. With the exception of aspen, eight conifers dominate these forests and make up 60% of the region's total vegetation.

Douglas firs, quaking aspens, shrubs and berry bushes blanket parts of the landscape from 6000 to 7000ft. Lodgepole pine forests, which range from 7600 to 8400ft, cover 60% of the park's broad plateaus. Above 8400ft, Engelmann spruce and subalpine fir predominate, interspersed with lodgepoles. Above tree line (10,000ft), alpine tundra supports lichen, sedges, grasses and delicate wildflowers.

For a leg up on spotting wildlife carry a field guide such as *Watching Yellowstone & Grand Teton Wildlife* by Todd Wilkinson.

Aspen has radiant silver-white bark and rounded leaves that 'tremble' in the mountain breezes and turn gold in fall. A regeneration species, aspen tends to reproduce by sending out root runners rather than by seeding. A stand of aspen is mainly cloned from an original parent tree.

Not a true fir, Douglas fir is a tall, adaptable and extremely widespread tree that ranges from the foothills to the subalpine zone and from

---

WILDFLOWER PRIMER

Look for a breathtaking variety of wildflowers peaking throughout June and July:

» **Trumpet-like gentian** A late-bloomer found above 10,000ft in moist arctic bogs, pretty arctic gentian has greenish-white flowers with purple stripes.

» **Columbine** Found at the edges of small, shaded clearings up to 9000ft. Colorado columbine has blue-white flowers with delicate long spurs carrying nectar attracting butterflies and hummingbirds.

» **Fireweed** A single-stem perennial that grows up to 6ft tall, crowned by clusters of pink, four-petaled flowers about an inch in diameter. It colonizes recent burn areas.

» **Succulent Indian hellebore** (aka corn lily) On subalpine slopes, these 7ft stalks have large leathery leaves crowned by maizelike flower tassels. Native Americans used it as an insecticide.

» **Delicate, yellow glacier lily** (aka dogtooth violet) Blankets entire tundra slopes. Bears eagerly extract their edible bulbs.

» **Beargrass** A fragrant lily relative with white starlike flowers on 4ft stalks in well-drained montane and subalpine clearings. Its waxy, bladelike leaves are favored spring forage among grizzly bears.

» **Bright red Indian paintbrush** Prolific in the Tetons and a favorite food source for hummingbirds.

very dry to quite moist locations. It has flattened, irregularly arranged needles, 4in-long cones, and thick, corky bark that protects it from fire.

True firs resemble spruces, but have flat, blunt needles and cones pointing upward on upper branches. The most widespread is subalpine fir with silvery-gray bark bearing horizontal blister scars.

Many lodgepole pines are dependent on periodic forest fires to melt the resins that seal their cones shut, ensuring seed dispersal after fire has prepared a fertile bed of ash. Lodgepoles sport needles in bunches of two and straight, narrow 'polelike' trunks that make for dense stands in recently regenerated forests.

Found in subalpine zones, the five-needled whitebark pine has small-ish, almost round cones that remain purple until maturity. Its seeds provide crucial autumnal forage for grizzly bears. Large individuals stand near Dunraven Pass in Yellowstone and South Cascade Canyon in Grand Teton National Park.

Dominating subalpine forests, Engelmann spruce is a towering, cold-tolerant conifer capable of withstanding winter temperatures of -50°F. Like other spruces, Engelmann has round, slightly pointed needles and pendant cones. Its resonant wood is used to make piano sounding boards.

For Everything There Is a Season, by Frank C Craighead, is a delightful account of wildlife through the seasons by one of Yellowstone's legendary naturalists.

SEASONS

Shrubs

These small woody plants may grow as heaths, form thickets or stand as single bushes on slopes and in meadows. But for herbivores, they are one thing: the bulk food aisle. Know your shrubs and you are one step closer to finding the wildlife.

Shrubby cinquefoil grows in meadows from the foothills to the tundra, sometimes in association with sagebrush. All summer long this multi-branched bush (up to 4ft high) is covered in yellow, buttercuplike flowers with five petals. Deer and bighorn sheep browse the foliage, but only when no other food is available.

Several dozen species of small willows are found in Greater Yellowstone, with fluffy, silky flowers like small bottlebrushes. Shrub willows, including the common gray-leafed willow, form thickets along subalpine and alpine stream basins. Moose eat willow year-round.

The scrumptious blueberry genus includes species locally known as bilberry, cranberry, grouseberry, huckleberry and whortleberry. Almost all produce small, round fruits of bright red to deep purple that sustain bears and other wildlife throughout the Rockies. One of the most common is the fragrant dwarf blueberry, which typically grows among lodgepole pines.

Junipers are aromatic, cedarlike conifers that generally thrive in dry, well-drained areas. Rocky Mountain juniper can approach the size of a small tree, and older shrubs (which may reach 1500 years) are gnarled and knotted. Birds feed on juniper 'berries,' allowing the seed to sprout by removing its fleshy covering.

Strongly aromatic sagebrush thrives on foothills and drier montane meadows. Since grazing mammals shun the bitter foliage, overgrazing results in the spread of sagebrush.

Conservation

A vast and complex wilderness, the Greater Yellowstone Ecosystem is home to a broad range of species that also includes humans. For the last century, our intervention has had positive and negative effects on conservation and wildlife. How to both preserve and inhabit this region remains of critical importance, even today.

Issues affecting the national parks are diverse and evolving. While preserving native species and their habitats is a priority, there is also the question of invasive species, which could look like anything from the New Zealand mud snail obstructing waterways to a snowmobile roaring through winter landscapes. Understanding these issues and managing them are an eternal process.

The Bigger Picture

The Greater Yellowstone Ecosystem is the largest intact temperate ecosystem in the world. We are only beginning to understand the intricate workings of this community, how individual species interact and how best to preserve this amazing environment.

The following is only an introduction to some of today's key issues. For a better understanding, download the free Yellowstone Issues and Resources handbook (www.nps.gov/yell/planyourvisit/resourceandissues .htm).

Protecting Wildlife

Given Yellowstone's mandate to protect wildlife, it's not surprising that some of the fiercest battles are fought over questions of how to manage it. One question is how to protect top-level predators like gray wolves (see the boxed text, p246) when they leave the park and run into conflict with local ranchers. Contributing to the confusion is the fact that each state has different laws on these issues. The slaughter of disease-carrying bison that wander out of the park is another vexing topic (see the boxed text, p248).

In Greater Yellowstone waterways, invasive species like whirling disease parasites, zebra mussels and New Zealand mud snails are threatening native species. Currently, the state of Wyoming requires boaters to purchase an invasive species decal as part of an education campaign. In addition, visiting boats and fishing equipment must be scrubbed of mud and plants that may carry exotics.

Migration Corridors

Protecting migration corridors allows elk and other migratory animals to move from their summer to winter habitats. As populations and road infrastructure increases, they become critical to ensure the survival of diverse species. The nonprofit initiative **Yellowstone to Yukon** (www.y2y.net) supports a dedicated migratory pathway through Grand Teton National Park all the way to Canada. Native pronghorn have been

Get a taste of Yellowstone, see spurting geysers and spy wildlife up close by taking a virtual nature tour at www.nps. gov/yell/photos multimedia/ virtual tour.htm.

using this corridor for 6000 years to undertake the second-longest animal migration in North America. By modifying livestock fences and creating road crossings, conservationists can help this millennial process to continue.

Can Fire Be Good?

In 1998, 30% of the park blazed in a major inferno that only ceased with the first snows of September. Front-page news, the event was more a public relations disaster than an environmental catastrophe (see the boxed text p99). Today's scientific views on land stewardship are evolving. Fire sparked by lightening hits is seen as a natural process that has been occurring for thousands of years. In Yellowstone, the current policy is to allow natural fires to burn under strict guidelines, as they encourage new growth in plant communities, restore nutrients to the soil and burn off accumulated deadwood.

Climate Change is Local

Climate change may be everywhere, but it appears to be happening at an accelerated pace in the region. With summer temperatures on the rise, scientists predict that the Yellowstone River, a renowned trout fishing stream, will become a warm-water fishery. Rising temperatures have also caused whitebark pines to die off at a rate of 85%, which in turn will impact grizzlies as it's an important food source. Researchers have also found much longer wildfire seasons, less snowpack and changing habitats.

While scientists study the issue, it's evident that reducing the stress we place on the environment is a clear step in maintaining it.

Sustainability

The Greening of Recreation

In recent years, snowmobile usage in both parks has been drastically reduced, though proponents decry its impact on winter tourism. In Yellowstone, snowmobilers are now only allowed on professionally guided tours. In Grand Teton, use has been reduced to the frozen Jackson Lake. Both parks require quieter and more efficient BAT (best available technology) snow machines. In addition, the two-stroke engines of rental boats have been replaced with cleaner and more efficient four-stroke versions.

Park Innovation

When Yellowstone approached its 125th anniversary in 1997, the park began planning for the next 125 years. One result was Yellowstone Environmental Stewardship (YES!), an ambitious project aiming to reduce greenhouse gases by 30%, electrical consumption by 15%, fossil fuel consumption by 18%, water consumption by 15% and divert all solid waste from landfills. Solar energy, composting and alternative fuels are a few ways the park has started meeting these goals. In 2010 alone, it was able to divert 80% of solid waste from landfills.

Concessions are an area of major improvement, with park concessionaire Xanterra employing corn-based biodegradables to help annually divert over 280,000 plastic bottles from landfills. Gift shops sell greener souvenirs and dining services pitch in by serving fair-trade coffee and naturally raised meats. In both Yellowstone and Grand Teton, park employees use some hybrid vehicles. LEED-certified park buildings also herald a new era, they include Xanterra employee housing and the new Old Faithful Visitor Education Center, as well as the new Laurance S Rockefeller Visitor Center in Grand Teton National Park.

The Greater Yellowstone Coalition (www.greateryellowstone.org) works on behalf of every major issue affecting the Yellowstone region, from environmental concerns to species survival.

To learn more about sustainable and ecofriendly options in the region, check out National Geographic's 'sustainable visit' map at www.yellowstonegeotourism.org.

Survival Guide

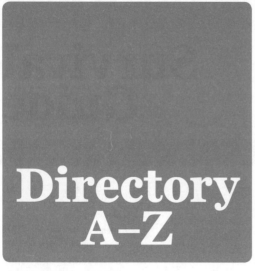

Directory A–Z

Accommodations

It will come as no surprise that rates for accommodations are noticeably higher in the Yellowstone region than in the surrounding areas of Wyoming, Idaho and Montana, particularly in the mad high-season months of July and August. Still, you'll find a wide range of places to stay, from the excellent National Park Service (NPS) and US Forest Service (USFS) campgrounds to private RV parks, simple motels, B&Bs and five-star luxury hotels, as well as that uniquely Western institution, the guest or dude ranch. You should be able to find something reasonably priced in most areas, especially off season.

Yellowstone itself remains the biggest headache, with noncamping accommodations limited to a handful of lodges or cookie-cutter cabins, both of which get booked up months in advance, despite there being almost 2200 rooms in the park.

Outside the parks you can normally find somewhere to stay if you just roll into town, but it's still a good idea to make a reservation at least a day or two in advance. The more popular hotels fill up a month or two in advance of high summer (July and August). Winter is also a prime season in Cooke City and West Yellowstone. The good news is that you can often score discounts of up to 50% on lodging outside the parks in the shoulder season months of April, May, late September through to mid-December, with winter discounts of at least 30% from January to March.

In this guide we use the following price ratings for a double room in high season, without tax:

budget	$	under $100
mid-range	$$	$100-200
top end	$$$	over $200

Camping

Camping is the cheapest, and in many ways the most enjoyable, approach to a Yellowstone vacation. Toasting marshmallows over an open fire, stargazing in the crisp mountain air and taking in an evening ranger talk are essential parts of the national park family bonding experience.

Around half of the campsites in Yellowstone and all sites in Grand Teton are on a first come, first served basis. In July and August campsites get snapped up quicker than you can find them on the map. Establish your campsite in the morning before you head off sightseeing (a 'site occupied' sign can be useful), and once you have a site that you like, hold onto it and use it as a base to visit neighboring sights.

If you have a tight itinerary and will be moving around a lot, try to plan at least a few overnight stays at Yellowstone's concession (Xanterra) campgrounds, where you can make site reservations in advance. Gamblers should remember that even if you manage to score a same-day site at a Xanterra campground, you may have to move out the next day if your spot is booked that night. Concessionaire campsites are around 50% pricier than the park service sites.

If all else fails, you'll find some great USFS campsites outside the park, and these generally only fill up on summer or holiday weekends.

Fishing Bridge in Yellowstone, Colter Bay in Grand Teton and Flagg Ranch in the John D Rockefeller Jr

Memorial Parkway are the only places with full hookups, though a couple of grounds have RV dumps. Generators are generally only allowed between 8am and 8pm, and no generators are allowed at any time at Yellowstone's Indian Creek, Lewis Lake, Pebble Creek, Slough Creek and Tower Fall sites.

CAMPSITE RULES

Some rules to remember from the National Park Service (NPS) and the United Stated Forest Service (USFS):

» Camping in pullouts, trailheads, picnic areas or anywhere except designated campgrounds is illegal.

» Wash dishes, hair, teeth etc away from the spigot. Camp wastewater must be disposed of in waste sinks, restroom sinks (no grease) or the toilet, not chucked into your neighbor's site.

» Campfires must be in established grates. Never leave a fire unattended.

» Cutting trees or shrubs for firewood is prohibited.

» Don't build trenches around campsites.

» A maximum of six people and two cars are allowed at each site (some USFS sites charge extra for a second car).

» No food, ice chests, food containers, utensils or camp stoves may be left outside unattended. If you are tenting, store all food and containers in bear boxes. Don't dispose of food in the camp area; put it in a bag or container and dispose of it in the trash. Don't put trash in the toilets.

» Pets must be physically controlled at all times. Please pick up after your pet.

» Bear restrictions require that only hard-sided campers (no pop-ups) can occupy sites at Fishing Bridge in Yellowstone and certain USFS grounds outside Cooke City and in the upper Wapiti Valley.

XANTERRA CAMPGROUNDS

Yellowstone's concessionaire, **Xanterra** (☎307-344-7311; www.travelyellowstone.com), runs five campgrounds, where sites can be reserved in advance. Reservations can be made over the phone or from other Xanterra campgrounds or facilities in the park. When you make a phone booking, you must pay by credit card and then receive a booking reference number. You'll need to show that credit card when you turn up at the campground. Xanterra doesn't take checks. A full refund of your deposit is possible if you cancel more than 48 hours in advance.

Be careful to specify the type of site you want: tent or non-tent site, reverse-in or pull-through site, and even the length of the site. If your site requirements change, you'll need to change the reservation. Some sites are designated tent-only: you don't *have* to put up a tent in these, but you can't roll up in a giant RV.

If the campground office is closed when you arrive, look on the notice board for your name on an envelope, which will contain your site allocation. If you arrive late at night without a reservation, look on the notice board to see if any sites are vacant and pay the next morning before 11am.

NATIONAL PARK SERVICE CAMPGROUNDS

Yellowstone and Grand Teton campgrounds usually have flush toilets (cheaper sites have vault toilets), drinking water, garbage disposal, fire pits (or charcoal grills) and picnic benches. Most sell boxes of firewood ($7) and kindling and most hold some kind of nightly campfire talk. Days, times and topics are prominently posted and are listed in the park newspapers.

The process of picking a site varies with the campground, but generally involves picking up an envelope from a box at the entrance, driving around the various loops until you find an available site you like, marking the site with either the tab from the envelope, some camp furniture, or the most agreeable family member, and then filling out the envelope and depositing it with the correct fee back at the entrance. Don't dally trying to find the world's best campsite – by the time you get back, the earlier one you liked may well have been snapped up. Some grounds ask you to keep the receipt tab displayed on your car windshield; others ask you to tag it to the campsite post. Rangers often come around at night to check receipts against vehicle number plates.

A 'site occupied' sign can be useful to mark your turf, and these are for sale in most campsites. In larger campgrounds such as Colter Bay in Teton and Mammoth in Yellowstone, you register and pay at the entrance and are computer-assigned a spot, so there's no need to mark your site.

NPS campsites generally do not accept checks or credit cards (with the exception of Signal Mountain in Grand Teton) and are self-service so make sure you bring plenty of $1 and $5 bills. Golden Age and Golden Access Passports give 50% reductions on most camping fees in national parks and national forests.

When choosing a site, discerning campers scrutinize its proximity to a bathroom, trash and water supply, whether the ground is level and, most importantly, the neighbors (a scattering of kids' toys or beer cans can be a very bad sign). In general, back-in sites offer a little more privacy; parallel sites are little more than car parks by the side of the road. A campground's outer loops are usually the most private.

A few campsites are normally reserved for hikers and cyclists at a discounted price.

DUDE RANCHES

Dude-ranch history dates back to the late 19th century, when visiting family and friends from eastern cities offered money to the informal accommodations supplied as a sideline by the region's ranches.

These days you can find anything from a working-ranch experience (5am wakeup calls included) to top-of-the-line resorts frequented by the rich and famous. Ironically, working cattle ranches are increasingly hard to find in the tourist-driven Yellowstone economy.

A few ranches offer nightly accommodations-only rates, but most require a minimum stay of three days to a week. Typical weekly rates run $150 to $200 per person per day, which includes accommodations, meals, activities and equipment. Ranches are proud of the connections they form with their clients, many of whose families return to the same ranch generation after generation.

While the highlight of dude-ranch vacations is horseback riding, many ranches have expanded their activity lists to include fly-fishing, hiking, mountain biking and cross-country skiing. Accommodations range from rustic log cabins to cushy suites with Jacuzzis and cable TV; meals range from steak and beans to four-course gourmet extravaganzas.

Yellowstone's dude ranches (increasingly called guest ranches) are concentrated in the Wapiti Valley near Cody, Jackson Hole and the Gallatin Valley northwest of Yellowstone. For more information contact the **Dude Ranchers' Association** (www.duderanch .org) or the **Wyoming Dude Ranchers' Association** (www.wyomingdra.com).

OUTSIDE THE PARKS

USFS campgrounds are generally less developed than NPS campgrounds; some don't have drinking water and require you to pack out all trash. A few of these sites are free. Many turn off the water supply about mid-September and then either close or run the site for a while at half-price. At any rate, it's always a good idea to bring a few gallons of water when camping.

Sites can be reserved in certain USFS campgrounds in the Gallatin Valley, Targhee National Forest and Custer National Forest (around Red Lodge) through the reservation service at **Recreation. gov** (☑877-444-6777, TDD 877-833-6777; www.recreation .gov). It's possible to select and reserve specific campsites online. Sites need to be booked a minimum three days and maximum eight months in advance.

Free dispersed camping (meaning you can camp almost anywhere) is permitted in some public backcountry areas. Sometimes you can pull off a dirt road and into a small lay-by where you can camp, especially in Bureau of Land Management (BLM) and national forest areas. In other places, you must be 0.25 miles from a developed campground and often not within 0.5 miles of a major highway. Check with the local district ranger office.

Private campgrounds outside the park are mostly designed with RVs in mind; tenters can camp, but fees are quite a bit higher than in public campgrounds, and sites are normally crushed together to maximize profits. Facilities can include hot showers, coin laundry, a swimming pool, full RV hookups with phone and satellite TV, games area, playground and a convenience store.

If you don't have kids, you'll find campgrounds to be much quieter outside school summer holidays.

Lodging

If you aren't camping, accommodations in Yellowstone and Grand Teton are limited to concession-run park lodges and cabins. Lodges are often grand reminders of a bygone era, but the rooms have usually been renovated and are generally quite comfortable. Not all rooms are equal, and there's often a vast range of different room permutations available.

Cabins are generally remnants from the 1950s, almost always jammed in a small area and resembling anything from an affluent suburb to a military barracks. The cheaper cabins haven't been renovated for decades but contain a modicum of rustic charm. The pricier cabins have modern interiors but are pretty charmless. Lodges in Grand Teton are generally more modern.

There are no TVs or radios in park accommodations (don't panic!), so bring a book. Children under 12 usually stay free.

In general, park accommodations are decent value considering the premium real estate. Lodge accommodations start around $80 for a double without bath and $120 for a double with bath. Cabins start at $65 for a double without bath, and $100 with bath. Room rates listed are without tax.

Check the Xanterra website for occasional internet specials, especially discounts of 20% for advance bookings in October and early winter (book before November 1 for mid-December).

In winter you'll save money by signing up for a joint accommodations and activities (normally snowmobile rental) package.

OUTSIDE THE PARKS
Accommodations outside the parks offer much greater variety, from hostels to top-of-the-line dude ranches and fly-fishing lodges.

USFS cabins are a little-known option and are particularly fun in winter, when you can either snowshoe or snowmobile into a basic cabin equipped with a wood-stove, cooking utensils and bunk beds. See the Around Yellowstone chapter for cabins in the vicinity of Hebgen Lake and the Paradise Valley.

Houses or condos are available for rent in ski-resort areas and can be good value for a large group or family, as they almost invariably include a kitchen and living room.

There are several B&Bs scattered around the gateway corridors to the parks, ranging from Victorian houses to wolf sanctuaries. Some offer rooms in the owner's house, while others offer stand-alone accommodations. Some B&Bs and cabins don't accept credit cards.

Some useful sites:

B&Bs, Ranches and Inns of Wyoming (www.wyoming bnb-ranchrec.com)

Jackson Hole Bed & Breakfasts (www.jackson holebnb.com)

Montana Bed & Breakfast Association (www.mtbba.com)

RESERVATIONS
Main reservation lines:

Grand Teton Lodge Company (☑advance reservations 307-543-3100, 800-628-9988, same-day reservations 307-543-2811; www.gtlc.com)

Xanterra Parks & Resorts (☑307-344-7311; www.travel yellowstone.com)

If you find yourself without a reservation, any of the parks' accommodations can tell you exactly what's available parkwide on the spot and can make bookings for up to two days ahead. If you are desperate, keep heading back to check, as cancellations open up a limited number of accommodations every day.

Make sure to let the hotel know if you plan on a late arrival – many places will give your room away if you haven't arrived or called by 6pm. Cancellation policies vary; inquire when you book.

Most of the gateway towns surrounding the parks have agencies that will gladly book your entire vacation, from car rental to hotel rooms and excursions:

Jackson Hole Central Reservations (☑888-838-6606; www.jacksonholewy.com; 140 E Broadway, Jackson, WY)

Yellowstone Tour and Travel (☑800-221-1151; www .yellowstone-travel.com; 211 Yellowstone Ave, West Yellowstone, MT)

Yellowstone Vacations (☑800-426-7669; www .yellowstonevacations.com; 415 Yellowstone Ave, West Yellowstone, MT)

Business Hours

Opening hours for all facilities are very seasonal. Outside of the high season, from Memorial Day to Labor Day, you can expect opening hours to be shorter by an hour or two than those listed

here. The park newspapers detail exact opening hours and dates. Reviews in this book don't include business hours unless they deviate from the following standards.

Banks, post offices and government offices 9am to 5pm weekdays, half day Saturday.

Park visitor centers Generally 8am to 7pm in summer.

Convenience stores Normally until 9:30pm within the parks.

Restaurants 7am to 10:30am, 11:30am to 2:30pm and 5pm to 9:30pm.

Shops 9:30am to 5:30pm.

Courses

Established in 1907, the non-profit **Yellowstone Institute** (☑307-344-2293; www. yellowstoneassociation .org/institute) conducts an educational field program offering one- to five-day outdoor courses in everything from identifying mammal tracks and wild edible plants to wolf behavior and Yellowstone's colorful history. It also runs multiday backpacking and horse-pack trips, kayaking, fly-fishing for teens and women, and backcountry trips, as well as courses on photography and wildlife-watching. 'Lodging and Learning Programs' are four- to five-day packages that include food and park accommodation. These are particularly popular in winter.

Most courses are conducted from late May to late September (plus some in January and February) at the historic Buffalo Ranch in

FREE PARK ADMISSION!

Admission to Yellowstone and Grand Teton National Parks is generally free on August 25, the founding of the National Park Service. There are over a dozen other free admission days, often including National Public Lands Day and Veteran's Day, but these change annually – see www.nps.gov/yell/planyourvisit/feefree.htm.

PARK PASSES

Several types of annual passes grant unlimited access to national parks. The passes admit a private vehicle and its passengers, or the pass holder, spouse and children. You'll need a photo ID to purchase and use the pass.

» **Annual Pass** Year-long access to Yellowstone and Grand Teton for $50.

» **Nationwide Annual Pass** Interagency Pass ($80) that gives access to any fee-paying site administered by the National Park Service (NPS), United States Forest Service (USFS), United States Fish & Wildlife Service (USFWS) or Bureau of Land Management (BLM).

» **Seniors Pass** A lifetime seniors' pass covering the same areas costs a one-off fee of $10 and is a great bargain. It allows US residents 62 years and older (and accompanying passengers in a private vehicle) unlimited entry to all sites, with a further 50% discount on most camping and other fees.

» **Access Pass** This free pass offers the same benefits to US residents who are blind or permanently disabled (proof is required). If you have an old Golden Age or Golden Access pass, there's no need to replace it with the new passes.

You can buy the passes at all park entrances or purchase one online at http://store .usgs.gov/pass. For more information see www.nps.gov/fees_passes.htm.

Yellowstone's Lamar Valley, though some day courses meet at the Yellowstone Association building in Gardiner. Courses start at $80 per day, excluding food and accommodations. Buffalo Ranch's self-catering log-cabin bunkhouses cost $25 per person and small groups can stay in the Yellowstone Overlook Field Campus cabins in Gardiner. View the course catalogues online.

The highly regarded **Teton Science School** (☎307-733-4765; www.teton science.org) in Kelly runs twice weekly natural-history seminars (from $65/35 for adult/child per day) for families, plus weeklong programs. It also houses the free Murie Natural History Museum; call for an appointment to visit.

If all of that sounds too much like school, try a fly-fishing course at the **Yellowstone Fly Fishing School** (☎406-220-5234; www.yellow stoneflyfishingschool.com; 271 Old Clyde Park Rd, Livingston, MT). Women-only courses, kid's courses, private lessons and four-hour clinics ($100 per person in a group of three) are available, some based at Chico Hot Springs.

Discount Cards

Always ask for some kind of discount, whether it be AAA, Good Sam, seniors, off-season, shoulder season, multiday or any other even half-credible reason you can imagine. Rates are notoriously flexible in the Yellowstone region. Student cards are of little use.

Food

Food in Yellowstone is generally more functional than fun, though you shouldn't have difficulty finding somewhere to eat whatever your budget. The parks offer a multitude of fast-food outlets and sandwich bars, as well as the occasional need-to-eat-something-different gourmet restaurant.

Outside the tourist-driven eateries in the parks, local cuisine is a stick-to-your-ribs diet of biscuits and gravy, chicken-fried steaks, turkey loaf and mashed potatoes, plus table-shaking half-pound burgers and bloody steaks. One local 'delicacy' that always gets foisted (with a grin) on tourists is Rocky Mountain

Oysters – deep-fried bison testicles, normally served in pairs.

If you plan on sticking to a strict vegetarian diet while traveling in Greater Yellowstone, you'll have to get used to two things: baked potatoes and grudging looks from local ranchers.

Given the lovely locations and abundant picnic areas, picnicking is a popular option. A cooler is an invaluable piece of equipment during the heat of summer, and ice is available at most park junctions. The majority of campers bring a dual-burner stove to speed along cookouts. At the end of the day, even the blandest can of beans tastes like heaven when cooked over an open fire and under a blanket of stars.

In this book we use the following definitions for a main course, not including tips or drinks:

budget	$	under $10
mid-range	$$	$10 to $20
top end	$$$	over $20

Insurance

Foreign visitors to the US should take out adequate travel insurance, purchased before departure. At a minimum, you need coverage for medical emergencies and treatment, including hospital stays and an emergency flight home if necessary. Medical treatment in the USA is of the highest caliber, but the expense could kill you.

You should also consider coverage for luggage theft or loss, and trip cancellation insurance. If you already have a homeowner's policy, see what it will cover and consider getting supplemental insurance to cover the rest. If you have prepaid a large portion of your trip, cancellation insurance is a worthwhile expense.

Finally, if you're driving it's essential that you have liability insurance. Car-rental agencies offer insurance that covers damage to the rental vehicle and separate liability insurance (which covers damage to people and other vehicles).

Worldwide travel insurance is available at www .lonelyplanet.com/travel_ services. You can buy, extend and claim online anytime – even if you're already on the road.

Internet Access

There is currently no public internet access in Yellowstone National Park. Most hotel rooms inside the park don't even have a telephone connection. Dornan's, at Moose in Grand Teton, has internet access at $5 per hour. An internet (@) and wi-fi (📶) icon is used in this book wherever internet access and/or wi-fi is available.

Most hotels, libraries, visitor centers, bookstores, cafes and McDonald's in the neighboring towns offer wi-fi internet access. Search www .wifiareas.com to find one near you.

Money

Yellowstone has 24-hour ATMs at almost all hotels and general stores.

In Grand Teton, look for 24-hour ATMs at Dornan's and Jackson Lake Lodge and other ATMs at Colter Bay grocery store and Signal Mountain.

Accommodation tax ranges from 4% to 8% and varies from county to county, even inside the parks. Sales tax is 4% in Wyoming (plus up to 2% county tax). There is no statewide sales tax in Montana, though a few places like Red Lodge, Big Sky and Cooke City impose a local 'resort' tax.

Bear in mind that tipping (around 15%) is generally expected on horse-packing and rafting trips and stays at dude ranches.

Post

The only year-round post office in Yellowstone is at Mammoth Hot Springs. Seasonal post offices are at Canyon,

YELLOWSTONE IN YOUR CELL PHONE (& OTHER NEAT GADGETS)

You can use a combination of MP3 players, smart phones and your car stereo to liven up the drive to the parks. If nothing else, it solves the festering debate over whose music to listen to!

» You can download the free National Park Service (NPS) video podcasts *Yellowstone in Depth, Visiting Yellowstone* or *Inside Yellowstone* from iTunes.

» Yellowstone and Grand Teton National Parks have developed free apps to help visitors plan their visits, available for download at http://tetonapp.com. A search will dig up other apps, from hiking guides to a list of park toilet facilities.

» Go old school with an audio book. Tim Cahill's *Lost in My Own Backyard* is available on audio CD or MP3 and is read by the author.

» The company Tourcaster (www.tourcaster.com) sells hour-long downloadable audio tours of both Yellowstone and Grand Teton parks for $10.

» For something even snazzier the Virtual Tour Guide (☎877-SELF TOUR; www.virtual tourguide.net; 116 Grizzly Ave, West Yellowstone) is a rentable GPS unit with a touch screen that gives you directions to points of interest and offers tips to spot wildlife. You can rent it at any of Yellowstone's gateway towns and drop it off at another, but it's not cheap at around $50/90 for one/two days.

» Several webcams offer interesting peeks into the park. Watch Old Faithful erupt online at www.nps.gov/yell/photosmultimedia/yellowstonelive.htm (refreshed every 30 seconds) and check out the amazing 360-degree panoramas at www.virtualguide books.com/Wyoming/Wyoming.php.

INTERNATIONAL VISITORS

See p261 for information about insurance.

Embassies & Consulates

British and Australian consulates are maintained in Denver, but they can't replace lost passports. For all other countries the nearest options would be in Washington, DC or San Francisco.

Entering the Country

If you have a non-US passport, you must complete an arrival/departure record (form I-94) before you reach the immigration desk. It's usually handed out on the plane along with the customs declaration. On arrival most visitors will have their photo taken and electronic fingerprints made of each index finger; the process takes less than a minute.

No matter what your visa says, US immigration officers have absolute authority to refuse admission to the USA or impose conditions on admission. They will ask about your plans and whether you have sufficient funds; it's a good idea to list an itinerary, produce an onward or round-trip ticket and have at least one major credit card.

Money

Foreign-currency traveler's checks can only be cashed in banks in the gateway towns, so do yourself a favor and bring US-dollar checks. They are by far the easiest to change and many businesses will simply accept them as cash. The front desks of all park accommodations exchange foreign currency cash 9am to 5pm weekdays.

Passports & Visas

Most visitors from Western Europe, Australia, New Zealand, Japan and Singapore can enter the US for stays of 90 days or less on a visa waiver program (VWP).

To qualify for this, your passport must meet one of the following conditions: it was issued before October 26, 2005, but is 'machine readable'; it was issued on or after October 26, 2005, and includes a digital photo as well as being machine readable; or it was issued on or after October 26, 2006, and contains a digital photo and 'biometric data,' such as digital iris scans and fingerprints.

As of January 2009, citizens of the 27 countries in the VWP need to register with the government online (https://esta.cbp.dhs.gov) three days before their visit. The registration is valid for two years.

For more details see the US State Department (www.travel.state.gov).

Practicalities

» **Electricity** Voltage in the USA is AC 110V. You'll need an AC adapter and probably a voltage converter to run most non-US electronics.

» **Measurements** The US uses the imperial system; ie miles, yards, pints and quarts. A US gallon is slightly larger than an imperial gallon and the US ton is slightly heavier than a metric tonne.

» **Media** *Jackson Hole News and Guide* (www.jhnewsandguide.com), *Bozeman Daily Chronicle* (www.bozemandailychronicle.com) and *USA Today* are available inside the parks.

Telephone

To dial interstate (long distance) dial ☎1 followed by the state code: Montana ☎406 or Wyoming ☎307. To call abroad dial the international code ☎011.

Time

All areas covered in this guide operate on US Mountain Time, which is -7 hours GMT. America subscribes to daylight savings time (DST): on the first Sunday in April clocks are set one hour ahead; on the last Sunday of October, clocks are turned back one hour.

Lake and Grant Villages, and Old Faithful.

In Grand Teton you'll find post offices at Colter Bay (summer only) and Kelly, Moose and Moran Junctions.

Public Holidays

On the following national public holidays, banks, schools and post offices are closed, and transportation, museums and other services operate on a Sunday schedule. Park visitor centers and facilities are open on the public holidays that fall within their normal opening dates. Holidays falling on a weekend are usually observed the following Monday.

January 1 New Year's Day

Third Monday in January Martin Luther King Jr Day

Third Monday in February Presidents' Day

Last Monday in May Memorial Day

July 4 Independence Day

First Monday in September Labor Day

Second Monday in October Columbus Day

November 11 Veterans' Day

Fourth Thursday in November Thanksgiving

December 25 Christmas Day

Telephone

Cell phone coverage is good in Grand Teton (except for the canyons) but patchy in much of Yellowstone, especially outside the major junctions. Bring yours along, but don't rely on it for emergency communications.

There are pay phones at most junctions but they can be expensive, especially for collect calls. Yellowstone General Stores sell prepaid phone cards that offer decent value.

Tourist Information

Visitors to Yellowstone and Grand Teton are well-supported with information from various organizations. See also On the Road chapters for details of visitor centers in individual towns and regions.

Yellowstone National Park

» **Albright Visitor Center** (☎307-344-2263)

» **Backcountry office** (☎307-344-2160)

» **Fire information** (☎307-344-2580)

» **Lost & found** (☎307-344-2109, for items lost in Xanterra accommodations or restaurants 307-344-5387)

» **Mammoth clinic** (☎307-344-7965)

» **Old Faithful clinic** (☎307-545-7325)

» **Old Faithful Visitor Center** (☎307-545-2750)

» **Park road updates** (☎307-344-2117)

» **Recorded campground & accommodation information** (☎307-344-2114)

» **Xanterra** (☎307-344-7311, 866-439-7375, TDD 307-344-5395, same-day reservations 307-344-7901)

» **Yellowstone National Park** (☎307-344-7381, TDD 307-344-2386)

Grand Teton National Park

» **Grand Teton Lodge Company** (☎307-543 3100, same-day reservations 307-543-2811)

» **Grand Teton National Park** (☎307-739-3300)

» **Jackson Hole & Greater Yellowstone Visitor Center** (☎307-733-3316)

» **Recorded campground information** (☎307-739-3603)

» **Recorded weather** (☎317-739-3611)

Greater Yellowstone

» **Recreation.gov reservation service** (☎1-877-444-6777)

» **State road & weather conditions** (☎Wyoming 307-772-0824, Montana 800-226-7623, Idaho 208-336-6600)

Travelers with Disabilities

Yellowstone has many accessible boardwalks and trails, and even several wheelchair-accessible backcountry campsites, including Goose Lake (OD5) south of Fountain Flats Drive in Geyser Country and Ice Lake on the Norris–Canyon road, which is half a mile from the trailhead and has a wheelchair-accessible vault toilet. The Madison River in the west of the park offers a wheelchair-accessible fishing platform.

The pamphlet *Visitor Guide to Accessible Features in Yellowstone National Park* lists accessible sights and facilities, and is available online at the 'Plan Your Visit' section of the park website. In Yellowstone there are wheelchair-accessible campsites at Bridge Bay, Canyon, Grant Village, Madison and Mammoth.

Deaf visitors can get information at TDD ☎307-344-2386 (Yellowstone) or TDD ☎307-739-3400 (Grand Teton). The park will provide sign language interpreters for ranger-led programs if booked three weeks in advance – call ☎307-344-2251.

Wheelchair-accessible trails in Grand Teton include the 6-mile paved trail along String Lake. Accessible accommodations are available at several campsites and all lodging facilities. For more details view the Accessibility brochure on the park's website.

Blind and permanently disabled people can get a free lifetime access pass, good for all federal parks (see the boxed text, p260). Get one at the park entrances.

Access Tours (☎208-787-2338; www.accesstours .org; PO Box 1320, Driggs, ID 83422) runs tours in Grand Teton and Yellowstone for those with physical disabilities.

Volunteering

The NPS runs a Volunteer in Parks (VIP) program. See the website www.nps.gov/ volunteer and www.nps.gov/ yell/supportyourpark/ volunteer.htm for details.

The USFS accepts a wider range of volunteers, from trail maintenance to campground hosts, and normally supplies rooms and board with a subsistence wage. Visit the websites www.fs.fed.us/fs jobs/volunteers.html or www .volunteer.gov.

The **Student Conserva-tion Association** (www .thesca.org) places student volunteers in the parks.

Youth Conservation Corps (YCC; www.nps.gov/ yell/parkmgmt/yccjobs.htm) offers month-long programs for teenagers (aged 15 to 18), who work in the park on jobs like trail construction, often in the backcountry. See p44.

For details of Grand Teton's volunteer program, contact the **Park Volunteer Coordinators** (☎307-739-3397, 739-3656; www.nps .gov/grte/supportyourpark/ volunteer.htm). Placements for 14 to 16 weeks as a park-ranger naturalist intern are available three times a year. You get free accommoda-tion and $120 a week for expenses.

Grand Teton's **Wildlife Brigade** takes a handful of volunteers and interns for its patrols, managing bear jams, and educating camp-ers on safe food storage, in an attempt to minimize bear encounters.

Other volunteering op-tions in the region:

Community Foundation of Jackson Hole (☎303-739-1026; www.volunteerjackson hole.org) Lists opportunities with dozens of local agencies, from therapeutic riding to art and wilderness organizations.

Continental Divide Trail Alliance (☎303-278-3177; www.cdtrail.org; PO Box 986, Golden, CO)

Wilderness Volunteers (☎928-556-0038; www.wilder nessvolunteers.org) Weeklong

trips helping maintain Ameri-ca's parks and wild lands.

Yellowstone Association (☎307-344-2293; www .yellowstoneassociation.org) Volunteers at the Buffalo Ranch center assist with courses for summer or winter seasons.

Work

Occasional seasonal jobs (for US citizens only) are available as rangers or labor-ers with the National Park Service, though competi-tion for these jobs is fierce. Check for openings at www. nps.gov/personnel, www. nps.gov/yell/parkmgmt/ ynpjobs.htm and www.usa jobs.gov.

Your first stop should be **Coolworks** (www.coolworks .com), which is an excellent clearing house for jobs both in and around the parks. The page www.coolworks.com/ yell.htm deals specifically with the Yellowstone region.

The main Yellowstone Concessionaire, **Xanterra** (☎human resources 307-344-5324, 24hr application request line 307-344-5627; www.yellowstonejobs.com), employs 3000 people in

---

PARK SUPPORT

Many visitors fall in love with the Yellowstone region, returning with their kids, and again with their grandkids. The following organizations do good work to ensure the parks' future:

» **Yellowstone Association** (www.yellowstoneassociation.org) Supports educational, historical, and scientific programs through memberships, book sales and courses at the Yellowstone Institute (p259).

» **Yellowstone Park Foundation** (www.ypf.org) Funds numerous park projects, from wolf monitoring to trail upkeep and raises funds through Yellowstone Park Visa cards and number plates.

» **Grand Teton National Park Foundation** (www.gtnpf.org) This organization's mis-sion is to enhance, preserve and protect the park, using member donations to fund park projects.

» **Grand Teton Association** (www.grandtetonpark.org) Book sales and membership dues fund educational, interpretive and scientific programs in Grand Teton.

» **Greater Yellowstone Coalition** (www.greateryellowstone.org) Monitors environmen-tal issues in areas around the park, from snowmobile use to mining concerns.

» **National Parks Conservation Association** (www.npca.org) This national organiza-tion strives to protect and enhance America's national parks. Members can subscribe to the magazine or sign up for an association credit card.

GETTING HITCHED

Thinking of getting married in the region? Weddings in the park require a $50 permit but you won't have far to travel for your honeymoon! Consider the following:

» The lovely, classic English-style church at Mammoth (p59), for a $100 reservation fee (☎307-344-2003).

» Church of the Transfiguration at Moose, a tiny chapel with huge Teton views.

» The gazebo or riverside site at the Canyon Wedding Chapel (www.canyonweddingchapel.com) in Red Lodge, in full view of the Beartooth Mountains.

summer and 300 in winter, who do everything from making beds to making soup. Pay starts at about $7 per hour and employee morale generally seems pretty low. Employee housing and food cost around $70 per week (RV sites $30 to $40 per week). Apply in December for summer jobs and in August/September for winter positions. Staff are a mix of students, overseas workers (who need to arrange their own work visas) or retirees living in their RVs.

You may also find opportunities with **Delaware North** (☎877-600-4308 in Bozeman; www.visityellowstonepark.com), who runs the Yellowstone General Stores and several gateway hotels. It employs around 800 people a year.

The third Yellowstone concessionaire, **Yellowstone Parks Service Stations** (www.coolworks.com/ypss), is based in Gardiner and has work for clerical as well as automotive technicians. For job opportunities in Grand Teton contact the following:

Dornan's (http://dornans .com/employment)

Flagg Ranch (www.flagg ranch.com/employment.html)

Grand Teton Lodge Company (☎800-350-2068; www .gtlc.com/employment/index .aspx)

Signal Mountain Lodge (www.coolworks.com/signalmt)

The **Association of National Park Rangers** (ANPR; www.anpr.org/publications .htm) publishes the booklet *Live the Adventure: Join the National Park Service* ($6), which gives advice on how to get a job as a park ranger.

Transportation

GETTING THERE & AWAY

The main gateways (and airports) nearest to Yellowstone National Park are Jackson (56 miles), Cody (52 miles), Bozeman (65 miles), Billings (129 miles) and Idaho Falls (107 miles). Grand Teton National Park sits right outside Jackson (13 miles). Depending on your direction of travel, it may be cheaper to land in Salt Lake City (390 miles) or Denver (563 miles) and rent a car there.

Flights, tours and rail tickets can be booked online at www.lonelyplanet.com/bookings.

Air

Airports & Airlines

Private planes can land at Jackson Hole Airport and several small airstrips, including Driggs and Mission Field, east of Livingston, Montana.

Billings Logan International Airport (BIL; ☎406-247-8609; www.flybillings.com) Service to Salt Lake City (Delta), Minneapolis (Delta), Denver (Frontier and United Airlines), Seattle (Alaska Airlines), Portland (Alaska Airlines), Phoenix, Los Angeles and Las Vegas (Allegiant Airlines) and other Montanan destinations (Gulf Stream Airlines).

Gallatin Field (BZN; ☎406-388-8321; www.bozeman airport.com) In Bozeman, service to Denver (United and Frontier), Minneapolis (Delta), Salt Lake City (Delta), Los Angeles (United) and Seattle (Horizon).

Idaho Falls Regional Airport (IDA; ☎206-612-8221; www.idahofallsidaho.gov/city/city-departments/idaho-falls-regional-airport.html) Service to Boise (SeaPort), Las Vegas (Allegiant Air), Long Beach (Allegiant), Phoenix (Allegiant), Salt Lake City (SkyWest/Delta) and Denver (United Express).

Jackson Hole Airport (JAC; ☎307-733-7682; www.jackson holeairport.com) Frequent service to Salt Lake City (Delta/SkyWest), Atlanta (Delta), Denver (United/Frontier), Dallas, Los Angeles (United), Minneapolis (Delta) and Chicago (American Airlines). It's 8.5 miles from Jackson and 4 miles inside Grand Teton National Park.

Yellowstone Airport (WYS; ☎406-646-7631; www.yellow stoneairport.org; ☉Jun-Sep) In West Yellowstone, the closest airport to Yellowstone National Park, with three daily summer flights (June through September) to and from Salt Lake City (SkyWest/Delta). Closes in winter.

Yellowstone Regional Airport (COD; ☎307-587-5096; www.flyyra.com) In Cody, connects to Salt Lake City (SkyWest and Delta) and Denver (SkyWest and Mesa).

CLIMATE CHANGE & TRAVEL

Every form of transport that relies on carbon-based fuel generates CO_2, the main cause of human-induced climate change. Modern travel is dependent on aeroplanes, which might use less fuel per kilometre per person than most cars but travel much greater distances. The altitude at which aircraft emit gases (including CO_2) and particles also contributes to their climate change impact. Many websites offer 'carbon calculators' that allow people to estimate the carbon emissions generated by their journey and, for those who wish to do so, to offset the impact of the greenhouse gases emitted with contributions to portfolios of climate-friendly initiatives throughout the world. Lonely Planet offsets the carbon footprint of all staff and author travel.

Airlines serving regional airports:

Alaska Airlines/Horizon (☎800-252-7522; www .alaskaair.com)

Allegiant Air (www.allegiant air.com)

American Airlines (☎800-433-7300; www.aa.com)

Big Sky Airlines (☎800-237-7788; www.bigskyair.com)

Continental (☎800-523-3273; www.continental.com)

Delta-Skywest (☎800-221-1212; www.delta.com)

Frontier (☎800-432-1359; www.frontierairlines.com)

Gulf Stream Airlines (☎800-499-7450; www.flygia .com)

Mesa (www.mesa-air.com)

Skywest (☎United connections 800-221-6903, Delta connections 800-325-8244; www.skywest.com)

SeaPort (☎888-573-2767; www.seaportair.com)

United (☎800-864-8331; www.united.com)

FLIGHTS FROM UK & IRELAND

British Airways (www .britishairways.com) The most direct route flies to Denver where US carriers connect to Jackson Hole (11 hours plus layover time). Also consider American, United, Delta and Virgin Atlantic.

FLIGHTS FROM AUSTRALIA & NEW ZEALAND

Route through Los Angeles or San Francisco before continuing on to regional airports. Via the Pacific route, the first leg is 12 to 14 hours. Flying through Asia probably means spending a night or considerable layover time in a connecting city.

Land

Bus

Unfortunately, long-distance bus services are a slow, somewhat infrequent and highly inconvenient way to get to Yellowstone and Grand Teton National Parks. But

they will get you to major cities, from where you could then rent a car or bicycle or book a local shuttle service.

Companies may charge extra to transport skis or bicycles.

Alltrans Jackson Hole Express (☎307-733-1719, 800-443-6133; www.jackson holebus.com) Daily service from Jackson to Salt Lake City.

Greyhound (☎800-231-2222; www.greyhound.com) The major long-distance bus company, with routes to Cody, Wyoming, and Bozeman, Montana. Greyhound's Discovery Pass (www. discoverypass.com) can be a good deal for traveling throughout the US and Canada. Passes are valid for anything from one week to two months. Consider purchasing two short-term passes if you're planning to stay in one place a while.

Karst Stage (406-556-3540; www.karststage.com) Airport shuttle service from Bozeman's Gallatin Field to Big Sky and West Yellowstone.

Rimrock Trailways (☎800-255-7655; www.rimrocktrailways .com) This division of Trailways travels to Billings, Montana.

Salt Lake Express (☎800-356-9796; www.saltlakeexpress .com) Daily minibus service to Idaho Falls, Salt Lake City and Boise.

Car & Motorcycle

The quintessential American road trip is practically a right of passage. Despite high fuel costs, this is the way to see the parks. Be aware that soft-shelled vehicles (like Jeeps) do not provide safe storage for food in bear country and parks require vehicles to have proper bear-proof canisters to carry food. Car and motorcycle drivers will need the vehicle's registration papers, liability insurance and an international driving permit or domestic license.

AUTOMOBILE ASSOCIATIONS

The following offer 24-hour roadside assistance, free maps and trip planning help.

American Automobile Association (AAA; ☎800-874-7532; www.aaa.com) The main US auto club. It has reciprocal membership agreements with several international auto clubs (check with AAA and bring your membership card).

Better World Club (☎866-238-1137; www.better worldclub.com) A smaller alternative, which donates 1% of earnings to environmental cleanups and offers ecologically sensitive choices for services.

DRIVER'S LICENSE

Visitors can legally drive in the USA for up to 12 months with their home driver's license. However, an International Driving Permit (IDP) will have more credibility with US traffic police, especially if your home license doesn't have a photo or is in a foreign language. Your automobile association at home can issue an IDP, valid for one year, for a small fee. You must carry your home license together with the IDP.

To ride a motorcycle you need a US state motorcycle license or an IDP appropriate for motorcycles. Helmets are required in most states.

RENTAL

Car rental rates in the towns around Yellowstone vary considerably throughout the year, with summer weekends bringing the highest rates. See the individual towns in the Around Yellowstone and Around Grand Teton chapters for car rental company contact details.

Jackson, Billings, Bozeman and Cody have the best selection of rental companies and thus slightly lower rates. All the airports have car rentals. The major companies are **Hertz** (www.hertz.com), **Avis** (www.avis.com), **Thrifty** (www

.thrifty.com) and **National** (www.nationalcar.com).

While renting an RV can save money in accommodations and dining out, higher RV campsite fees and the cost of gas can quickly negate these savings. Between gas consumption (most RVs average between 5 and 10 miles per gallon) and the electricity they use at campsites, RVs are not exactly a green option, though they can be convenient.

For a range of RVs, **Cruise America** (☎800-671-8042; www.cruiseamerica.com) rents through local dealers in Salt Lake City. Renters face a three-day minimum, and costs for one week start at $1155 for the smallest RV in high season (mid-June to mid-August), not including mileage fees. Summer rentals should be reserved well in advance.

INSURANCE
Don't put the key in the ignition if you don't have auto insurance. In most states it's compulsory; moreover, you risk financial ruin if you have an accident without insurance. If you already have auto insurance, make sure it will cover your rental car. Rental companies provide limited insurance, usually charging extra for collision damage. Check to see if your credit card covers collision damage coverage for rental cars; most do and it saves a bundle of money.

ROAD RULES
Most US natives know that cars drive on the right side of the road, but bear this mind if you're from the UK, Australia, New Zealand or Japan. Seatbelts and child-safety seats are required in every state. The speed limit is generally 65mph to 75mph on western highways, 25mph in cities and 15mph in school zones. Littering brings fines of up to $1000. Most states don't allow you to transport open containers of alcohol, and penalties for driving under the influence of drugs or alcohol (DUI) are severe.

Train
In its heyday the *Union Pacific* pulled right into West Yellowstone and Gardiner; now this social event is preserved as a quaint memory by the local historical society. If you are not intimidated by the fact that the closest passenger trains to this region service destinations over 300 miles away (Denver and Salt Lake City), contact **Amtrak** (☎800-872-7245 www.amtrak.com) for more information.

GETTING AROUND
It's almost impossible to visit Yellowstone without your own vehicle. There's no public transportation of any kind inside the park and only minimal transportation in the gateway corridors. What's surprising is that despite the volume of traffic trundling through the park, there appears to be little movement in the direction of a mass transit system inside the park.

Bicycle
Touring by bicycle is popular, although traveling through Yellowstone National Park presents its own special challenges. Specifically, many riders report that cycling can be very unpleasant due to narrow roads jammed with RVs – whose side mirrors and wide loads present a real danger to the little guy. For more on safe biking, traffic and road conditions, see the Health & Safety chapter (p271).

Cyclists using national-park campgrounds usually pay the same fee as walk-ins, which can be considerably lower than the fee for a vehicle. Mountain biking in areas around the national parks is outstanding; however, bike travel on national-park trails is severely limited and wilderness areas may also have restrictions. Bike shops frequently have group rides and can provide information on local trails. **Better World Club** (☎866-238-1137; www.betterworldclub.com) offers a bicycle roadside assistance program.

Rental
Long-term bike rentals are easy to find; recommended rental shops are listed throughout the guide. Rates run from $100 per week and up, and a credit-card authorization for several hundred

ROAD DISTANCES

CITY	DISTANCE TO YELLOWSTONE (WEST ENTRANCE)
Boston	2450 miles
Chicago	1450 miles
Denver	640 miles
Los Angeles	1010 miles
Miami	2600 miles
New York	2300 miles
Salt Lake City	325 miles
San Francisco	950 miles
Seattle	750 miles
Washington DC	2200 miles

dollars is usually necessary as a security deposit.

Buying a bike and reselling it before you leave may be a more economical option. Check out local yard sales or message boards in local coffee shops for used bikes, and be sure to tune up your ride before hitting the road.

Bus

Although some long-distance touring companies visit the parks, only Jackson has regular bus service.

Yellowstone National Park

Xanterra (☏307-344-7311; www.travelyellowstone.com) Runs interpretive tours that leave from the visitor centers. The Yellowstone in a day tour ($62 adults/$31 children), which starts in Mammoth or Gardiner, is free for kids under eight years old.

Old Yellow Bus tours (☏866-439-7375; 1hr tour adult/child $12/8; ☽Jun-Sep) Reinstate classic vintage vehicles for tours ranging from one hour to all day.

Both services should be reserved in advance.

Grand Teton National Park National Park

Jackson has a free town shuttle that runs every 20 to 30 minutes and the Start Bus (www.startbus.com) public service to Teton Village.

Alltrans Park Shuttle (☏800-443-6133, 307-733-3135; www.alltransparkshuttle.com; daily pass to-from park $12; ☽7am-7pm Jun-Sep) Operates several buses a day in summer between Jackson, Moose, Jenny Lake Lodge, Signal Mountain Lodge, Jackson Lake Lodge and Colter Bay. Riders can pay with cash or credit cards. Rides are unlimited on the daily pass. The service is free for guests of Grand Teton Lodging Company (GTLC) properties. Call

for airport shuttle service (one way from Jackson is $16).

CART (☏208-354-2240) Idaho Falls–based bus services between Jackson and Idaho Falls via Teton Valley.

Jackson Hole Express (☏307-733-1719, 800-443-6133; www.jacksonholebus.com) For regional shuttle service, Alltrans shuttles daily from Jackson to Idaho Falls (one way/round-trip $40/70, 2½ hours), Salt Lake City (one way/round-trip $75/140, 4½ hours) and points in between. Reservations are recommended.

Car & Motorcycle

While drivers in this region tend to be lead-footed on the interstate, traffic in the park is exasperatingly slow, typified by lumbering RVs wheezing over the Continental Divide. At the slightest whiff of a bison or moose, traffic slams to a halt. For this reason, it pays be extra-attentive when driving.

Fuel & Spare Parts

Gas prices inside the park are slightly higher than elsewhere in Wyoming and Montana. Prices rise as you get closer to the park, peaking at Red Lodge and Cooke City. Most gateway towns have an auto-parts store (Napa or Checker) and bicycle shop. Yellowstone has a car-repair garage in Bridge Bay, next to the gas station, but if your car is struggling, it is best to take it to a shop outside the park.

Road Conditions

Harsh winter conditions create frost heaves and potholes that mar even recently repaved roads. Grand Teton National Park's roads are generally in better condition than Yellowstone's. At Yellowstone, there's usually one section of the Grand Loop under construction, causing delays of up to an hour.

Sometimes sections of road are closed between certain hours; make sure you check the parks' newspapers or websites for current road conditions.

For road closures and conditions outside the parks, contact www.fhwa.dot.gov/traffic info/index.htm or state agencies:

Idaho (☏888-432-7326; www.511.idaho.gov)
Montana (☏800-226-7623; www.mdt.mt.gov/travinfo)
Wyoming (☏800-996-7623; www.wyoroad.info)

Road Rules

Practice courteous driving etiquette. If you're driving a slow vehicle, use one of the numerous pullouts to let faster traffic pass. If you don't want your open driver's side door torn off by a passing bus, pull off the road fully when watching wildlife. Wildlife always has the right of way.

Speed limits in the park are generally 45mph, dropping to 25mph or less at popular pullouts or junctions. Hwy 191 in Grand Teton National Park has a limit of 55mph. Roads outside the park generally have limits between 55mph and 65mph, with highways up to 65mph or 75mph.

The use of seat belts and child-safety seats is required. On motorcycles, helmets are required for anyone under 18 in Montana and Idaho or under 19 in Wyoming.

Road Hazards

Every year hundreds of wild animals meet their fate on the grill of a car. Keep an eye out for crossing animals and drive with particular care at dawn and dusk.

Higher-risk areas have signs marked with a deer, though all areas, even those outside the park, may have animals crossing. Bison should be passed very carefully – they are not nearly as passive as cattle.

Hitchhiking

Hitchhiking is potentially dangerous and not recommended. While it is prohibited on highways, you'll see more people hitchhiking (and stopping) on rural roads, especially near hiking trailheads.

If you are hiking a long loop, it's sometimes difficult to encounter a ride for those last few road miles, although more likely at the most popular trailheads.

You can check ride-share boards at ranger stations and in hostels.

Snowcoach Tours

In Yellowstone National Park only, converted vans on snow tracks provide transportation in and around the park in winter, also providing a useful service for skiers. Snowcoach tours depart daily from West Yellowstone (p169), Flagg Ranch Resort (p202), Wapiti Valley and Mammoth; most stop at Old Faithful and all stop for wildlife-watching opportunities. **Xanterra** (www.travel yellowstone.com; prices from $55) operates park-based tours. Other operators are listed in the Around Yellowstone chapter.

Tours

Buffalo Bus Co (☑406-646-9353, 800-426-7669; www .yellowstonevacations.com/ yellowstone-park-tours/ buffalo-bus-tours; both loops adult/teen $120/98) Northern or southern loops of Yellow-stone from West Yellowstone; free pickup from hotels or campgrounds.

Flagg Ranch (☑800-443-2311; www.flaggranch.com; full-day tour $225) Visits Yellowstone.

Grand Teton Lodge Company (☑800-628-9988; www .gtlc.com; tour $45) Half-day Grand Teton tours, full-day tours of Yellowstone or a combination of both parks.

Gray Line National Park Tours (☑307-733-3135, 800-443-6133; www.graylinejh.com; full day adult/child $100/50) Full-day park tours from Jackson.

Xanterra (www.gtlc.com) Yellowstone concessionaire offering coach tours, including the classic Old Yellow Bus, wildlife-viewing and photography, plus transport and accommodation packages.

Health & Safety

Keeping healthy depends on your predeparture preparations, your daily health care while traveling and how you handle any medical problems that develop. While the potential problems can seem daunting, in reality few visitors experience anything worse than a skinned knee. Read this chapter in preparation.

BEFORE YOU GO

The best preparation for a hiking vacation is to embark on some regular, dedicated exercise at least three weeks prior to travel. To lessen the chances of getting sore shoulders, blisters and foot fatigue, wear in your boots thoroughly by undertaking long walks with a loaded pack. You can also try out different pack adjustments, socks and footwear.

Those coming from sea level should wait several days after arriving before undertaking any strenuous activity at altitude. Prepare your metabolism for acclimation to the higher elevations by drinking more water and laying off the alcohol.

Medical Checklist

First-aid kits should include:
» acetaminophen (paracetamol) or aspirin
» adhesive or paper tape
» antibacterial ointment for cuts and abrasions
» antibiotics
» anti-diarrhea drugs (eg loperamide)
» anti-inflammatory drugs (eg ibuprofen)
» antihistamines (for hay fever and allergic reactions)
» bandages, gauze swabs, gauze rolls and safety pins
» insect repellent with DEET
» iodine tablets or water filter (for water purification)
» moleskin (to prevent chafing of blisters)
» non-adhesive dressing
» oral rehydration salts
» paper stitches
» pocket knife
» reverse syringe (for snakebites)
» scissors, safety pins, tweezers
» sterile alcohol wipes
» steroid cream or cortizone (for allergic rashes)
» sticking plasters (Band-Aids)
» sunscreen and lip balm
» thermometer

Further Reading

If you're hiking in remote areas, consider the following detailed health guides:
» *NOLS Wilderness Medicine* by Tod Schimelpfenig and Joan Safford prepares you for just about any major or minor medical emergency in the outdoors.
» *Medicine for the Outdoors* by Paul Auerbach is a general reference with brief explanations of many medical problems and practical treatment options.
» *Wilderness 911* by Eric A Weiss is a step-by-step guide to first aid and advanced care in remote areas with limited medical supplies and no professional help.

IN THE PARKS

Availability & Cost of Health Care

Health-care costs will vary widely depending on your insurance. Be sure to travel with your insurance card and know the co-payments and conditions of coverage before traveling.

Yellowstone National Park

Yellowstone Park Medical Services operates three clinics:
Lake Hospital (☑307-242-7241; ◉8:30am-8:30pm mid-May–mid-Sep) Has a 24-hour

---

EMERGENCIES

In an emergency of any sort dial ☑911. If you need to contact friends or family, emergency messages can be posted at the parks' entry stations and at visitor centers.

BEARS IN THE PARKS

TYPE	COLOR	BODY	FACE	TRACKS	AGILITY
Grizzly Bears	blonde to black	larger with distinctive shoulder hump	dish-shaped face with short, rounded ears	long, straight front claws (2–4in)	can't climb trees well
Black Bears	blonde to black	no shoulder hump	straight profile from nose to ears; tall, pointed ears	short, curved front claws (1–2in)	climb trees

emergency service through 📞911.

Mammoth Clinic (📞307-344-7965; ⊙8:30am-5pm) The only year-round clinic.

NPS emergency medics (📞307-344-2132) On call 24 hours a day, year-round. First aid is available at visitor centers and ranger stations. In an emergency, call 📞911. Emergency messages can be left on boards at park entrances and visitor centers.

Old Faithful Clinic (📞307-545-7325; ⊙7am-7pm mid-May–mid-Sep)

Grand Teton National Park

Grand Teton Medical Clinic (📞307-543-2514, 307-733-8002; ⊙10am-6pm mid-May–mid-Oct) Near Jackson Lake Lodge.

Infectious Diseases

Amoebic Dysentery

Fluid replacement is the mainstay of management for serious diarrhea. Weak black tea with a little sugar, soda water or soft drink allowed to go flat and 50% diluted with water are all good. With severe diarrhea, a rehydrating solution is necessary to replace minerals and salts. Commercially available oral rehydration salts (ORS) are very useful. You should stick to a bland diet as you recover.

Lyme Disease

A bacterial infection, in the Rocky Mountains Lyme disease is mainly transmitted by the deer (wood) tick. Although the number of cases reported in the US has skyrocketed during the last two decades, Lyme disease remains relatively uncommon over large parts of the Rockies. Early symptoms, which may take months to develop, are similar to influenza – headaches, stiff neck, tiredness and painful swelling of the joints. If left untreated, complications such as meningitis, facial palsy or heart abnormalities may occur, but fatalities are rare. A safe vaccination is not yet available, but Lyme disease responds well to antibiotics.

West Nile Disease

Unknown in the United States until a few years ago, this disease has now been reported in almost all 50 states. It's transmitted by culex mosquitoes, which are active in late summer and early fall, and generally bite after dusk. Most infections are mild or asymptomatic, but the virus may infect the central nervous system, leading to fever, headache, confusion, lethargy, coma and sometimes death. There is no treatment for West Nile virus. See currently affected areas at the US Geological Survey website (http://west nilemaps.usgs.gov/).

Environmental Hazards

Altitude

In the thinner atmosphere of the Rockies, a lack of oxygen may cause headaches, nausea, nosebleeds, shortness of breath, physical weakness and other symptoms. These can lead to serious consequences, especially if combined with heat exhaustion, sunburn or hypothermia. Most people adjust to altitude within a few hours or days. Be careful (especially with children) when driving and overnighting on the Beartooth Plateau, where altitudes reach 10,000ft. In mild cases of altitude sickness, everyday painkillers such as aspirin may relieve discomfort. If symptoms persist, descend to lower elevations.

COMMON AILMENTS

Fatigue Stay within your capabilities, take breaks and eat properly.

Blisters Wear broken-in boots and moisture-wicking socks, and carry special blister bandages.

Knee pain Use hiking poles and descend with shorter steps without twisting or hyperextending your foot.

Bears

Bears live a sedentary life and will typically avoid contact if given sufficient warning of an approaching individual. Yet travelers need to be bear aware. The main causes of human-bear conflict include the animal's instinctual protection of its young, the presence of food and surprise encounters. In July 2011, a man was killed when he surprised a female with her cubs. In the same summer, a grizzly fatally attacked a lone hiker on an infrequently used trail for unknown reasons. In Yellowstone history, the year of 2011 was unique, since very high snowpack meant spring conditions (with high bear activity) in mid-summer, which increased human encounters. Hikers should follow all suggested precautions. But remember, there's a 1 in 3-million chance of being attacked by a grizzly in Yellowstone.

BEARS & HIKING

When hiking in grizzly country, always stay alert and make plenty of noise on the trail. Never hike after dusk. While grizzlies have a highly acute sense of smell, they may not catch your scent if you approach from downwind. Some hikers wear 'bear bells' to announce their approach, but bears are better able to hear deeper sounds like shouting or clapping. The human voice is effective: while some prefer a medley of show tunes, many shout, 'Hey Bear!' when approaching a blind corner.

Here's some advice if you happen to encounter a bear at close range:

» Do not run – bears can easily outrun humans and will instinctively pursue a fleeing animal.

» Do not drop your pack as a decoy – this may teach the bear that threatening humans is a good way to get food.

» Back away slowly, talking soothingly to the bear while avoiding direct eye contact.

» Bears very often 'bluff charge' an intruder, veering away at the last instant.

Using a pepper spray (see p274) may deter a charging bear, but here's what to do if an attack does ensue:

» If the attack is imminent, play dead.

» Lie down and pull your knees against your chest, and (if not wearing a large backpack) pull in your head and shield your neck with your hands.

» In most cases the bear will eventually leave the scene once assured that you present no danger.

» In extremely rare cases, grizzly bears with clear predatory intent have attacked humans. Such attacks tend to occur around campsites at dusk or during the night, and are the only time when you should fight back against an aggressive grizzly.

BEARS & FOOD

Bears are obsessed with food and rarely 'unlearn' knowledge acquired in finding it. In the past, Yellowstone's bears were regularly fed and given access to garbage dumps while tourists watched in grandstand seating. While this tradition no longer continues, visitors are unnecessarily careless and the problem persists. Conditioned to associate humans with food, large numbers of 'habituated' bears have harassed picnickers or aggressively raided camps. Nowadays, even mildly troublesome bears are usually destroyed. Don't let your carelessness result in the death of one of these magnificent creatures.

» Never leave food unattended, even in a backpack.

» Use the bear boxes at developed campgrounds or lock food in your car.

» Never store food or eat in your tent.

» Don't sleep in clothes worn while fishing or cooking.

» Don't camp downwind of your food stash.

In Yellowstone National Park, backcountry campers must hang food and scented items such as garbage, toothpaste, soap and sunscreen at least 10ft above the ground, 4ft from trunks and 200ft from their tents. Carry a robust stuff-sack attached to a 35ft length of rope. First weight the sack with a rock and throw it over a high, sturdy limb at least 4ft from the tree trunk. Gently lower the sack to the ground with the rope, stash everything with food smells and perfumes, and then pull the sack back up close to the tree limb. Finally, tie off the end of the rope to another trunk or tree limb well out of the way. Backcountry campgrounds usually supply a food pole, which simplifies the process.

In Grand Teton National Park, the park regulations have changed. Hanging food is no longer a prerequisite; instead, backpackers must purchase and use approved bear-resistant canisters. Backcountry permitting locations have these available for free.

Bison, Moose, Mountain Lions & Wolves

One of the memorable sights in Yellowstone is watching an amateur photographer encourage their loved one to edge toward a seemingly tame, fuzzy bison for an exclusive photo op. These 2-ton creatures can sprint at 30mph and have actually harmed more visitors than bears have.

Moose usually flee intruding humans but if a moose feels cornered or otherwise threatened, it may suddenly charge. Moose cows with calves are especially dangerous, as they will aggressively defend their young. Moose can inflict severe injuries by

USING PEPPER SPRAY

» Pepper sprays' effectiveness in deterring charging or attacking bears remains controversial, but experts agree they are a useful last line of defense. Remember that carrying pepper spray is not a substitute for vigilance or other safety precautions – always keep a distance of 300ft if you see a bear. Spray is sold in backpacking stores (for around $55).

Spray Requirements

» Buy a minimum size of 7.9oz (225g)
» Concentration should be 1.4% to 1.8% capsaicin
» Spray jet should reach 30ft

Proper Use

» Carry within easy and immediate reach – not in your pack
» Wait for the bear to be in close range to use
» Aim spray toward the ground
» Make sure you are not downwind

striking out with their powerful front hoofs.

Your chances of encountering an aggressive mountain lion remain extremely small, but as humans encroach on their territory attacks appear to be on the increase. Avoid hiking alone in prime mountain-lion habitats. Keep children within view at all times. If you happen to encounter a mountain lion, raise your arms and back away slowly. Speak firmly or shout. If attacked, fight back fiercely.

There have been no reliable documented cases of fatal wolf attacks on humans for more than a century. Attacks on humans by wild wolves are believed to be attributable to either rabies infection or habituation – when a wolf has lost its fear of people.

If you stay aware and keep a respectful distance from all wildlife, most encounters will be avoided.

Bites & Stings
LEECHES
Sometimes present in lakes, leeches attach themselves to your skin to suck your blood. Salt or a lit cigarette end will make them fall off. Do not pull them off, as the bite is then more likely to become infected. Clean and apply pressure if the point of attachment is bleeding.

MOSQUITOES
Mosquitoes can be a major irritant in early and midsummer (until around mid-August), so remember to carry mosquito repellent. The most effective sprays contain DEET (the higher the percentage of DEET, the more effective the spray). DEET is powerful stuff and should be kept away from plastics. Citronella is a kinder (to the skin at least) alternative.

SNAKES & SPIDERS
In the history of the park there have been only two recorded snakebites. The prairie rattlesnake is the only poisonous snake in the region, found in the driest and warmest river areas of Yellowstone. There are some spiders with dangerous bites but antivenoms are usually available.

For snakebites, immediately apply a reverse syringe (Sawyer Extractor). Keep the victim calm and still, wrap the bitten limb tightly and immobilize with a splint. Get the victim to a doctor as soon as possible.

TICKS
Ticks may be present from mid-March through July. Always check all over your body if you have been walking through a potentially tick-infested area, as ticks can cause skin infections and other more serious diseases. Ticks are most active from spring to autumn, especially where there are plenty of sheep or deer. They usually lurk in overhanging vegetation, so avoid pushing through tall bushes if possible.

To remove, press down around the tick's head with tweezers, grab the head and gently pull upward; avoid pulling the rear of the body. Smearing chemicals is not recommended.

Cold
HYPOTHERMIA
This occurs when the body loses heat faster than it can produce it and the core temperature of the body falls.

It is frighteningly easy to progress from very cold to dangerously cold due to a combination of wind, wet clothing, fatigue and hunger, even if the air temperature is above freezing. If the weather deteriorates, put on extra layers: a wind and/or waterproof jacket, plus a wool or fleece hat and gloves are all essential. Have something energy-rich to eat and ensure that everyone in your group is fit, feeling well and alert.

Symptoms of hypothermia are exhaustion, numb skin (particularly toes and fingers), shivering, slurred speech, irrational or violent behavior, lethargy, stumbling, dizzy spells, muscle cramps and violent bursts of energy. Irrationality may take the form of sufferers claiming they are warm and trying to take off their clothes.

The early recognition and treatment of mild hypothermia is the only way to prevent severe hypothermia, which is a critical condition.

For mild hypothermia, get the person out of the elements, remove clothing if it's wet and replace it with dry, warm clothing. Give hot liquids (not alcohol) and high-energy, easily digestible food. Allow the victim to slowly warm – don't rub.

FROSTBITE

This refers to the freezing of extremities, including fingers, toes and the nose. Pain and swelling are inevitable. Signs of frostbite include a whitish or waxy cast to the skin, or even crystals on the surface, plus itching, numbness and pain.

For frostbite, warm affected areas by immersion in warm (not hot) water or warm with blankets or clothes (only until skin becomes flushed). Frostbitten parts should not be rubbed, and blisters should not be broken. Get medical attention right away.

Heat

DEHYDRATION & HEAT EXHAUSTION

Dehydration is a potentially dangerous and generally preventable condition caused by excessive fluid loss. Sweating combined with inadequate fluid intake is one of the most common causes of dehydration in trekkers, but other important causes are diarrhea, vomiting and high fever – see Amoebic Dysentery (p272) for more details about appropriate treatment in these circumstances.

The first symptoms are weakness, thirst and passing small amounts of very concentrated urine. This may progress to drowsiness, dizziness or fainting on standing up, and, finally, coma.

It's easy to forget how much fluid you are losing via perspiration while you are trekking, particularly if a strong breeze is drying your skin quickly. You should always maintain a good fluid intake – a minimum of 3L a day is recommended.

Dehydration and salt deficiency can cause heat exhaustion. Salt deficiency is characterized by fatigue, lethargy, headaches, giddiness and muscle cramps. Salt tablets are overkill; just adding extra salt to your food is probably sufficient.

HEATSTROKE

This is a serious, occasionally fatal, condition that occurs if the body's heat-regulating mechanism breaks down and the body temperature rises to dangerous levels. Long, continuous periods of exposure to high temperatures and insufficient fluids can leave you vulnerable to heatstroke.

The symptoms include feeling unwell, not sweating very much (or at all) and a high body temperature ($102°F$ to $106°F$ or $39°C$ to $41°C$). Where sweating has ceased, the skin becomes flushed and red. Severe, throbbing headaches and lack of coordination will also occur, and the sufferer may be confused or aggressive. Eventually the victim will become delirious or convulse.

Hospitalization is essential but in the meantime get victims out of the sun, remove their clothing, cover them with a wet sheet or towel and then fan continually. Give fluids if they are conscious.

Snow Blindness

This is a temporary painful condition resulting from sunburn of the surface of the eye (cornea). It usually occurs when someone walks on snow or in bright sunshine without sunglasses.

Treatment is to relieve the pain – cold cloths on closed eyelids may help. Antibiotic and anesthetic eye drops are not necessary. The condition usually resolves itself within

---

GEOTHERMALS

You'll see plenty of signs warning you to stay on existing boardwalks and maintain a safe distance from all geothermal features. Thin crusts of earth can break, giving way to boiling water. Even warm springs can be dangerous; temperatures often fluctuate, sometimes dramatically, so what is safe one day may not be safe the next. About 20 people have died in Yellowstone's hot springs since the 1880s; some have backed into hot springs while taking photos, and more than one unknowing pet has jumped into a boiling pool.

The park service warns that spring waters can cause a rash and that thermophilic amoebas in the water can transmit amoebic meningitis (though there are no recorded cases). If you do swim in any of the areas mentioned in this guide, keep your head above the surface and don't take in any water.

a few days and there are no long-term consequences.

Sun

Protection against the sun should always be taken seriously. Sunburn occurs rapidly in the rarified air and deceptive coolness of the mountains. Slap on the sunscreen and a barrier cream for your nose and lips, wear a broad-brimmed hat and protect your eyes with good-quality sunglasses with UV lenses, particularly near water, sand or snow. If you get sunburned, calamine lotion, aloe vera or other commercial sunburn-relief preparations will soothe.

SAFE HIKING

For more suggestions on hiking safely, see p31.

Trail Safety Tips

» Allow plenty of time to accomplish a walk before dark, particularly when daylight hours are shorter.

» Study the route carefully before setting out, noting possible alternate routes and the point of no return (where it's quicker to continue than to turn back). Monitor your progress against the time estimated for the walk, and keep an eye on the weather.

» It's wise not to walk alone. Always leave details of your intended route, the number of people in your group and the expected return time with someone responsible before you set off; later announce your return.

» Before setting off, make sure you have a relevant map, compass and whistle, and that you know the weather forecast for the area for the next 24 hours.

» Be aware of whether the trail should be climbing or descending.

» Check the north-point arrow on the map and determine the general direction of the trail.

» Time your progress over a known distance to monitor further progress with reasonable accuracy.

» Watch the path – look for boot prints and other signs of previous passage.

Crossing Streams

Sudden downpours are common in the mountains and can speedily turn a gentle stream into a raging torrent. If you're in any doubt about the safety of a crossing, look for a safer passage upstream or wait. If the rain is short-lived, it should subside quickly. Late in the day, crossing may be essential.

» Look for a wide, shallower stretch (not a bend).

» Keep boots on to prevent injury.

» Store clothes and a towel in a plastic bag near the top of your pack.

» Unclip the chest strap and belt buckle of your pack (in case you have to swim).

» Use a hiking pole, grasped in both hands, on the upstream side as a third leg.

» With a companion, clasp at the wrist and cross side-on to the flow in short steps.

Fire

Fire danger in the Rockies varies from year to year, but is often extreme in July and August. Local park and USFS offices can advise hikers about forest fires, and fire warnings are usually posted at wilderness access points. For fire updates contact the parks at ☎307-739-3300, stop at a visitor center or check out their websites. Also contact the **National Interagency Fire Center** (☎208-387-5050; www.nifc.gov).

Lightning

Getting struck by lightning during a summer afternoon storm is a real possibility. Your best bet is to undertake long hikes early. Follow these tips during lightning storms:

» Avoid exposed ridges, open areas and lone trees.

SAFE WATER

Giardia

» This microscopic, waterborne parasite causes intestinal disorders.

» Symptoms – which can appear weeks after exposure – include chronic diarrhea, cramps, bloating and appalling gas.

» See a doctor if you have symptoms. Treatment requires a course of antibiotics.

Prevention

» Don't drink any snowmelt, stream, lake or ground water without filtering it.

» Boiling water for 10 minutes is effective against most microbes *except* giardia.

» Use a filter at 0.5 microns or smaller, a Steripen or treat with water tablets.

BEAR JAMS

For some reason, perfectly reasonable adults lose all their sense when sighting wildlife: it's happened to us and it will probably happen to you. Rubbernecking at wildlife doesn't just cause traffic jams; along with speeding, it's the main cause of more than 600 annual vehicular accidents in Yellowstone. Trust us when we tell you, the bear, bison or moose you're stalking won't be the last one you see in the park. If you absolutely must get that rutting elk snapshot, pull completely off the road. If there's no room to park, just wait for a better opportunity.

Also, vehicles dispatch about 100 animals a year in Yellowstone, so watch your speed and the road, especially at dusk.

» Move away from bodies of water or beaches.

» If camping, crouch on a sleeping pad with your arms around your knees.

Rockfall

Even a small falling rock could shatter your hand or crack your skull, so always be alert to the danger of rockfall. Don't dally below cliffs or on trails fringed by large fields of raw talus. If you accidentally let a rock loose, loudly warn other hikers below. Mountain goats and bighorn sheep sometimes dislodge rocks, so be vigilant.

Rescue & Evacuation

Search-and-rescue operations are expensive and often require emergency personnel to risk their own welfare. Self-evacuation should be your first consideration.

For serious accidents or illness, seek help, but don't leave the injured party alone. If that's impossible, leave sufficient warm clothing, food and water. Leave a whistle and flashlight, and mark the position with something conspicuous.

SAFE CYCLING

Bicycles are subject to the same traffic rules as cars. While cycling is permitted on established public roads, parking areas and designated routes, it is prohibited on backcountry trails and boardwalks.

Yellowstone is not an easy place to bike. Road shoulders are slim and many a cyclist has been threatened by an encroaching RV mirror. Cyclists must be very aware. For this reason, it's best to bike early in the morning or after 6:30pm when traffic thins out. Drivers sometimes pass on hill crests, blind curves or in oncoming traffic. Wearing a helmet and using high-visibility clothing and mirrors is essential. Never use headphones while cycling.

Bison may be a hazard to cyclists. If you come upon some, dismount and walk far around them or wait for a vehicle to drive through (the bison will follow it).

Visitor centers will have additional information. For more cycling suggestions, see p31.

Road Conditions

Use extreme caution when cycling in the park; roads are winding and narrow, and shoulders are either narrow or nonexistent. Vehicle traffic is heavy most of the time. There are no bicycle paths along roads.

Road elevations range from 5300ft to 8860ft, and services and facilities are relatively far apart – typically 20 to 30 miles.

Cyclists should take advantage of shoulder seasons. A great time to bike is between October and mid-November, when there is little traffic and less wind. Springtime cyclists can enjoy some roads closed to motorized vehicles. While roads are plowed and summer preparations are made, cycling is permitted between the West Entrance and Mammoth Hot Springs from about mid-March (weather allowing) through to the third Thursday in April. Note that high snow banks from April to June can make travel more dangerous. August is typically the windiest month.

General road closures are posted at www.nps.gov/yell/planyourvisit/open_close dates.htm.

Clothing & Equipment

It takes a masterful plan to sort out what clothing and equipment is indispensable for a trip and what will become only a needless addition to an already brimming backpack. Those overnighting on the trail should pay special mind to dividing their belongings into necessities and luxuries. Weigh the benefits of a freshly laundered shirt versus an achy back and you will see why most experienced backpackers choose to harmonize with the riper smells of nature.

Make sure you devote adequate time to this phase of trip planning. Sampling the load beforehand and using a checklist can help.

CLOTHING

The Right Layers

In the mountains layering is essential. Be prepared for changeable weather, including flash thunderstorms and frosts even in summer.

Synthetic, silk or wool base layers (not cotton) are the most effective. Depending on the weather, thermal underwear, wind pants or waterproof shell pants (for winter conditions) may be appropriate. Rain gear should be light, breathable and waterproof. A rain jacket and rain pants are recommended for fall through spring conditions. In cooler weather, wear over an insulating layer, usually fleece, down or wool.

Prepare for wind and cooler temperatures above the tree line. Even on a cloudless summer day, it's smart to pack a shell jacket and a knit cap.

Footwear & Socks

Light to medium hiking boots are recommended for day hikes, while sturdy boots are necessary for demanding hikes or extended trips with a heavy pack. Most important, they should be well broken in with a nonslip (such as Vibram) sole.

Snow persists in spring and early summer, so use waterproof boots then. In mid-summer, running or hiking shoes can work for easier hikes in dry conditions.

Buy boots in warm conditions and walk around while trying them on. Save your feet from soaking and carry sandals to ford rivers and wear at night.

Synthetic and wool-blend hiking socks are the most practical option. They should be free of ridged seams in the toes and heels.

EQUIPMENT

Backpacks & Daypacks

For day hikes, daypacks (30L to 40L) will usually suffice, but multiday hikes require an internal frame pack (45L to 90L). Line with heavy-duty liners or a trash bag.

Tents & Tarps

A three-season tent will suffice in most conditions. The floor and the fly should have taped or sealed seams and covered zips to stop leaks. Weight ranges from 1kg for a stripped-down, low-profile tent to 3kg for a roomy four-season model.

Dome- and tunnel-shaped tents handle blustery conditions better than flat-sided tents. Bring a tarp and short lengths of rope to make a covered cook shelter in rain.

Sleeping Bags & Mats

Goosedown bags are warm, lightweight and compact but useless if they get wet. Synthetic bags are cheaper and better wet, but bulkier. Mummy-shaped designs prove best for weight and warmth. The rating (-5°C, for instance) is the coldest temperature at which a person should feel comfortable in the bag. For extra warmth, purchase a liner.

Self-inflating sleeping mats provide comfort and insulate from the cold. Foam mats are low-cost but less comfortable.

Stoves & Fuel

When buying a stove, think lightweight and easy to operate. Most outdoors stores sell and rent stoves. Butane stoves are the easiest to operate. Multifuel stoves are versatile but need pumping, priming and lots of cleaning.

In general, liquid fuels are efficient and cheap; look for high-performance, cleaner-burning fuel. Gas is more expensive, cleaner and a reasonable performer. When using canisters be sure to pack yours out. Fuel can be found at outdoor gear shops, hardware stores (white gas) and some supermarkets.

Airlines prohibit flammable materials and may well reject empty liquid-fuel bottles or even the stoves themselves.

Water Purifiers & Tablets

Mountain streams may look crystal clear, but with the prevalence of bacteriological contamination, sipping from the source has become a thing of the past. Boiling water rapidly for 10 minutes is effective, but uses precious fuel.

When buying a filter, note that giardia requires a filter with a rating of 1.0 to 4.0 microns and *E Coli* requires a microfilter rating 0.2 to 1.0 microns. When filtering, go for clear water in the current of a stream instead of stagnant water and avoid silty water. A Steripen (laser-based purifier) is a useful alternative.

The two-step iodine tablets come with a neutralizing tablet that improves the taste. If you don't plan to be in the backcountry often, these tablets are the most convenient solution.

For more on water safety and purification, see the boxed text p276.

Buying & Renting Locally

A hotbed for outdoor-gear innovation and consumption, the Rocky Mountain area offers high-quality products, though in-park selection is usually poor.

All winter resorts have good rental shops with ski, snowboard and Nordic equipment, as well as mountain bikes in summer. Most have a program to 'demo' new equipment models.

More listings can be found in town sections.

Grand Teton National Park & Around

Outside the park, Jackson Hole has a number of outdoor shops selling and renting gear.

NAVIGATION EQUIPMENT

Maps & Compass

You should always carry a good area topographical map and know how to read it properly. Before setting off, familiarize yourself with the contour interval, the map symbols and the magnetic declination (difference between true and grid north), plus the main ridge and river systems in the area and the general direction in which you are heading. On the trail, try to identify major landforms such as mountain ranges and valleys, and locate them on your map.

Compasses require some knowledge and practice. The attraction of magnetic north varies in different parts of the world, so compasses need to be balanced accordingly. Compass manufacturers have divided the world into five zones: have yours balanced for your destination zone. There are some 'universal' compasses on the market, which can be used anywhere in the world.

How to Use a Compass

For simplicity, this basic introduction doesn't take magnetic variation into account. Before using a compass we recommend you get further instruction.

READING A COMPASS

Hold the compass flat in the palm of your hand. Rotate the bezel so the red end of the needle points to the N (north point) on the bezel. The bearing is read from the dash under the bezel.

ORIENTING THE MAP

To orient the map so that it aligns with the ground, place the compass flat on the map. Rotate the map until the needle is parallel with the map's north–south grid lines and the red end is pointing to north on the map. You can now identify features around you by aligning them with labeled features on the map.

TAKING A BEARING FROM THE MAP

Draw a line on the map between your starting point and your destination. Place the edge of the compass on this line with the direction of travel arrow pointing towards your destination. Rotate the bezel until the meridian lines are parallel with the north–south grid lines on the map and the N points to north on the map. Read the bearing from the dash.

Adventure Sports OUTDOOR GEAR
(☎307-733-3307; Moose Village, WY; ☺9am-7pm) Rents kayaks ($48 per day), mountain and road bikes ($36 to $48 per day), as well as kids' bikes and racks, with discounted weekly rates. Winter rentals include Nordic skis, snowshoes and sleds.

Colter Bay Marina BOAT RENTAL
(☎307-543-2811; ☺8am-5pm) Rents motorboats ($35/175 per hour/day), rowboats and canoe rentals ($15 to $17 per hour).

Moosely Mountaineering OUTDOOR GEAR
(☎307-733-6094; Moose Village, WY; ☺8am-7pm) At Dornan's, sells mountaineering and camping equipment. Rentals include rock-climbing shoes ($7 per day), snowshoes ($15) and poles ($6), with discounted weekly rates.

Signal Mountain Marina BOAT RENTAL
(☎307-543-2831; ☺7am-7:30pm mid-May–early Sep) Rents canoes ($17/85 per hour/day), kayaks ($15/79), motorboats ($36/175) and pontoon cruisers ($80/480).

Skinny Skis OUTDOOR GEAR
(☎307-733-6094; 65 W Deloney Ave, Jackson) A top Nordic shop that also rents sleeping bags ($5), backpacks ($5) and tents ($10).

Snake River Angler OUTDOOR GEAR
(☎307-733-3699, 800-998-7688; Moose Village, WY; ☺7am-7pm) Sells and rents fly rods and reels, offers fishing licenses and guided trips.

Yellowstone National Park & Around

This list is partial. Kayak rentals are available in Cody, Jackson and Gardiner; ski and snowshoe rentals are available at ski centers and

FOLLOWING A BEARING

Rotate the bezel so that the intended bearing is in line with the dash. Place the compass flat in the palm of your hand and rotate the base plate until the red end points to N on the bezel. The direction of travel arrow will now point in the direction you need to walk.

DETERMINING YOUR BEARING

Rotate the bezel so the red end points to the N. Place the compass flat in the palm of your hand and rotate the base plate until the direction of travel arrow points in the direction in which you have been walking. Read your bearing from the dash.

GPS

Originally developed by the US Department of Defense, the Global Positioning System (GPS) is a network of more than 20 earth-orbiting satellites that continually beam encoded signals back to earth. Small, computer-driven devices (GPS receivers) can decode these signals to give users an extremely accurate reading of their location – to within 10m, anywhere on the planet, at any time of day, in almost any weather. The cheapest hand-held GPS receivers now cost less than $100 (although these may not have a built-in averaging system that minimizes signal errors). When purchasing, also consider a GPS receiver's weight and battery life.

A GPS receiver is useful only when used with an accurate topographical map. The receiver gives your position, which you must then locate on the local map. GPS receivers only work properly in the open. The signals from a crucial satellite may be blocked (or bounce off rock or water) directly below high cliffs, near large bodies of water or in dense tree cover and give inaccurate readings. GPS receivers are more vulnerable to breakdowns (including dead batteries) than the humble magnetic compass – a low-tech device that has served navigators faithfully for centuries – so don't rely on them entirely.

Altimeter

An altimeter gives one piece of information: the elevation. Watch altimeters can be easier to use than traditional models with a needle and dial. They help keep track of your progress and pinpoint your location on the map. By noting the elevation of points along the way, it is easier to find these unmarked places again. It is also useful to note progress: if in the first hour you gained 800ft and only 500ft in the second, you can predict your pace for the next 1000ft of a steady slope with better accuracy. And if you summit a peak in the clouds, it's one way to be sure you've truly arrived!

popular Nordic locations like West Yellowstone.

Absaroka
Bicycles　　　BICYCLE RENTAL
(☎307-527-5566; 2201 17th Street, K-mart Plaza, Cody, WY; ◎10am-6pm Mon-Sat) Offers riders tips, rentals and repairs.

Bear Den Bike BICYCLE RENTAL
(Old Faithful Snow Lodge, Yellowstone National Park) This small booth inside the hotel's gift shop at Old Faithful rents out kids' and adults' bikes during the summer, and snowshoes, skis and other equipment in the winter.

Bridge Bay
Marina　　　　BOAT RENTAL
(☎307-242-3880; ◎8am-8pm mid-Jun–early Sep) Rowboat ($10/45 per hour/day) and outboard ($47 per hour) rentals.

Free Heel &
Wheel　　　OUTDOOR GEAR
(☎406-646-7744; www.free heelandwheel.com; 40 Yellowstone Ave, West Yellowstone, MT; ◎9am-8pm Mon-Sat, 9am-7pm Sun) Rents mountain bikes ($25 per day), skis ($20 per day) and snowshoes ($15), and offers touring, skate-ski lessons and free women's rides.

Lava Creek
Adventures　　KAYAK RENTAL
(☎reservations only 406-209-7452; www.paddleonadventures .com; West Yellowstone area) Rents canoes and sit-on-top kayaks with lifejackets and paddles.

REI　　　　OUTDOOR GEAR
(☎406-587-1938; www.rei .com/bozeman; 2220 Tschache St, Bozeman) Yellowstone topo maps, backpacking rentals and popular weekly talks/workshops.

Sunlight
Sports　　　OUTDOOR GEAR
(☎307-578-9517; www.sunlight sports.com; 1131 Sheridan Ave, Cody WY) Cody's best gear shop also offers rentals.

behind the scenes

SEND US YOUR FEEDBACK

We love to hear from travelers – your comments keep us on our toes and help make our books better. Our well-traveled team reads every word on what you loved or loathed about this book. Although we cannot reply individually to postal submissions, we always guarantee that your feedback goes straight to the appropriate authors, in time for the next edition. Each person who sends us information is thanked in the next edition – and the most useful submissions are rewarded with a free book.

Visit **lonelyplanet.com/contact** to submit your updates and suggestions or to ask for help. Our award-winning website also features inspirational travel stories, news and discussions.

Note: We may edit, reproduce and incorporate your comments in Lonely Planet products such as guidebooks, websites and digital products, so let us know if you don't want your comments reproduced or your name acknowledged. For a copy of our privacy policy visit lonelyplanet.com/privacy.

OUR READERS

Many thanks to the travelers who used the last edition and wrote to us with helpful hints, useful advice and interesting anecdotes:
Emma Leung, Robin Muskal, Rose Shirey

AUTHOR THANKS

Bradley Mayhew

Carolyn McCarthy was a great coauthor and helped with all parts of the text. Thanks to Kirsten Rawlings and Kathleen Munnelly for much style assistance. Thanks to Kelli for helping me test restaurants across the Yellowstone region.

Carolyn McCarthy

Many thanks go out to friends who helped support my trip and writing process, especially Claire, who will never again sing 'Yellow Submarine.' Once again, working with Bradley Mayhew has been a pleasure. I am particularly grateful to Jenny Anzelmo-Sarles and Jackie Skaggs at the park offices, plus Christian Santelices and Eric Henderson. The Climbers' Ranch continues to be an incredible resource. I heartily thank God for my hand-me-down pillow, and the staff and co-campers who shared both tips and time. My gratitude also goes to Drew Hardesty and the elusive Black George, an inspiration in absentia.

ACKNOWLEDGMENTS

Climate map data adapted from Peel MC, Finlayson BL & McMahon TA (2007) 'Updated World Map of the Köppen-Geiger Climate Classification', *Hydrology and Earth System Sciences,* 11, 163344.

Cover photograph: Snake River slithers through an autumnal aspen grove, Grand Teton NP, Wyoming /Willard Clay/Photolibrary

Many of the images in this guide are available for licensing from Lonely Planet Images: www.lonelyplanetimages.com.

This Book

This 3rd edition of Lonely Planet's Yellowstone & Grand Teton National Parks guidebook was researched and written by Bradley Mayhew and Carolyn McCarthy, who both also authored the 2nd edition. The 1st edition was also written by Bradley Mayhew, along with Andrew Dean Nystrom and Amy Marr.

This guidebook was commissioned in Lonely Planet's Oakland office, and produced by the following:

Commissioning Editor Kathleen Munnelly
Coordinating Editors Kate James, Pat Kinsella
Coordinating Cartographers Joelene Kowalski, Marc Milinkovic
Coordinating Layout Designer Yvonne Bischofberger
Managing Editor Kirsten Rawlings
Senior Editors Susan Paterson, Angela Tinson

Managing Cartographers Shahara Ahmed, Alison Lyall
Managing Layout Designer Jane Hart
Assisting Editors Eli Arduca, Andrea Dobbin, Martine Power
Assisting Layout Designers Mazzy Prinsep, Jacqui Saunders, Wendy Wright
Internal & Cover Image Research Sabrina Dalbesio
Thanks to Helen Christinis, Ryan Evans, Liz Heynes, Heather Howard, Trent Paton

NOTES

index

000 Map pages
000 Photo pages

how to use this book

These symbols will help you find the listings you want:

- 👁 Sights
- 🏄 Beaches
- 🏃 Activities
- 🥾 Courses

- 👉 Tours
- 🎎 Festivals & Events
- 🛏 Sleeping
- 🍴 Eating

- 🍷 Drinking
- ☆ Entertainment
- 🛍 Shopping
- ℹ Information/ Transport

These symbols give you the vital information for each listing:

- 📞 Telephone Numbers
- 🕐 Opening Hours
- 🅿 Parking
- 🚭 Nonsmoking
- ❄ Air-Conditioning
- @ Internet Access

- 📶 Wi-Fi Access
- 🏊 Swimming Pool
- 🥗 Vegetarian Selection
- 📖 English-Language Menu
- 👪 Family-Friendly
- 🐾 Pet-Friendly

- 🚌 Bus
- ⛴ Ferry
- Ⓜ Metro
- Ⓢ Subway
- 🚇 London Tube
- 🚊 Tram
- 🚆 Train

Reviews are organised by author preference.

Look out for these icons:

- TOP CHOICE — Our author's recommendation
- FREE — No payment required
- 🌿 — A green or sustainable option

Our authors have nominated these places as demonstrating a strong commitment to sustainability – for example by supporting local communities and producers, operating in an environmentally friendly way, or supporting conservation projects.

Map Legend

Sights
- 🏖 Beach
- 🛐 Buddhist
- 🏰 Castle
- ✝ Christian
- 🕉 Hindu
- ☪ Islamic
- ✡ Jewish
- 🗼 Monument
- 🏛 Museum/Gallery
- 🏚 Ruin
- 🍷 Winery/Vineyard
- 🐘 Zoo
- 👁 Other Sight

Activities, Courses & Tours
- 🤿 Diving/Snorkelling
- 🛶 Canoeing/Kayaking
- ⛷ Skiing
- 🏄 Surfing
- 🏊 Swimming/Pool
- 🚶 Walking
- 🏄 Windsurfing
- 🎯 Other Activity/ Course/Tour

Sleeping
- 🛏 Sleeping
- ⛺ Camping

Eating
- 🍴 Eating

Drinking
- ☕ Drinking
- ☕ Cafe

Entertainment
- ☆ Entertainment

Shopping
- 🛍 Shopping

Information
- 📮 Post Office
- ℹ Tourist Information

Transport
- ✈ Airport
- ⊗ Border Crossing
- 🚌 Bus
- Cable Car/ Funicular
- Cycling
- Ferry
- Ⓜ Metro
- Monorail
- Ⓟ Parking
- Ⓢ S-Bahn
- Taxi
- Train/Railway
- Tram
- Tube Station
- Ⓤ U-Bahn
- • Other Transport

Routes
- Tollway
- Freeway
- Primary
- Secondary
- Tertiary
- Lane
- Unsealed Road
- Plaza/Mall
- Steps
- Tunnel
- Pedestrian Overpass
- Walking Tour
- Walking Tour Detour
- Path

Boundaries
- International
- State/Province
- Disputed
- Regional/Suburb
- Marine Park
- Cliff
- Wall

Population
- 🟊 Capital (National)
- ◉ Capital (State/Province)
- 🔴 City/Large Town
- 🔴 Town/Village

Geographic
- 🛖 Hut/Shelter
- 🗼 Lighthouse
- 👁 Lookout
- ▲ Mountain/Volcano
- Oasis
- Park
-)(Pass
- Picnic Area
- Waterfall

Hydrography
- River/Creek
- Intermittent River
- Swamp/Mangrove
- Reef
- Canal
- Water
- Dry/Salt/ Intermittent Lake
- Glacier

Areas
- Beach/Desert
- Cemetery (Christian)
- Cemetery (Other)
- Park/Forest
- Sportsground
- Sight (Building)
- Top Sight (Building)

OUR STORY

A beat-up old car, a few dollars in the pocket and a sense of adventure; in 1972 that's all Tony and Maureen Wheeler needed for the trip of a lifetime – across Europe and Asia overland to Australia. It took several months, and at the end – broke but inspired – they sat at their kitchen table writing and stapling together their first travel guide, *Across Asia on the Cheap*. Within a week they'd sold 1500 copies. Lonely Planet was born.

Today, Lonely Planet has offices in Melbourne, London and Oakland, with more than 600 staff and writers. We share Tony's belief that 'a great guidebook should do three things: inform, educate and amuse'.

OUR WRITERS

Bradley Mayhew

Coordinating Author, Yellowstone National Park, Around Yellowstone An expat Brit, Bradley currently calls Yellowstone County, Montana home and he hikes nearby Yellowstone Park and the Beartooth Mountains every chance he gets. Half a lifetime of travels through Central Asia, Tibet and Mongolia has made him feel quite at home in Big Sky country. He is the coordinating author of a dozen Lonely Planet guides, including *Tibet, Bhutan, Nepal, Central Asia* and *Trekking in the Nepal Himalaya*. See what he's up to at www.bradleymayhew.blogspot.com.

Read more about Bradley at:
lonelyplanet.com/members/nepalibrad

Carolyn McCarthy

Grand Teton National Park, Around Grand Teton When not strolling the wildflower meadows of Grand Teton scanning for grizzly scat, author Carolyn McCarthy makes her home in Chile. In the last seven years she has contributed to over a dozen Lonely Planet titles. She has also written for *National Geographic, Outside,* and *Lonely Planet Magazine,* among other publications. You can follow her Americas blog at www.carolynswildblueyonder.blogspot.com.

Read more about Carolyn at:
lonelyplanet.com/members/carolynmcc

Published by Lonely Planet Publications Pty Ltd
ABN 36 005 607 983
3rd edition – Feb 2012
ISBN 978 1 74179 407 6
© Lonely Planet 2012   Photographs © as indicated 2012
10 9 8 7 6 5 4 3 2 1
Printed in China

Although the authors and Lonely Planet have taken all reasonable care in preparing this book, we make no warranty about the accuracy or completeness of its content and, to the maximum extent permitted, disclaim all liability arising from its use.